LEGACY

New Perspectives on the Battle of the Little Bighorn

Proceedings of the Little Bighorn Legacy Symposium,
held in Billings, Montana, August 3–6, 1994

LEGACY

New Perspectives on the Battle of the Little Bighorn

**Edited by
Charles E. Rankin**

MONTANA
HISTORICAL
SOCIETY
PRESS

Helena

Paperback—front cover image: detail of *Custer & 20,000 Indians*, by Fritz
Scholder, 1969 (full image reproduced as fig. 9, following page 230); back cover
image: 1994 Little Bighorn Legacy Symposium logo, by John Potter.

Cover and book design by Kathryn Fehlig

Typeset in Adobe Garamond and ITC Usherwood

Printed by Rose Printing Co., Tallahassee, Florida

This book was made possible with partial funding by the Wyoming Council for
the Humanities and the Montana Historical Society Foundation.

The findings, conclusions, etc., do not necessarily reflect the views of the Montana
Historical Society Foundation, Wyoming Council for the Humanities, or National
Endowment for the Humanities.

97 98 99 00 01 02 03 04   9 8 7 6 5 4 3 2 1

Library of Congress Cataloging-in Publication Data

Legacy : new perspectives on the Battle of the Little Bighorn / edited by Charles
E. Rankin.
    p. cm.
    "Proceedings of the Little Bighorn Legacy Symposium, held in Billings, Montana,
August 3–6, 1994" —Half t. p.
    Includes bibliographical references and index.
    ISBN 0–917298–41–1 (casebound : alk. paper).
    ISBN 0–917298–42–X (softcover : alk. paper)
    1. Little Bighorn, Battle of the, Mont., 1876—Congresses. I. Rankin, Charles
E. II. Little Bighorn Legacy Symposium (1994 : Billings, Mont.)
E83.876.L44 1996
973.8'2—dc20
96–24512
CIP

This book was made possible with partial funding by the Wyoming Council for the Humanities, the Montana Historical Society Foundation, and Mrs. Helen Hornby, to whose memory it is dedicated.

Contents

Illustrations

Text Illustrations

Illustrations following page 230

Preface

Throughout the western United States are scores of sites relating to a conflict of cultures we know as the Indian wars. While a few are public parks today, most sites remain relatively obscure, isolated spots, unknown but to the most diligent of frontier historians and a handful of elder Native Americans. Each of these places, in its own way, speaks of the struggle to control the western plains. Yet, one site relating to the western Indian wars—the Little Bighorn battlefield—is unique and unabated in its sheer power.

Little Bighorn is preeminent as an icon of controversy and as an event of legendary, if not mythical proportions. Hardly more than a skirmish by military standards, it ranks with the likes of Pearl Harbor, Gettysburg, and the Alamo as a defining moment in America's heritage. It seems to embody all that was either right or wrong about America's conquest of the Trans-Mississippi West. This austere scene of life-and-death struggle evokes both pride and sadness. It is a lonely place that haunts the American conscience.

For most of a century, this battle was perceived largely in a single dimension. Lieutenant Colonel George Armstrong Custer and his men achieved immortality by dying for the cause of America's western empire. At least that was what most Americans of European ancestry believed until nearly three-quarters of the way through the twentieth century.

This was not, however, the way that Native Americans remembered it. They knew it as the fight at Greasy Grass, a great, yet fleeting victory that signaled the doom of their traditional way of life. For subsequent generations of Native Americans, it meant the beginning of a dispiriting life of confinement on reservations and dependence on the United States Government.

In the wake of the battle, the site quickly became the focus of an effort by the United States Army to memorialize the fallen Custer and his men. The site was formally designated a national cemetery in 1879, and an enormous granite obelisk was placed atop the most important terrain feature, Custer Hill, a mere five years after the event. Commemorative ceremonies held periodically at the battlefield served to affirm that Little Bighorn was exclusively a military memorial. This theme was perpetuated when the War Department transferred the site to the National Park Service in 1940. The appointment of Edward S. Luce, an avid student of the battle and ex-Seventh Cavalryman, to be the first park service superintendent of the battlefield insured a military emphasis at what had already become a national shrine.

It was not until the 1970s and several generations of superintendents later, however, that anyone questioned the inherent bias of the story being conveyed at the National Monument. True enough, the Indian victors had become nearly invisible in the story, merely backdrop to a center-stage George Custer. Public attention focused sharply on this issue when members of the American Indian Movement led demonstrations at the battlefield during the centennial observance in 1976. Revisionist literature and motion pictures, if not general social unrest and perceived parallels with the Vietnam War, caused many white Americans to reassess traditional interpretations of the western Indian wars. Consequently, the National Park Service came under intense pressure to take a more balanced approach to the way it related the Little Bighorn story.

A new era dawned, one in which successive superintendents consciously endeavored to be more evenhanded in conducting educational activities at the Little Bighorn monument. But not everyone agreed with this trend. Traditionalists attempted to have the park service stay the course and resist what they perceived as the transformation of history into political correctness. Thus began in earnest a symbolic battle to determine whose shrine the Little Bighorn battlefield would be. As the official steward of the monument, the National Park Service was caught in the middle. To the present day, advocates on opposite sides of the issue attempt to pressure the park service to advance their particular agenda, to the end that the National Park Service continues to be embattled on one front after another, and often on several simultaneously.

During my tenure as the historian at the battlefield, like others before me, I wrestled with the weighty question of how the park service might achieve greater objectivity in conveying to the public the powerful and inherently controversial story at Little Bighorn. One day early in 1992, while making the long and none-too-inspiring drive from the battlefield to Forsyth, Montana, to attend a meeting, I found time once again to ponder the issue. It occurred to me that despite our best intentions and efforts to be objective, the park staff might simply be too near the eye of the hurricane. I began to wonder how scholars outside the park service viewed Little Bighorn. And, what did Native Americans really think about it? Would it not be great, I asked myself, if we could gather some of the best minds to consider these issues and share the benefit of their thinking in a public forum?

Upon my return to the park, I discussed the concept with Superintendent Barbara Booher (now Sutteer), the soft-spoken but steely woman of Ute-Cherokee ancestry who made headlines as the first Native American manager of the battlefield. Certainly no stranger to controversy, Barbara enthusiastically endorsed the idea. The easy part was done. Now, came the more difficult act of transforming the concept into reality.

I found a valuable ally in my long-time friend, Jon James, a historian then serving at Bighorn Canyon National Recreation Area, just over the mountain to the southwest. When I told him of the project, Jon offered to assist me in any way possible. Allowing him no time to retreat, I immediately drafted him as cochair in charge of the administrative aspects of the project. The choice could not have been a better one. Jon's energy, coupled with his expertise in grantsmanship, proved to be an invaluable combination. To him go the laurels of garnering much of the funding needed to bring the project to fruition, as well as for refining the themes and objectives of the symposium.

We then proceeded to poll several of our colleagues in the field of frontier history to outline the concept of a symposium and to solicit their suggestions. This eventually led to the formation of a steering committee that would further define the program and assist with the innumerable planning and logistical details for the conference. Included were: Paul L. Hedren, superintendent of Fort Union Trading Post National Historic Site; Joseph M. Marshall III, Lakota historian and educator; Charles E. Rankin, editor of *Montana The Magazine of Western History*; John D. McDermott, retired National Park Service historian and author; and Paul Fees, chief curator at the Buffalo Bill Historical Center.

The combined knowledge and talents of this team at an organizational meeting in Billings in the fall of 1992 lent form and substance to the Little Bighorn Legacy Symposium. It was to be a gathering to examine the context, historical significance, and cross-cultural impacts of the Battle of the Little Bighorn. In contrast to the frequently held conferences in which "Custer buffs" rehash the minutiae of June 25, 1876, the legacy conference would be a one-of-a-kind symposium taking a scholarly, interdisciplinary approach to a broad spectrum of topics relating to the Little Bighorn, and we would attempt to attract the best scholars in the field to address them.

Momentum built in the months that followed. With encouragingly few exceptions, the committee's first choices for presenters enthusiastically accepted the invitation to participate. Before we knew it, the program was not only filled, but others asked to be included. Word had spread that this conference would be truly unique, and that Billings was the place to be during the first week of August 1994.

The very fact that this volume has been published attests to the success of the conference. Some 350 people attended, representing the academic and public history communities, as well as interested lay persons from across the nation. Their evaluations of the conference were uniformly enthusiastic, and many urged that it become an annual event. Our primary purpose, however, was to examine the "state of the Little Bighorn" at the present time and to compile a body of thought on the subject that might aid the National Park Service in its efforts to better interpret the site. Nonetheless, this was not an end, but rather a beginning.

Many have asked us if another such symposium will be held. We hope so, but probably not right away. In a wrap-up evaluation meeting, the committee agreed that another legacy symposium is warranted but that it should remain a truly special event. Without question, this sort of milepost examination deserves to be repeated whenever cross-cultural communication, research, and scholarship have generated fresh perspectives on the Little Bighorn.

In the meantime, we wish to acknowledge the contributions of the following individuals and organizations for making possible the 1994 Little Bighorn Legacy Symposium. First and foremost are Southwest Parks and Monuments Association, Wyoming Committee for the Humanities, and Montana Committee for the Humanities, all of which provided major funding to underwrite the conference. The legacy symposium would not have happened without their generosity. Special thanks also to the Montana Historical Society for allowing Chuck Rankin to participate as a member of the steering committee and for publishing this volume so that the presentations at the symposium might be more widely disseminated and collectively preserved for future reference.

We owe a great debt to the presenters themselves, a group of people without whom this symposium could not have succeeded to the high degree that it did. Their enthusiasm for and professional treatment of their respective topics truly made the Little Bighorn Legacy Symposium a memorable experience in initiating scholarly, cross-cultural analysis of this timeless subject.

Other contributors to the effort included: John Potter, an artist of Chippewa-Cree ancestry, who donated his considerable talent to design the symposium logo; the Billings *Gazette* for donating the conference badges; Tom Fenske and Fenske Printing of Billings for a superb job of designing and printing program materials; Linda Stevens and the staff of the Billings Sheraton Hotel for their assistance "above and beyond the call" in providing the fine accommodations; Edith McCleary of Custer Country Tourism Region, Hardin, and the G. L. Ness Agency, Billings, for promotional assistance; and Cook Travel Agency and Continental Airlines.

Both of my former bosses, Superintendent Gerard A. Baker and previous superintendent Barbara A. Sutteer, Little Bighorn Battlefield National Monument, deserve thanks for their encouragement and support of this project, and for allowing me to take time away from my regular duties to see it through.

Samantha Hugs, clerk-typist at Little Bighorn battlefield, deserves special recognition. Sam, with her usual energy and attention to detail, organized and coordinated the registration system, accounted for the receipts, supervised the registration table at the conference, and cheerfully handled an endless number of other details over many months. To Sam, my personal and profound thanks.

Douglas C. McChristian
December 1995

Introduction

Charles E. Rankin

L ittle Bighorn. Long ago, the name became a symbol for much
more than the small high plains stream that courses its way
northward through southeastern Montana. The battle that
occurred along its banks 120 years ago easily eclipsed any
geographical designations. In the collective American mind, the
site of George Armstrong Custer's demise became an absorbing,
enigmatic symbol that reverberates to this day in the national
consciousness.

Still, the Battle of the Little Bighorn can be described, aptly
perhaps, as a mere skirmish by military standards. Indeed, as
Richard S. Slotkin argues, it was a relatively minor military
engagement involving a man of marginal historical importance,
although others insist that the battle ultimately, if ironically, was
crucial to the defeat of the resistant Lakotas and their allies.
Questionable historical significance notwithstanding, Little
Bighorn has become, in the words of various contributors to this
volume: the preeminent icon of controversy; a military monument;
a national shrine; the symbol for a defining national moment; a
multifaceted, malleable story fraught with ironies; a mirror of
contemporary social, political, and cultural values and at times a
window on the historical past and what we might make of it; a
lonely place that haunts the American consciousness. The Little

Bighorn's power, it would seem, is that it continues to be all these things; indeed, more than their sum. Hence, the fascination.

The hundreds of books on George Armstrong Custer and his famous denouement on June 25, 1876, are ample testimony to the Little Bighorn story's enduring appeal. But this volume is about more than that fascination. Rather, it reflects change, or more accurately an attempt to fashion a proper response to change. It is based on the lectures and presentations offered by leading scholars and writers from a diversity of disciplines during the three-day Little Bighorn Legacy Symposium held in Billings, Montana, in August 1994. Collectively, those who advanced their thoughts at the conference sought a broader, more inclusive story. For a century, the conventional interpretation of the Little Bighorn had been decidedly narrow. As Paul L. Hedren documents in an essay included here, in the aftermath of the battle at the Greasy Grass the United States Army quickly appropriated both the story and the battlefield, making the one a testament to blood sacrifice for a worthy cause and the other a national cemetery. To the nation, the story became one of a heroic offering on behalf of the advance of white civilization, the archetype for the winning of the West from what were perhaps wronged, but nonetheless uncivilized people who inevitably had to be swept from the path of progress.

During the past twenty years, however, new scholarship and a growing awareness—as well as acceptance—of Native American historical voices has exposed the inadequacy of such a limited view. Unable to accommodate cross-cultural and multicultural viewpoints, the conventional interpretation of the battle's meaning has impeded understanding by excluding Native American perspectives on the story—their views on why they fought, why they won that day, why the aftermath of their ultimate defeat was so tragic—in brief, what the Little Bighorn has meant to them. The use of the plural—Indian perspectives—is intentional, for as Colin G. Calloway shows, many native groups—from Lakota, Cheyenne, and Arapaho to Crow, Shoshone, Pawnee, and Arikara—were caught up in the events surrounding the Little Bighorn, some fighting against each other. As a consequence of new scholarship, new investigative techniques, new evidence, and especially because of a growing Native American insistence on

inclusion in the Little Bighorn story, the conventional interpretation has become hopelessly outmoded. No longer can it
accommodate such a diversity of perceptions and potential
meanings for so many different groups. A reinterpretation is needed.
The legacy symposium in Billings, then, in conjunction with the
renaming of the battlefield and planning for an Indian memorial,
represented a tentative step toward fashioning a new, more inclusive
explanation.

As Douglas C. McChristian explains in his preface, the purpose
of the legacy symposium was to obtain a historiographical cross-
section of state-of-the-art scholarship on the Little Bighorn with
which the National Park Service might better interpret the site.
Assembling scholars and writers from a broad range of disciplines,
the park service was able to draw from the work of Native American
authors, historians, and narrators; environmental historians;
archaeologists; communications scholars; historians of federal
Indian policy and military strategy; and approaches ranging from
the anthropological to the myth historical and art historical. From
these presentations, the park service and the more than three
hundred people who attended the symposium heard appeals for
reinterpreting the Little Bighorn in a larger context, for using other
disciplines and other sources to enhance and deepen our
understanding, especially material evidence and Indian testimony,
and for greater appreciation of the significance of myth—what it
can reveal as well as what it often obscures. More than anything
else, the symposium underscored the need for greater recognition
of Native American perspectives and their meaningful
incorporation into the story. Responsible for interpreting as well
as administering the Little Bighorn Battlefield National
Monument, the National Park Service sought and found guidance
on how it might convert the site from a place enshrined for a single,
celebratory purpose into a national monument where, as Edward
T. Linenthal puts it, different groups might play a role in
constructing a collective memory.

In keeping with such a worthy undertaking, creation of a
permanent record seemed imminently fitting. Consequently, the
Montana Historical Society, one of the symposium's several
sponsors, tape recorded the entire proceedings for its oral history

collections. These tape recordings are on file with the state archivist at the Society in Helena and are available to anyone upon request. In addition, the Montana Historical Society Press has undertaken to publish in one volume the essays that grew out of the lectures and discussions offered in Billings those three days in August. Sixteen essays appear here. As one would expect, such a diversity of approaches required a certain standardization for editorial consistency. Little Big Horn, for example, became Little Bighorn. Otherwise, the essays and their scholarly citations, which are grouped for the sake of continuity into three parts—the Context, the Battle, and the Myth—appear as the authors crafted them.

In the book's opening essay, Dan Flores deploys an interdisciplinary approach to provide context on a grand ecological scale. He shows how the Great Sioux War perhaps hastened somewhat but nonetheless played only a small part in a much larger drama. Victim to a convergence of ecological, cultural, and technological forces, the bison ecology that had flourished in North America for ninety centuries and on which the Plains tribes had based their buffalo cultures came crashing to an end in a mere twenty-five years. Next, Alvin M. Josephy, Jr., explains how the Little Bighorn was the logical result of an Indian policy that, however fraught with independent actions, corruption, and well-intentioned philanthropy, offered only three alternatives to Native American societies: become white on your own accord; be driven onto reservations where you will assimilate to white ways or starve; or die. As Josephy asserts, the Little Bighorn battle was supposed to achieve the policy's third alternative.

If the policy-making in Washington was rigid, Joseph C. Porter shows how the Native American response on the high plains was surprisingly fluid. Through the life and times of the enigmatic Lakota warrior Crazy Horse, Porter relates the Indian worldview, one in which proud people sought to defend their homeland, their families, and their way of life against invading armies of another culture and in so doing, changed their own culture even as they defended it. As Colin G. Calloway cautions, however, the world created by white invasion was not a simple one with fixed racial lines. There were, he reminds us, "other Indians." The Crows, Shoshones, Pawnees, and Arikaras intentionally allied themselves with strength—with the United States Army—to defeat their traditional enemies, the Lakotas and Cheyennes. Hardly the white man's fools, these Indian allies, like the Indians they fought against, struggled against formidable odds for cultural survival. For these native groups, the Little Bighorn represented disaster, but for reasons much different than for the United States military.

From the army's perspective, meanwhile, as disastrous as the Little Bighorn was, it represented a turning point in the larger Sioux war. As Jerome A. Greene argues, the Little Bighorn, a battle among skirmishes, was a pivotal moment that shaped all subsequent events. Until the Little Bighorn engagement in late June 1876, the army's fortunes during its campaign that year were in decline and those of the opposing tribes in ascendancy; afterward, it was just the reverse. Rounding out this section, John D. McDermott describes why the Little Bighorn is so multifaceted as a historical event. The Little Bighorn says as much about flawed federal policies and national attitudes toward settlement, Indian prowess, national mythology, and a standing military as it does about individual personalities and unique circumstances.

In part two, Native American author Joseph M. Marshall III shifts the focus to a different set of heroes by providing an insider's view from the village Custer opposed that Sunday in June 1876. Those who fought Custer as well as generations of their descendants have felt pride for having won and defended themselves well that day, and sadness for ultimately losing the clash of cultures. Such views are best expressed through the memories and histories of Native Americans, and Margot Liberty argues for the indispensability of such information. As with all historical sources, using Indian testimony can be problematic, but such evidence is essential if we are to arrive at a fuller understanding of the events surrounding Little Bighorn.

Building on Liberty's appeal for putting Native American evidence to greater use, Richard A. Fox, Jr., argues that when combined with archaeological data, these sources help begin to resolve such questions as the location and size of the Indian village, which in turn is critical to interpreting Custer's strategy as well as the actions the Indians took on the west side of the river. Similarly, Douglas D. Scott explains just how archaeological evidence has been gathered at the battlefield to reveal a number of insights and confirm other evidence. As well, the archaeological techniques pioneered at Little Bighorn have served more contemporary investigations, including cases of suspected human rights violations in Iraq, El Salvador, and Croatia. Finally, as noted earlier, Paul L. Hedren traces the army's efforts to render the Little Bighorn battlefield holy ground in a fashion similar to the nation's response to the sites of Civil War engagements.

Beyond the context and the battle itself lies what is arguably Little Bighorn's most powerful legacy, its mythology. Creation of the Custer myth had many sources but none perhaps more influential than the visual record fabricated by artists. In a study of the art of the Little Bighorn, Brian W. Dippie contends that in creating Custer's Last Stand, artists made real in the public mind a gloriously heroic fiction that no one could effectively prove or wholly disprove. Ironically, to accommodate their dedication to accuracy in the minute details of saddles, firearms, and uniforms, artists fashioned a larger context—and a mythology—that assumed enduring power. Similarly, Paul Andrew Hutton shows how Hollywood, ever dedicated to entertainment, paid little heed to historical accuracy in its many depictions of the events surrounding the Little Bighorn. Rather than *historical* fidelity, Hollywood's treatment of Custer and the Little Bighorn over time reveals with surprising precision the nation's willingness to use historical characters and events to reflect changing perceptions of its villains and heroes.

If the mythology surrounding Custer has provided a window on popular notions of our national identity, it also has obscured dangerous fallacies embedded in American self-perceptions and hindered needed cultural reconciliation. As John P. Hart shows, the Little Bighorn provides rich potential for communications studies, especially in how the myth complicates the problems of intercultural communication. Underscoring this theme, Richard S. Slotkin asserts that if Custer and the Little Bighorn are important to understanding the nation's wrenching transition to modernity, they are important to Native Americans also as symbols of the intercultural clash over values and beliefs. The myth of exclusion, which identified Native Americans as "alien others" and justified their elimination, Slotkin argues, not only led the nation to Little Bighorn–style confrontations but perpetuated exclusion of Indian peoples from the American social compact thereafter.

If exclusion is the obscurant myth, Edward T. Linenthal believes we have taken the first steps toward a more inclusive reality by renaming the battlefield and attempting to convert it from a shrine to manifest destiny to a historic site where a variety of peoples and perspectives might construct multifaceted memory. The act of naming a place, Linenthal asserts, is an act of ownership. Renaming the battlefield, and thereby allowing for a broader ownership, constructing an Indian monument, a process still ongoing as this book is being published, and the Little Bighorn Legacy Symposium itself all reflect attempts to fashion a more inclusive approach to interpreting a site that is and will remain a powerful symbol.

As these essays show, the mystery and irony of Little Bighorn give the story remarkable staying power. Indeed, the battle and its participants are being reassessed with an increasingly complex array of evidence and from a widening range of viewpoints. To be sure, in inviting not one but many cultural perspectives, we complicate what once seemed a comfortably familiar story, but the gains would seem worth the risk. The fabric of national memory has never been uniform, one dimensional, or solo-voiced, though it may have seemed so at times. All along, other historical meanings waited for a chance to become known. By adding more voices, Little Bighorn will gain relevance to an ever-widening audience and become more truly universal. That, at least, is the hope.

PART I
The Context

Hide hunters shipped about ten million bison hides east from the Great Plains in the 1870s–1880s. L. A. Huffman captured this buffalo skinning scene circa 1880 in eastern Montana. (Montana Historical Society Photograph Archives, Helena)

The Great Contraction

Bison and Indians in Northern Plains Environmental History

Dan Flores

Sometime in the early 1830s (the year is variously given as 1830 and 1832), a band of the Yanktonai division of the Lakota that was encamped on the east side of the Missouri River opposite Fort Pierre destroyed with in a few minutes' time a buffalo herd of about fifteen hundred animals.[1] At first glance this event would hardly seem to be noteworthy or particularly important. Indians had been hunting bison in that country for eleven thousand years, often killing far greater numbers of animals using the technique of the buffalo jump. Nor was the stratagem these Sioux employed—a mounted version of the communal "surround"—in any way unusual or startling. Highly sophisticated and organized communal hunt strategies had been worked out on the northern plains millennia before.

What was unusual about this hunt, and the reason it became reported and widely known, was what the Yanktonais did with the slain animals. Rather than carefully butchering the carcasses and skinning the animals out, they are reported to have done no more than cut out the tongues, with which they then crossed the river and offered in trade to the engagés of the American Fur Company.

Looking back on this disturbing scene two decades later, Edwin T. Denig, bourgeois at the American Fur Company's Fort Union, thought this may have been a turning point in the long history of the relationship between bison and Indians on the northern plains. "Since that time buffalo have gradually retired from the eastern territory," he wrote, and as their range contracted to the west the Plains tribes were naturally compelled to follow.[2]

Denig's inference that the Yanktonai hunt over the river from Fort Pierre had acted as a catalyst to the retreat of the bison herds was almost certainly in error, but the event nonetheless can stand as a kind of watershed in the environmental history of the northern plains. Certainly, as Denig and other observers on the nineteenth-century northern plains noticed, *something* was happening to the bison herds by midcentury. Accustomed as we are to thinking of forty million or sixty million or one hundred million bison thriving on the Great Plains until the arrival of white hide hunters with their Sharps rifles in the 1870s, it is a bit disturbing to think that the bison may have been disappearing earlier, and under a different and far more complex set of circumstances. But in fact, that is almost certainly what happened.

My search to try to unravel the ecological mysteries of the wilderness plains came from a discovery of several enigmas in the traditional historical story of what happened to the buffalo. What puzzled me most were the following contradictions in the primary sources. First were the widespread stories by Indian agents and other sources, including calendar histories kept by some of the tribes themselves, of lengthening spans of time on the plains by the 1840s and 1850s when bison were becoming harder to find and the tribes were increasingly compelled to compete for the animals. The second puzzler was that documented records existed for only about ten million bison hides shipped east by hide hunters in the 1870s and 1880s. If the pre–hide hunter plains had presented a harmonious cycle of sunlight and grass, bison and Indians, why were so many groups complaining of starvation and consciously shifting their ranges to the high plains decades before the end? And what had happened to the other thirty million or fifty million or ninety million bison by the time the hide hunters got around to wiping them out?

Until recently, environmental history had yet to tackle this set piece in western history. Existing secondary literature took no cognizance of the riddles in the story, so that attempting a systematic analysis of the circumstances of buffalo ecology— determining how many bison there *really* were, what their population dynamics had been on the wilderness plains, how the herds were affected by natural mortality, predation, and climate change, and piecing together the long span of Native American interaction with the bison—essentially required a new cookbook. On the southern plains, the story has turned out to be far more complex than anyone could have imagined.[3] This preliminary article indicates no less for the northern plains, and demonstrates that in the years leading up to that fateful encounter on the slopes above the Greasy Grass River, bison, Plains Indians, and the entity called the United States were joint captives in a spiraling whirlwind that demanded release, and got it.

Among some of the issues requiring investigation for a reinterpretation of the bison and Indians in northern plains environmental history are these:

1. How many bison were there, really, and how does one estimate their numbers?

2. How many Indians hunted bison, and what factors affected their bison kill?

3. What other factors, both long-term and short-term, might have affected bison populations?

4. Did Plains Indian world views function, as we have often been told, to give native peoples special insights into how nature *worked*, and to keep Indians in harmonious balance with the natural world? Or were there other forces afoot in the West by the nineteenth century that influenced the Indian relationship to nature in even more compelling ways?

In researching these questions, one of the things I discovered was that understanding the bison story requires a perspective on history that bites off chunks of time much larger than the ones we are used to dealing with, and acknowledges forces that traditional history often has been too myopic to see. Understanding nineteenth-century northern plains environmental history, then, is impossible without addressing *la longue durée*.

To begin with, the core homeland of the American bison and of the peoples who over nine thousand years have linked their lives to this great animal has always been the vast dry pastures of the interior continent. The Great Plains, however, is not a singular landscape, but is recognizably three different physiographic provinces: the hot, desert-influenced southern plains, extending from the Blackland prairies of Texas and Oklahoma across the Llano Estacado to the Sangre de Cristo Mountains in New Mexico, and reaching from the Concho River in southwestern Texas north to the Arkansas River; the grassland empire of the central plains, lying northward from the Arkansas River to the North Platte and Niobrara Rivers, and bounded irregularly on the west as the Front Range of the Rockies falls off into island mountains in a sagebrush sea in Wyoming; and the broken and diverse northern plains, stretching northward from central Wyoming across Montana to the aspen parklands of Saskatchewan and Alberta, and westward from the Missouri River to the Rocky Mountain Front.

The topography of the northern plains is dominated by the Missouri Plateau, capped by a Tertiary tableland that has been bisected by the Missouri and major tributaries like the Yellowstone, and otherwise scored into canyonlike coulees that finger down from the grassy divides and, where conditions are right, lay open brilliant stretches of striped badlands. The Little Missouri Badlands of North Dakota were formed when that drainage was diverted by the advance of glaciers, but both the upper Missouri and the lower Yellowstone surge through badlands terrain, while the most extensive badlands of the northern plains are the Big or White River Badlands southeast of the Black Hills. Other river drainages that have scored deep topography along the boundaries of the northern plains are the North Platte River and its tributaries as it arcs across present-day Wyoming, and the Saskatchewan River drainage of the northern border. Along most all these rivers are green-ribbon corridors of silt-loving cottonwoods and willows and limber pine. In such a dry, cold, and open world, that has made the rivers both ancient arteries of travel and protected and fertile oases for Great Plains life of both the four-legged and two-legged varieties.[4]

The Anglo-American perception of the western plains as a flat, desert waste was formed in the early nineteenth century by travelers such as Zebulon Pike and Stephen Long, who in Long's case were exposed to the southern high plains in the heat mirages of August during a drought year.[5] Both "flat" and "desert" are far more appropriate to the Great Plains south of the thirty-fifth parallel than north of it. Not only are the badlands of the northern plains far more extensive in area than the dissected country (such as the canyons and breaks of the Llano Estacado) farther south, the face of the northern uplands generally is choppier and more broken, streams are more reliable in their flows, and annual evaporation is far less.

With the exception of the Wichita Mountains and a few scattered volcanic peaks and remnant mesas, moreover, the southern plains generally lack mountain ranges until the wall of the Front Range looms on the west. But in the north, the plains are mountainous, and the mountains are important additions to the ecological landscape. The Black Hills, the Bighorns, the Absarokas and Winds and Tetons, the Big Belts and Little Belts and Highwood and Bears Paw, even smaller ranges like the Sweetgrass and Cypress Hills and the Killdeer Mountains, add a biotic and ecological diversity to the northern plains and make the region less a monotonous plain than a mosaic of ecotones.

The northern plains, then, for at least the last nine thousand years has been the most topographically diverse and ecologically rich province on the American Great Plains. For a very long string of human cultures here, the movements of bison were determinative. The yearly cycle for both four-legged and two-legged was summering and overwintering, the latter essentially lasting from October to May. During that season a majority of the herds was on the western and northern edges of the northern plains, sheltered in the aspen parklands, the more broken country to the west, down in the woodlands along the river trenches, and sometimes in the Cypress and Sweetgrass Hills and the Black Hills. In summer, especially late summer, water became the critical resource, and the same pattern held true—the great beasts and their human predators crowded into the valleys of the more dependable river courses.

There ought, then, to be no surprise in the historical circumstances that made the northern plains the scene of the nineteenth-century endgame for both bison and Plains Indians.

In the scheme of unfolding western environmental history, it seems to me almost inevitable that the country just north of the Little Bighorn, along the Yellowstone on the Montana plains, should feature the final acts of almost ninety centuries of Indian/bison interactions in western America. When circumstances both internal and external to this world brought it crashing, like the shorelines of a pothole shrinking under the summer sun, it imploded to its final essence in this kernel of country.

The animal that came to dominate this world of sunlight and grass and wind was a creature whose origins lay elsewhere. In an evolutionary sense, bison, like humans, are not true natives of North America. The giant species of bison from which our modern animal springs were Eurasian in origin and arrived in North America via the Bering Land Bridge during the Pleistocene glaciations. But North America shaped the evolution of the modern animal, for between nine and twelve thousand years ago, the giant species *Bison latifrons*, *B. antiquus*, and other ancestors of modern bison disappeared in a wave of large fauna extinctions that swept some parts of the world, including North and South America. Exactly why thirty-two genera of large mammals and birds (including mammoths, mastodons, horses, camels, sloths, and most of their predators) became extinct in Pleistocene North America is a hotly debated topic in paleontological circles. A warming, drying climate seems certain to have played a role, but some of the most respected paleobiologists believe that the arrival of the Indian big-game hunters we call the Clovis people was critical. Possessed of a remarkable flint tool kit, the Clovis people were specialist hunters whose concentration on female and juvenile animals perhaps pushed animals with long gestation periods and few defenses against human predation into extinction.[6]

That great extinction crash of one hundred centuries ago set in motion ecological ripples that enormously affected later centuries. Nature's response to all those vacant grazing niches and to the new ecological pressure of human hunting was to set in motion a dwarfing within the genus *Bison*, producing by about seven thousand years ago a far smaller species (our modern animal) that possessed a much faster reproductive turnover time than its progenitors. In the absence of grazing competition, *Bison bison* multiplied into the vast herds that the earliest European explorers recorded seeing thousands of years later. In an evolutionary sense, then, the modern bison was a "weed species" that proliferated as a result of a major ecological disturbance. Subsequent Indian societies that hunted bison thus were exploiting a situation that has had few parallels in world history.

That bison were still here when the Europeans arrived is obvious evidence that a nine-thousand-year-old ecology had achieved, in a broad-scale sense, a dynamic ecological equilibrium. Bison populations, grassland carrying capacity, and predation—including Indian hunting—had achieved a working balance that, to the Indian mind, seemed to operate at the same level as forces that governed the heavens and the seasons.

In many Indian religions, bison joined the winds and the stars as supernatural in origin. According to the mythologies of many Plains Indian groups, bison had their origins in the earth itself. Every spring immense herds of new animals swarmed like bees from a hive out of specific landforms that were sacred to particular tribes, and which, in fact, constituted part of the transferable cosmologies of the tribes when they migrated across the plains. The canyons of the Llano Estacado on the southern plains, for example, were often singled out to nineteenth-century observers as the wellspring of the bison herds, but once the tribes there were removed to Oklahoma, the sacred point of emergence was transferred to Hiding Mountain in the Wichita range.[7] Given such a belief system, the reemergence and return of the bison long had stood at the center of Plains Indian religious ceremony. Like the sun, the stars, and the winds, bison could never be made to disappear.

The metaphors were not only poetic, but insofar as the long sweeps of time were concerned, this imagery was (and is) substantially realistic. Across the long spans of time that native peoples had inhabited the Great Plains, however, we now know that there had been times when the bison actually had diminished significantly in number, and probably disappeared regionally altogether. For one thing, bison obviously were influenced by climate, and the Great Plains for as long as humans have lived here and before have been notorious for climatic swings, the effects of which are noticeably pronounced in such a semiarid landscape. So, responding to droughts particularly and probably to Indian land-use practices as well, the Great Plains bison herds sometimes moved out of their core range to wetter regions against the Rockies and farther east.[8]

Droughty episodes that undoubtedly curtailed bison populations on the northern plains and produced demonstrable effects on human adaptations include:

- The Atlantic episode 8,500 to 4,730 years ago, otherwise known as the Altithermal because it was a Great Plains drought that lasted almost 4,000 years. This climate swing was so severe that across extensive expanses of the plains, particularly the southern high plains, there was virtual human abandonment.
- The 400-year Scandic episode from A.D. 280 to A.D. 870.
- The 300-year Pacific episode from A.D. 1250 to A.D. 1525, the drought that led to the famous abandonment of the Four Corners area by the Anasazi.

Conversely, there exists in the pollen and dendrochronological records episodes of moist, cool climate swings that evidently produced bumper crops of bison, including:

- The two-century Sub-Atlantic episode before the time of Christ, during which grasslands and bison spread far to the south of the present Great Plains, as evidenced by use of the most southerly buffalo jump so far discovered in the West—the Bonfire Shelter jump site on the Pecos River near the present-day Mexican border—about 500 B.C.[9]
- The 400-year Neo-Atlantic episode from 850 to 1250, producing favorable weather that not only grew the herds but extended the range over which corn grew far up the river corridors of the Great Plains.
- The Neo-Boreal, or Little Ice Age, which happened to commence at the time of first contact with Europeans in the early 1550s and came to an end, ominously for nineteenth-century Plains Indians, around the year 1850.

At one time in Native American studies, such scholars as Alfred Kroeber asserted that until the reintroduction of the horse to the Americas, the Great Plains had been a thinly occupied hinterland. While this view may capture the southern plains during certain environmental episodes, it does not square with the evidence we have from the northern plains, where a continuous sequence of bison-hunting cultures stretches back to the Folsom and Cody cultures of Paleolithic times, and gathers momentum 3,500 years ago with the Pelican Lake and (1,000 years later) the Besant peoples, the latter regarded by some scholars as the most sophisticated communal bison hunters on the plains prior to horse days. The momentum of bison hunting further accelerated with the bow-wielding Avonlea hunters, perhaps Athabaskans, who arrived on the scene about 700 years before the first European intrusions, and specifically sought out badlands topography for impounding bison.[10]

Yet even within this pattern of accelerating cultural momentum, climate always intruded. During the wet intervals, larger herds meant the possibility for more organized, complex, hierarchical societies that made possible—or perhaps were made necessary by—*communal* bison hunts. The Besant hunters were the last northern plains peoples to rely on the atlatl, but evidence shows their hunt to have been highly ritualized and communal, a type of hunt that in Wyoming, at least, came to an end around A.D. 400 and did not resume until the 1500s. Similarly, there is actually a gap in the jump record, from A.D. 305 to A.D. 760, at Head-Smashed-In jump in Alberta. Both these cultural intervals correspond neatly with the Scandic Episode droughts.[11]

As was true in southern plains bison/Indian interactions, it was not only the peoples living directly amongst the herds that influenced them, and were shaped by them. Along the tall-grass prairie perimeter of the northern plains, the evolution towards the fairly dense settlements of historic times began with the Neo-Atlantic climate of about A.D. 800. It was at this time and in the southernmost reaches of the northern plains that Plains Villager culture began, with storage pits, ceramics, the bow, and sedentary lifestyles. Over the years from A.D. 800 to A.D. 1250, conditions were wetter than now, and the spread of corn-growing made possible the chief adaptive strategy of the peoples of the prairie, the laying up of surplus dried corn. Yet village sites were chosen in woodlands along rivers in part because bison liked to winter there, and bison remained the dietary mainstay of these prairie groups.

It was during these years that the ancestors of the Siouan-speaking Mandans, Hidatsas, and River Crows emerged as horticultural hunters of the northern plains.[12]

The great western droughts that commenced around 1250 produced a measurable effect on these people. After 1250 their village sites were almost always fortified, and the supposition is that human carrying capacity had been achieved under the previous wetter conditions, and that the droughts now led to food shortages, malnutrition, and warfare. Arrival of groups (like the Caddoan Arikaras) from the central plains into the Missouri River trench around A.D. 1300 are probably related to the widespread drought.[13]

At the onset of the period of European contact, yet another major weather sequence set in on the northern plains and indeed across the entire Northern Hemisphere. By 1500 the much cooler and probably moister climate of the Little Ice Age was devastating agriculture in Europe and advancing glaciers in the Alps and Rockies. But for buffalo hunters on the Great Plains of the American West an efflorescence began. In the villages of the middle Missouri, trade networks were being linked up with other cultures across the continent, and many kinds of native technologies and art forms were reaching their highest expression. Recovering from centuries of drought, human population in these villages is estimated to have been no more than about fourteen thousand in 1500. In the face of arriving European diseases and the colder, corn-nipping climate of the Little Ice Age, these villages would not reach their previous population levels again. But they did launch some of their divisions onto the plains to become full-time bison hunters.[14]

The patterns thus were set in motion for what has to be judged the most extraordinary period in the long span of northern plains history. First, the three centuries that preceded the fateful encounter at the Little Bighorn were marked by two converging patterns that functioned to grow an enormous biomass of bison—herds so large that they spilled over into the Rocky Mountain valleys and followed the prairies created by Indian burning practices virtually to the Atlantic seaboard. The first was the grazing-beneficent onset of the weather of the Little Ice Age, the second an easing of hunting pressure across much of the continent traceable directly to the impact of European disease on the continental Indian population. During these years, organized, communal bison hunting reached its absolute zenith on the northern plains; hundreds of jumps and corrals are known for the period from 1500 to 1850.[15] Reflecting the bison boom and other factors whose origins lay with the European presence, Indians were in flux, with many groups moving to the plains, many others converging and coalescing there. The stage was being set not only for the intense and glorious heyday of the great buffalo hunt, but for the great contraction as well, a collapse so sudden that the shock waves of it are palpable on the plains into our own time.

In 1500, at the time of first European contact, there were probably in excess of 30 million bison in North America. Extrapolations from later (1900 and 1910) United States agricultural censuses have indicated that the average bison carrying capacity of the Great Plains below the Arkansas River was somewhere around 8.2 million animals at the end of the nineteenth-century. The entire Great Plains in those years probably had a carrying capacity of about 22 to 25 million buffalo, and although I have not yet made a systematic estimate of bison on the northern plains, my supposition is that during much of the Little Ice Age this stretch of the Great Plains likely held as many as 5 to 6 million animals.[16]

But changes resulting from contact between Europeans and Indians quickly began to shrink both the bison's range and its numbers. Although those changes had their origins with the arrival of Europeans, they were very much implemented by the native peoples. Horses, reintroduced to the Americas after an absence of more than eight thousand years, through intertribal trade became widely distributed after the Pueblo Indians successfully revolted against Spanish rule in New Mexico in 1680. Feral horses reestablished themselves in their old grazing niche in a fraction of ecological time; by 1800 an estimated two million horses roamed wild below the Arkansas River and an undetermined number farther north, competing directly with the bison for grass.[17] And horses had transformed the life of Indians in the West. Some groups, like the Flatheads and other Rocky Mountain tribes, used horses to intensify their central adaptation—seasonal movement between salmon and buffalo—eradicating local bison herds in valleys like the Bitterroot and Flathead in the process.[18] Although the women and entrenched upper classes often resisted, across the plains, among the horticultural tribes, some three dozen groups ended up flocking to the buffalo herds as mounted hunters.[19]

After 1700 a new ecological situation began to emerge. Reflecting the shrinkage in the northern plains bison range, the Sioux not only were pressing westward towards the bison core on the Montana plains, they were engaging in wars over hunting territories with the Blackfeet, Crows, and other groups. And beginning in the Missouri River villages in 1738, the northern plains were opened to direct trade with Europeans.[20] Trade between plains buffalo-hunting peoples and groups on the periphery of the prairies, such as the village tribes of the middle Missouri, had been going on certainly since A.D. 1000 and probably much longer. The exchange of villager garden products for plains dried meat and leather was a symbiotic gift exchange, cementing alliances and establishing new contacts. But when the Euramerican agents of organizations such as the Missouri and American fur companies began probing the plains with the metalwares of the Industrial Revolution, they acquired from the buffalo Indians items specifically geared to flow through the network of the global market economy.

What the Plains Indians got in return in this entrée into the Euramerican market economy—particularly from the French and American traders—were guns and ammunition to prosecute their increasing wars over access to the plains. But the observant among the Plains tribes also saw their cultures altered in subtle ways as they grew increasingly dependent on the products of the Industrial Revolution. And when tribal cultures were saturated with metalware, there was always alcohol as an inducement to continued trade.[21]

By the 1820s the buffalo-hunting tribes were learning that there was one other item the Euramericans found desirable in trade. Indian women worked long hours to produce beautifully tanned bison robes, different from later dried hides in that they were softly pliable and finished with the hair on. Traded at posts like Fort Benton or Fort Union or the Hudson's Bay Company posts across the border, robes met an insatiable demand in the eastern United States and eastern Canada as cold-weather covering. They became a major hunting motive for Plains Indians at least as early as 1825, when 25,000 robes a year were going down the Missouri. By the 1840s, 85,000 to 100,000 Indian-produced bison robes were arriving in St. Louis yearly. The Hudson's Bay Company trade also reached its zenith of 73,278 robes between 1841 and 1845.[22]

Bison had been built by the evolutionary pressures of climate and predation to be prolific. Maintaining the herds in dynamic equilibrium with the grasslands required that their 18 percent annual natural increase be harvested by some means. On the wilderness plains natural mortality from disease, weather, and fire, took care of about half that 18 percent. The Pawnees noticed that wolves got three to four out of every ten bison calves, and wolf predation does seem to have accounted for a third or more of the bison's natural increase.[23] The remaining 20 percent of the yearly increase (almost 200,000 animals a year would have been available given the probable size of the historic northern plains herd) long had been harvested for subsistence by the Plains, village, and Rocky Mountain tribes of the region. Careful calculations have indicated that the subsistence requirements of buffalo specialists on the southern plains were roughly 6.5 bison per person per year.[24] This probably varied only slightly, if at all, in the north. With approximately 42,000 souls amongst the northern plains bison tribes in the 1850s—a figure that omits entirely the village and Rocky Mountain tribes that were seriously working the bison herds in those years—the *subsistence* harvest alone would have been nearly 275,000 animals a year.[25]

So it is not surprising to find observers like Edwin Thompson Denig and George Catlin and John James Audubon and Father Pierre-Jean de Smet aware of and disturbed by the fact that at midcentury the bison herds were dwindling rapidly. Farther south, the Kiowa Calendars (historical records painted on bison robes) record a year of "many bison" only once after 1841. The Texas Comanches were reduced in the late 1840s to consuming some 20,000 animals out of their own horse herds. Denig reports that the Assiniboines ate many of their horses, too, in 1846.[26]

In the long history of the bison, what was happening was an unprecedented confluence of historical forces. Not only were bison now competing with horses for grass and water, it seems very clear that they were being reduced by the onset of a major drought on the plains that began in 1846, briefly abated, then set in for more than a decade, and now is seen as the start of the endgame for the Little Ice Age.[27] By the mid-nineteenth century the herd's ancient drought refuges in the tall-grass prairies and the Rockies were beginning to fill in with homesteaders. Another threat, although the details of its timing are not clear, is presently understood to have arrived with the domestic cattle brought by American emigrants on the overland trails. However they were exposed, most of the bison remaining alive at the end of the century were infected with the exotic bovine diseases brucellosis (*Brucella abortus*), bovine tuberculosis (*Mycobacterium bovis*), and anthrax. The impact of these diseases on the viability of the herds is unknown, but easily could have acted in concert with other factors to produce a major dimunition.[28] Like the long-term oscillations of the climate, these new diseases—including the human scourges that had seemed the only dark cloud across the Little Ice Age in the West—were changes in the circumstances of the Plains tribes that were beyond their abilities to influence.

Finally, and very likely the *pièce de résistance*, the consumer goods of the worldwide market economy had by the 1840s lured the northern plains tribes heavily into the robe business. Unlike wolves, who killed calves and sick and injured animals, Indian market hunters focused on prime, breeding-age cows. There is an upper limit for cow selectivity in a healthy bovine herd, beyond which a population decline will set in.[29] And perhaps it is in that relationship that the Yanktonai buffalo hunt at Fort Pierre in the 1830s constitutes a watershed. Prior to 1825, many of the buffalo tribes had practiced a kind of Zen affluence: except for horses, they eschewed the accumulation of goods.[30] But the persistent wooing of the traders—and the attraction of alcohol—eventually wore down their resistance, so that it is hard to escape the conclusion that the native hunters willingly and even enthusiastically pursued their sacred beast literally to the point of its extinction.

All these factors produced a stressed and a seriously depleted northern plains bison herd fully a quarter century before the arrival of the white hide hunters. Observing the result as nearly fifteen thousand Lakotas pressed relentlessly westward and twelve thousand Métis hunters rolled their cart *caravanes* onto the northern plains in the 1860s, many of the white inhabitants of the northern plains worried about the trend. In 1856 the agent for the Blackfeet would write of them that "They annually destroy much more game than they require to subsist and clothe themselves, but as yet there is no sensible decrease in the number of buffalo in their country, it is impossible, at present, to induce them to be more economical." Beginning in the year 1858, agents Alexander Redfield at Fort Union and Alfred Vaughan at Fort Benton began to call on the government to ban the robe trade. But the government hewed to its traditional policy of *laissez-faire* in the fur trade.[31]

As for the Indians, it may be—as on the southern plains—that their belief that bison had supernatural origins and were governed by supernatural sanctions did not sufficiently alert them to the danger of the new situation. Plains buffalo hunters, in reality, were probably not conservationists in the modern sense. In quest of optimal efficiency, some of their hunting strategies probably did have the *inadvertent* effect of conserving animals or even increasing their numbers. But to practice conservation, a culture has to possess the idea that concrete actions towards elements of nature (like buffalo herds) in the *present* will influence their prospects for the *future*. While Plains Indians possessed this idea in the spiritual sense, they did not appear to translate it into practical game management. And finally, since bison were a commons for which there was an extraordinary and mounting competition, to cut back the harvest was only to disadvantage one's own people.[32]

By the time Sitting Bull (p. 114) and Custer were circling one another in 1876, the white hide hunt was essentially over in Kansas and on the southern plains. The year before in New York and Boston, robe supply had surpassed demand, saturating the market and plunging prices. But the result on the northern plains was classic Keynesianism. The drop in the value of their skins prompted groups like the Métis to *increase* the harvest.[33] The result was that in spring 1879, Canadian hunters found no bison at all, and surged into Montana, where a final hunt—this time in competition with white hide hunters—took place in the core area between the Yellowstone and the Sweetgrass Hills. At the beginning of the 1880s the remnant of the northern plains herd is estimated at only about

1.5 million animals, from which white commercial hunters produced about 320,000 hides. The Blackfeet had their last great hunts in 1881, taking some 100,000–150,000 animals—two to three times the number their bands needed for subsistence. By the spring of 1883, when Blackfeet hunters netted their last *six* animals, it was all over.[34]

The bison ecology of the American Great Plains was a natural system, and like all natural systems it was capable of considerable variation, considerable resiliency, within its normal equilibrium. Such systems can continue operating within their established parameters so long as no agglomerate of forces pushes them beyond their boundaries.[35] Weather, new technologies, the coming and going of cultures over the millennia—these factors had disrupted but never *erased* Great Plains bison ecology. But I submit that a quarter century before the hide hunters and the Battle of the Little Bighorn counted final coup on the northern plains, that agglomeration of forces had been assembled on the northern plains. The twenty-five-year shift to a new paradigm was a remarkably swift contraction for a system that had been in place for ninety centuries.

Notes

1. Both George Catlin and Edwin Denig reported this incident. I follow Denig. See Edwin Thompson Denig, *Five Indian Tribes of the Upper Missouri: Sioux, Arickaras, Assiniboines, Crees, Crows*, ed. John C. Ewers (Norman: University of Oklahoma Press, 1961), 30. Also, George Catlin, *Letters and Notes on the North American Indians* (2 vols.; New York: Dover edition, 1973), 1:216-17.

2. Denig, *Five Indian Tribes*, 30.

3. Dan Flores, "Bison Ecology and Bison Diplomacy: The Southern Plains from 1800 to 1850," *Journal of American History*, 78 (September 1991), 465-83.

4. See L. Adrien Hannus, "Cultures of the Heartland: Beyond the Black Hills," in *Plains Indians, A.D. 500–1500: The Archaeological Past of Historic Groups*, ed. Karl Schlesier (Norman: University of Oklahoma Press, 1994), 176-98; Walter Prescott Webb, *The Great Plains* (Boston: Ginn and Co., 1931), chap. 1; Sven Froiland, *Natural History of the Black Hills and Badlands* (Sioux Falls, S. Dak.: Center for Western Studies, 1990).

5. Merlin Lawson and Charles Stockton, "Desert Myth and Climatic Reality," *Annals of the Association of American Geographers,* 71 (December 1981), 527-35. See especially their discussion of conditions on the plains at the time of the Long Expedition.

6. Paul Martin and Richard Klein, eds., *Quaternary Extinctions* (Tucson: University of Arizona Press, 1985); Jerry McDonald, *North American Bison: Their Classification and Evolution* (Berkeley: University of California Press, 1981), 150-63; Michael Wilson, "Bison in Alberta: Paleontology, Evolution, and Relations with Humans," *Alberta,* 3 (1992), 1-17.

7. See Richard I. Dodge, *Our Wild Indians* (Hartford, Conn., 1882), 286, for a description of this belief. Peter Powell, in *Sweet Medicine* (2 vols.; Norman: University of Oklahoma Press, 1969), 2:281-82, describes the Kiowas' Hiding Mountain in Oklahoma, identified in other Kiowa accounts as Mount Scott.

8. Unless otherwise noted, the paragraphs on climate come from: Sally Greiser, "Late Prehistoric Cultures on the Montana Plains," 34-55; Michael Gregg, "Archaeological Complexes of the Northeastern Plains and Prairie-Woodland Border, A.D. 500–1500," 71-95; R. Peter Winham and Edward Lueck, "Cultures of the Middle Missouri," 149-75, all in Schlesier, *Plains Indians, A.D. 500–1500.* Greiser notes that two sources refer to dental and other skeletal anomalies in bison during the dry episodes, an indication of considerable nutritional stress. On the southern plains the key sources are Timothy Baugh, "Holocene Adaptations in the Southern High Plains," ibid., 264-89; Tom Dillehay, "Late Quaternary Bison Population Changes on the Southern Plains," *Plains Anthropologist,* 19 (August 1974), 180-96.

9. Solveig Turpin, "Bonfire Shelter: An Ancient Slaughterhouse," 88-91; and Vaughn Bryant, "Pollen: Nature's Tiny Capsules of Information," 53, 78; both in Harry Shafer, ed., *Ancient Texans: Rock Art and Lifeways along the Lower Pecos* (Austin: Texas Monthly Press, 1986).

10. George Frison, "The Changing Western Environment," lecture presented at the University of Wyoming, Laramie, October 8, 1993; George Frison, "The Foothills-Mountains and the Open Plains: The Dichotomy in Paleoindian Subsistence Strategies Between Two Ecosystems," in *Ice Age Hunters of the Rockies,* ed. Dennis Stanford and Jane Day (Niwot: University of Colorado Press, 1992), 323-42; Hannus, "Cultures of the Heartland," 184-90.

11. Greiser, "Late-Prehistoric Cultures on the Montana Plains," 42.

12. Gregg, "Archaeological Complexes of the Northeastern Plains and Prairie-Woodland Border," 83-95; Winham and Lueck, "Cultures of the Middle Missouri," 159-72.

13. Winham and Lueck, "Cultures of the Middle Missouri," 159-72.

14. Gregg, "Archaeological Complexes of the Northeastern Plains and Prairie-Woodland Border," 95; Stanley Ahler et al., *People of the Willows: The Prehistory and Early History of the Hidatsa Indians* (Grand Forks: University of North Dakota Press, 1991).

15. Greiser, "Late Pre-Historic Cultures on the Montana Plains," 51.

16. My methodology was worked out in Flores, "Bison Ecology and Bison Diplomacy." This involved compiling the horse, mule, and cattle grazing totals from the counties of the southern plains using Bureau of the Census, *Thirteenth Census of the United States, Taken in the Year 1910*, vols. VI and VII, *Agriculture, 1909 and 1910* (Washington, D.C.: Government Printing Office, 1913).

17. L. J. Krysyl et al., "Horses and Cattle Grazing in the Wyoming Red Desert, I. Food Habits and Dietary Overlap," *Journal of Range Management*, 37 (January 1984), 72-76; Frank Roe, *The Indian and the Horse* (Norman: University of Oklahoma Press, 1955); J. Frank Dobie, *The Mustangs* (New York: Bramhall House, 1934), 108-9.

18. Philip Duke and Michael Wilson, "Cultures of the Mountains and Plains: From the Selkirk Mountains to the Bitterroot Range," in Schlesier, *Plains Indians, A.D. 500–1500*, 59.

19. For a discussion, see Preston Holder, *The Hoe and the Horse on the Plains* (Lincoln: University of Nebraska Press, 1970).

20. W. Raymond Wood and Thomas Thiessen, eds., *Early Fur Trade on the Northern Plains: Canadian Traders among the Mandan and Hidatsa Indians, 1738–1818* (Norman: University of Oklahoma Press, 1985), 3-5.

21. What is known as "dependency" was the result, and is the particular topic of Richard White, *Roots of Dependency: Subsistent, Environment, and Social Change among the Choctaws, Pawnees, and Navajos* (Lincoln: University of Nebraska Press, 1983).

22. David Wishart, *The Fur Trade of the American West, 1807–1840: A Geographical Synthesis* (Lincoln: University of Nebraska Press, 1979), 109; William Dobak, "Driving the Buffalo Out of Canada" (unpublished paper in possession of Dan Flores).

23. See Flores, "Bison Ecology and Bison Diplomacy," 481-82; L. N. Carbyn, "Wolves and Bison: Wood Buffalo National Park—Past, Present and Future," *Alberta*, 3 (1992), 167-78.

24. Bill Brown, "Comancheria Demography, 1805–1830," *Panhandle-Plains Historical Review*, 59 (1986), 8-12; H. Paul Thompson, "A Technique Using Anthropological and Biological Data," *Current Anthropology*, 7 (October 1966), 417-24.

25. My 1850s population figures for the Sioux divisions and bands (11,835), Crows (2,250), Assiniboines (3,200), and Plains Crees (11,500) are averages from Denig and the sources, primarily Indian agents, which editor John C. Ewers cites in his footnoting of Denig. See Denig, *Five Indian Tribes of the Upper Missouri*, along with Ewers's notes. For estimates of the Blackfeet (7,630, down from 16,000 to 20,000 in the early 1830s) I rely on John C. Ewers, *The Blackfeet: Raiders on the Northwestern Plains* (Norman: University of Oklahoma Press, 1958), 60, 212; and for the Métis (12,000), Dobak, "Driving the Buffalo Out of Canada."

26. James Mooney, *Calendar History of the Kiowa Indians* (Washington, D.C.: Government Printing Office, 1979), 287-95; Jerold Levy, "The Ecology of the South Plains," in *Symposium: Patterns of Land Utilization and Other Papers, American Ethnological Society Proceedings, 1961*, ed. Viola Garfield (Seattle: University of Washington Press, 1961). The description of widespread Comanche horse eating is in William Bollaert, *William Bollaert's Texas*, ed. W. Eugene Hollon (Norman: University of Oklahoma Press, 1989), 361. On Assiniboine starvation and horse eating, see Denig, *Five Indian Tribes of the Upper Missouri*, 96.

27. See Edmund Schulman, *Dendroclimatic Data from Arid America* (Tucson: University of Arizona Press, 1956), 86-88; Harry Weakley, "A Tree-Ring Record of Precipitation in Western Nebraska," *Journal of Forestry*, 41 (November 1943), 816-19; Lawrence Loendorf, "The Chilling Effect of the Little Ice Age on North Dakota," *North Dakota Quarterly*, 59 (Fall 1991), 192-99; David Stahle and Malcolm Cleaveland, "Texas Drought History Reconstructed and Analyzed from 1698 to 1980," *Journal of Climate*, 1 (January 1988), 59-74. The latter article points out that the years 1856–1864 rank with the 1780s and 1950s as one of the three driest decades on record on the southern plains.

28. See Stacy Tessaro, "Bovine Tuberculosis and Brucellosis in Animals, Including Man," *Alberta*, 3 (1992), 207-24. Brucellosis was discovered in 1897 by Bernhard Bang, hence "Bang's Disease." In humans it is known as undulant fever. It may well have been an occupational hazard for Indians butchering infected buffalo. The disease causes spontaneous abortions in both cattle and bison, but rarely does in humans, although the symptoms include a general malaise.

29. See Flores, "Bison Ecology and Bison Diplomacy," 480 and n. 38 for a discussion of how cow selectivity worked on the southern plains.

30. The argument over the motives for Indian hunting, much debated by scholars like Calvin Martin and Shepard Krech III, can benefit from these two Canadian sources: J. E. Foster, "The Metis and the End of the Plains Buffalo in Alberta," *Alberta*, 3 (1992), 61-62; Paul Thistle, *Indian-European Trade Relations in the Lower Saskatchewan River Region to 1840* (Winnipeg: University of Manitoba Press, 1986). In 1877 the Council of

the North-West Territories in Canada passed regulations outlawing pounds and prohibiting the killing of buffalo under two years of age. But it was too late. See Ewers, *The Blackfeet*, 278.

31. On the Sioux advance I rely on Richard White, "The Winning of the West: The Expansion of the Western Sioux in the Eighteenth and Nineteenth Centuries," *Journal of American History*, 65 (September 1978), 319-43. The Blackfeet agent reports are cited in Dobak, "Driving the Buffalo Out of Canada." The Blackfeet, for one, were not easy to convince that the herds were disappearing. See James Willard Schultz, *Blackfeet and Buffalo: Memories of Life among the Indians*, ed. Keith Seele (Norman: University of Oklahoma Press, 1962), 41. However, their agent wrote in 1877 that "They admit the time approaches fast when buffalo will disappear, but until then the excitement of the chase . . ." Cited in Ewers, *The Blackfeet*, p. 281.

32. Raymond Hames, "Game Conservation or Efficient Hunting," 92-120, and Robert Brightman, "Conservation and Resource Depletion: The Case of the Boreal Forest Algonquians," 121-41, both in *The Question of the Commons: The Culture and Ecology of Communal Resources*, ed. Bonnie McKay and James Acheson (Tucson: University of Arizona Press, 1987).

33. Foster, "The Metis and the End of the Plains Buffalo in Alberta," 73.

34. Ewers argues that a prairie fire pushed the Canadian herd into Montana, and it never returned. Ewers, *The Blackfeet*, 279. Estimates on the last herd on the plains and the 1881 Blackfeet hunt are discussed in Rudolph Koucky, "The Buffalo Disaster of 1882," *North Dakota History*, 50 (Winter 1983), 23-30. In 1874 G. C. Doan had estimated the northern herd at 4 million.

35. See Daniel Botkin, *Discordant Harmonies: A New Ecology for the Twenty-First Century* (New York: Oxford University Press, 1990); Donald Worster, *The Wealth of Nature: Environmental History and the Ecological Imagination* (New York: Oxford University Press, 1993), 152, 165, 169.

Indian Policy and the Battle of the Little Bighorn

Alvin M. Josephy, Jr.

A mid the accelerated interest in westward expansion that followed the Civil War, the editor of the *Army and Navy Journal* in New York City was moved to contemplate the status of the government's policy in dealing with the still unconquered western Indian tribes. To say the least, he found the situation messy and confusing—certainly not reassuring to those who hoped that, like the end of slavery, the long conflict with Indians would also become a thing of the past. "We go to [the Indians] Janus-faced," the disheartened editor wrote. "One of our hands holds the rifle and the other the peace-pipe, and we blaze away with both instruments at the same time. The chief consequences is a great smoke—and there it ends."[1]

If anything, this was not only an understatement of a situation that would continue to produce grave conflicts and tragedies, but the reflection of a continuation of a legacy that doomed Indians, as well as whites, to policies—or a lack of them—that inexorably and inevitably led to the tragedies. At the heart of Indian-white relations since the earliest colonial days lay the most simple of facts—often unrecognized or unacknowledged by whites, but always recognized by the Indians: the whites wanted the Indians' lands and resources, and most Indians did not want to give them up.

In addition, the Eurocentrism, or white convictions of superiority, that stemmed back to the days of Columbus, laid down from the beginnings of what is now the United States three unspoken, but understood, options for the previously free Indian nations and their peoples: first, they could abandon everything that constituted their Indianness and turn into whites, accepted as whites by the white population; second, if they refused to adopt that option, they would have to move far away from the whites, out of sight and out of mind, giving up their land and resources and becoming in no way a physical or cultural threat to the whites; and, third, if they refused to become whites or move away from them, they would have to be exterminated.

Such basic underpinnings of Indian-white relationships—with the various exceptions that have made them rules—have often been overlooked or deemed contentious generalizations unworthy of consideration by many persons who have preceded me in viewing the subject matter of this paper. But they were the heritage of those who struggled with Indian policies that led to the Little Bighorn, and they must be kept in mind as engines—still existing in the nineteenth century—that drove the contestants to the Little Bighorn.

Among the various Sioux nations, the four tribes of the Eastern, or Santee, Sioux of Minnesota were the first to experience the adverse impacts of a mixed bag of government policies, better described as independent government actions, including formal treaties, payments, and promises of education and various types of services—all usually designed, twisted, or administered to serve immediate goals of white men, rather than the needs and desires of the Indians. Throughout the 1850s and into the 1860s, colluding local politicians, Indian agents, traders, and settlers, often with the connivance of administration and congressional cronies in Washington, penned the Sioux tribes in Minnesota on smaller and smaller reservations, cheating them and stealing their treaty payments and supplies almost at will, while missionaries worked tirelessly to turn the Indians into whites. Finally, brought to the brink of starvation, told by an arrogant trader that if they were hungry, they should eat grass, and humiliated otherwise beyond endurance, the desperate Santees rose up in August 1862 and slew more than 350 whites before punitive armies overwhelmed them.

At first, 307 Indians and halfbreeds were sentenced to be hanged. But Episcopal Bishop Henry B. Whipple, one of the few tolerant whites in Minnesota, who blamed the sins of the traders and politicians as much as the Indians for what had happened, managed to visit President Abraham Lincoln in Washington, D.C., and describe to him the causes of the outbreak and the evils of the reigning government system of dealing with Indians that had permitted the victimization of the Sioux. Lincoln, who was busy trying to save the Union, gave little thought to Indians or to an Indian policy. Nevertheless, he reported that Bishop Whipple "talked with me about the rascality of this Indian business until I felt it down to my boots," and, according to Whipple, he promised that "if we get through this war, and I live, this Indian system shall be reformed."[2] Following Whipple's visit, Lincoln personally reviewed the charges against the Indians scheduled to be hanged in Minnesota and, despite the anger of citizens and the military in that state, trimmed the list of condemned men down to 38.

Meanwhile, many of the defeated Santees had fled from Minnesota, seeking safety among the more westerly bands of Yankton, Yanktonai, and Lakota Sioux, who hunted buffalo on the Dakota prairies and the central and northern plains. Directed by General John Pope, military expeditions in 1863 and 1864 pursued the refugees into the western lands, attacking innocent bands of Lakotas and other Sioux who had had nothing to do with the Santee uprising. Pope believed strongly that the way to deal with Indians was to stop the long-established policy of making treaties with them and paying them to keep the peace (which, he maintained, made them targets of swindling, trouble-making traders and other whites), and to transfer control over them from the corrupt Office of Indian Affairs in the Department of the Interior to the War Department, whose no-nonsense power could make them sue for peace and go on reservations where the army could hasten their assimilation. Ironically, however, Pope's expeditions of 1863 and 1864, far from proving to be a showcase of the military's effectiveness in ending the Indians' power, only spread hostilities with the Sioux farther west, invading the hunting grounds of some of the most powerful of their nations and starting a period

of aggression against them that would reach its climax at the Little Bighorn.

As the Civil War came to a close, other high officers in the military, including Generals William Tecumseh Sherman and Philip Sheridan, shared some or all of Pope's notions of how to deal with the Sioux and other still-unconquered western tribes. Sherman and Sheridan, both believers in total war that would speed the defeat and surrender of an enemy, ardently supported getting relations with so-called hostile Indians out of the hands of civilians and under the control of the army. Various factors, however, frustrated them.

First of all, the military's conduct of relations with western Indians during the Civil War produced a number of scandals that had shocked much of the nation and brought on congressional and other investigations that undermined support for turning the Indians over to army control. Most notable were revelations of the savagery accompanying the massacre of Cheyenne and Arapaho Indians at Sand Creek, Colorado Territory, in 1864, and recognition of the true causes of the Minnesota Sioux uprising of 1862 and various events surrounding it. But critical newspaper accounts and other inquiries and complaints of General Patrick E. Connor's massacre of Shoshone Indians at Bear River in Idaho Territory, General James Carleton's brutal roundup and exiling of the Navajo Indians in the Southwest, army participation in genocidal warfare against Indians in Nevada and northern California, and numerous smaller episodes all to a greater or lesser degree hobbled the case for army control of the tribes.

In the second place, dating from before the Civil War, but now emerging with great strength and influence, particularly in the East, was a "peace" movement of humanitarians, philanthropists, churchmen, lecturers, and others, who advocated reforming the Indian Bureau, eradicating the injustices and abuses which drove the tribes to hostilities, and ending Indian wars by "conquering the Indians with kindness," rather than with force. Fed in part by a crusading humanitarian spirit that had helped free the slaves and in part by an abhorrence of continued warfare now that the Civil War was over, the peace movement agreed with military leaders like Sherman that the civilian control of Indian affairs was hopelessly corrupt and responsible for most of the problems afflicting the tribes. But to the peace movement—which also like the army carried on the old legacy of confronting Indians with the three options of assimilation, segregation, or death—the answer was reform to achieve an honest and just civilian control with the goal of turning the Indians into whites, and not the transfer of the Indians to the mailed-fist control of the army, which more likely would lead only to hostility and wars.

Despite an aversion to tinkering with a boodle-producing Indian system in which many members of Congress and their friends had vested interests, the angry reaction of the peace forces to the Sand Creek massacre and other military excesses against Indians moved Congress on March 3, 1865, to authorize a joint special committee of the House and Senate, headed by Senator James R. Doolittle of Wisconsin, to conduct a field study of the condition of the western tribes "and especially into the manner in which they are treated by the civil and military authorities of the United States."[3] After travels through the West, accumulating a mass of information about the tribes, the committee submitted its findings on January 26, 1867. The report noted a rapid decline in the Indians' population resulting from a variety of causes, including wars started by white men's aggressions, and recommended a number of proposals designed to cope with the pervasive corruption of the current system. Congress, however, was preoccupied with a Reconstruction bill for the South and with its own growing controversy with President Andrew Johnson, and little came of the report's recommendations save a restirring of the conscience of the reform-minded peace proponents.

Meanwhile, the Janus, or contradictory, nature of the government's dealing with the western tribes, noted by the editor of the *Army and Navy Journal*, had become painfully clear. In 1865, while government commissioners, offering peace to the Indians, met with the Sioux and other tribes, attempting to win their approval to settle down in lasting peace on reservations, General Pope and other military leaders in the West prepared large, new expeditions to drive the same tribes onto the reservations by force. The peace commissioners managed to abort some of the campaigns, and those that got underway floundered ineffectually against bands of Lakotas in their Powder River hunting country of present-day Wyoming. Eventually, these expeditions' unsuccessful efforts were deemed too expensive and were also called off.

Still, the simultaneous and competing carrot-and-stick approach went on. Opposition, as well as support, came to both sides from many sources, from hordes of frontier homesteaders, politicians, newspaper editors, speculators, and builders of new towns in the West, and from powerful financial circles in the eastern cities and their allies in Congress who were involved, honestly or dishonestly, in western money-making schemes. The latter were unrestrained and rampant, ranging from the grandiose building of a transcontinental railroad and other rail and wagon roads to the dispensation of lucrative Indian Service jobs, supply contracts, and grants and leases of reservation and other lands and resources for timber, mineral, and other exploitation. Most in the West wanted army control to clear the Indians out of the way and safeguard the building of the railroad and other developments. Many people in the East supported civilian rule, not necessarily because they were crusaders for peace, but because of their belief that it would be more difficult for them to manipulate the army and continue their own illegalities and swindles.

Among the Sioux and other affected tribes, the two-faced approach bore the marks of forked-tongued lying, deceit, and treachery. In 1866, the confusion came to a head when the government decided to fortify and protect the Bozeman Trail, a shortcut route pioneered by John M. Bozeman and another white man that ran from the Oregon Trail directly through the Powder River country of Wyoming, the most favored hunting grounds of some of the Lakotas and Northern Cheyennes and Arapahos, to the newly discovered gold mines of western Montana. Both the army and the peace advocates, employing different approaches to attain the same end—getting the Indians away from the trail, even though it was still their own country, and onto reservations—went simultaneously at the Indians. Relying on force, the army dispatched Colonel Henry B. Carrington and a battalion of seven hundred officers and men of the Eighteenth Infantry to Fort Laramie with orders to establish a chain of forts along the trail in the Indians' Powder River country. At the same time, a government "peace" commission, journeying separately, reached Fort Laramie ahead of Carrington. Sitting down with Red Cloud (p. 31) and other Lakota chiefs, the commissioners hoped to persuade the Indians with gifts and other inducements to allow white travelers to use the Bozeman Trail without interference. To the Sioux, the subject—and the payments the whites promised them—was worthy of consideration, and after a postponement to allow more Indians to reach Fort Laramie, the conference was reconvened. In the peaceful atmosphere generated by the commissioners, things went smoothly until suddenly Colonel Carrington and his troops, on their way to assert control over the Powder River country, marched into the fort. The Sioux were furious at the white men's duplicity.

"Great Father sends us presents and wants new road," Red Cloud exclaimed. "But white chief goes with soldiers to steal road before Indian says yes or no!"[4] Breaking up the conference with the peace commissioners, Red Cloud and most of the other Lakota chiefs left the fort, vowing to drive Carrington's men from the Powder River country.

The Indians made good their vow. Although Carrington established three forts along the Bozeman road, besieging Sioux warriors made it unsafe for troops to leave the posts. As a result, without the army's protection, few travelers or freight wagons dared use the trail. On December 21, 1866, catastrophe struck Carrington when Sioux decoys ambushed and wiped out a unit of eighty-one of his men under Captain William J. Fetterman, who had ventured recklessly out of Fort Phil Kearny. The disaster, which shocked the country, played into the hands of the peace advocates, some of whom found themselves appointed, along with military officers, to a presidential commission to investigate the Fetterman affair. On July 1, 1867, the commission reported that, in its opinion, most of the western Indians would welcome peace, and it recommended an end to aggressive campaigns against them. The army thought differently, however, and in the same year, trying to allay the fears of settlers who were overrunning the buffalo-hunting grounds of the central plains, it launched unprovoked and bumbling attacks on Cheyenne villages in western Kansas.

At the same time, in response to the growing strength of the peace advocates and the report of the committee that had investigated the Fetterman affair, Congress on July 20, 1867, authorized a formal peace commission to meet with aggrieved "hostile" tribes, including those fighting to retain the Powder River country, to make treaties that would end the Indians' "just causes of complaint."[5] In addition, the commission was directed to secure the safety of the transcontinental railroad route and select permanent reservations on which the Indians would be forced to settle. Chaired by Commissioner of Indian Affairs Nathaniel G. Taylor, the commission was composed of four noted peace advocates and four army officers, including General Sherman, who as commander of the Division of the Missouri was in charge of military affairs in the West.

Twice in the fall of 1867, the commission tried to meet with Red Cloud, but that chief and those allied with him in the fighting in the Powder River country refused to sit down with the whites until the government dismantled the forts and the troops left the Indians' country. The commissioners managed to persuade the Brulé leader, Spotted Tail, and a number of lesser Sioux chiefs, whose bands had no interest in the Powder River country and hunted elsewhere, to make their marks on treaties. Then they went on to deal with other tribes.

On January 7, 1868, the commission submitted its report, which smacked strongly of the influence of the "peace" members, including Commissioner Taylor. It blamed most of the troubles with the western tribes on whites but, supporting western settlement and the development and use of the West's natural resources, recommended hastening the assimilation of the Indians by getting them on reservations under the influence of educators and Christian missionaries and abolishing immediately the payment to the Indians of all money annuities, which made them susceptible to victimization by corrupt whites and caused many of the resentments and conflicts. At the same time, it recommended that the Indians remain under civilian control.

Although all the members of the commission signed the report, much of it, especially the endorsement of civilian control, did not sit well with Sherman and the other military members. "We did not favor the conclusion arrived at," Sherman later wrote to a

In 1866 Oglala leader Red Cloud demanded closure of the Bozeman Trail and abandonment of the military forts that violated Sioux territory on the Great Sioux Reservation. (Montana Historical Society Photograph Archives)

senator, "but being out-voted, we had to sign the report."[6]

Meanwhile, with the westward advance of the railroad providing safer and shorter routes to the Montana mines from rail points farther west, the government—beset by an economy-minded Congress, a need for troops to police the South, and a growing demand in the East for an end to wars with Indians—was deciding that trying to hold onto the Bozeman Trail was no longer worth the trouble and expense. On March 2, 1868, amid the confusion in Washington over impeachment of President Johnson, General of the Army U. S. Grant wrote Sherman: "I think it will be well to prepare at once for the abandonment of the posts Phil Kearney [sic], Reno, and Fetterman [he meant Fort C. F. Smith] and to make all the capital with the Indians that can be made out of the change. . . . We will have, hereafter, to rely upon inspections by competent officers to govern us in our disposition of troops and dealings with the Indians. . . . I am where a President, a Secretary of War, a Secretary of the Interior and Superintendent of Indian Affairs can all be approached by politicians in the interests of traders and speculators. I will try to embarrass you as little as possible by their suggestions."[7] Sherman was in no hurry to carry out the evacuation of the Bozeman Trail forts, but the die was cast. Runners were sent to Red Cloud and his allies with word of the government's decision, and Taylor invited the chiefs again to meet with the peace commission at Fort Laramie to sign a peace treaty. Red Cloud, however, refused to come until the troops actually left the forts. In July and August 1868 the troops finally did so, and Red Cloud, proud of having forced the army out of his people's hunting grounds, at last came in to Fort Laramie and signed a treaty of peace.

The treaty was a highly legalistic and confusing document, laced with ambiguous and contradictory provisions, and showing the strong hand and strategic and tactical thinking of Sherman, who, far from Washington and the peace advocates, would be in charge of the practicalities of the treaty's administration and enforcement. It is unlikely that an interpreter could have conveyed the meaning of much of the treaty's substance to Red Cloud, or that the chief or any other Indian comprehended all to which they were agreeing. Red Cloud later insisted that he was told lies about what was in the document and that all he thought it conveyed was the government's promise to get out of the Powder River country and leave its Indian owners in peace.

Whatever the Indians did or did not know about it, the treaty, in fact, established all of present-day South Dakota west of the Missouri River as a reservation, on which the commission intended to confine all the western Sioux, peaceably or by force, making them report to an agency at Fort Randall on the Missouri River at the reservation's southeastern tip, far from their buffalo ranges. Secondly, in a confusing and expedient arrangement, which the government, but not the Indians, viewed as temporary, the land north of the North Platte River and east of the Bighorn Mountains, including the Powder River hunting grounds so vigorously defended by Red Cloud's forces and now not included in the reservation, was designated unceded Indian territory barred to white entry without the permission of the Indians.[8] And, finally, other clauses contradicted these provisions, opening ways for scores of trespasses on the Indians' country, as well as for the removal of the Indians from the valley of the Platte River and all other lands, including the unceded territory, outside of the reservation.

Following the signing of the treaty with Red Cloud, Sherman moved determinedly to increase the military's control over the Indians. Congress gave him authority to disburse the funds voted for carrying out the treaties, and he created separate military districts for the Sioux and for the southern Plains tribes and directed their commanders to act as agents for Indians who had not yet gone onto reservations. In October 1868 the peace commission met again. This time Sherman and the military members had the upper hand, voting to use force, if necessary, to drive the Indians onto reservations; to cease observing Supreme Court Justice John Marshall's definition of tribes as "domestic dependent nations," dealt with as equals by treaties; and, reversing their previous stand, to recommend the transfer of the control of Indian affairs to the War Department. A month later, Custer's attack on Black Kettle's sleeping village of Southern Cheyennes on the Washita River highlighted a campaign to drive the tribes of the central and southern plains onto reservations. Farther north, the Sioux who had not gone onto their new reservation, but still hunted, according to their treaty rights, in the Powder River country or in other parts of their unceded lands, also experienced Sherman's sternness. On June 29, 1869, ignoring the treaty made at Fort Laramie with Red Cloud only a few months before, General Sheridan, at Sherman's direction, announced that Sioux who were found outside the borders of their reservation—for example, hunting in their unceded territory—were "under the original and exclusive jurisdiction of the military [not the civilian] authority, and as a rule will be considered hostile."[9] Congress played no role in this decision. In a way, on the western frontier, the military representatives of the

War Department of the executive branch of the government had embarked on a course of setting Indian policy unilaterally, even to the extent of breaking a solemn treaty, the highest law in the land.

Meanwhile, in the East, the peace movement had continued to gain strength from each report of a new campaign or battle against Indians. In New York, Philadelphia, and other cities, private humanitarian organizations like the self-styled United States Indian Commission enlisted the support of wealthy, religious-minded business and professional leaders in a growing crusade to reform the Indian Service and bring peace and justice to the Indians.

In the weeks before his inauguration in 1869, President-elect Grant met with groups of Quakers who pleaded for a new Indian policy based on peace and Christian morals and urged the use of religious employees by the Indian Service as a means of ending its flagrant corruption. The Quakers found Grant surprisingly sympathetic, anxious to end the Indian wars and, like Sherman, sharing their disgust with corrupt, trouble-making traders and agents. Telling one of their groups that their advice was good and he would accept it, he asked them to submit names of Quakers and he would appoint them as Indian agents. "Let us have peace," he told them.[10]

The Quakers and Grant both followed through, inaugurating a unique era in Indian affairs. At first, Grant, ignoring implications of the government's abdicating its responsibilities or violating the Constitutional principle of the separation of church and state, appointed Quaker nominees to run the entire affairs of certain superintendencies and reservations. On other reservations, he appointed army officers, thinking that they, like the Quakers, had the morals and integrity necessary to cope with corruption and restore faith in the Indian Service. Eventually, however, congressional and civilian members of the Indian Ring of grafters saw patronage and sources of boodle slipping away, and in 1870 Congress forbade army officers to accept civil appointments. Grant refused to let the grafters have their way. At the suggestion of the reformers, he turned all the reservations over to church administration, allotting the agencies to the various major denominations. The scheme had mixed results. Not all the men the churches sent to the reservations were any better or more honest than their nonreligious predecessors. Some were misfits, ill-equipped for the job. Others were fanatical in their religious beliefs and became tyrannical over the Indians. Some churches quarreled jealously over the number and importance of the reservations allotted to them, and others proved unable or unwilling to fund the persons they sent to the reservations and withdrew from the program. But though there were both good men and bad and successes as well as failures, the policy as a whole was unable to cope with the continued systemic corruption that permeated Indian affairs. The churches themselves gradually lost interest, the Indian Ring scandal involving Secretary of War William Belknap in 1876 was disillusioning, and Congress continued attempts to regain the right of patronage and spoils. All worked to undermine support for the policy, which finally during the Hayes administration died without a whimper and was replaced by one more satisfactory to the politicians and vested interests.

In the meantime, a second device of reform—the establishment of a Board of Indian Commissioners, composed of prominent, public-spirited peace advocates who served without pay and were given great powers by Congress to investigate, advise, and oversee the government's conduct of Indian affairs—became associated in the public's mind, along with the church rule on the reservations, as constituting the major elements of what was known as Grant's peace policy. For five years, the first board worked with great dedication to try to solve almost every problem in Indian affairs—inspecting records of purchases and payments, exposing incidents of graft and corruption, meeting with Indians to hear and try to end their grievances and injustices, studying and making recommendations on treaty making, the payment of annuities, and the respective roles of the military and civilian officials in dealing with Indians, and providing proposals and plans for "civilizing" and assimilating the tribes.

The board—which Grant had proposed and Congress on April 10, 1869, had authorized—was a force for improvement and moral leadership and made many recommendations for reforms that were later adopted. It was often harried, however, and was opposed by powerful members of the Indian Ring and by officials of the Department of the Interior who resented having to be accountable to, and share their authority over Indians with, the "watchdog" civilian board. In 1871, the board clashed with Ely Parker, a Seneca Indian and Grant's Commissioner of Indian Affairs, questioning some of his dealings in the procurement of Indian supplies. Parker was absolved but resigned in anger. Later, in turn, the secretary of the board was forced to resign when his investigations on the conduct of Indian affairs in the Southwest incurred the wrath of the secretary of the interior. Finally, in 1874, when the secretary of the interior ignored its recommendation that Indian affairs be transferred from his department to a new, independent Indian office, the entire board resigned and was replaced by one composed of less critical members.

In its initial report in 1869, the Board of Indian Commissioners had recommended unanimously the abolishment of the treaty system, an impediment—as the peace-minded reformers viewed it—to the much-desired destruction of tribal organizations and the assimilation of Indians as "wards of the government." On March 3, 1871, a conflict between the House and the Senate over the lack of House participation in the treaty-making process finally resulted in the implementation of the board's recommendation and brought an end to the making of further treaties with the tribes, although the legislation recognized the continued legality of all existing Indian treaties.

In the meantime, on the frontier, after numerous difficulties, the military had cajoled or coerced many of the western Sioux, including Red Cloud, to settle on the Dakota reservation and had built agencies for them. Other bands, however, including the Oglalas of Chief Crazy Horse, Sitting Bull's Hunkpapas, and allied groups of Northern Cheyennes and Arapahos, refused to come onto the reservation and continued to hunt buffalo in the unceded territory. Following Sherman's edict, which violated their treaty right to be in the unceded territory, they were called hostiles by the whites. Such distinctions made no difference to many of the reservation Sioux, who frequently left the agencies to join the hostiles on hunts and then returned to the reservations in the cold season to live on government rations.

The nation would not have supported a determined campaign to round up the hostiles, and for a while, relative peace reigned on the northern plains. At the same time, a buildup of pressure from gold prospectors and others to open up the unceded lands was accompanied by numerous trespasses into the territory, none of which particularly bothered whites, in or out of government. After all, whether the Indians understood it or not, under the treaty the unceded lands would eventually have to be denied to the Indians. Meanwhile enough loopholes had been written into the treaty to rebuff protests by Indians or eastern peace advocates against most of the trespassing.

In summer 1871, a more serious trespass began, when surveyors for the Northern Pacific Railroad, accompanied by army escorts, entered the unceded territory to explore a right-of-way along the Yellowstone River that would slice through the hunting grounds of Sitting Bull's Hunkpapas and other northern off-reservation Sioux. In the following summer, angry Sioux bands, knowing that the railroad would also bring settlers into the country, tried to force the surveyors and their military escorts to leave. An attempt by the Board of Indian Commissioners to gain Sitting Bull's consent to the railroad, which the development-minded commissioners supported, failed, and in 1873, a greatly enlarged military force, including Custer's Seventh Cavalry, appeared on the Yellowstone to protect the surveyors. After two sharp engagements between Custer and the Indians, the sudden financial panic of 1873 brought an abrupt halt to construction of the railroad, and the surveyors withdrew.

In the meantime, the growing need to get the off-reservation bands under control and onto the reservation concerned General Philip Sheridan, who had become commander of the Military Division of the Missouri. In the fall of 1873, Sheridan received permission from Grant and the War Department to build a fort in the Black Hills, from which he could better cope with the hostile bands. This was serious, for it was not a trespass of the unceded lands, but an invasion of the most sacred part of the permanent Sioux reservation, in blatant disregard of the 1868 treaty. In addition, when Sheridan ordered Custer on a reconnaissance into the Black Hills in the summer of 1874, Custer turned it into a prospecting tour that announced to the world the discovery of gold. The resulting gold rush and overrunning of the Black Hills by whites, which the army could not stem, presented Grant with a problem. Westerners would condemn him if he tried to protect the Indians against the invasion of their reservation by enforcing their legal treaty rights, and peace advocates, the courts, and the Board of Indian Commissioners would condemn him if he failed to do so.

After first trying unsuccessfully to browbeat a delegation of Sioux chiefs visiting Washington in May 1875 into ceding the Black Hills part of their reservation to the government, and perhaps moving their people to the Indian Territory, Grant sent a special commission west in September 1875 to negotiate with the Sioux for the sale of both the Black Hills and the unceded territory. Representatives of Sioux bands, both on and off the reservation, met in tense sessions with the commissioners, but refused to sell their lands. The frustrated commissioners returned east and reported that the government would be unable to settle the Black Hills issue until the Sioux had been taught a lesson. Somewhat desperately, Grant chose the only option that seemed open to him: to force all the Sioux bands onto the reservation and keep them under control. In November, the Indian Bureau ordered all the off-reservation hunting bands to come into the Sioux agencies by the following January 31 or be driven in by troops. Behind the order lay Grant's hope that once the bands were brought under control and cowed, they could be induced to give up the Black Hills, the Bighorn Mountains, and the Powder River country. That is, give up these areas on the government's terms—which is what the ensuing history tells us is what happened.

From the Indians' point of view, it can now be seen that in the long run, it really did not matter so much who was in control of Indian policy—the military or peace-advocating civilians. Both shared the same ends; only methods and procedures differed. Both were inheritors of the same legacy and offered the Indians the same three choices: become whites; stay on reservations, isolated from the rest of us, until you can be assimilated; or resist both choices and die. The Little Bighorn was meant to be the policy's third choice.

Notes

1.   Robert G. Athearn, *William Tecumseh Sherman and the Settlement of the West* (Norman: University of Oklahoma Press, 1956), 219.

2.   David A. Nichols, *Lincoln and the Indians: Civil War Policy and Politics* (Columbia: University of Missouri Press, 1978), 141.

3.   Francis Paul Prucha, *The Great Father: The United States Government and the American Indians* (abridged ed.; Lincoln: University of Nebraska Press, 1986), 154.

4.   Frances C. Carrington, *Army Life on the Plains* (Philadelphia: J. B. Lippincott, 1910), 46-47.

5.   Francis Paul Prucha, ed., *Documents of United States Indian Policy* (Lincoln: University of Nebraska Press, 1975), 105-6.

6.   Francis Paul Prucha, *American Indian Policy in Crisis: Christian Reformers and the Indian, 1865–1900* (Norman: University of Oklahoma Press, 1976), 22.

7.   James C. Olson, *Red Cloud and the Sioux Problem* (Lincoln: University of Nebraska Press, 1975), 71-72.

8.   Prucha, ed., *Documents of United States Indian Policy*, 114.

9.   John S. Gray, *Centennial Campaign: The Sioux War of 1876* (Fort Collins, Colo.: Old Army Press, 1976), 15.

10.   Prucha, *American Indian Policy in Crisis*, 48.

The warrior Red Horse depicted the Sioux fighting Custer's battalion in this drawing, reproduced in the Tenth Annual Report of the Bureau of Ethnology, 1888–'89 (Washington, D.C.: Government Printing Office, 1893), plate 43.

Crazy Horse, Lakota Leadership, and the Fort Laramie Treaty

Joseph C. Porter

C razy Horse symbolizes the Native American military struggle to preserve their lands and cultures against the Europeans and their descendants. His life span almost exactly fits the years of the most violent confrontations between the Lakotas and their allies and the whites. The death of Crazy Horse in 1877 marked the end of a chapter in American history that began four hundred years earlier with the arrival of the first Europeans in North America. By the early 1840s white incursions into the lands of the Lakotas and their Cheyenne allies triggered three decades of confrontation. Lakota and Cheyenne resistance only crumbled in 1877 when, after using the "hard war" strategy perfected against the Confederacy during the Civil War, the United States Army destroyed the resource base and the economic infrastructure of the nomadic Lakotas and Cheyennes.[1]

Lakota leaders from the 1860s to the 1880s bore this burden. Crazy Horse, Red Cloud (p. 31), Spotted Tail, Lone Horn, American Horse, Sitting Bull (p. 114), Touch the Clouds, Lame Deer, and other tribal and band leaders knew that the Lakota survival depended upon their decisions as chiefs. Lakota and Cheyenne leaders were men at a crucial turning point in their peoples' histories. Each of the nearly three hundred tribes in North America in 1500 reached a historic crisis during which they faced the terrible realization that the whites were creating a future bereft of the resources—the land and its creatures of earth, sky, and water—that not only met the material needs of their tribes but were also the bedrock of their religion, culture, and sense of tribal being. For the Lakotas, this crisis began in the 1840s.

Crazy Horse was born in 1840 into an Oglala Lakota band camped near Bear Butte, South Dakota. The year, according to one Lakota winter count, was one in which the Oglalas stole a hundred horses.[2] The infant boy was the son and grandson of men also called Crazy Horse,[3] and during his childhood he was called Light Hair. His mother was a Minneconjou woman named Rattle Blanket Woman. She was a member of the prestigious Lone Horn family among the Minneconjous; indeed, she may have been a sister or cousin of the Minneconjou chief Lone Horn whose portrait George Catlin painted in 1832. Grieving the loss of his only son, Lone Horn permitted himself to be gored to death by a buffalo bull in 1836. His younger brother then became a chief, taking the name Lone Horn.[4]

A shrewd politician and diplomat, this second Lone Horn became a prominent Minneconjou leader, perhaps best known for forging a seven-year truce from 1851 to 1858 with the Mountain Crows.[5] Lone Horn played a critical role in Lakota affairs during the events of 1875–1876. He had four sons, including Big Foot, who was killed at Wounded Knee in 1890, and Touch the Cloud, a significant figure in the adult life of Crazy Horse.[6]

The elder Crazy Horse and Rattle Blanket Woman had at least two children, a girl born about 1838, and the boy born in 1840. In 1844 the Crows defeated the Oglalas in battle, killing between twenty-six and thirty-eight Oglala warriors from Crazy Horse's band. The elder Crazy Horse's brother, an uncle to the boy, was among the Oglala casualties. One winter count (that of Cloud Shield) notes that the elder "Crazy Horse says his prayer and goes on the warpath." Grief stricken at the deaths of so many in her band, Rattle Blanket Woman committed suicide.[7] Eventually, her widower Crazy Horse married two Brulé women, sisters of Spotted Tail. One became the mother of Little Hawk, the reckless and daring half-brother of young Crazy Horse.

Crazy Horse and his wives raised young Crazy Horse in the

traditional Lakota culture. Seven tribes comprised the Lakotas: the Oglalas; Brulés (or Sicanjus); Minneconjous; Blackfeet; Two Kettles; Sans Arcs (No Bows); and Hunkpapas. The seven tribes had the same language, religion, and culture, and they shared similar histories. Like any other nation (Indian or non-Indian) the Lakotas sought to control the economic resources essential to their existence, and by 1840 the Lakotas were a formidable military power at the zenith of their strength.

By 1840 the resources essential for Lakota survival were buffalo herds and the grazing grounds that supported the buffalo and horse herds. As early as the mid-1840s, however, the buffalo herds in the eastern part of Lakota country were declining. The herds were moving west toward the mountains, compelling the Lakotas to send hunting parties north and south.[8] The Lakotas required the game populations not only for their sustenance, clothing, shelter, and religion, but also to maintain their involvement in the extensive trade networks crucial to tribal survival.

Lakota efforts to dominate this territory pitted them against other tribes who lived in or hunted in the region, including Crows, Shoshones, Pawnees, Hidatsas, Mandans, and Omahas. These tribes required the same territory for their own survival, and competition led to warfare. In the 1840s an increasing tide of Oregon Trail emigrants across Lakota lands exacerbated the situation. Then came the United States Army with orders to protect the emigrants and the wagon roads in Indian country.

War against other tribes and against the whites dominated Lakota history during Crazy Horse's lifetime, and it was as a war leader that Crazy Horse served his people. Indeed, threats to their way of life so escalated during the 1860s that Lakota chiefs redefined their meaning of war, and some attempted to modify the nature of chieftainship to better stop the white challenge.

Some authors have misunderstood the underlying dynamics of warfare on the northern plains, and earlier generations of scholars trivialized the military history of the northern plains tribes. In some cases, the last non-Indians to take Indian warfare seriously were the soldiers who fought them. Early twentieth-century scholars reduced Plains Indian warfare to a glorified *machismo* game. As anthropologist Robert Lowie wrote in 1920, "The Plains Indian fought not for territorial aggrandizement nor for the victor's spoils, but above all because fighting was a game worth while because of the social recognition it brought when played according to the rules." In 1940 Lowie reemphasized, "though the desire for loot and revenge played their part, the outstanding goal of these tribes was glory. . . . [T]he motives of primitive warfare seldom coincided with those familiar to us. . . . Plains Indian warfare . . . loomed as an exciting pastime played according to established rules, the danger lending zest to the game. . . . Wherever men fight for glory, practical ends are bound to recede."[9]

Warfare was "exciting," bringing "glory" to Crazy Horse, but it was not a game bereft of "practical ends" any more than was the combat at Gettysburg or at Omaha Beach on D day. War for the survival of one's own people is the most eminently practical reason to fight. Indeed, war between tribes and against the whites was a fundamental contest for survival.

In 1854, when he was fourteen, Crazy Horse first encountered these new antagonists who were appallingly different from traditional tribal enemies of the Lakotas. On August 19, 1854, Crazy Horse was in the Brulé (Sicanju) village of Chief Conquering Bear near Fort Laramie when a cow limped away from a passing Mormon wagon train. Young Lakota men killed and ate the cow. The next day a brash, arrogant brevet second lieutenant named John L. Grattan led thirty-one men and two artillery pieces to Conquering Bear's village and ordered Conquering Bear to surrender the warrior who shot the cow. When Conquering Bear, a wise chief, tried to negotiate, Grattan ordered the cannons fired. Grattan was as inept at artillery as he was at negotiation. The rounds flew harmlessly through the tops of tepees. Retaliating warriors killed Grattan and his entire command in minutes. Chief Conquering Bear later died from wounds he sustained during the battle.[10]

Crazy Horse witnessed this bloody episode, and it profoundly affected him. Soon thereafter the fourteen year old had a vision that guided him the rest of his life and empowered him later as a war chief. The boy's vision, which was complicated and difficult to interpret, became a remarkably detailed prediction of his adult life. Once Crazy Horse became an adult, the Oglala holy man

Chips continued to interpret the vision for Crazy Horse.[11]

The Grattan affair was only the first in a series of clashes between the Lakotas and the army. On September 3, 1855, General William S. Harney attacked a Brulé (Sicanju) village on the Blue Water in western Nebraska. The soldiers killed at least eighty-six Brulés, many of them women and children. During the attack, Crazy Horse, who was visiting the village, was away hunting. When he returned he discovered a smoldering wreckage filled with dead and mutilated corpses. Amongst the carnage he found a severely wounded Cheyenne woman whom he nursed to health and returned to her own people. Indeed, Crazy Horse may have lived periodically among the Cheyennes for some years after 1855.

During these years his name became Horse Stands In Sight, and by 1861 he had his warrior name, Crazy Horse. Years before, his grandfather, a medicine man also named Crazy Horse had predicted that his grandson would someday carry the name.[12] Crazy Horse's younger brother took the old name, Horse Stands In Sight, that same year. As an adult this same brother eventually took the adult name of Little Hawk. Their father became Worm, and he is best known to posterity as Worm.

Declining game populations, especially buffalo, increased pressure on the Lakotas and surrounding tribes. The overland trail migrations, which began in 1842, split the buffalo herds, and the migrants' animals depleted the grass, making adjacent areas empty of game.[13] The migrants also killed game, and as early as 1846 Lakota chiefs along the Platte River bitterly complained that the whites were maliciously destroying buffalo. That same year, Congress passed the Oregon Trail Act authorizing military protection for the migrants and making the army a fixture along the southern border of Lakota country. In 1849 the California gold rush greatly increased travel on the trails, further exacerbating the situation for the Lakotas. The struggle for resources intensified as Crazy Horse grew up. As one historian writes:

> rather than a clash over the remaining buffalo, the struggle had been joined over the grazing areas where the last herds would wander. By 1864 the bands of the Teton Sioux, the most numerous and powerful of the tribes in this region,

had begun to push back all competition, forcing other tribes to withdraw from adjacent territories. Only the Sioux now resided in the secluded grazing grounds of the wandering herds. Thus, only the remote bands of Sioux could believe that the independence of their traditional way of life might be prolonged.

However, even the western Sioux, the Tetons, were not united in their assessment of the situation. Not all Sioux leaders believed that their people could resist the changes demanded by the invasions of the whites.[14]

Crazy Horse, who lived with and led these more remote Lakotas, believed deeply that resistance was possible.

Amidst the turmoil along the Platte River, and in the wake of the Grattan affair and Harney's punitive expeditions through Lakota country, the warfare that involved the Lakotas and their Cheyenne allies in the 1860s, and the aftermath of the Sioux War in Minnesota, some Lakota chiefs began to think that the whites now posed the supreme danger. These chiefs believed the Lakotas had to rethink their very definition of white men as enemies because it was apparent that the whites more threatened Lakota survival than any of their tribal antagonists.

The core of Lakota culture sanctioned tribal support for their warriors. When White Buffalo Woman brought the sacred pipe to the Lakotas, she also gave them precise instructions about the pipe as an agent of prayer and of peace. One contemporary of Crazy Horse, the Oglala George Sword wrote: "Then she [White Buffalo Woman] told them that those who fought each other within the tribe must be friends instead. But those who were enemies were not to be friends, but enemies; and then as enemies they will remain. And she said everything done in warfare [against these enemies] was to be accounted as good deeds."[15]

According to Raymond J. DeMallie, who is translating George Sword's writings, Sword shows that White Buffalo Woman "provides what can only be considered a religious justification for intertribal warfare." For the Lakotas the traditional conferring of enemy status on Indian foes meant that "enemies" were "common men" or Indians, like themselves. Thus, for the Lakotas, fighting tribal enemies was the "most honorable duty of a man's life . . . [whereas] white people had no place in this classification. In fact, the first whites with whom the Sioux came in contact were considered to be not human in the same way as the Sioux."[16]

Like the other Plains tribes, the Lakotas developed an elaborate system of war honors to recognize and promote the reputations of their bravest men. "But if warfare against enemy tribes was a natural state of affairs for the Lakotas, what about fighting the whites? They were not '*toka*', therefore there was no honor in fighting them and the scalps of white people were not valued as trophies," explains DeMallie. "If the Lakotas were to be successful in resisting the white advance on their territory, then in cultural terms they needed to transform white people into enemies."[17]

Sword described how the Lakotas transformed the whites into enemies. About 1863 the Minneconjous and Hunkpapas decided to fight the whites. Some did not want to "transform white people into enemies," but, as DeMallie translates Sword:

> Red Cloud wanted to fight the whites, and many agreed; that winter they decided definitely to fight the whites. What the Lakotas principally resented, they said, was that the whites were advancing and taking the land, and that by continuing they would annihilate the Lakota people, they said, and this frightened them. So they planned a big fight, and the tribal council had the crier make this announcement:
>
> "All of you young men, listen well! The white people are about to take over our land completely, and we will no longer be a people. Therefore we will fight them, so anyone who strikes a white man will strike an enemy!
>
> Anyone who is wounded by a white man will be considered to be wounded by an enemy!" So the crier said, and "if you take their horses; all these deeds will count as honors, so they say!"[18]

Thus the Lakotas joined their collective need for defense to the culturally sanctioned combat honors so essential to a warrior's prestige and standing among the Lakotas. Crazy Horse had already entered his most active years as a warrior. Certainly he was superlative at warfare. His growing reputation was based on his fights against the whites as well as against enemies like the Crows and Shoshones. The Lakotas had recognized the singular ability of Crazy Horse before Red Cloud's War of 1866–1868 when the Oglala Red Cloud and other leaders refused whites the use of the Bozeman Trail, which led north through the Powder River region—through Lakota country—to the goldfields in Montana. Determined to compel the army to abandon its forts along the Bozeman Trail, Red Cloud was the primary architect of the war to preserve the Powder River country for the Lakotas.

Crazy Horse led war parties against the soldiers throughout the Powder River country. Between August and December of 1866 Lakota warriors killed 154 soldiers and travelers along the Bozeman Trail. On December 21, 1866, Crazy Horse was instrumental in the Lakotas' most stunning victory over the army until the annihilation of George Armstrong Custer's Seventh Cavalry a decade later. That day Crazy Horse lured Captain William Fetterman into a trap where 1,500 to 2,000 Lakota, Cheyenne, and Arapaho warriors killed Fetterman and his entire command in twenty minutes. Fetterman had once boasted that with 80 men he could ride through the entire Lakota nation. The army lost 81 men that day.

The Oglala warrior Eagle Elk's remarks to poet John G. Neihardt illustrate that Crazy Horse had those qualities essential for any great military commander.[19] According to Eagle Elk, Crazy Horse was not only an inspired warrior, he worried about mundane but important things such as the rest and feeding of his men and the care of their weapons and horses. Like other great battlefield commanders, Crazy Horse remained calm in the worst of situations. His mere presence on the battlefield heartened his men for the grim business ahead. For similar examples of such poised leadership we need only to think of the bearing of such Crazy Horse contemporaries as General Stonewall Jackson on the battlefields of Virginia, General William T. Sherman's coolness amidst the unbelievable carnage at Shiloh, or Colonel Joshua Chamberlain's uncanny clearheadedness at the Battle of Little Round Top at Gettysburg. Here we see the impact that such leaders as Crazy Horse have on their men in the merciless crucible of combat.

The victory over Fetterman in 1866 shocked the country, prompting a searching debate over federal Indian policy. General William T. Sherman wanted the full force of the army thrown against the Lakotas, "even to their extermination, men, women, and children."[20] Desiring negotiation, other officials in 1867 invited the Lakotas to meet with government commissioners at Fort Laramie. While some Lakotas showed up, most members of the Powder River country bands and the northern Lakotas did not. Red Cloud would come to Fort Laramie only when he saw the soldiers abandoning the Bozeman Trail forts. "He assured us," reported the commissioners, "that whenever the military garrison at Fort Phil Kearny and Fort C. F. Smith were withdrawn, the war on his part would cease."[21]

Only in the autumn of 1868 did Red Cloud and chiefs of the Brulés, Hunkpapas, Blackfeet Lakotas, and Sans Arcs arrive at Fort Laramie. Red Cloud and about 125 chiefs and leading men attended, including several who had already signed the treaty. The various Lakota chiefs signed a draft treaty that provided for a large reservation to include all of present-day South Dakota west of the Missouri River. It designated the Powder River as "unceded Indian territory" closed to all whites. The government clearly expected the Lakotas to abandon their nomadic culture for life on the reservations. Government commissioners wanted to establish agencies, to supply clothes and rations, and to educate the Lakotas to become farmers. The government expected them to cease being Lakotas and become red white men.[22]

Red Cloud, the most prominent Lakota signatory of the treaty, remains a controversial figure. He was a brilliant warrior and war leader. Red Cloud is the only Indian leader in the American West to win a war against the United States Army. Indeed, Red Cloud's victory was, in the words of one historian, "the only instance in the history of the United States where the government has gone to war and afterwards negotiated a peace conceding everything demanded by the enemy and exacting nothing in return."[23] Red Cloud was as shrewd a negotiator as he was a gifted war leader. His great abilities confused government officials who mistakenly believed that Red Cloud's success determined his status among his own people. Many Lakotas distrusted Red Cloud, however, because they believed he was too ambitious personally, and they were concerned with internal conflicts in Oglala history going back to Red Cloud's earlier years.

While government officials were unclear about what to do with Red Cloud, army officers regarded the 1868 treaty as a temporary expedient because they thought future developments would render the treaty meaningless. Army officers predicted that completion of the transcontinental railroad in 1869 would open more direct routes to Montana and thus render the Bozeman Trail useless. Likewise, army officers knew the growing western railroad network would make it easier to concentrate troops and supplies if fighting erupted in the region. The grazing grounds and buffalo herds in the unceded territory meant that the Lakotas could live there traditionally rather than on the "government dole" at the agencies, which "neatly postponed a dispute over going to the reservation," writes Robert M. Utley, "but white officials confidently looked to the day when the extinction of the buffalo would eliminate the issue."[24]

The 1868 treaty gave the Lakota leadership what Utley presents as three options: they could

> surrender most of what made them [Lakota], settle on the Great Sioux Reservation, and yield their independence to white officials. Or they could try to keep a foot in each world, following the herds in the unceded territory but also exploiting the agency system to whatever limits the government would tolerate. Or, like Sitting Bull [and Crazy Horse], they could fiercely reject all relations with whites (except traders, of course), hold to the old ways as distant from the whites as possible, and meet any further white encroachments with force.
>
> A hard core of each tribe, possibly one-third of the total Lakota population, chose the last course.[25]

Divided Lakota opinion about the controversial Red Cloud further complicated the Oglalas response to the treaty. In later years historians mistakenly viewed the Oglalas as polarized, gravitating to one fixed group or another: to the so-called "agency" Lakotas that were at Spotted Tail and Red Cloud Agencies in

Nebraska; and to the "northern" Indians or so-called "hostiles" under the leadership of Crazy Horse, Sitting Bull, and other chiefs. In fact, the situation was quite fluid as chiefs, bands, and family groups moved from the agency to the north country and back again as best fit their particular band or family interests.

The Fort Laramie Treaty of 1868 confronted the Lakota leaders with an extraordinary challenge. As before, when whites were redefined as enemies, some chiefs in the late 1860s proposed radical changes to the traditional Lakota system of leadership. Four Horns, a Hunkpapa chief, proposed to bring the nonreservation Lakotas from all bands to the banner of the Hunkpapas. Four Horns suggested that his nephew, Sitting Bull, become not only the head chief of the Hunkpapas but be elevated "to nothing less than a supreme chieftainship of all the Lakota tribes, with the Yanktonais included as well."[26] Four Horns's revolutionary proposal went against the ingrained independence of Lakota bands and tribes, but in the aftermath of the 1868 treaty all the nonreservation factions of all the Lakota bands were thrown together in the Powder River country. Sometime in 1869 along Rosebud Creek a large camp of nonreservation Lakotas from all bands and Northern Cheyennes held a ceremony to appoint Sitting Bull, as Utley terms it, "supreme chief of the Sioux confederation."[27]

The prominence of Sitting Bull paralleled the rise of Crazy Horse, who had become one of the most renowned and respected warriors among the Lakotas. In 1868 some Oglalas formally recognized his status when, a few months after some chiefs signed the treaty, a large camp of Oglalas gathered about forty miles northeast of present-day Lusk, Wyoming. According to one contemporary, they "were camped in the hereditary manner followed by [them] when they are moving, viz, in a large circle with an opening in the east or the southeast, so that it is in a general direction toward the rising sun."[28] The "old men or leaders" of this large camp selected four warriors, Crazy Horse and three others as shirt wearers, or "head warriors of their people."[29] The four head warriors received broad powers from their leaders. They "represented in their commands and acts the entire power of the nation."[30] In 1944 the Oglala Black Elk described the responsibilities of the these four men:

The four chiefs had the power to care for the people, for the tribe as a whole. Next is the land; look after the land. Next is the helpless; see that they are taken care of. Remember you probably [will] have your graves in four different places; you [will] probably die on a plain or a hill [in warfare]; it might be in a gulch; it might be the woods. They were elected to give their lives for the people, so they may have to die for the people.

Crazy Horse, concluded Black Elk, "is the last big chief, and then it's all over."[31]

Crazy Horse remained a shirt wearer until 1870, a devastating year of personal loss for him. That year Black Buffalo Woman left her husband, No Water, and eloped with Crazy Horse, accompanying him on a war party.[32] Enraged, No Water did not accept this abrupt divorce from Black Buffalo Woman. Borrowing a revolver, No Water trailed the lovers. He finally caught up with the war party, quickly entered the lodge of Crazy Horse, and shot him. The bullet struck Crazy Horse in the face just below his left nostril and exited out the back of his skull, scarring him terribly but not killing him.[33] No Water was three to four feet from Crazy Horse when he fired, and severe powder burns also permanently marked Crazy Horse's face. Crazy Horse spent several months recovering. Plains Indians expected their chiefs to rise above personal conflicts that might disrupt the tribe or a band, and the uproar over Black Buffalo Woman cost Crazy Horse his formal position as a shirt wearer. He also lost Black Buffalo Woman, because No Water, after shooting Crazy Horse, compelled her to return to him.

The No Water episode was only the first personal tragedy to overtake Crazy Horse in 1870. Eagle Elk told Neihardt that Crazy Horse was still recuperating from his wound when Little Hawk, his beloved half-brother, was killed in battle.[34] The two brothers were devoted to each other, and both were fearless and superb warriors. Some Lakotas believed that had Little Hawk lived, his reputation as a warrior and war leader would have rivaled that of Crazy Horse.

The death of Little Hawk devastated Crazy Horse, already lying

wounded and helpless, despondent over the loss of both Black
Buffalo Woman and his position as a shirt wearer. That same
summer the Shoshones killed Hump, a Minneconjou chief.[35] Older
than Crazy Horse, Hump had been a close mentor and confidant
of Crazy Horse since the latter's childhood. Hump had planned
the tactics that destroyed Fetterman and his command, and he
had selected his young protégé, Crazy Horse, to lead the decoys
who lured Fetterman to his end.

Certainly with the embarrassing situation concerning Black
Buffalo Woman and the grievous losses of Little Hawk and Hump,
the summer of 1870 was a ruinous period for Crazy Horse. Indeed
1870 was such a disastrous year for Crazy Horse that some of his
closest friends decided he should marry, and in 1871 they arranged
for Crazy Horse to marry an Oglala, Black Shawl Woman.[36] Black
Shawl Woman bore Crazy Horse's only child, a daughter named
They Are Afraid of Her. The child died in 1873, and her death
deeply affected her doting father. After his daughter's death, Crazy
Horse became even more introverted than before. After her death,
possibly in her honor, Crazy Horse created the Last Child Warrior
Society. Eagle Elk, whose comments to Neihardt are our best source
on the Last Child Warrior Society, said Crazy Horse selected the
warriors for their bravery and that they were the younger or
youngest children in their families.[37]

While Crazy Horse despaired over these personal losses, relations
between the Lakotas and the government continued to deteriorate.
Crazy Horse lost the formal status of shirt wearer, but his absolute
opposition to the whites assured him a considerable following
among those who now looked to him and Sitting Bull for
leadership. By 1870 Sitting Bull and Crazy Horse and other leaders
decided to attack the whites only to repel them from Lakota
country. Crazy Horse and Sitting Bull adhered to this strategy of
defensive war until the end of the fighting in 1877.

Havoc at the agencies ignited Lakota distrust while government
officials accused warriors of raiding outside Lakota domain.
Circumstances further deteriorated when surveyors marked a route
for the Northern Pacific Railroad along the northern fringes of
the unceded territory, infuriating the more northerly Hunkpapas.
Their outrage increased when in 1874 the government sent

Lieutenant Colonel George Custer on an expedition into the Black
Hills, an area clearly part of the Great Sioux Reservation.

By the mid-1870s Crazy Horse's firm resistance to white
incursions into Lakota lands had earned him his own considerable
following, especially among the Oglalas, Brulés, and Minneconjous.
Government officials and army officers recognized Crazy Horse
as one of the prominent Lakota chiefs. The Lakotas, including
those like Crazy Horse who had refused to sign the treaty or
recognize the authority of the Lakota chiefs who did, knew that
the 1868 treaty gave the Lakotas the right to live and hunt in their
territory south of the Yellowstone River in Montana and Wyoming.
The 1868 treaty clearly confirmed Lakota ownership of the Black
Hills of South Dakota, but by 1875 the United States government
wanted them because gold had been discovered there. The Lakotas
adamantly rejected all government offers for the Black Hills, and
the Brulé chief Spotted Tail suggested that whites would not loan
a team of mules on the kind of terms that the government
proposed.[38]

Negotiations collapsed in late 1875, and in December the Indian
Bureau sent an ultimatum to the Lakotas and Cheyennes living in
the region of the Powder and Bighorn Rivers, bluntly ordering
Crazy Horse and the others to be on the reservations in Nebraska
within six weeks (by January 31, 1876) or face military action. The
order was absurd. Had the Lakotas and Cheyennes intended to
comply immediately, which they did not, severe winter weather
and the possibility of deep snow could have prevented them from
reaching the Nebraska reservations before the deadline. Some of
the chiefs, including Crazy Horse, decided to wait until the better
spring weather to go to the reservations to see what government
officials had to say. Five years before, Sitting Bull and Crazy Horse
had concluded to fight only defensively against the whites, and in
the winter of 1875–1876 Crazy Horse was not going to attack unless
soldiers entered Lakota country first.

The government insisted upon the deadline, however, and
ordered the army to proceed. Army generals decided upon a winter
campaign against the Indians in the Powder River country. Winter
conditions on the northern plains made terrible demands on
soldiers and their mounts, but winter also held advantages for the

army. The mobile Lakotas and Cheyennes settled into fixed villages during the winter, and these winter camps held tons of dried buffalo meat as well as robes and other essentials to get the people through the winter. One army officer explained the army strategy succinctly: "If a single one of these villages could be surprised in the depth of winter, the resulting loss of property would be so great that the enemy would suffer for years; their exposure to the bitter cold of the blizzards would break any spirit, no matter how brave."[39]

Army attacks on villages that included old people, women, and children has created controversy from then until now. Critics charged that the soldiers were butchers who needlessly involved noncombatants. If a village was destroyed, women, children, and old people were subject to starvation, freezing, or death in the fighting. The strategy's principal architects (Generals Sheridan, Crook, and others) first came to prominence as Union officers during the Civil War. In the Civil War these generals, following the lead of President Abraham Lincoln, and Generals Ulysses S. Grant and William T. Sherman, had fought not only the Confederate armies but also the Southern economic infrastructure; they waged war against agricultural plantations, railroads, factories, warehouses, cities, and towns, in effect, against the Southern population.

Lincoln, Grant, and Sherman decided that once a civilian population loses the will to fight, their armies will crumble, no matter how brave or how victorious they may be on the battlefield. We need only to remember Grant's campaigns in Mississippi and his intense bombardment and siege of Vicksburg, Sherman's burning of Atlanta and his devastating march through Georgia and South Carolina, or Sheridan and Crook's destruction of the Shenandoah Valley of Virginia. This strategy worked against their own people during the Civil War, and in 1876 these same officers adopted it against the Lakotas and Cheyennes. Like Southerners during the Civil War, the Lakotas and their allies were to feel the brunt of "hard war."

The army decided upon a three-pronged military offensive into southern Montana and northern Wyoming. Some army officers predicted that it would all be over by the spring of 1876, but the weather ruined the army's plans. Two of the army's three columns were snowed in and never left their home forts, but on March 1, 1876, General George Crook moved a third column into the field. Known to the Lakotas as Three Stars and to other tribes as Grey Fox, Grey Wolf, or Morning Star, Crook led his men north from Fort Fetterman in Wyoming. Crazy Horse once reportedly said that Crook was to be feared more than any other general. Crook's men marched into the teeth of a fierce Great Plains winter. After sixteen bitterly miserable days in the field, they were close to starving.[40]

On March 17 a colonel and six companies of cavalry from Crook's command found a Cheyenne village and attacked it. Army scout Frank Grouard mistakenly assured army officers that this village belonged to Crazy Horse's Lakotas. The battle was an embarrassing debacle for the army and an utter catastrophe for the Cheyennes, who lost their village. The soldiers' attack initially surprised the Cheyennes, but the warriors' counterattacks were coordinated, disciplined, and fierce. They fought so well that the commanding officer entirely lost his composure and abandoned his instructions from General Crook. Making this situation even worse was the fact that these Cheyennes were waiting for spring weather to go to Red Cloud Agency in Nebraska because their chiefs wanted to avoid the fighting that they feared would come with summer.[41]

The army attack galvanized the Lakotas and Cheyennes in the Yellowstone country. Crazy Horse, Sitting Bull, and other chiefs prepared for defensive war against the army. General Crook did not find Crazy Horse in the Cheyenne village in March. Rather, Crazy Horse and Lakota and Northern Cheyenne warriors found Crook and his army column on Rosebud Creek in Montana on June 17, 1876. The hard-fought six-hour Battle of the Rosebud was a strategic victory for Crazy Horse and his Lakota and Cheyenne warriors. Crazy Horse stopped Three Star's advance, forcing this army column out of action for six crucial weeks.[42]

By then, another army column, commanded by Brigadier General Alfred Terry and including Custer's Seventh Cavalry, was also in the Yellowstone River Country. On June 25, 1876, Custer and units of the Seventh Cavalry attacked an immense Lakota and Cheyenne village along the Little Bighorn River. Crazy Horse was in the fighting at the south end of the village, and then the action shifted to the north where Crazy Horse led charges that shattered whatever unit cohesion remained among the Seventh Cavalry units.[43] The Battle of the Little Bighorn stunned the country. Initially in the press and in public perception, Sitting Bull, one of the great Lakota chiefs and religious leaders, received credit for destroying Custer. Sitting Bull lived until 1890, becoming well known because of his self-imposed exile in Canada, his appearance in Buffalo Bill's Wild West show, and his untimely death at the hands of Indian police during the Ghost Dance movement. His fame over the years obscured the role of Crazy Horse in the minds of non-Indians. Certainly, Sitting Bull was a major figure whose religious leadership and political skill was instrumental in keeping together the formidable Lakota/Cheyenne coalition during the summer of 1876, but Crazy Horse was the leading Lakota military figure that summer.

In a period of eight days Crazy Horse and his warriors defeated George Crook and destroyed Custer's command. At the Battle of the Rosebud, Crazy Horse bested a general recognized in his own lifetime and today among historians as a skilled, innovative battlefield commander. In Crook, Crazy Horse defeated one of the army's best. While Custer's ability as a commander remains hotly debated, he was certainly the best-known army officer in the West. With their overwhelming victory at the Battle of the Little Bighorn, Crazy Horse and Lakota and Cheyenne warriors had destroyed the army's most controversial and prominent Indian fighter.

The army continued its "hard war" against the Lakotas and Cheyennes throughout the summer of 1876 and into the ensuing autumn and winter. Resupplied and with reinforcements, Crook sought to vanquish the warriors who defeated him at the Rosebud. Tenaciously he stayed on the trail of the Lakotas throughout August and September, and on November 26, 1876, units from his command attacked the large Cheyenne village of Chief Morning Star (or Dull Knife, p. 82). The army defeated the Cheyennes and destroyed their village of more than two hundred lodges. Cast into the bitter northern plains winter, some Cheyennes made it to the village of Crazy Horse.[44] Other army units along the Yellowstone

River kept after the Lakota villages in that area, and Crazy Horse had several sharp fights against the army that winter.

Despite the bravery of the Lakotas and Cheyennes and the genius of Crazy Horse, the army's campaign of attrition worked. Army patrols kept the Indians on the move, which kept them from hunting, and over the winter starvation wore on the families of the warriors. Finally, emissaries representing Chiefs Red Cloud and Spotted Tail reached Crazy Horse in the spring of 1877.[45]

A military realist, Crazy Horse saw that his women, children, and old people faced starvation, whereas continued fighting meant annihilation of his fighting force. By spring 1877 the army's strategy had brought Crazy Horse to the same position Robert E. Lee had faced in April 1865. With the army cordon tightening around him, Crazy Horse knew that further fighting meant only the eventual annihilation of his fighting force and their families. As it had successfully ground the Confederacy and its armies into submission a decade earlier, the army's war of attrition had brought Crazy Horse's people to the brink of starvation.

Crazy Horse surrendered with his band at Camp Robinson, Nebraska, in spring 1877. Deep distrust quickly developed between Crazy Horse and army officers. Careless and inexperienced army officers, incompetent and conniving interpreters, and the open jealousy of other Lakota chiefs poisoned relations between Crazy Horse and the officers. On September 5, 1877, Crazy Horse came to Camp Robinson, expecting to meet the commanding officer. Instead, Lakota escorts took Crazy Horse to the guardhouse. Recognizing the deception, he fought against entering the guardhouse door, and as one of his own war chiefs pinned Crazy Horse's arms from behind an army sentry fatally bayoneted Crazy Horse in the groin. Crazy Horse died just before midnight on September 5, 1877. He was thirty-seven years old.

Twenty-three years earlier, the fourteen-year-old Crazy Horse had a vision that he would never die in battle. Rather his vision had forewarned of his death while being held by some of his own people. Crazy Horse had fought for his people, and his defense of their Lakota birthright measured his greatness. After his death, other tribes fought the army, and army campaigns against the Chiricahua Apaches continued until 1886. But never again did an

Indian nation wage a military struggle of the magnitude of that of the Lakotas and their Cheyenne allies between the mid-1860s and 1877. Standing as an embodiment of patriotism, boldness, and determination, Crazy Horse and his generation of warriors ended a four-hundred-year saga of Native American military resistance.

Notes

The author gratefully acknowledges the receipt of a research grant from the Omaha, Nebraska, Corral of Westerner's International given in memory of Omaha-based writer, the late Budington Swanson. This grant made it possible for the author to conduct the research upon which this essay is based.

1.   For a discussion of the "hard war" strategy of "directed severity" see Mark Grimsley, *The Hard Hand of War: Union Military Policy toward Southern Civilians, 1861–1865* (New York: Cambridge University Press, 1995).

2.   Encouraging Bear or Chips, interview by Eli S. Ricker, 1907, Pine Ridge Reservation, South Dakota, tablet 18, Eli S. Ricker Collection, Nebraska State Historical Society, Lincoln (hereafter Ricker Collection).

3.   Victoria Conroy to Superintendent McGregor, December 18, 1934, Burnside Papers, State Historical Society of Iowa, Des Moines. This letter is also printed in full in Richard G. Hardorff, *The Oglala Lakota Crazy Horse* (Mattituck, N.Y.: J. M. Carroll and Company, 1985), 29-31.

4.   He Dog, Chips, and William Garnett were quite specific that the mother of Crazy Horse was Minneconjou. Chips interview, Ricker Collection; William Garnett, interview by Eli S. Ricker, tablet 1, Ricker Collection; He Dog, interview by Mari Sandoz, 1931, Pine Ridge Reservation, South Dakota, box 31, part 2, Mari Sandoz Collection, Special Collections, University of Nebraska Library, Lincoln. Others commented upon the kinship between Crazy Horse and Touch the Clouds, the Minneconjou chief and a member of the Lone Horn family, which further substantiates He Dog, Chips, and Garnett. See also Hardorff, *The Oglala Lakota Crazy Horse*, 27, 32. Compiling and evaluating evidence from winter counts and statements from contemporaries of Crazy Horse, Hardorff makes a compelling case for Crazy Horse's relationship to the Minneconjou through his mother. Certainly Hardorff is the first to

systematically review these items, many of which have been in the historical record since the nineteenth and early twentieth centuries. For Lone Horn's portrait, see George Catlin, *Letters and Notes on the Manners, Customs, and Condition of the North American Indians* (2 vols.; 1841; reprint, Minneapolis: Ross and Haines, 1965), 1:221-22, pl. 86.

5. Kingsley M. Bray, "Lone Horn's Peace: A New View of Sioux-Crow Relations, 1851–1858," *Nebraska History*, 66 (Spring 1985), 28-47.

6. He Dog and William Garnett called Touch the Cloud a relative of Crazy Horse: He Dog called Crazy Horse and Touch the Cloud "close" relatives; Garnett noted that Touch the Cloud was the son of Lone Horn and that the band of Touch the Cloud spent most of 1875 and 1876 with the Oglalas and Sicanjus with Crazy Horse. See Robert A. Clark, ed., *The Killing of Chief Crazy Horse: Three Eyewitness Views* (Lincoln: University of Nebraska Press, 1988), 66, 69, 115.

7. Conroy to McGregor, December 18, 1934. The Battiste Good winter count calls 1844–1845 "The Crows-came-and-killed-thirty-eight-Oglalas Winter." The Cloud Shield winter count, 1844–1845, notes "Crazy Horse says his prayers and goes on the war-path." Garrick Mallery, *Picture-Writing of the American Indians* (2 vols.; 1893; reprint, New York: Dover Publications, 1972), 1:fig. 401, 2:fig. 641. See also Hardorff, *The Oglala Lakota Crazy Horse*, 27.

8. Richard White, "The Winning of the West: The Expansion of the Western Sioux in the Eighteenth and Nineteenth Centuries," *Journal of American History*, 65 (September 1978), 319-43.

9. Robert L. Lowie quoted in W. W. Newcomb, Jr., "A Re-examination of the Causes of Plains Warfare," *American Anthropologist*, 52 (July-September 1950), 318. See also Bernard Mishkin, *Rank and Warfare among the Plains Indians* (1940; reprint, Lincoln: University of Nebraska Press, 1992). Fraser J. Pakes, *Making War Attractive* (London: English Westerner's Society, 1990) provides an insightful evaluation of the economic and cultural forces that affected the Plains Indian war complex of the nineteenth century.

10. George E. Hyde, *Red Cloud's Folk: A History of the Oglala Sioux Indians* (1937; reprint, Norman: University of Oklahoma Press, 1976), 72-77; Mari Sandoz, *Crazy Horse: The Strange Man of the Oglalas* (1942; reprint, New York: Hastings House, 1975), 22-23.

11. Garnett interview, Ricker Collection.

12. Author interviews, 1989, Rosebud Sioux Reservation, South Dakota; Chips interview, Ricker Collection. Crazy Horse also had the names of Buys A Bad Woman, Crushes Man, and Horse Partly Showing. See He Dog in Clark, ed., *The Killing of Chief Crazy Horse*, 68.

13. For an excellent summary of the environmental context affecting the buffalo herds, see Dan Flores, "The Great Contraction: Bison and Indians in Northern Plains Environmental History" in this volume.

14. John J. Killoren, S.J., *"Come Blackrobe": De Smet and the Indian Tragedy* (Norman: University of Oklahoma Press, 1994), 256.

15. Sword quoted from Raymond J. DeMallie, "Sioux Warfare: An Ethnohistorical Appraisal," paper, Rosebud Battle Symposium, Sheridan, Wyoming, August 15, 1990, p. 5. I am indebted to Professor DeMallie for permission to quote from his paper. DeMallie translated from Lakota to English the writings of George Sword (c. 1847–1909). Sword was the younger brother of Man That Owns A Sword, who was appointed a shirt wearer along with Crazy Horse in 1868.

16. Ibid.

17. Ibid.

18. Ibid.

19. Eagle Elk, interview by John G. Neihardt, November 1944, John G. Neihardt Collection, Western Historical Manuscripts Collection, University of Missouri–Columbia (hereafter Neihardt Collection).

20. Sherman quoted in Robert M. Utley, *The Indian Frontier of the American West, 1846–1890* (Albuquerque: University of New Mexico Press, 1984), 105.

21. Red Cloud, quoted in James C. Olson, *Red Cloud and the Sioux Problem* (Lincoln: University of Nebraska Press, 1965), 65.

22. For an excellent review of the historical context behind the 1868 Fort Laramie Treaty see Alvin M. Josephy, Jr., "Indian Policy and the Battle of the Little Bighorn" in this volume.

23. Doane Robinson, *A History of the Dakota or Sioux Indians* (1904; reprint, Minneapolis, Minn.: Ross and Haines 1956), 387.

24. Robert M. Utley, *The Lance and the Shield: The Life and Times of Sitting Bull* (New York: Henry Holt and Company, 1993), 82.

25. Ibid., 85.

26. Ibid.

27. Ibid., 87.

28. Garnett interview, Ricker Collection. William Garnett was in this camp; Garnett was the son of Confederate Brigadier General Richard Garnett (who died in Pickett's Charge at the Battle of Gettysburg) and a Lakota mother. Garnett was living with his mother's people in this camp at this time. Garnett was thirteen years old. Raymond J. DeMallie, ed., *The Sixth Grandfather: Black Elk's Teachings Given to John G. Neihardt* (Lincoln: University of Nebraska Press, 1984), 322.

29. In addition to Crazy Horse, the three other shirt wearers were Young Man Afraid of His Horse, American Horse, and Man That Owns A Sword (also known as Knife); the latter was brother of George Sword.

30. Garnett interview, Ricker Collection.

31. DeMallie, *The Sixth Grandfather*, 322.

32. Eagle Elk interview, Neihardt Collection.

33. Chips interview, Ricker Collection.

34. Eagle Elk interview, Neihardt Collection.

35. DeMallie, *The Sixth Grandfather*, 158.

36. Red Feather, interview by Eleanor H. Hinman, July 8, 1930, Pine Ridge, South Dakota, in Eleanor H. Hinman, "Oglala Sources on the Life of Crazy Horse," *Nebraska History*, 57 (March 1976), 29.

37. Eagle Elk interview, Neihardt Collection.

38. Edward Lazarus, *Black Hills, White Justice: The Sioux Nation Versus the United States, 1775 to the Present* (New York: Harper Collins, 1991), 81.

39. John G. Bourke, quoted in Joseph C. Porter, *Paper Medicine Man: John Gregory Bourke and His American West* (Norman: University of Oklahoma Press, 1986), 28.

40. Ibid.

41. Ibid., 42-46; Neil C. Mangum, *Battle of the Rosebud: Prelude to the Little Bighorn* (El Segundo, Calif.: Upton and Sons, 1987).

42. Porter, *Paper Medicine Man*, 55-58.

43. Richard Allan Fox, Jr., *Archaeology, History, and Custer's Last Battle: The Little Bighorn Reexamined* (Norman: University of Oklahoma Press, 1993).

44. For an excellent study of the military offensive against the Lakotas and their allies during winter of 1876–1877 and the spring of 1877, see Jerome A. Greene, *Yellowstone Command: Colonel Nelson A. Miles and the Great Sioux War, 1876–1877* (Lincoln: University of Nebraska Press, 1991).

45. Ibid., 187-88.

Army Allies or Tribal Survival?

The "Other Indians" in the 1876 Campaign

Colin G. Calloway

I n the late 1750s, as France battled to save her crumbling North American empire, the army of the Marquis de Montcalm was a polyglot crew, composed of regular troops, Canadian militia, volunteers, and Indians. The Indian contingent comprised, at one time or another, warriors from various Iroquois tribes, Indians from Catholic mission villages on the St. Lawrence River, Hurons, Algonkins, Nipissings, Penobscots, Abenakis, Maliseets, Ottawas, Chippewas, Menominees, Mississaugas, Potawatomis, Delawares, Shawnees, Sauks, and Mesquakies. The diplomacy and expense of keeping together such a coalition, most of whose members spoke mutually unintelligible languages and many of whom harbored ancient hostilities, taxed French resources and resilience to the limit. The French devoted considerable effort to cultivating and maintaining their Indian alliances—they had to: their North American empire depended on it.[1] The British likewise employed Indian allies—mainly Mohawks, Mahicans, and Mohegans. In some campaigns, Indians constituted as much as one-seventh or one-eighth of New England's colonial armies.[2] The British developed the administration, personnel, and expertise to deal with their Indian allies.

Nevertheless, the Indians who participated in the so-called "French and Indian Wars" were neither mercenaries nor pawns.

They fought by their own rules and mostly for their own reasons, as indicated by the frequent frustrations of their European allies, who were never quite sure what they were up to. In some cases, the prime motive for going to war was to strike enemy Indians in traditional patterns of culturally motivated war, not to fight European troops in imperially driven conflicts. Some of Montcalm's Indian allies canoed a thousand miles to fight, then paddled home after a brief skirmish had netted them a few scalps. Others perpetrated the slaughter of the English garrison at Fort William Henry in 1757, an event made infamous by *The Last of the Mohicans*. The French had secured their objective when they took possession of the fort, but the Indians felt betrayed that *their* objectives had been frustrated. They took matters into their own hands to secure the scalps and plunder they felt their services warranted.[3] These people fought for their own reasons.

Looking back at the wars in the eastern woodlands, most of us can jettison the racist views of writers like Francis Parkman and Theodore Roosevelt that this was a simple story of conflict between natural enemies, with Anglo-Saxon "civilization" destined to defeat Indian "savages" and French Catholics. The "French and Indian Wars" were complex and messy affairs, in which international rivalries, intercolonial disputes, intertribal foreign policies, and intratribal politics overlapped in a kaleidoscope of conflicts and competitions.

More than a hundred years later and a thousand miles west, we rarely see such confusion. Instead, we often still get simple stories. European rivals have long since fallen out of the picture, and the United States alone engages in a straightforward campaign of whites against Indians. What is more, you do not have all those trees to obscure your vision: Indian war parties and United States cavalry units move across an uncluttered canvas, like easily distinguishable teams on an open playing field. Add to that star quarterbacks like Custer and Crazy Horse whose "parallel lives" as representatives of cultures in inevitable conflict culminate in the encounter, and it's easy to see why the Little Bighorn has captured our imagination as an epic, an elemental struggle with clear life-and-death issues and obvious resolution.[4]

But simple stories distort human realities. Serving as scouts and soldiers for the United States Army was a fairly common practice among Plains Indians.[5] Other Indian peoples besides the Sioux and Cheyenne participated in the Battle of the Little Bighorn, which, after all, was fought on the Crow reservation. On the day after the battle, as Lieutenant James Bradley's column approached the scene of the fight, the Crow scouts he had sent ahead met three Crow scouts who had been with Custer. They came back singing a mourning song and in tears. As the Crow scout Little Face struggled to tell Bradley his story, the other Crows went off a ways and "sat down alone, weeping and chanting that dreadful mourning song, and rocking their bodies to and fro. They were the first listeners to the horrid story of the Custer massacre, and, outside of the relatives and personal friends of the fallen, there were none in this whole horrified nation of forty millions of people to whom the tidings brought greater grief."[6]

Why? I doubt it was for love of Custer. What Native American interests and foreign policies caused Crows—and Arikaras, and Shoshones, and Pawnees—to be involved on the "wrong side" in the 1876 campaign, and what caused them to be so mortified at the outcome of this classic Indian-white encounter? These people were not lost, they were not confused, and they had not "sold out" to the Americans. We think we know what the soldiers and the Sioux were doing at the Little Bighorn and, of course, they were the main protagonists. But unless we include as actors in their own right the other Indians who were there as allies of the United States we cannot appreciate the different meanings that this "Indian victory" had for different Indian peoples. The Little Bighorn was a battle between cavalry and Sioux, but it was also an Indian-Indian conflict and occurred in the context of competing strategies for survival.

I thought of calling this essay "Oh, and by the way, Custer was there as well." Thankfully, I thought better of it, but perhaps we can move Custer aside for a moment and pay some attention to those Indian participants whose stories have been rather forgotten. If we leave the lens of our historical camera focused squarely on Indian-white conflict, with Little Bighorn as its dramatic culmination, we see these people but faintly, off to the side, and their actions make no sense to us. But if we move our lens half a turn, or better still put these people center-screen, things fall into place. Crow tears become understandable as a response to a perceived *Crow* tragedy, and not as the paean of "faithful allies" to a departed American hero.

Let's muddy the picture somewhat. Indians are usually the victims in American history. At the Battle of the Little Bighorn we see them in the unaccustomed role of victors, but we know the end of the story and we know, as they knew, that this was a late-in-the-game rally, not a final result. In a broader sense, however, everyone at the Little Bighorn was a victim. Industrializing America, with immigrant factory workers to feed in the East, demanded that cattle and settlers replace buffalo and Indians in the West. The instrument of this policy, the frontier army, was manned in large part by people from the margins of American society, casualties of similar economic and demographic changes. For many of the soldiers who died there, the Little Bighorn was the final stage in a journey of economic victimization that drove them from Europe or the East to death at the hands of other peoples fighting to escape their victimization. Charles Windolph, who was with Reno, had fled Prussia six years before to avoid being drafted to fight in the Franco-Prussian war. Unable to find steady work in New York, he joined the United States Army and got the kind of life he had come to America to escape.[7] I am not suggesting we should see American soldiers and American Indians as class allies, sacrificed to the capitalist goals of eastern elites, but it is worth a thought to break up some of the racial battle lines so deeply impressed in our historical memory.

The actions and motivations of the Indians involved in the 1876 campaigns poke additional holes in those racial battle lines. In August, about six weeks after the battle, Crow and Arikara scouts with General Alfred Terry came racing back to the main command, occasionally running their ponies in circles to signify they had sighted the enemy. They galloped through the columns to the rear, stripped to their loin cloths, painted their faces, mounted fresh ponies, and dashed back to the front, ready to fight the Sioux. In this event, the "enemy" Indians turned out to be General George Crook's Shoshone scouts.[8] But notice that in this incident the United States Army is irrelevant: Indian warriors prepare, Indian fashion, to fight Indian enemies. Four months later, these Crows killed five Minneconjou chiefs who came in under a flag of truce. General Nelson Miles was furious at an act that threatened to prolong the war. He confiscated the Crows' horses and sent them to the relatives of the slain chiefs with a message "that no white man had any part in the affair." A month after that, when the army had rounded up a group of Sioux women, the Crows took turns counting coup on them.[9] American concerns and objectives did not govern the actions of Crow warriors.

On close examination, the lines of tribal conflict can become as fuzzy as those of racial conflict. When the Sioux smashed in the head of a fallen Arikara scout and thrust a willow branch into his chest, the mutilation had as much to do with old tribal enmities as with participation on different sides of a United States Army campaign, and stories of a vendetta between the Hunkpapa Gall and Custer's Arikara scout Bloody Knife have become part of Little Bighorn lore.[10] But five Sioux rode with Custer's Arikara scouts, apparently Hunkpapas who had married Arikara women. One of them returned to the Sioux in the course of the campaign and was killed, evidently fighting the soldiers he had previously scouted for.[11] According to Chief Plenty Coups, the only Crow death at the Battle of the Rosebud "was a Cree who had lived with us for years, so that we looked upon him as a Crow."[12] Mitch Boyer, Custer's scout, was of mixed Sioux-white parentage, but a Crow by choice and adoption. He went to his death with Custer and his body was found "in the middle of the troopers."[13]

The series of scattered skirmishes, charges, and retreats we know as the Battle of the Rosebud was so much a battle between Indians that American troops were afraid of confusing Crow and Shoshone allies with Sioux and Cheyenne enemies. Some Sioux remembered it not as the day they turned back Crook's force but as "the battle with our Indian enemies."[14] Before the "Sioux War" of 1876–1877 was over, Crows, Shoshones, Arikaras, Utes, Bannocks, Pawnees, Northern Arapahos, Cheyennes, and Sioux had all served with the United States Army, and one hundred Winnebagoes even offered their services.[15] The comparison with Montcalm's coalition of tribes 120 years earlier begins to seem less farfetched.

The reasons for the presence of Arikaras, Pawnees, Crows, and

Shoshones in this war are not hard to find. The westward expansion of the Sioux in the late eighteenth and early nineteenth century placed them all on the defensive.[16] Not dependent for their supplies of guns and ammunition on the trade network that centered on the upper Missouri River, and growing in population while other peoples declined, the Sioux reduced trade systems and power balances on the northern and central plains to a shambles.[17]

By 1804, smallpox and Sioux attacks had reduced the once-powerful Arikaras (four thousand warriors in thirty-two villages, according to fur trader Jean Baptiste Truteau; eighteen villages, according to trader Pierre Antoine Tabeau) to five hundred warriors in a couple of villages. The Sioux pushed them upriver, blocked their trade routes with the Kiowas, stole horses, curtailed their hunting expeditions, kept the buffalo away from Arikara villages, and evidently browbeat the Arikaras into trading on Sioux terms.[18] Americans contributed to the Arikara misfortune. In 1823, in a reversal of the situation half a century later, United States troops and fifteen hundred Sioux launched a united assault on the Arikara villages. The Americans performed poorly in Sioux eyes, and the Sioux finished the removal of the Arikaras themselves, forcing them out of their Missouri River villages. The Yanktonai Sioux took over the old Arikara territory.[19] In response to the 1831 smallpox epidemic on the central plains, the United States initiated a vaccination program. The most heavily vaccinated groups were the Yankton, Yanktonai, and Teton Sioux, and they escaped relatively lightly from the massive smallpox epidemic of 1837. Lack of funds meant that tribes farther up the Missouri River remained unvaccinated and hence susceptible to mass destruction in 1837.[20]

The surviving Mandans, Hidatsas, and Arikaras congregated in Like-a-Fishhook village on the Fort Berthold reservation. Cholera struck Fort Berthold in 1851 and 1853, smallpox returned in 1856, and periodic crop failures increased the Indians' dependence on the Americans. Sioux attacks contributed to the steady attrition of their population. In December 1862, a Sioux war party burned much of Like-a-Fishhook village. Arikaras could continue to fight old Sioux enemies only if they had strong allies. The United States fulfilled that role. In 1868 Arikaras enlisted as scouts with the American army to fight the Sioux.[21]

The Arikaras still faced insurmountable odds, however, in confronting the Sioux. The Arikara scouts at the Little Bighorn, many of them young and inexperienced, spat on clay they had brought from their homeland and rubbed it on their chests as good medicine. But the thin line of Arikaras extending on the left of Reno's men was overwhelmed by a mass of Sioux horsemen. A bullet blew out Bloody Knife's brains and Bob-tailed Bull, who as leader wore three stripes on his sleeves, was killed, "a solitary horseman facing scores of circling warriors."[22]

The fact that Arikaras supplied scouts for American campaigns into Sioux country and fought and died at the Little Bighorn did not mean they were any more enthusiastic than their Sioux enemies to accept white American attempts to "civilize" them and to reeducate their children.[23] Like their enemies, the Arikaras were struggling on several fronts to survive as a people.

The Arikaras' relatives, the Pawnees from the Loup and Platte Rivers in Nebraska, had experienced similar calamities. Brulé Sioux winter counts record skirmishes with the Pawnees in the first decade of the nineteenth century; by the 1830s, Pawnee conflicts with Sioux, Cheyennes, and Arapahos were becoming a common occurrence.[24] Decimated by disease, the Pawnees were in no position to withstand the growing Sioux assaults. In 1839, they lost 180 warriors in a pitched battle. American missionaries John Dunbar and Samuel Allis witnessed a major attack by several hundred Sioux on a Pawnee village just a mile from their mission in June 1843. The Pawnees defended themselves as well as they could, but the Sioux were all mounted and nearly all had guns. The Sioux drove off two hundred horses, killed or captured sixty-eight people, and burned half the lodges in the village. Allis said the Sioux shot down women and children as they fled from the burning lodges. The burning homes, mutilated bodies, and cries of women and children made a desolate sight. The Pawnees hastily buried their dead and departed the village, leaving some of their cornfields unhoed. The Sioux boasted that they would exterminate them, and the Pawnees were constantly on the lookout for enemy war parties. Hunting and horticulture were disrupted. That spring alone, the Pawnees lost four hundred horses and more than two hundred people to Sioux attacks. The missionaries despaired of what they could do for "the perishing Pawnees," who were "at the entire mercy of the Sioux." Three years later, they closed their mission.[25] In 1873, just three years before the Battle of the Little Bighorn, the Sioux killed one hundred Pawnees on the Republican River. In 1875–1876, the Pawnees abandoned their Nebraska homelands and moved to Indian territory (now Oklahoma).[26] Pawnees had good reason to fight the Sioux in 1876.

So had Shoshones. Having been pushed off the plains in the late eighteenth century by more powerful and better-armed enemies, especially the Blackfeet, the Shoshones welcomed American trade and allied themselves with growing American power in the West.[27] As competition for diminishing hunting grounds increased in the second half of the nineteenth century, Shoshones went less often to war with longtime Crow enemies and more often confronted new threats from Sioux, Cheyennes, and Arapahos. According to the Shoshone chief Washakie, the Sioux troubled them, "but when the Sioux are taken care of, we can do well."[28] Eighty-six Shoshone warriors led by Wisha, Naaki, and a French-Shoshone mixed-blood named Luisant or Luishaw, joined Crook's command in June 1876, making a striking impression as they galloped into camp.[29] Some writers believe that the Shoshone charge at the Battle of the Rosebud saved the day for the Americans by preventing the Sioux from splitting the command in two. Captain John Bourke characterized the behavior of his Shoshone and Crow allies in the battle as "excellent."[30] Shoshones also served with United States troops in the assault on Dull Knife's Northern Cheyenne village in November 1876. Shoshone soldier scouts scalped Crow Split Nose, the chief of the Elk Scraper society, and carried off his sacred shield in triumph.[31]

But the Shoshones were motivated by more than just traditional enmity in turning out on campaign. At a time when United States agents on the Shoshone agency were pressuring the tribe to give up the old ways and accept a sedentary farming life, going to war against the Sioux and Cheyennes offered young Shoshone men a chance to pursue traditional activities, to *avoid* becoming farmers. Not only did they get to fight old enemies, the United States Army provided them with soldiers' rations while they were on campaign and arranged for their wives and children to be fed. Bourke noted that they were also armed with the latest model .45 caliber rifles.[32]

When the Shoshone contingent reached Crook's command prior to the Battle of the Rosebud, they galloped into camp in what John Bourke described as a "barbaric array" of feathers, beads, bells, scarlet cloth, and flashing lances. The Shoshone chief charged into the battle on a fiery pony with an eagle feather headdress sweeping the ground behind him. The Crows were just as flamboyantly attired. Bourke said Medicine Crow "looked like a devil in his war-bonnet of feathers, fur, and buffalo horns." After the battle, the Crows and Shoshones each held a scalp dance.[33] Back on the reservations, this was exactly the kind of behavior the United States government was intent on eradicating. The American need for Indian allies gave the Crows and Shoshones the opportunity to fight old enemies, celebrate their warrior culture, and get paid for doing it. These people were hardly the white man's fools.

In the past, Shoshones and Crows had fought each other, but in 1876 they made common cause against the Sioux and Cheyennes. From time immemorial, it seemed, the Crows had battled to defend the Yellowstone valley. Few in number, they fought off predatory tribes who encroached on their rich hunting lands. By the mid-nineteenth century, American traders and travelers predicted the Crows were on the verge of extermination, and Sioux pressure was increasing steadily. "Look at our country, and look at our enemies," Crow chiefs declared in 1870, "they are all around it; the Sioux, Blackfeet, Cheyennes, Arapahos, and Flatheads, all want our country, and kill us when they can." In such circumstances, it is a tad misleading to speak of the United States employing Crow allies; the Crows employed the United States as allies in their war for survival.[34]

The Crows faced a difficult situation in 1876. The year before, President Ulysses S. Grant had placed them on a reduced reservation south of the Yellowstone, opening traditional hunting grounds in the Judith Basin in the north to white farmers and stockmen, and opening the upper Yellowstone to miners. The Crows moved eastward from the Yellowstone to a new agency at the junction of the Stillwater River and Rosebud Creek. There, in 1876, "temptingly closer" to the Sioux, they were starting over again.[35]

When Colonel John Gibbon came that spring to ask for Crow

scouts to serve as his eyes because "[t]he white man goes through the country with his head down and sees nothing," there was no rush to enlist. The chiefs sat silent with bowed heads. When Gibbon pressed them for an answer, Old Crow retorted angrily, "You have said what you had to say; don't be too fast! We are studying within ourselves and will talk after awhile." Mountain Pocket declined the request. "I have fought the Sioux till I am tired," he said. "You want to fight now—I'll let you go alone." The chiefs tried to explain to Gibbon that it was up to each Crow to make his own decision. Twenty-three young warriors and two "squaw men" did enlist as "wolves for the blue soldiers," swearing allegiance on the point of a knife and placing red bands on their left arms to distinguish them from the enemy. Blackfoot said the Crows did not understand the whiteman's ways, but he explained their reasons for enlisting: "The land we tread belongs to us, and we want our children always to dwell in it. All other Indian tribes do evil to the whites, but I and my people hold fast to them with love. We want our reservation to be large, we want to go on eating buffalo, and so we hold fast to the whites."[36]

According to Chicago *Times* war correspondent John Finerty, Old Crow later reviewed his people's sufferings at the hands of the Sioux and declared his support for the United States. The Great Spirit had given the Crows their lands, he said,

> but the Sioux stole them from us. They hunt upon our mountains. They fish in our streams. They have stolen our horses. They have murdered our squaws, our children. What white man has done these things to us? The face of the Sioux is red but his heart is black. But the heart of the pale face has ever been red to the Crow. . . . Our war is with the Sioux and only them. . . . The Sioux have trampled upon our hearts. We shall spit upon their scalps.[37]

The Crows made invaluable scouts. James Bradley recorded: "Crows scouted excellently today, scouring the country for a breadth of ten or twelve miles and holding themselves well in front." Charles Varnum, Custer's chief of scouts, recalled they "were in their own country and knew it thoroughly."[38]

One hundred and seventy-six Crows eventually joined General Crook and, according to John Bourke who was impressed by them, "they were soon on terms of easy familiarity with the soldiers."[39] Medicine Crow and Alligator Stands Up led the warriors at the Battle of the Rosebud where, according to Pretty Shield, a Crow woman and a berdache participated in the fighting. The woman, Other Magpie, rode into battle with her forehead painted yellow and wearing a stuffed woodpecker on her head. Determined to avenge her brother's death at the hands of the Sioux, she counted coup, taunted her enemies, and spat on them. This was not exactly the kind of ally the United States Army had in mind when it recruited the Crows for the campaign.[40] Like her male counterparts, Other Magpie turned an American campaign into an occasion for Crow warfare.

Six Crow scouts from Gibbon's column were selected to accompany Custer: Half Yellow Face, White Swan, Curley (p. 75), Goes Ahead, White Man Runs Him (p. 74), and Hairy Moccasin. Five days before his death, Custer wrote his wife:

> I now have some Crow scouts with me, as they are familiar with the country. They are magnificent looking men, so much handsomer and more Indian-like than any we have ever seen, and so jolly and sporting, nothing of the gloomy, silent redman about them. They have formally given themselves to me after the usual talk. In their speech they have heard that I never abandon a trail; that when my food gave out, I ate mule. That was the kind of man they wanted to fight under; they were willing to eat mule too.[41]

As the Seventh Cavalry started up the Rosebud, Custer had thirty-five Indian scouts: twenty-five Arikaras; six Crows; and four Sioux. At the Little Bighorn, all the Indian scouts except four Crows served with Reno.[42]

Reporting what her husband Goes Ahead had told her, Pretty Shield said that while White Swan and Half Yellow Face went with Reno, Goes Ahead, White Man Runs Him, Hairy Moccasin, and Curley led Custer to the Little Bighorn, telling him several times there were more Sioux and Cheyennes than soldiers' bullets. But, said Pretty Shield, Custer "was like a feather blown by the

Crow Scout White Man Runs Him (Richard Throssel, photographer, Montana Historical Society Photograph Archives, Helena)

wind, and *had* to go." She said that Goes Ahead, White Man Runs Him, and Hairy Moccasin saw Custer fall at the river and then left, but Goes Ahead himself denied seeing any part of Custer's battle. John Gray, who appears to have followed everyone's movements around the Little Bighorn battlefield with a stop watch, found the claim "impossible."[43] Nevertheless, the Crows knew what was happening to Custer. On reaching Reno's command, they told the Arikara scouts "the Dakotas kill the soldiers easy." On June 28, Curley brought news of the defeat to the steamer *Far West* at the mouth of the Little Bighorn River.[44]

Crows continued to serve in the mopping up operations the

Fred E. Miller photographed Crow Scout Curley circa 1900.
(Montana Historical Society Photograph Archives, Helena)

following year. On one occasion in the winter they brought corn to the Americans' suffering livestock; on another they brought news, inaccurate as it turned out, of the presidential election results.[45]

When Plenty Coups was a boy the Sioux had killed his brother, and he had sought a vision to avenge the death.[46] But, like Blackfoot, Plenty Coups in later life explained the Crows' allegiance to the United States as motivated by love of homeland, not blind revenge or misplaced loyalty: "Our decision was reached, not because we loved the white man who was already crowding other tribes into our country, or because we hated the Sioux, Cheyenne, and Arapaho, but because we plainly saw that this course was the only one which might save our beautiful country for us. When I think back my heart sings because we acted as we did. It was the only way open to us."[47] Tribal historian Joe Medicine Crow echoes Plenty Coups's sentiments: "We were looking for our survival and I think we played it smart."[48] Like the Shoshones, the Crows held on to a reservation in their precious homeland. They used the United States as allies to secure their survival as a people, and it paid off.

But an American alliance was a mixed blessing. Fighting alongside American soldiers did not protect the Crows from steadily mounting assaults on their culture. Nor did it guarantee them the boundaries of the reservation they had fought so hard to secure. Plenty Coups's recollection of his visit to President Rutherford B. Hayes in Washington in 1880, along with Old Crow, Pretty Eagle, Long Elk, and Medicine Crow, aptly conveys the point:

> The President asked how we had treated the soldiers, and I said that we had been friendly to them. When their horses feet were sore, so were ours. When they had to drink alkali, we shared their misfortune. When they suffered, we suffered, and I said we would continue to have friendly relations. Then the President said that he would grant our requests to remain in the country where we lived, but in return he expected us to let them build a railroad through the valley of the Yellowstone.[49]

After the delegation returned from Washington, the Crows ceded a four-hundred-foot right-of-way through the reservation to the Northern Pacific Railroad. They also ceded the extreme western portion of their reservation, which the Great Father thought it "might be better for you to dispose of" because it contained mines. Adding insult to injury, an executive order in 1886 set aside land from the Crow Reservation for a national cemetery and the "Custer Battlefield."[50] "We helped the white men so we could own our land in peace. Our blood is mixed in the ground with the blood of white soldiers," said Crow warrior Two Leggings. "We did not know they were going to take our land. That is what they gave us for our friendship."[51]

History, like popular trends, tends to go in cycles. Today's heroes often become tomorrow's villains and vice versa. Most of us now recognize the Sioux and Cheyennes not as the killers of a great

American hero but as people fighting to defend their lands, their families, and their way of life against alien aggression. But if in this post–*Dances with Wolves* era the Sioux and Cheyennes are today's heroes, where does that put the people who used to be "good Indians" because they fought against them? Was the struggle of the Crows, Shoshones, and Arikaras any less heroic because they sided with those whose historical reputation has taken a beating lately? These "other Indians" knew as well as anyone the threat the Americans posed to their way of life. The Crow struggle to preserve their culture would continue long after the Battle of the Little Bighorn and all that happened there. But in 1876, Crows were fighting an old battle of simply surviving against the odds.

In the long view of Indian relations with Euramericans, the foreign policies of the Crows, Arikaras, Shoshones, and Pawnees were more typical than we have acknowledged. Open resistance was only one strategy for survival and few Indian peoples resisted constantly. All across America and across the centuries, capable Indian leaders tried policies of accommodation at one time or another: Squanto of the Patuxets; the Pennacook Wanalancet; Hagler of the Catawbas; Red Shoes of the Choctaws; Keokuk of the Sauks; the Miami war chief turned government chief Little Turtle; Cornstalk and Black Hoof, chiefs of the Maquachake division of the Shawnees; White Eyes of the Delawares; Little Carpenter of the Cherokees; Sioux chiefs Little Crow and Red Cloud (p. 31); the Arapahos Black Coal and Sharp Nose; Washakie and Plenty Coups. The world created by white invasion was not a simple world, with rigid battle lines fixed along racial lines. If it had been, the story would have been very different, and the Battle of the Little Bighorn would have been very different as well.

Notes

1.   Edward P. Hamilton, ed. and trans. *Adventure in the Wilderness: The American Journals of Louis Antoine de Bougainville, 1756–1760* (1964; reprint, Norman: University of Oklahoma Press, 1990), passim; Richard White, *The Middle Ground: Indians, Empires and Republics in the Great Lakes Region, 1650–1815* (New York: Cambridge University Press, 1991), chaps. 1-6.

2. Richard R. Johnson, "The Search for a Usable Indian: An Aspect of the Defense of Colonial New England," *Journal of American History*, 64 (December 1977), 640.

3. Ian K. Steele, *Betrayals: Fort William Henry and the "Massacre"* (New York: Oxford University Press, 1990).

4. Stephen E. Ambrose, *Crazy Horse and Custer: The Parallel Lives of Two American Warriors* (Garden City, N.Y.: Doubleday, 1975).

5. Thomas W. Dunlay, *Wolves for the Blue Soldiers: Indian Scouts and Auxiliaries with the United States Army, 1860–1890* (Lincoln: University of Nebraska Press, 1982); Registers of Enlistments in the United States Army, Microfilm no. 233, roll 70, vols. 150-51, 1866–1877: Indian Scouts, National Archives (hereafter NA).

6. Lieutenant James H. Bradley, *The March of the Montana Column*, ed. Edgar I. Stewart (1961; reprint, Norman: University of Oklahoma Press, 1991), 153-54.

7. Charles Windolph, *I Fought with Custer: The Story of Sergeant Windolph, Last Survivor of the Battle of the Little Big Horn, as told to Frazier and Robert Hunt* (Lincoln: University of Nebraska Press, 1987).

8. Jerome A. Greene, *Yellowstone Command: Colonel Nelson A. Miles and the Great Sioux War, 1876–1877* (Lincoln: University of Nebraska Press, 1991), 41-42.

9. Miles to Assistant Adjutant General, December 17, 1876, Letters Received by the Adjutant General's Office, National Archives Microfilm, M666, reel 280, NA; Greene, *Yellowstone Command*, 150-52, 164; Thomas B. Marquis, ed., *Memoirs of a White Crow Indian by Thomas H. Leforge* (1928; reprint, Lincoln: University of Nebraska Press, 1974), 270.

10. O. G. Libby, "The Arikara Narrative of the Campaign against the Hostile Dakotas, June 1876," *North Dakota Historical Collections*, 6 (1920), 110; Joseph Henry Taylor, "Bloody Knife and Gall," *North Dakota Historical Quarterly*, 4 (April 1930), 165-73; Edgar I. Stewart, *Custer's Luck* (Norman: University of Oklahoma Press, 1955), 180.

11. Dunlay, *Wolves for the Blue Soldiers*, 140-41.

12. Frank B. Linderman, *Plenty Coups, Chief of the Crows* (1930; reprint, Lincoln: University of Nebraska Press, 1962), 170.

13. John S. Gray, *Custer's Last Campaign: Mitch Boyer and the Little Bighorn Reconstructed* (Lincoln: University of Nebraska Press, 1991).

14. John G. Bourke, *On the Border with Crook* (New York: Scribner's Sons, 1891), 313; Dunlay, *Wolves for the Blue Soldiers*, 116.

15. Bourke, *On the Border with Crook*, 357, 391-92, 395.

16. Richard White, "The Winning of the West: The Expansion of the Western Sioux in the Eighteenth and Nineteenth Centuries," *Journal of American History*, 65 (September 1978), 319-43.

17. Colin G. Calloway, "The Intertribal Balance of Powers on the Great Plains, 1760–1850," *Journal of American Studies*, 16 (April 1982), 44-46.

18. White, "The Winning of the West," 325-26, 331-32; J. Daniel Rogers, *Objects of Change: The Archaeology and History of Arikara Contact with Europeans* (Washington, D.C.: Smithsonian Institution Press, 1990), 44, 87-88; Annie Heloise Abel, ed., *Tabeau's Narrative of Loisel's Expedition to the Upper Missouri* (Norman: University of Oklahoma Press, 1939), 123-25, 131-33; Douglas W. Owsley, "Demography of Prehistoric and Early Historic Northern Plains Populations," in *Disease and Demography in the Americas*, ed. John W. Verano and Douglas H. Ubelaker (Washington, D.C.: Smithsonian Institution Press, 1992), 75. George A. Dorsey, comp., *Traditions of the Arikara* (Washington, D.C.: Carnegie Institution, 1904), 159-71, recounts instances of hostilities with the Sioux.

19. Roger L. Nichols, "Backdrop for Disaster: Causes of the Arikara War of 1823," *South Dakota History*, 14 (Summer 1984), 93-113; Edwin Thompson Denig, *Five Indian Tribes of the Upper Missouri*, ed. John C. Ewers (Norman: University of Oklahoma Press, 1961), 54-59; White, "The Winning of the West," 332-33.

20. White, "The Winning of the West," 329; Michael K. Trimble, "The 1832 Inoculation Program on the Missouri River," in Verano and Ubelaker, eds., *Disease and Demography in the Americas*, 260-63.

21. Roy W. Meyer, *The Village Indians of the Upper Missouri: The Mandans, Hidatsas, and Arikaras* (Lincoln: University of Nebraska Press, 1977), 104-8, 119, 127.

22. Libby, "The Arikara Narrative of the Campaign against the Hostile Dakotas," 11-12, 84. The names of the Arikara scouts are given in Libby, 49-51; in David Humphreys Miller, *Custer's Fall: The Indian Side of the Story* (1957; reprint, London: Corgi Books, 1965), 202-3; and Col. W. A. Graham, comp., *The Custer Myth: A Source Book of Custeriana* (New York: Bonanza Books, 1953), 27-28. Biographies of some of the scouts are in Libby, 177-209, together with photographs of survivors taken in old age.

23. Meyer, *Village Indians of the Upper Missouri*, 143, 145.

24. George E. Hyde, *The Pawnee Indians* (new ed., Norman: University of Oklahoma Press, 1974), 157, 180-87, 197, 199-201.

25. White, "The Winning of the West," 337-38; Waldo R. Wedel, ed. *The Dunbar-Allis Letters on the Pawnee* (New York: Garland, 1985), x, 656-60, 663, 730-31.

26. White, "The Winning of the West," 339.

27. Colin G. Calloway, "Snake Frontiers: The Eastern Shoshones in the Eighteenth Century," *Annals of Wyoming*, 63 (Summer 1991), 82-92.

28. Quoted in Dunlay, *Wolves for the Blue Soldiers*, 115.

29. Bourke, *On the Border with Crook*, 303, 306, 312; John F. Finerty, *War-Path and Bivouac: The Bighorn and Yellowstone Expedition*, ed. Milo Milton Quaife (Chicago: R. R. Donnelley and Sons Co., 1955), 103.

30. Dunlay, *Wolves for the Blue Soldiers*, 116; Bourke, *On the Border with Crook*, 312-13, 316.

31. Peter J. Powell, "High Bull's Victory Roster," in *The Great Sioux War 1876–77*, ed. Paul L. Hedren (Helena: Montana Historical Society Press, 1991), 160.

32. Agents on the Shoshone reservation no doubt encouraged young men to enlist: army rations reduced the demand on agency beef. Henry E. Stamm IV, "Community, Economy, Policy and Spirituality: A History of Shoshones, Arapahoes, and Settlers in the Wind River Valley, Wyoming, 1868–1885," (doctoral diss., University of Wyoming, 1994); Bourke, *On the Border with Crook*, 305.

33. Bourke, *On the Border with Crook*, 303, 316, 318; Quaife, ed., *War-Path and Bivouac*, 101.

34. Colin G. Calloway, "'The Only Way Open to Us': The Crow Struggle for Survival in the Nineteenth Century," *North Dakota History*, 53 (Summer 1986), 25-34, quote at 33. See also, Katherine M. Weist, "An Ethnohistorical Analysis of Crow Political Alliances," *Western Canadian Journal of Anthropology*, 7 (no. 4, 1977), 34-54.

35. Michael P. Malone and Richard B. Roeder, "1876 on the Reservations: The Indian Question," in Hedren, ed., *The Great Sioux War*, 56-57; Gray, *Custer's Last Campaign*, 118.

36. Gibbon's council with the Crows is reported in Stewart, ed. *The March of the Montana Column*, 39-46, see esp. 40-43, 48. See also Bourke, *On the Border with Crook*, 300-301, and Marquis, ed., *Memoirs of a White Crow Indian by Thomas H. Leforge*, 206-8. Pretty Shield used the term "wolves for the blue soldiers"; Frank B. Linderman, *Pretty-Shield, Medicine Woman of the Crows* (1932; reprint, Lincoln: University of Nebraska Press, 1972), 225.

37. Speech attributed to Old Crow by John Finerty of the Chicago *Times*, one of five correspondents with Crook, in Quaife, ed., *War-Path and Bivouac*, 104.

38. Stewart, ed., *March of the Montana Column*, 52; John M. Carroll, ed., *Custer's Chief of Scouts: The Reminiscences of Charles A. Varnum, Including his Testimony and the Reno Court of Inquiry* (Lincoln: University of Nebraska Press, 1982), 60.

39. Bourke, *On the Border with Crook*, 300-302.

40. Joseph Medicine Crow, *From the Heart of the Crow Country: The Crow Indians' Own Stories* (New York: Orion Books, 1992), 47; Linderman, *Plenty Coups*, 166-69; Linderman, *Pretty Shield*, 228-31. The medicine power of the woodpecker is discussed in Peter Nabokov, *Two Leggings: The Making of a Crow Warrior* (1967; reprint, Lincoln: University of Nebraska Press, 1982), 110.

41. Quoted in Gray, *Custer's Last Campaign*, 202.

42. Ibid., 204, 296-97.

43. Miller, *Custer's Fall*, lists Custer's Crow scouts but says only White Swan was present at the battle that day, 157, 203; cf. Linderman, *Pretty Shield*, 236-39; Gray, *Custer's Last Campaign*, 348-49.

44. Gray, *Custer's Last Campaign*, 351. According to Pretty Shield, Curley said he was sick and ran away. John Gray, however, using maps and time-motion analysis to check Curley's accounts, believed the much-maligned scout to have been a reliable informant. Ibid., 373-82.

45. Greene, *Yellowstone Command*, 45, 131, 219.

46. Linderman, *Plenty Coups*, 34.

47. Ibid., 154.

48. Film interview with Joseph Medicine Crow, Hardin, Montana, March 1, 1991, quoted in Paul Stekler, "Custer and Crazy Horse Ride Again . . . And Again, And Again: Filmmaking and History at Little Bighorn," *Montana The Magazine of Western History*, 42 (Autumn 1992), 68.

49. Peter Nabokov, ed., *Native American Testimony* (New York: Harper, 1979), 180-81.

50. Burton M. Smith, "Politics and the Crow Indian Land Cessions," *Montana The Magazine of Western History*, 36 (Autumn 1986), 30-34.

51. Nabokov, *Two Leggings*, 187.

Following the Indians' June victory on the Little Bighorn, the village of Northern Cheyennes led by Dull Knife (right) and Little Wolf (left) suffered a crushing reprisal when they were attacked by troops under the command of Colonel Ranald S. Mackenzie in November 1876. (Nebraska State Historical Society, Lincoln)

A Battle among Skirmishes
Little Bighorn in the Great Sioux War

Jerome A. Greene

An objective here is to gain an understanding of the legacy of the Battle of the Little Bighorn—what that event has meant to subsequent generations and societies and what it means to people today. Many scholars today tend to view the battle in the context of George Armstrong Custer's life. I would like to deal with another form of context. My charge is to provide some perspective on that signature episode through its relationship to events preceding and following in the Great Sioux War of 1876–1877. For that kind of context—where it all fits—is what this episode has sorely lacked since its occurrence. It is a foregone conclusion that Little Bighorn stands above all else in the history of the Indian wars, the salient encounter beside which all others pale. Looming alone, it has survived without notable supporting cast, due mainly to the factors of its magnitude, mystery, controversy, psychology, and finality, as well as to the symbolism its leading army protagonist—Custer—has come to project to different people.

Certainly and properly, the Battle of the Little Bighorn dominated the spectrum of the Sioux War because of its sheer magnitude. Yet Custer, it seems, has become the transcendent reason for the continued attraction of the Little Bighorn battle in the popular mind. Now mythic in stature, he was in fact no more than part of the leadership and followership in 1876–1877, part of the mosaic of the war. Through time he has assumed a dominance that continues to fuel the magnification of the battle. And I would submit that the Custer persona has distracted historians from illuminating the other aspects of the war, to the ultimate detriment of not only all of its collateral actions but of its entire essence as well. (Furthermore, statistics show that, if current trends continue, by the year 2013 everybody in the United States will have written a book about Custer!)[1]

The result of all this, perhaps understandably, has been the segregation of this battle historically from the other encounters that composed the Great Sioux War, with the exception of the Rosebud Creek action. Our understanding of the sequential engagements of the war remains murky, largely because of the reasons cited and because lesser actions, at least compared to the Custer phase of the battle, yielded army survivors and little comparable controversy. Yet each battle, each skirmish of the Great Sioux War has its own story, and, taken together, they afford a compelling overview of what happened in 1876–1877 to the army and, more importantly, to the Lakota and Northern Cheyenne people and of what precipitated their cultural upheaval. As we shall see, the first encounters of the Great Sioux War set the stage for the Battle of the Little Bighorn, just as that battle triggered all subsequent encounters. In effect, Little Bighorn, occurring when and under the circumstances it did, became the pivot on which turned the balance of the war.[2]

The Great Sioux War began early in 1876 as the result of lengthy deteriorating relations between the United States government and the Lakota Indians. Many so-called "Northern Sioux" had refused to recognize the Treaty of 1868 establishing the Great Sioux Reservation in southwestern Dakota Territory. Known as the "non-treaty bands," these Lakotas, headed by such leaders as Sitting Bull (p. 114) and Crazy Horse, continued to roam the lands adjoining the lower Yellowstone River rather than submit to an uncertain agency existence. Government inroads into their domain in the summer of 1873 by a surveying expedition for the Northern Pacific Railroad provoked their resistance. Similarly, the invasion of miners onto reservation lands during the Black Hills gold rush confirmed

to the tribesmen the dubious sanctity of government treaty promises
and brought their armed reaction. Both events symbolized to the
Lakotas the expansive designs of white Americans. The subsequent
government decision to militarily prosecute the tribesmen brought
about the Great Sioux War.[3]

By their nature and result, the three encounters that preceded
the Little Bighorn battle in the Great Sioux War quite explicitly
anticipated that event. The first engagement of the conflict, an
assault by troops under Colonel Joseph J. Reynolds, of Brigadier
General George Crook's command, on the Northern Cheyenne
village of Old Bear, occurred on March 17, 1876. Reynolds thought
he had struck a village of Lakotas under Crazy Horse. Primarily,
the encounter succeeded only in aggravating the Northern
Cheyennes to further cement their security alliance with the Oglala
Lakotas, while likely compounding problems inherent in the
government roundup of the so-called non-treaty bands by
providing additional Indians with which the troops must contend.
Secondarily, the Powder River battle was a tactical miscarriage that
did not bode well for the army. The strong fighting of the
Cheyennes, coupled with Colonel Reynolds's destruction of the
camp's provisions and his failure to secure the all-important pony
herd, left the army's winter initiative in ruin.[4] Although casualties
on both sides were light, the action at Powder River precipitated a
downward spiraling of army fortunes as well as a corresponding
burgeoning of Indian military successes that would propel them
to their respective destinies.

The trends continued in June, after army operations resumed.
General Crook once more headed north. On June 9 he bivouacked
his one-thousand-man force at the confluence of Prairie Dog Creek
with the Tongue River, where that evening emboldened warriors
fired on his camp, inflicting little damage but announcing their
intention to stiffly contest Crook's advance. Eight days later came
the confrontation at Rosebud Creek, where more than one
thousand Lakota and Cheyenne warriors initiated yet another attack
on Crook's command, this time a major offensive strike that
resulted in heavy soldier casualties. More important, Rosebud
effectively crippled army strategy for the next two months. This
victory by the growing Indian coalition prevented an anticipated

union of Crook's command with that of Brigadier General Alfred H. Terry and promoted an even greater victory little more than a week later. While the Battle of the Little Bighorn might have occurred regardless of what happened at Rosebud Creek, Crook's defeat certainly assured the enormity of that army loss.[5] It is impossible to divine the result had Crook joined Terry as planned, but the likelihood is that the circumstances that impelled Custer forward would have been decidedly different by June 25 with Crook's one thousand soldiers added to the mix.

On June 25, as we all know, Lieutenant Colonel George A. Custer led his Seventh Cavalry troops to defeat and death when he directed an attack on an intertribal encampment estimated to contain as many as eight thousand people, including perhaps twenty-five hundred warriors. The Little Bighorn loss was complete and resounding; it raised the confidence of the Lakota-Cheyenne union and demoralized the army. Suffice it to say that Little Bighorn was emblazoned in the collective consciousness of all Sioux War participants, soldier and Indian, for the balance of the conflict. But as Little Bighorn proved the crowning military accomplishment for the Lakotas and Northern Cheyennes, it presaged the breakup of the very coalition that had orchestrated the victory, denying to its achievers any sustainability because of economic reality. Simply put, the tribesmen could not share limited natural resources, such as grass for their ponies and game for sustenance; and their reliance on what, for them, were nonrenewable resources such as firearms and ammunition, proved determinants ultimately in promoting the end of the warfare. Immediately after the Little Bighorn battle, dispersal of the various bands of Lakotas and Cheyennes became essential for their survival, and while dispersal made the subsequent army pursuit difficult, it nonetheless made it achievable.

Just as all engagements that preceded Little Bighorn anticipated that battle, all that came afterward bore its significant imprint. The phase that followed the Indian victory at Little Bighorn was a lengthy one marked by persistent military retribution. None of the subsequent engagements assumed that battle's scale, but their cumulative impact, coupled with the eventual near-starvation of the tribesmen, effectively destroyed Indian unity and drove most bands to yield to the government. With few exceptions, army-

Indian engagements after the Little Bighorn battle consisted of widely scattered actions in which troops defeated piecemeal the once powerful Indian alliance.

Despite the stupendous military loss, Little Bighorn quickly became the battle cry of the stunned field command, as evinced in Colonel Wesley Merritt's rout of Cheyennes at Warbonnet Creek, Nebraska, in July ("Buffalo Bill" Cody's widely acclaimed "First Scalp for Custer!") and Captain Anson Mills's (of Crook's command) strike against a village of Sioux and Cheyennes at Slim Buttes, Dakota Territory, in September. Slim Buttes represented the first major army victory in the Sioux War. Most of the people in the camp fled in the misty dawn. A few were forced to surrender while the village, which contained booty stripped from Custer's troopers, was destroyed.[6] Similar discoveries in other villages attacked by soldiers during the following fall, winter, and spring seemingly provided justification and incentive for those assaults.

Preventing a reunion of the disparate elements of the tribal coalition figured uppermost in the strategy of Colonel Nelson A. Miles, who, together with a contingent of Fifth and Twenty-second infantrymen, assumed a permanent station along the Yellowstone River in the autumn and winter of 1876–1877. Miles's strategy stemmed directly from knowledge of the intertribal composition represented at the Little Bighorn in June; it looked to forestall any such future assembly of the Indians. His conference with Sitting Bull at Cedar Creek in late October represented the first meeting of a federal representative with a leader of the warring tribes since the conflict began. Unable to convince the Lakota leader to bring his people into the army cantonment at the mouth of Tongue River on the Yellowstone, Miles opened hostilities and sent his soldiers after the tribesmen in the rugged divide country between the Missouri and Yellowstone Rivers. The Cedar Creek affair, little more than an extended skirmish, exhibited the army's resolve to prosecute the Indians until they surrendered or were killed. Within days of the encounter, several hundred Indians yielded to Miles, although Sitting Bull and his immediate followers eluded the troops and fled north. Many of the Indians who surrendered to Miles later recanted and remained afield.[7]

In another venue of the war, General Crook in November

launched an offensive from Fort Fetterman, Wyoming Territory. On November 25 part of his command under Colonel Ranald S. Mackenzie struck a village of fifteen hundred Northern Cheyennes under Chiefs Dull Knife and Little Wolf (p. 82) nestled in a red-walled canyon along a branch of the Powder River. Mackenzie's dawn attack was swift, vengeful, and complete, and left more than forty warriors dead and hundreds of people, including many women and children, fleeing hopelessly into the cold.[8] The attack on Dull Knife, one of the largest engagements of the war, ended large-scale Northern Cheyenne participation and sent the refugees wallowing through snowdrifts to seek the shelter of Crazy Horse's village along the upper Tongue River in Montana.

Meantime, Miles continued his prosecution through the winter along both sides of the Yellowstone. His expedition to the Fort Peck Indian Agency in November and December ended with successive assaults on Sitting Bull's people, the last one of which, led by Lieutenant Frank D. Baldwin, destroyed the Indian camp and drove them into the snow with no property amid freezing temperatures. Soon afterwards, Sitting Bull and his followers crossed the international boundary into Canada, thereafter constituting only a peripheral element of the war.[9]

In January 1877, in the Wolf Mountains below the Yellowstone River, Miles sought out Crazy Horse's village. On the morning of January 8, along the upper Tongue River, warriors from that camp, hoping to preempt Miles, met his soldiers in a major clash of several hours' duration until a blinding snowstorm swept in to end it. The warriors withdrew up the Tongue River, and Miles returned to his cantonment. Nonetheless, the Wolf Mountains battle proved to be an important army victory that, coupled with their mounting problems securing game, clarified for the Indians the futility of prolonged resistance. Wolf Mountains was a powerful inducement for the wholesale capitulation of the tribesmen that followed in the spring of 1877.[10]

In May a final engagement occurred with Chief Lame Deer's band of Minneconjou Lakotas, after the Indian surrenders at the agencies were well underway. Miles's attack on Lame Deer's sleeping village was once more brutal and complete. The chief's determination to remain free symbolized a final protest by the

Lakotas against their continued harassment since the Little Bighorn battle.[11] Just as symbolic, Crazy Horse's surrender that same month, following Sitting Bull's passage into Canada, marked the end of the conflict. While the Battle of the Little Bighorn thus became the climactic event in the Indians' struggle to maintain their independence, it proved a progenerative force for subsequent events of the Great Sioux War. And while the army's fortunes took an upturn within weeks of one of its greatest disasters, Lakota and Cheyenne prospects for sustaining their victory—and their way of life—dissipated on the plains of Dakota, Montana, Nebraska, and Wyoming during late 1876 and early 1877.

We should not lose sight of context in our studies of the Battle of the Little Bighorn. Context, of course, is ultimately influenced by evidence, and the broadest context is built upon the broadest foundation of evidence. One means of insuring context is to consider *all* sources of information from *all* quarters. For too many years Indian testimony won little acceptance among non-Indians as a creditable means of determining what happened at the Little Bighorn, despite the fact it was the *only* participant testimony that could describe Custer's demise.

Fortunately, with time and distance from the event and the emergence of a generation of scholars aided by technological advancements in data recovery, the study of events at, and surrounding, the Little Bighorn battle has been pursued with more reason and objectivity than ever before. Truly, the acquisition and appreciation of Lakota and Cheyenne perspectives is now essential to achieving a holistic view of not only the Little Bighorn battle but of the entire Sioux War. While it is recognized that the Indian reports possess inherent difficulties in use, mostly related to translation and the circumstances under which they were derived, it is vital that these accounts always be carefully considered in the final analysis.[12] Doing so will insure impartial judgment and enable scholars to provide broad battle and war contexts. Recent scholarship has shown how greatly Indian reminiscences, carefully weighed along with other sources, can affect long-standing interpretations of the Custer battle.[13] Yet much remains to be done with these materials, especially as they pertain to the remainder of the Great Sioux War and other Indian-white and even intertribal conflicts. As historians, we must welcome this diverse and often elusive evidence and cultivate it to gain as much insight as possible about such engagements as the Little Bighorn, Slim Buttes, Cedar Creek, and Wolf Mountains and to really learn about the human beings of both sides who fought there. Above all else, no more should the Lakotas and Cheyennes remain faceless contestants in these struggles.

Finally, the matter of context should quite properly extend to the historic sites in question. We need to improve the interpretation of context in Indian wars sites just as we have promoted it at Revolutionary War and Civil War sites. Interpretively, Gettysburg does not stand alone; neither should the Battle of the Little Bighorn. As indicated, there exist numerous places where other events occurred that relate directly to the *rest* of the story. There are at least ten sites, including the Little Bighorn, that together can provide an understanding not only of the geographical scope of the warfare but also the lesser engagements and how they relate to the whole. All are important properties that must be seen and understood both individually and contextually. Experiencing these sites and their interrelationships can enhance our appreciation of the Little Bighorn and the rest of the Great Sioux War as part of our heritage.

Surprisingly, many of the sites of the Great Sioux War, or significant parts of them, lie on federal and state land. Others are privately owned. Most—not all—are memorialized with markers, but this is not always sufficient to insure their protection and proper interpretation. Eventually, some of these sites will face the inexorable tide of population growth and development—the same force that has either destroyed or continues to threaten Civil War battlefields in the East, and that seems to be the inevitable by-product of an ever-expanding society. A consortium of interested preservation entities might see opportunities in exploring potential interpretive linkages of Great Sioux War sites, an initiative that might not only encourage a broader understanding of the conflict but could protect these sites from irrevocable loss. Such an effort would seem an appropriate contribution to the legacy of the Little Bighorn, the crown jewel of them all.[14]

Notes

1.   For discussions of Custer and the Little Bighorn relative to their evolving prominence and symbolism, see Edward Tabor Linenthal, *Sacred Ground: Americans and Their Battlefields* (Urbana: University of Illinois Press, 1991), chap. 4; Brian W. Dippie, *Custer's Last Stand: The Anatomy of an American Myth* (Missoula: University of Montana Press, 1976); Bruce A. Rosenberg, *Custer and the Epic of Defeat* (University Park: Pennsylvania State University Press, 1974); and Robert M. Utley, *Custer and the Great Controversy: The Origin and Development of a Legend* (Los Angeles: Westernlore Press, 1962).

2.   There remains to be written a comprehensive study of the Great Sioux War. Partial efforts that deal with elements beyond Little Bighorn include some of my own products, particularly, *Slim Buttes, 1876: An Episode of the Great Sioux War* (Norman: University of Oklahoma Press, 1982), and *Yellowstone Command: Colonel Nelson A. Miles and the Great Sioux War, 1876–1877* (Lincoln: University of Nebraska Press, 1991). See also, Paul L. Hedren, *First Scalp for Custer: The Skirmish at Warbonnet Creek, Nebraska, July 17, 1876* (Glendale, Calif.: Arthur H. Clark Company, 1980); Neil C. Mangum, *Battle of the Rosebud: Prelude to the Little Bighorn* (El Segundo, Calif.: Upton and Sons, 1987); and earlier works on the Rosebud and Powder River battles by Jesse W. Vaughn as cited below. John S. Gray's *Centennial Campaign: The Sioux War of 1876* (Fort Collins, Colo.: Old Army Press, 1976) concentrates on operations centering on the Little Bighorn battle and omits many subsequent events. An anthology that connects the diverse Sioux War engagements from the army standpoint is Jerome A. Greene, comp., ed., *Battles and Skirmishes of the Great Sioux War, 1876–1877: The Military View* (Norman: University of Oklahoma Press, 1993). See also, Paul L. Hedren, ed., *The Great Sioux War, 1876–77: The Best from Montana The Magazine of Western History* (Helena: Montana Historical Society Press, 1991).

3.   The best treatment of the events leading to the Great Sioux War remains Edgar I. Stewart, *Custer's Luck* (Norman: University of Oklahoma Press, 1955), chaps. 1, 2, and 3. See also, however, Paul A. Hutton, *Phil Sheridan and His Army* (Lincoln: University of Nebraska Press, 1985), chap. 13; Paul L. Hedren, *Fort Laramie in 1876: Chronicle of a Frontier Post at War* (Lincoln: University of Nebraska Press, 1988), chap. 1; Gray, *Centennial Campaign*, chaps. 1, 2, 3, and 4; and Greene, *Yellowstone Command*, chap. 1.

4. J. W. Vaughn, *The Reynolds Campaign on Powder River* (Norman: University of Oklahoma Press, 1961); Greene, *Battles and Skirmishes*, chap. 1; Jerome A. Greene, comp., ed., *Lakota and Cheyenne: Indian Views of the Great Sioux War, 1876–1877* (Norman: University of Oklahoma Press, 1994), chap. 1.

5. Mangum, *Battle of the Rosebud*; Jesse W. Vaughn, *With Crook at the Rosebud* (Harrisburg, Penn.: Stackpole Company, 1956); Greene, *Battles and Skirmishes*, chaps. 2, 3; Greene, *Lakota and Cheyenne*, chap. 2.

6. Hedren, *First Scalp for Custer*; Greene, *Slim Buttes, 1876*; Greene, *Battles and Skirmishes*, chaps. 6, 7; Greene, *Lakota and Cheyenne*, chaps. 5, 6.

7. Greene, *Yellowstone Command*, chaps. 4, 5; Greene, *Battles and Skirmishes*, chap. 10; Greene, *Lakota and Cheyenne*, chap. 8.

8. Sherry L. Smith, *Sagebrush Soldier: Private William Earl Smith's View of the Sioux War of 1876* (Norman: University of Oklahoma Press, 1989); Greene, *Battles and Skirmishes*, chap. 13; Greene, *Lakota and Cheyenne*, chap. 9.

9. Greene, *Yellowstone Command*, chap. 6; Greene, *Battles and Skirmishes*, chaps. 11, 12.

10. Greene, *Yellowstone Command*, chaps. 7, 8; Greene, *Battles and Skirmishes*, chap. 14; Greene, *Lakota and Cheyenne*, chap. 10.

11. Greene, *Yellowstone Command*, chap. 9; Greene, *Battles and Skirmishes*, chap. 15; Greene, *Lakota and Cheyenne*, chap. 11.

12. "The Great Sioux War and Indian Testimony," in Greene, *Lakota and Cheyenne*, xiii-xxvi.

13. Douglas D. Scott, Richard A. Fox, Jr., Melissa A. Connor, and Dick Harmon, *Archaeological Perspectives on the Battle of the Little Bighorn* (Norman: University of Oklahoma Press, 1989); Richard Allan Fox, Jr., *Archaeology, History, and Custer's Last Battle: The Little Big Horn Reexamined* (Norman: University of Oklahoma Press, 1993).

14. Information about protection strategies is outlined in the following documents: *Proposal for an American Heritage Area System* (Washington, D.C.: National Park Service, 1991); Legislation for the Heritage Partnership Program Act of 1993; "Civil War Sites in the Shenandoah Valley of Virginia: A Regional Assessment of Fifteen Battlefields" (draft, Washington, D.C.: National Park Service Interagency Resources Division, 1991); "Protecting Battlefields: American Battlefield Protection Program," *CRM Bulletin*, 13 (no. 5, 1990), 1-2.

Custer and the Little Bighorn Story
What It All Means

John D. McDermott

The purpose of this paper is to answer two questions: Why did the battle happen and why is it remembered? One hopes the answers will reveal what it all means.

Why Did It Happen?

When viewed from the historian's perspective, the deaths of George Armstrong Custer and his immediate command at the Little Bighorn were the logical outcome of nineteenth-century attitudes, cumulative circumstance, and inexplicable coincidence. In the broadest sense, the event may be seen as a consequence of historical forces that were at work in the United States 120 years ago. In essence, conflict grew out of differing ideas of land use: Custer and his troopers representing Euramerican beliefs of ownership in fee simple, that Nature needed reshaping for the betterment of humankind, and that expansion was prearranged in heaven; and, on the other hand, Sitting Bull (p. 114) and his allies holding that Mother Earth needed no help and that her breadth and bounties belonged to those who had cherished them from time's memory.[1] Among those nineteenth-century observers who commented on the Indians' special view of the land was George Armstrong Custer. Writing in the New York *Herald* in 1875, he explained that Indians had a strong attachment for the ground containing the bones of their ancestors. "Love of country is almost a religion with them," he wrote. "It is not the value of the land that they consider," he noted, "but rather [it] is a strong local attachment that the white man does not feel, and consequently does not respect."[2] When technology in the form of the deep breaking plow extended possibilities for intensive agriculture and white occupation to the prairies and plains, confrontation over land was only a matter of time.[3]

Perhaps as much to blame for the conflict was United States immigration policy. The great numbers of land hungry newcomers from the Old World in the nineteenth century created pressures for expansion to which the president and the Congress responded. By 1860 there were 4 million foreign-born people in the United States. In the decade of the 1870s, the peak year of immigration was 1873 when 459,803 persons landed on American shores. Compare these numbers with population figures for native peoples and the inevitability of it all becomes clear. Estimates are that American Indians totaled about 500,000 at the time of Columbus and declined to 248,253 by 1890. During the 1870s, the Teton Sioux numbered about 31,650, the Northern and Southern Cheyennes about 4,000, and the Arapahos even fewer.[4] The latest infusion of whites into eastern Montana and the Black Hills was simply that which triggered this last major conflict. An important tool of migration on the northern plains was the railroad, and because the Sioux were perceived as a threat to construction of the Northern Pacific, they had to be subdued. Here again, Euramerican technology in the form of the steam engine had made rapid expansion possible, and development of the high-speed printing press had increased the ability to disseminate settlement propaganda, firing migration and creating new pressures.[5]

Another important determinant was the lack of respect by the United States government for the fighting skills of its adversary. Recent studies of warfare have concluded that the most important single factor in precipitating armed conflict is misperception, especially as it is manifested in a leader's view of his opponents' capabilities and power.[6] The strategy adopted by army commanders evidenced this view. Rather than sending one overwhelmingly large force to accomplish its mission, it sent three supposedly self-sufficient columns led by Crook, Terry, and Gibbon. Custer's division of his command simply reflected this strategy. At least Custer based his actions on the valid principle that Indians fled when attacked in their villages.

Disrespect lay in views concerning the Indians' nature and abilities. One method of denigrating your opponent is to treat him as something different and apart. The "Alternity Theory" teaches that one common way to confirm your opponent as "the Other" is to feminize him, make him into a woman or a child. Lieutenant Eugene F. Ware in his book *The Indian War of 1864* does this in his description of some of the first Indians he met when traveling west in Nebraska. Of the Omaha males he encountered, he wrote: "It seemed to me that . . . the men were about fifty-five percent feminine. I think that some of the contempt which the early settlers had for the Indian was due to his effeminate actions and appearance. In addition to this, the Indians grew no whiskers and had a general inefficient manner, and was not in stature and build the equal of the white boys that were in our company."[7]

Ware's pronouncement was preceded by centuries of misinformation about and depreciation of Native Americans, from the castigations of Cotton Mather, the seventeenth-century New England divine who believed that Indians were active disciples of Satan, to the eighteenth-century French biologist Comte de Buffon who saw them as an underdeveloped species or race, to a contemporary of Custer who wrote in a frontier newspaper: "In peace they are rough and brutal . . . showing no affection whatever for their families. In war cruelty and torture are their chief study . . . they fight like demons and show no mercy."[8] Such views did not engender patience or compassion in Indian wars, and military leaders in the heat of battle occasionally expressed radical views. For example, after Modocs killed peace commissioners under a flag of truce in 1873, General William Tecumseh Sherman telegraphed his commander of troops in California: "You will be fully justified in their utter extermination."[9]

Another attitude contributing to the failure of the military in the 1876 campaign was the ingrained distrust of a new democratic republic for a large standing army. Signer of the Constitution Elbridge Gerry succinctly stated this belief in 1783 when he wrote: "Standing armies in time of peace are inconsistent with principles of Republican Government, dangerous to the liberties of a free people, and generally converted into destructive engines for establishing despotism."[10] Thus, following the Revolutionary War, the United States Army consisted of one company of artillery, retained to guard West Point, Pittsburgh, and a few other posts. By 1790, the force had grown to 1,216 men. In 1849, the number had increased to 10,320, and at the beginning of the Civil War, the army contained 13,024 combatants. After the war in 1866, the number of regular army troops stood at 43,059, but by 1870, it had fallen back to 37,313, and by 1875, the force had been reduced to 27,525. Just before the Battle of the Little Bighorn, the strength of the United States Army stood at 25,331, and on June 19 the Democratic House voted to reduce the number further to a new postwar low of 22,000 officers and men.[11] Compared to other countries during this period, the military forces of the United States were infinitesimal. According to one estimate, the population of the United States on June 1, 1876, was 46,284,344.[12] This meant that .05 percent of the population was in the army. In England troops represented .51 percent of its population, in Prussia 1.26 percent, in Russia 1.82 percent, and in France 1.9 percent. To put it another way, the army in England was ten times the size per capita of American forces, Prussia twenty-five times; Russia thirty-six times; and France thirty-eight times.[13]

What were the consequences of this predisposition against large standing armies? It meant that only in times of crises did the country marshal its great human resources for combat. In the case of the Indian wars, the conflict was not considered a threat to the Republic; therefore, military forces remained the same. If the United States government had wished to conquer all Indians by feat of arms, and had the full support of American voters, it could have done so with great rapidity. Instead, it relied on small numbers of soldiers on the frontier to enforce its policy, which vacillated between rewards and punishments. At the same time, it used troops from this small pool to defend its coastlines and borders and impose Reconstruction on the South. In reviewing the experience of the

Indian wars in 1878, General Philip Sheridan declared: "No other nation in the world would have attempted reduction of these wild tribes and occupation of their country with less than 60,000 to 70,000 men, while the whole force employed and scattered over the enormous region . . . never numbered more than 14,000 men. The consequence was that every engagement was a forlorn hope."[14] While Sherman might bemoan the fact of insufficient troops to do the job, he was responsible in part for their sometimes inadequate performance. The general and other military leaders of the day had not developed a coherent military policy or strategy regarding Indians. There were no manuals on tactics for conducting Indian campaigns, and the army remained more interested in fighting wars against future conventional enemies than in developing an effective system to handle the guerrilla warfare of the Plains Indians.[15]

This distrust of the military is also seen in the bifurcation of authority in Indian policy. Congress removed Indian affairs from the War Department in 1849, and in 1876 when the House voted to return the bureau to its original home, the Honorable John A. Logan of Illinois rose in opposition when the bill reached the Senate floor. Speaking on June 24, just one day before the Battle of the Little Bighorn, Logan declared:

> I have learned from history, by my reading from my childhood, that the downfall of governments was by putting power in military hands. I have learned that the republics must and can only be maintained by civil authority, not by military. Put the Indian Department under the War Department, the Pension Bureau next, then the Land Office next, then abolish the Interior Department next, and then you have got one fourth of the government under the charge of the military, and thus a long step toward the resumption of military authority in this country. Remember the voices of Clay and Webster, of the great statesmen in this land, against the usurpation and inroads of military authority.[16]

Senator Logan's viewpoint prevailed and the transfer did not take place. The results of the division of responsibility for Indian affairs are well known. Marcus A. Reno summarized the problem in the concluding paragraph of his July 15 report on the Battle of the Little Bighorn. "The harrowing sight of the dead bodies crowning the height on which Custer fell," Reno wrote, "is too recent for me not to ask the good people of this country whether a policy that sends opposing parties in the field armed, clothed, and equipped by one and the same Government, should not be abolished."[17] While many correctly point to programmatic schizophrenia as a major difficulty in conducting nineteenth-century Indian affairs, many detractors forget that structural divisiveness probably prevented a stronger military effort that would have resulted in the loss of many more lives.

Not only was Indian policy inherently divisive, it was criminally inefficient. For example, records show that no supplies worth mentioning had been issued at Red Cloud and Spotted Tail Agencies since April 10, 1876, and that the Sioux were on the verge of starvation due to the failure of Congress to vote an appropriation and failure on the part of the Indian Bureau to forward the supplies needed.[18] Certainly inefficiency, indifference, and graft were factors in forcing the dramatic showdown on Custer Ridge. It was no coincidence that the campaign of 1876 took place during the Grant administration, the most corrupt in our history.

Just as there were impersonal causes that propelled both groups toward deadly confrontation, there were nonstrategic and nontactical reasons why the Sioux and their allies performed so well in combat during the summer of 1876. One of them was that, man-for-man, the Plains Indian warrior was more skilled than his adversary in horsemanship and use of firearms, equestrian warfare being endemic to his culture. Furthermore, the number of whites who possessed prior familiarity with firearms had diminished as the East industrialized and farming families provided fewer recruits because of the manpower needed to survive. Lack of training compounded the problem, due in part to lack of funds. Beginning in 1874, the army was able to issue only 120 cartridges per man for target practice, and it was not until after the Nez Percé War of 1877 that enlisted men received any instruction whatsoever in the theory of marksmanship. In 1893 Captain James Parker of the Fourth Cavalry observed that the lack of success of his branch of the service in the Indian wars had often been rationalized on the grounds that the enemy had possessed superior weapons. He declared that in truth the Model 1873 Springfield was the best military rifle in the world, but the Indians were simply better shots. According to Parker, when a warrior fired his weapon, he fired it to kill; each cartridge represented a life.[19]

Was Custer's regiment part of the Little Army That Couldn't Shoot Straight? It is true that about 15 percent of those in the Seventh Cavalry were generally unskilled recruits, while many of the rest were ill-prepared for battle through neglect of target practice.[20] However, in his latest work, *Archaeology, History, and Custer's Last Battle*, Richard Fox does not attribute Custer's ultimate defeat to troopers' poor firing and riding skills. Rather he finds the key in the shock firepower of Henry repeating rifles brought by Sioux warriors to bear on Calhoun's line, whose disintegration spread to the rest of the command. Thus, in the case of the Custer fight, poor training among the troops seems to have been less of a factor than concentrated short-range firepower on the Indian side.[21]

Why Is It Remembered?

Why does the Little Bighorn story continue to be remembered? After all, it was only one of 938 skirmishes in which regular army troops engaged native peoples.[22] Obviously, the totality of the event is a factor. The casualties suffered there were great in proportion to other battles, and the fact that no soldiers survived engenders continuing fascination. John Urquhart and Klaus Heilman in their new study, *Risk Watch: The Odds of Life*, have documented the strange way people perceive risk: sudden surprising news triggers horror, while people find greater misfortune in group tragedy than in individual calamity; ten people dying alone will receive less attention than ten dying in a group.[23] Another factor is our present view of death—that it is a mistake. Daniel Callahan recently noted that our contemporary belief that most causes of death are curable if science tries hard enough heightens the horror of contemplating sudden death and no survivors.[24]

While these studies may provide insights into the enduring interest in the Battle of the Little Bighorn, there is a deeper, less primitive reason for the power of its memory: the malleability of the myth. More interpretive possibilities exist in the Little Bighorn story, including its personalities and antecedents, than in any other dramatic episode in the history of the United States in the nineteenth century, and its capacity for mirroring diverse, even conflicting, social and political values qualifies it for recognition as a great American epic. The story is played in the vast setting of one of the world's great panoramas; it is replete with countervailing heroes whose strengths are their weaknesses; and it embodies all that is good and bad in our history.

An epic must have heroes and villains. On one side, we have George Armstrong Custer, hero and antihero in the same form. Already famous for his exploits in the Civil War and on the southern plains, he was a dashing figure who rode to the sound of the guns at the head of his command. As one former Michigan cavalryman put it, "When Custer was not in front there was no front."[25] Eloquent with pen as well as sword, Custer was not above taking on the mighty when conscience dictated. On the other hand, he was vain, brash, occasionally insubordinate, cruel at times, often tasteless, and morally suspect. Unfaithful to his mate, he participated in questionable business practices and was given to repeating hearsay damaging to other men's reputations.[26]

These attributes, then as now, earned him detractors. "Few men had more enemies than Custer," wrote his first biographer Frederick Whittaker, who added, however, that "no man deserved them less," testifying to the strong emotions precipitated by this dichotomous figure.[27] Perhaps Custer's greatest critic surfaced after his death. This was his immediate superior, Colonel Henry Sturgis, who blamed the officer for the death of his son. The embittered Sturgis unleashed his fury in a long letter to the St. Louis *Globe-Democrat* and in doing so summarized the feelings of many in past and present generations. In his letter, Sturgis declared: "I have said that General Custer possessed unbounded and selfish ambition; I say so now. I have said he was tyrannical in his intercourse with his officers and men; I say so now. I have said his knowledge of Indian warfare was extremely limited and overrated; I say so now. I have said that all these combined led to the useless and unpardonable sacrifice and cruel butchery of 300 gallant men; I say so now."[28]

To have a tale of epic proportions, both opponents have to be worthy and exhibit comparable resolve.[29] In Sitting Bull we have Custer's counterpoint, a renowned warrior, courageous, intractable, and mystical, whose importance has been reaffirmed in Robert Utley's recent biography.[30] In remaining true to the values and principles that guided his tribe, Sitting Bull achieved greatness. There were other Indian heroes present as well. With the exception of Red Cloud (p. 31) and Spotted Tail, all the famous chiefs of the Lakotas were in the Indian village when the trumpets sounded on June 25. As mentioned above, the fighting skills of the Sioux and their allies finally have been recognized, giving new power to the story.

The ability of the story to accommodate contradictory values is one of the secrets of its viability. This capacity may be expressed in irony, a state of affairs wherein the end result is often opposite to that which is appropriate. The commonly repeated irony of the story has become a cliché: while the Sioux and their allies won the battle, they lost the war. Others are less widely discerned. For example, there is irony in using troops to insure freedom for African Americans in the South while using troops to take away freedom from Native Americans in the West. There is irony in that Custer was a spokesman against cheating Indians out of their personal property through illegal trading practices and an agent of the government in taking away their real estate. There is great irony in the fact that the technology which gave whites the advantage in the conflict of cultures, in the hands of the Sioux and their allies in the form of Henry repeating rifles, a significant factor in the defeat of Custer's troops at the Battle of the Little Bighorn.

The greatest strength of the Little Bighorn story is its ability to accommodate disparate social and political values. As Brian Dippie has pointed out, the Democratic party immediately blamed Custer's defeat on the duplicity, corruption, and incompetence of the Grant administration, while Republicans pointed to the antimilitary posture of its opposition, exemplified in the vote of the Democratic House to reduce the size of the army to 22,000 men.[31] Over time the most often invoked interpretations of the story have been as a lesson of personal sacrifice and martyrdom from the white perspective and as subjugation and repression from the Indian point

On July 25, 1988, the 112th anniversary of the battle, American Indian Movement activists led by Russell Means (center) placed a plaque honoring Indian patriots near the Custer Monument. The plaque now hangs in the battlefield's visitor center. (Judy Tell, photographer, Billings Gazette)

of view. In popular culture, the former is best seen in the 1941 film, *They Died with Their Boots On* (fig. 37), where Custer, played by Errol Flynn, sends the Seventh to certain death in order to save Terry and Gibbon. Conversely, in the 1970 film *Little Big Man* (p. 260), Custer's actions in attacking the Indian village manifested a destructive racism that directors of the film felt still abided in American society, revivified in the Vietnam War.[32]

This theme of repression has been dramatized in the past two decades through protests by Indian activists, principally by American Indian Movement (AIM) leader Russell Means. The last protest of note occurred in 1988, ending in the placement of a plaque within the grassy area next to the soldier monument on Custer Hill. According to the text, the plaque honored Indian patriots who had successfully fought to save Indian women and children from mass murder and to secure their people's homeland.[33]

It is interesting to note that Indian reaction to the end of nomadic freedom and the repression of their culture seems to follow a pattern discerned by contemporary psychologist Elisabeth Kübler-Ross in those having suffered great loss.[34] The first stage is denial, seen in the Ghost Dance movement that promised a return to previous conditions. The second stage is anger, which appeared in the 1960s with the Second Wounded Knee and other acts of violence. The third stage is bargaining, evidenced in the continuing effort to obtain appropriate compensation for the loss of the Black Hills, to memorialize the Indian side of the story at Little Bighorn battlefield, and to secure the return to the tribes of skeletal remains held by museums. Steps four and five are grieving and acceptance, still to come. In the 1990s the national monument continues to serve as a place for catharsis, a stage upon which Indian peoples can act out their feelings.

A third major use of the story has been for reconciliation. The initial ceremonial attempt at the battlefield was in 1926, when Brigadier General E. S. Godfrey, with naked sword, led five troops of Seventh Cavalry to meet an Indian column led by White Bull, son of Sitting Bull. At their meeting, the warrior raised his open hand in the sign of peace, and the old soldier sheathed his sword. Godfrey presented White Bull with a large American flag which, according to one historian, the chief cherished until the day of his death.[35] The most recent attempt at reconciliation was in 1986 when remains of troopers found on the battlefield through archaeological investigation were reinterred in a public ceremony. A Sioux speaker noted that the battle site was not alien ground but was steeped in tribal history and pride, while a white speaker reminded listeners that those who had faced each other more than a century before had fought side by side in recent wars.[36] A new sign of the increasing power of reconciliation was the passage of federal legislation in 1993 to change the name of the National Park Service monument from Custer Battlefield National Monument to Little Bighorn Battlefield National Monument and to authorize a monument on the site to honor Indian dead.[37]

A fourth use of the Little Bighorn story is gaining prominence.

Perhaps best described as the secularization of the myth, the dramatization of the story and its subplots is being used to make money. For some time, the Crow tribe has been holding a pageant in which the Custer fight is reenacted with Crow men and women playing the part of their enemies and opponents in the battle—the Sioux, Cheyennes, and Arapahos. In 1993, the tribe opened a gambling casino about a mile from the battlefield, invoking the Custer name to encourage betting. An advertisement appearing in local newspapers declares that "Custer Would Have Had a Much Better Chance of Winning" if he had visited the casino instead of the Indian village.[38] Does commercialization of the myth spell its weakening? I think not; rather, it proves again its malleability.

In 1992 yet another commercial possibility materialized. North Shield Ventures, Inc., backed by Time-Warner Records, offered to pay the National Park Service and the Crow tribe millions of dollars in royalties over a thirty-year period in return for exclusive rights to conduct battlefield tours, sell products on site, and build a historical theme park in the area. Besides a cash return, benefits offered to the National Park Service (NPS) included additional land for the battlefield, a new visitor center, staff housing, and relief from some administrative duties. Billed as a total living experience, the theme park was to include a herd of one hundred buffalo with Indian hunting parties stalking them; Crow, Northern Cheyenne, and Sioux villages; a portrayal of "Thomas Jefferson's World" of 1803; a depiction of the Lewis and Clark Expedition; reenactment of daily life around Fort Laramie; and the signing of treaties between the United States and Indian tribes. Regional Director Bob Baker noted that the park would include vignettes depicting "the incredible arrogance of the white man's values." The firm promised six hundred full-time summer jobs for Indians—four hundred for the Crows and one hundred each for the Northern Cheyennes and Sioux—and a smaller operation during the rest of the year.[39] While the National Park Service has tabled the project, one may expect other offers in the future, as developers continue to calculate the monetary value of history.[40]

Another factor nurturing the life of the Little Bighorn story is its uncanny ability to remain relevant from age to age. For instance, Custer was one of the first soldiers to venture into space. In spring

1863, he spent time in General William F. Smith's balloon corps, participating in the army's first program of aerial reconnaissance.[41] Recent coverage of gays in the military reminds us that Corporal John A. Nunan (also known as "Noonan"), the trooper who committed suicide after his wife was revealed to be a man, was a trooper in Custer's regiment, and that the only known photographs of him were taken with his commander, posed with a grizzly bear killed in the Black Hills in 1874.[42] Finally, Custer has an interest for some of those in the New Age movement, for in 1877 a medium claimed that he had been reached in the nether world. In other words, he had been channeled long before Seth and Lazarus. On November 23, 1877, the Cheyenne, Wyoming, *Daily Leader* published a 541-word spirit message, which concluded as follows:

> You would expect me, perhaps from the ideas I expressed while I dwelt in the form, to speak harshly of the Indian; but since I have come to spirit life I have learned a lesson that none can ever take from me; that I was mistaken in regard to the red man's character that the selfishness and barbarity of the white man has made him what he is; that the Indian has been outrageously wronged. . . . Then be true to the letter of all agreements . . . strive to give homes, peace and contentment to the red man. I would plead with you my country men, my brother officers, my friends, to be lenient and endeavor to bring peace and good influence to bear upon this man, that he may become civilized like his white brother. Do not seek to annihilate them, but try and make them better if possible.[43]

In effect, Custer declared that he hoped that he had died for the last of our sins.

In conclusion, what can we say of the Little Bighorn story? It is an episode in American history that is only understood when placed in the context of its time. More important than any orders issued in Washington in sending Custer to the Little Bighorn were the assumptions held by the Euramerican populace and its leaders about land, the country's destiny, the nature of native peoples, and large standing armies. Demographics, new technology, bifurcation of authority, bureaucratic ineptitude, and the power of other national priorities had as much to do with Custer's demise as the Sioux and their allies or tactical misjudgment.

Why is the story remembered? Certainly we can say that it is an American epic, embodying grand themes and great heroes. It accommodates differing social and political views. It is complex, malleable, laced with irony, and remains mysteriously relevant. In the end it is difficult to judge its ultimate meaning. To use a term in contemporary literary criticism, the story possesses that interpretation engendering quality known as "indeterminacy." That is, more than other stories, it rewards our interest in ways so various that we cannot hope to predict what future paths Custer scholarship will take—what new meanings, informed by what new currents in intellectual history or new communal values, will be codified through reasoned arguments as Custer-truths.[44] And as historians, we know that our judgments are colored by cultural milieu, academic fashion, and idiosyncrasies of taste.[45] In contemplating the meaning of the Little Bighorn story, I am reminded of the last words of Gertrude Stein, who, when musing about her imminent death, asked her companion Alice B. Toklas, "What is the answer?" When no reply came, she said, "In that case, what is the question?"[46] In the end, we can ask many questions of the Little Bighorn story and get many answers, and as long as there are historians capable of looking with fresh eyes, it will be possible to uncover new meanings. This is the predicament, and this is the challenge.

Notes

1.   James Oliver Robertson, *American Myth, American Reality* (New York: Hill and Wang, 1980), 106-11; Jay P. Kinney, *A Continent Lost— A Civilization Won: Indian Land Tenure in America* (Baltimore: Johns Hopkins Press, 1937), 1-5; Emmerich de Vattel, *The Law of Nations; or Principles of the Law of Nature, Applied to the Conduct and Affairs of Nations and Sovereigns* (Northhampton, Mass.: n.p., 1820), 158-59; Julius W. Pratt, "The Ideology of American Expansion," in *Essays in Honor of William E. Dood*, ed. Avery Craven (Chicago: University of Chicago Press, 1935), 333-48.

2. Quoted in Charles Francis Bates, "The Red Man and the Black Hills," *The Outlook*, 146 (July 27, 1927), 411.

3. Ellsworth Huntington, *The Red Man's Continent: A Chronicle of Aboriginal America* (New Haven: Yale University Press, 1919), 150-53, 172.

4. Steve Ambrose, "Custer Had It Coming," *Harvard Magazine*, 78 (June 1976), 46; Russell Thornton, *American Indian Holocaust and Survival: A Population History since 1492* (Norman: University of Oklahoma Press, 1987), 17, 120, 160; Kingsley M. Bray, "Teton Sioux: A Population History, 1655–1881," *Nebraska History*, 75 (Summer 1994), 172. For a table that dramatically shows increases in immigration in the United States from 1820 to 1880 see Harold Underwood Faulkner, *American Economic History* (5th ed., New York: Harper and Brothers Publishers, 1943), 300-301.

5. Frederick Merk, *Manifest Destiny and Mission in American History: A Reinterpretation* (New York: Vintage Books, 1963), 24, 33, 53-55, 265.

6. John G. Stoessinger, "War Is a Human Sickness," in David L. Bender and Bruno Leone, *War and Human Nature: Opposing View Points* (St. Paul: Greenhaven Press, 1983), 71.

7. Eugene F. Ware, *The Indian War of 1864* (New York: St. Martin's Press, 1960), 28.

8. *The Miners Journal*, November 19, 1867. For similar views see E. J. Goodspeed, *History of the Great Fires in Chicago and the West* (New York: H. S. Goodspeed and Co., 1871), 36-37; Thomas Sturgis, *Common Sense View of the Sioux War with True Method of Treatment as Opposed to both the Exterminative and the Sentimental Policy* (Cheyenne, Wyo.: Leader Steam Book and Job Printing House, 1877), 52. For the history of Euramerican attitudes towards Indian see Antonello Gerbi, *The Dispute of the New World: The History of a Polemic, 1750–1900*, trans. Jeremy Moyle (1955; rev. and enlarged, Pittsburgh: University of Pittsburgh Press, 1973), 250 ff; Ray Allen Billington, *Land of Savagery, Land of Promise: The European Image of the American Frontier in the Nineteenth Century* (1981; reprint, Norman: University of Oklahoma Press, 1985), 12-13; Roderick Nash, *Wilderness and the American Mind* (New Haven: Yale University Press, 1967), 36. For comprehensive works on attitudes towards Indians in the eighteenth and nineteenth centuries see Merle E. Curti, *Human Nature in American Thought* (Madison: University of Wisconsin Press, 1986), 13-23, 83, 144-45; Bernard W. Sheehan, *Seeds of Extinction: Jeffersonian Philanthropy and the American Indian* (Chapel Hill: University of North Carolina Press, 1973), esp. 66-116; Roy Harvey Pearce, *The Savages of America: A Study of the Indian and the Idea of Civilization* (Baltimore: Johns Hopkins Press, 1965); Robert F. Berkhofer, Jr., *The White Man's Indian: Images of the American Indian from Columbus*

to the Present (New York: Alfred A. Knopf, 1976); and Francis Paul Prucha, "Scientific Racism and Indian Policy," in *Indian Policy in the United States, Historical Essays* (Lincoln: University of Nebraska Press, 1981).

9.   Edward Howland, "Our Indian Brothers," *Harper's*, 56 (April 1878), 773.

10.   Walter Mills, *A Study of American Military History* (New York: G. P. Putnam's Sons, 1956), 37, 41-43; Ralph H. Gabriel, *The Course of American Democratic Thought: An Intellectual History since 1815* (New York: Ronald Press Company, 1940), 90-91.

11.   *Report of the Secretary of War, 1876* (Washington, D. C.: Government Printing Office, 1876).

12.   "Population of the United States," Chicago *Inter-Ocean*, July 13, 1876.

13.   See entry for "Army" in *Index Rerum* (n.p., 1883). A copy of this rare volume is found in box 7, Luther P. Bradley Papers, U.S. Military History Institute, Carlisle, Pennsylvania. English traveler Richard Burton noted that Americans looked upon a standing army "as a necessary nuisance; they are ever listening open-eared to projects for cutting and curtailing army expenditures and when they have weakened their forces by a manner of atrophy, they expect them to do more than their duty, and if they cannot command success, abuse them." Richard Burton, *The City of the Saints and across the Rocky Mountains to California* (1862; reprint, Niwot, Colo.: University Press of Colorado, 1990), 44.

14.   *Report of the Secretary of War, 1878* (4 vols., Washington, D.C.: Government Printing Office, 1878), 1:36.

15.   Robert Wooster, *The Military and United States Indian Policy, 1865–1903* (New Haven, Conn.: Yale University Press, 1988), 144, 170-71; Thomas T. Smith, "Introduction," in *A Dose of Frontier Soldiers: The Memoirs of Corporal E. A. Bode, Frontier Regular Infantry, 1877–1882*, ed. Thomas T. Smith (Lincoln: University of Nebraska Press, 1994), 10.

16.   "Indian Affairs," Chicago *Inter-Ocean*, June 24, 1876. This was not the first time the House had acted, having voted to make the transfer in December 1868. See *Army and Navy Journal*, December 12, 1868, 264.

17.   "Little Big Horn," Chicago *Tribune*, August 7, 1876.

18.   "The Indians," Chicago *Tribune*, April 29, 1876.

19.   John D. McDermott, *Forlorn Hope: The Battle of White Bird Canyon and the Beginning of the Nez Perce War* (Boise: Idaho State Historical Society, 1978), 152; James S. Hutchins, "Mounted Riflemen: The Real Role of Cavalry in the Indian Wars," in *Probing the American West*, ed. K. Ross Toole et al. (Santa Fe: Museum of New Mexico Press, 1962), 83;

Allan R. Millett and Peter Maslowski, *For the Common Defense: A Military History of the United States of America* (New York: Free Press, 1984), 338; Philip Weeks, *Farewell, My Nation: The American Indian and the United States, 1820–1890* (Arlington Heights, Ill.: Harlan Davidson, 1990), 120-21.

20. Douglas C. McChristian, *An Army of Marksmen: The Development of United States Marksmanship in the 19th Century* (Fort Collins, Colo.: Old Army Press, 1981), 33-34.

21. Richard Allan Fox, Jr., *Archaeology, History, and Custer's Last Battle: The Little Big Horn Reexamined* (Norman: University of Oklahoma Press, 1993), 262-64.

22. Don Russell, "The Army of the Frontier: 1865–1891," *The English Westerners' Brand Book*, 2 (January 1960), 7.

23. Billings *Gazette*, May 12, 1993.

24. Daniel Callahan, *The Troubled Dream of Life: Living with Mortality* (New York: Simon and Schuster, 1993); Washington [*Post*] *Book World*, August 22, 1993.

25. "What an Old Michigan Trooper Remembers," Chicago *Inter-Ocean*, July 7, 1876.

26. For implicating the brother of President Grant in selling of post traderships, he earned the president's anger and was temporarily suspended from his command. To many he was a hero for speaking out. Personally he knew nothing, or next to nothing; however, he knew a great deal that had been told to him by others of matters commonly rumored at frontier posts. See "The Custer Tragedy," Chicago *Inter-Ocean*, July 9, 1876; "General Custer's Testimony," Chicago *Inter-Ocean*, March 30, 1876; *Army and Navy Journal*, October 12, 1879, 1.

27. Frederick Whittaker, *A Complete Life of Gen. George A. Custer* (New York: Sheldon and Co., 1876), 1. The biography was reprinted in two volumes in 1993 by the University of Nebraska Press, with introductions by Gregory J. W. Urwin (vol. 1) and Robert M. Utley (vol. 2). For a contemporary review of the volume, see "General Custer," New York *Herald*, November 30, 1876.

28. "General Sturgis," Chicago *Inter-Ocean*, August 12, 1876.

29. Bryan Perrett, *Last Stand! Famous Battles against the Odds* (London: Arms and Armour Press, 1991), 9.

30. Robert M. Utley, *The Lance and the Shield: The Life and Times of Sitting Bull* (New York: Henry Holt and Company, 1993), 314.

31. Brian Dippie, "The Southern Response to Custer's Last Stand" in *The Great Sioux War, 1876–77*, ed. Paul L. Hedren (Helena: Montana Historical Society Press, 1991), 234-36, 339-40.

32. Edward Tabor Linenthal, "Ritual Drama at the Little Big Horn: Persistence and Transformation of a National Symbol," *Journal of the American Academy of Religion*, 51 (June 1983), 279; Paul A. Hutton, "From Little Bighorn to Little Big Man: The Changing Image of a Western Hero in Popular Culture," *Western Historical Quarterly*, 7 (January 1976), 35-36, 41; Bruce A. Rosenberg, "Custer: The Legend of the Martyred Hero in America," *Journal of Folklore Research*, 9 (Fall 1972), 110, 115, 123-26; Robert M. Utley, *Cavalier in Buckskin: George Armstrong Custer and the Western Military Frontier* (Norman: University of Oklahoma Press, 1988), 11.

33. Edward Tabor Linenthal, *Sacred Ground: Americans and Their Battlefields* (Urbana: University of Illinois Press, 1991), 159. The history of protests began at the hundredth anniversary of the battle on June 25, 1976, when Means and two hundred followers arrived on the scene dragging an American flag upside down (p. 294). At one point Means threatened to burn down the park visitor center, since it contained Custer memorabilia. Negotiations avoided violence. For a description of this event by a program participant that day, see Utley, *Cavalier in Buckskin*, 11.

34. Elisabeth Kübler-Ross, *On Death and Dying* (New York: Macmillan Publishing Company, 1969), 39-137.

35. Stanley Vestal, "White Bull and One Bull—An Appreciation," *The* (Chicago) *Westerners Brand Book*, 4 (October 1947), 47.

36. Los Angeles *Times*, June 26, 1986.

37. 105 Stat. 1631.

38. Sheridan *Press*, May 2, 1994.

39. The NPS and North Shield Ventures, Inc., signed a memorandum of understanding about the plan in September 1992, before the public knew that negotiations were underway. The NPS did not reveal the agreement until forced to do so by a formal request under the Freedom of Information Act. See Billings *Gazette*, May 12; December 1, 1993. For samples of arguments in opposition to the proposal see *Custer Little Bighorn Battlefield Advocate*, 1 (Fall 1993), 1, 4-5, 7-8.

40. Cultural heritage tourism has become a significant segment of the travel industry, with places associated with the history of the American West in the forefront. For a discussion of the phenomenon and its growing economic appeal see John D. McDermott, "Why Cultural Heritage Tourism?" *Trail Talk: Newsletter of the Old West Trail Association* (February 1994), 3; "Spreading the Word," *Association of Montana Newsletter*, 25 (Winter 1994), 9; "The Challenge of History," *Great Plains Tourism Connection*, 2 (Spring 1993), 3; "Never Underestimate the Power of History," *Tourismreader*, 2 (April 1991), 12-13.

41. Jay Monaghan, *Custer: The Life of General George Armstrong Custer* (Boston: Little, Brown and Company, 1959), 70-72; Morris M. Thompson, *Maps of the Americas* (Washington, D.C.: Geological Survey, 1979), 10.

42. For a short life of Nunan, see James V. Schneider, *An Enigma Named Noonan* [Fort Wayne, Ind.: James V. Schneider, 1988]. The two photographs of Nunan appear on pp. 19-20.

43. Cheyenne *Daily Leader*, November 23, 1877.

44. J. Hillis Miller, "The Critic as Host," in *Critical Theory since 1965*, ed. Hazard Adams and Leroy Searle (Tallahassee: Florida State University Press, 1986), 468.

45. For a discussion of this issue, now much in vogue, see Michel Foucault, "What Is an Author?" in Adams and Searle, eds., *Critical Theory Since 1965*, 140 ff; Stanley Fish, *Doing What Comes Naturally: Change, Rhetoric, and the Practice of Theory in Literary and Legal Studies* (Durham: Duke University Press, 1989), 30; and Stefan Collini, ed., *Interpretation and Overinterpretation: Umberto Eco with Richard Rorty, Jonathan Culler, and Christine Brooke-Rose* (Cambridge, UK: Cambridge University Press, 1992).

46. John Bartlett, *Bartlett's Familiar Quotations* (14th ed., Boston: Little, Brown and Company, 1968), 933.

LEGACY

PART II
The Battle

Hunkpapa holy man and leader Sitting Buffalo [Sitting Bull] received a vision that foretold the Indian victory at the Battle of Greasy Grass River [Little Bighorn River]. (D. F. Barry, photographer, Montana Historical Society Photograph Archives, Helena)

A Battle Won
and a War Lost
A Lakota Perspective

Joseph M. Marshall III

A s a Lakota and a person intensely interested in the history of the West—and especially *how* that history is reported—I am always appreciative of an opportunity to offer a Lakota perspective; but I am most appreciative of the willingness of non-Indians to listen to an Indian perspective and accord that perspective its rightful voice in the entire human history of this continent. And if there is one single event which should logically be the catalyst and an initial focal point for the presentation of several viewpoints and several voices, it is the Battle of the Greasy Grass River (Little Bighorn).

As a Lakota I am glad that more and more voices are raised which speak *for* the Indian or Native American viewpoint in history. The next logical step would be to vigorously seek out those Indian people with knowledge of their specific tribal histories as well as history in general, so that those voices can be added. Indian opinion and Indian history should be articulated by Indian people. And that has nothing to do with a command of the English language; it has to do with knowledge. No individual or group is a single omniscient source when it comes to history. It is a composite, and we need the true voices from each part to tell a complete and realistic story. Anything less is an insult to all of the people who lived that story and contributed to the history we study and tell about in our times.

Mila Hanske kin Peji Slusluta Wakpa el wicaktep he itokabna tehi slolunyapi, na iyohankap hecena tehi slolunyapelo. "Life was difficult for us before the Long Knives were killed at Slippery Grass River, and it was still difficult for us after that." These are the words of Isaac Bear Looks Behind, a Sicangu Lakota. He spoke them to me in 1954 a few months before he died. He was born in 1883, seven years after the Battle of Greasy Grass River and two years after the Spotted Tail Agency became known as the Rosebud Sioux Indian Reservation. At the age of seventy-one, his sad retrospect was a preface to the last time he ever told me about what he knew of the battle. But it is also an accurate assessment of life for the Lakotas during that period called the "Plains Indian Wars" or the "Great Sioux War." (These are eclectic misnomers that, in my opinion, rank with the one which labels us all generically as Indians; but that is another discussion entirely.)

Grandfather Bear Looks Behind's words do aptly describe that period which was the final fifty years of what is commonly called the "buffalo culture" or the "horse culture" of the Great Plains: from 1840 to 1890. Those ethnological characterizations include many different tribes, of course, one of which is the Lakota.

The different groups of the Lakotas were, and are, the Oglalas, Mniconjus, Sihasapas, Itazipa colas, Oohenunpas, Hunkpapas, and Sicangus. And if some of these names are not familiar to some of you, it is probably because the names are *all* in Lakota and not a mixture of English, French, and Lakota.

By 1840 there was a definite Euramerican presence both at the fringes of Lakota territory and inside of it as well: Fort Laramie, for example, and the steamboat landing at Fort Pierre. The Lakotas were apprehensive and uncertain about that presence. A major reason for those feelings was the smallpox epidemic of 1837, which spread from contact with a steamboat traveling upriver on the Great Muddy or Missouri (in what is now central South Dakota) and killed nearly two thousand people.

According to Grandfather Bear Looks Behind, life was difficult for the Lakotas before and after the Battle of Greasy Grass River because of the whites. And the difficulty increased with the increase in white activity, such as the migrations on the Holy Road (Oregon Trail) and the Powder River Road (Bozeman Trail).

By the end of 1890, except for a few scattered incidents, armed conflicts between the Plains tribes and Euramericans had ceased. Indigenous cultures, which had existed for hundreds of years on the Plains and as part of a race that existed for tens of thousands of years on this continent, were changed forever by the persistent encroachment and invasion and dogged imperialism of the Euramericans. Even those tribes that did not militarily resist the invasion—such as the Poncas who once lived near the southern reaches of Lakota territory—were swept up in the policy of control and assimilation. Imperialism took the lands; control and assimilation took the spirit. Among those who chafed within the pressing boundaries and limits of reservation life were the Lakota warriors who handed the United States Army its worst defeat in the nineteenth century.

During the Moon of Cherries Ripening in the year of Winter When the Long Knives Were Killed at the Slippery Grass River, the largest gathering of Lakotas ever assembled in the memories of those who were there conducted a Sun Dance and moved camp from Ash Creek to the western side of Slippery or Greasy Grass Creek. Among them were the Sahiyelas (the Northern Cheyennes) and a few from the Mahpiya Tos (Northern Arapaho). Days before, nearly a thousand Lakota and Sahiyela warriors had stopped the northerly advance of Three Stars (General George Crook) at Rosebud Creek. Flush from that victory and because of the sheer size of the camp, the number of people overall, and the number of fighting men, there was a feeling of relative security. There was a feeling that no one would be foolish enough to attack such a large encampment.

Of course, at this point, no one in the encampment knew that they were on the eve of an event that would certainly accelerate the change in their lives and effect the lives of their descendants for generations to come. Even after the battle, many who were there regarded the event as just one of several over the course of many years that underscored their relationship with the Euramericans, such as the migration along the Holy Road, the Grattan Fight, Woman Killer's Coming (William S. Harney's campaign), the cholera outbreak of 1849, the Treaty Councils on Horse Creek (1851 and 1868 Fort Laramie treaties), the wagons on the Powder River Road, the forts along the Powder River Road, the Battle of the Hundred in the Hand (the Fetterman battle), and Long Hair's (George Armstrong Custer) expedition into the Black Hills. The Sahiyelas, of course, could add to that list Sand Creek and Washita River. Therefore, while there might not have been any worry about imminent attack, there was definitely a concern for the long-term future.

The great encampment along the Greasy Grass, with its horse herd of about fifteen thousand head, stretched for miles along the river with its middle near an old creek bed called Medicine Tail Coulee, which sloped down to the river from the east.

A gathering this size was unusual, but so was the reason for it. Months before, the Hunkpapa holy man and leader, Sitting Bull (actually, the precise translation of his Lakota name is Sitting Buffalo), had sent out messengers urging the people to gather to talk about something that concerned them all: The steady encroachment of the whites and what that fact meant for the future of all the Lakota people. The response to the Hunkpapa leader's call indicates the extent to which other Lakotas shared his concern.

While still at the Ash Creek camp, Sitting Bull (p. 114) conducted a Sun Dance and offered one hundred pieces of his flesh; he received the vision of blue uniformed soldiers falling head first into a Lakota camp. The vision foretold the death of soldiers and victory over them. Although the Lakota and Sahiyela warriors who had defeated Three Stars carried the certainty of the vision with them, there were many others who felt and said that Sitting Bull's vision had not come to pass at Rosebud Creek. And they, of course, were right.

One version of history says that the battle occurred on June 25, 1876. In the Lakota calendar, it took place in the first few days of the Middle Moon, and the fighting lasted for two days until the Lakotas and Sahiyelas exercised a military option open to them and broke off the fighting—by virtue of their fierce counterattacks and subsequent decisive suppression of two direct thrusts at the encampment. The enemy did not have that option, and those who survived owed their lives to the Lakota decision to move women and children to safety because of scouting reports of soldiers moving south from the Elk River (Yellowstone River). Had it not been for those enemy soldiers, the remaining soldiers at the Greasy Grass, forced into a limited defensive posture behind barricades on a hill, sooner or later would have been wiped out by relentless guerrilla tactics or mounted charges by some of the finest light cavalry in the world—or the simple but inevitable depletion of food, water, and medical supplies.

The Battle of the Greasy Grass River was a victory for the Lakotas and Sahiyelas (although someone informed me four years ago that Reno was the victor since he held the field when the relief column arrived). The prism of some contemporary opinions notwithstanding, everyone who has looked at the reality of the battle agrees that it was a victory for the Lakotas and Sahiyelas and a defeat for the Seventh Cavalry. And there are at least three major factors that account for the reality of the Battle of the Greasy Grass. First, the invading force did not know the size of the Lakota and Sahiyela encampment. Second, the invading force was not physically and emotionally prepared to engage in intense combat (because of an exhaustive forced march). Third, the stakes were much higher for the defending force than they were for the invaders. The first two factors speak for themselves. The third is often overlooked or only superficially explored in many discussions of the battle, if at all. It warrants closer scrutiny, if for no other reason than the fact that history is more than the obvious aspects of any given event or period. Events and conditions occur because of human action and reaction, human decisions and mistakes.

When the invading force launched its assault on the encampment on the Greasy Grass, the defending forces did not care that the enemy and their horses were worn out from a forced march. Neither did they know or care that the enemy had underestimated the size of the encampment. The defending forces knew only that they had to do what was necessary to protect what was nearest and dearest. That knowledge and that commitment was the deadliest weapon they carried into combat.

The action of the invading enemy was to launch an attack against a Lakota and Sahiyela encampment populated mostly by women, children, and old people. The reaction of the defending force was to counterattack swiftly.

The actual number of Lakota and Sahiyela warriors will never be known. But my best guess based on family composition of the time—taking into account the presence of a small percentage of unmarried and unattached warriors—is that the males who were physically able and adequately equipped to go into combat made up 10 to 15 percent of the total population of the Greasy Grass encampment. But those counterattacks were much more than the reactionary deployment of a military unit; it was grandfathers, fathers, sons, uncles, brothers, and cousins making a commitment to defend family and friends. But, in a sense, they were defending much more than that.

It is ironic that during a gathering whose primary purpose was to discuss concerns about the increasing encroachment of whites into Lakota territory, that gathering would be attacked by whites. Therefore, the Battle of the Greasy Grass occurred on two levels, if you will, at the same time. The first level was the immediacy of the situation. The camp—women, children, and old people—had to be protected at all costs. And they were. On the second level, the warriors were fighting to protect against another Blue Water, another Sand Creek, another Washita. They were fighting to protect a way of life. They won the battle to protect the camp. In the end they lost the war to protect a way of life.

The Battle of the Greasy Grass has been discussed, studied, reenacted, and told in many versions through visual art and the written word. In most of the stories I have heard or read, it has been characterized more as a loss for one side and less as a victory for the other. It has given us heroes and villains, and has been the springboard for myth and legend. It has been memorialized more as a monument to the losers than to the winners. And I suspect that it will continue to have the power to entangle us in argument, draw us into scholarly discussion, and reveal our personal and racial biases, while *it* remains behind a veil of mystery. I hope that in this process we continue to look for the reality of the Battle of the Greasy Grass River. And in the opinion of at least one Lakota, that reality is this: The Battle of the Greasy Grass River was a human event. It was a turning point which more than likely hastened the end of a lifestyle (though not of a people). It was probably inevitable because there have always been two basic reactions to imperialism: capitulation without conflict; or a fight for freedom. The Lakotas, given that we were one of the most powerful indigenous groups (if not the most powerful) of the pre-reservation era on the northern plains, were not about to do anything else but defend ourselves. So we chose to fight for our freedom, our way of life, and our very lives. Our victory at the Greasy Grass was, to us, part of a continuing struggle. Yet, the saddest reality of Greasy Grass was that we thought it was enough to teach the invaders to stay out of our territories and our lives.

In my boyhood I listened to many stories about the Greasy Grass fight told by several old men and women. Without exception the two most obvious emotions were pride and sadness. Pride because the battle was won. Pride because of the specific role of a close or distant ancestor in the battle. But sadness because the victory and the heroics did not ultimately preserve the freedom to be Lakota.

Indeed. The twenty-twenty hindsight of time has revealed that this, of all battles, in the eventual fifty-year struggle to repel Euramerican encroachment and invasion of the Plains was the turning point, but not because it was a Lakota victory. I believe that the planners of that summer's campaign against the Lakotas were expecting nothing short of a decisive army victory, to break the Lakotas' will and ability to resist militarily and force them onto reservations. Although the Greasy Grass was a loss for the United States Army, it still turned out to be that turning point and became a rallying cry for many Euramericans on the same level as the Alamo. And the eventual intended result was that the Lakotas were forced onto reservations. I think that was the reason I saw such sadness in the eyes of those old storytellers. And I think that is the reason for Grandfather Bear Looks Behind's words. "Life was difficult for us before the Long Knives were killed at Slippery Grass River, and it was still difficult for us after that."

I looked up the word *patriot* in an English language dictionary, and the definition is simply "one who loves his country." That same thought is expressed in many of the Lakota warriors' honoring songs, with the words *Oyate kin nipi kta ca lecamu.* "I do this so that the people may live." In my opinion and in my heart, there is no higher commitment than to defend one's country—one's people, and their way of life and their right to exist. To me, all of the people who did what they had to to survive and face an invading enemy at the Greasy Grass were patriots.

Many of the mothers and grandmothers, and the grandfathers who were too far past their prime to ride into battle, not knowing what the outcome of the battle would be, gathered the young and other helpless ones and fled to safety. Some stayed in the camp to be of whatever assistance they could to the fighting men. I have heard stories of wives, mothers, and grandmothers who stood at their lodges holding the lead ropes of their husbands', sons', and grandsons' second and third war horses, and singing and praying as the battle progressed. And knowing full well that they were endangering themselves if the enemy should come into the camp. I have heard stories of small boys who had to be physically restrained by mothers and older sisters to prevent them from sneaking into the fighting. And I have heard the same story from several different sources that the defenders who repelled an attempted incursion at Medicine Tail Coulee were mostly old men and young boys. In my opinion, the warriors who fought and defeated the enemy that day had a lot of help and certainly no monopoly on courage and commitment. All of those people who faced that terrible day on the Greasy Grass are *my* heroes. Each one who put something on the line that day was defending his or her people, his or her family, his or her way of life. Each one who took any action did so, so that the people would live. Each one was a patriot. And in the end, the fact that we lost the so-called "clash of cultures" does not diminish that patriotism.

The Battle of the Greasy Grass took place 120 years ago. Of course, there are some Lakotas who feel that the final engagement happened at Wounded Knee Creek 14 years later. In any case, Greasy Grass will live on in memory and imagination. We will continue to learn more about it and perhaps one day we will know the complete story. Whatever happens, we should remember that the final shot at Greasy Grass has been fired. Personally, I am not interested in debating or arguing about Greasy Grass. I am, however, interested in ways that we can learn the reality of Greasy Grass and tell the story fairly from all viewpoints. The only way we can do that is to realize that history belongs to all of us. It is not the domain of those who consider themselves to be the "winners" to the exclusion of those who are perceived to be the "losers." It belongs to all of us because all of our ancestors lived it then, and we live with it now. Therefore, our collective obligation is to know the reality of history and report it completely—with all of its victories and defeats, with all of its compassion and brutality. To do anything less would be to deny the humanity of it.

Sources

Sicangu Lakota Interviews
   Isaac Bear Looks Behind
   Albert Little Bird Two Hawk
   Paul No Two Horns
   Isaac Knife
   Richard Mouse
   Maggie Little Dog née Little Bird
   Moses Rattling Leaf
   Lucy Rattling Leaf née Little Bird
   Eunice Black Wolf
   Harris Lodgeskin Menard
   George Brave Boy

Oglala Lakota Interviews
   Wilson Janis
   Alice Janis

Secondary Sources
Sandoz, Mari. *The Battle of the Little Bighorn*. New York: J. B. Lippincott Company, 1966.

Scott, Douglas D., Richard A. Fox, Jr., Melissa A. Conner, and Dick Harmon. *Archaeological Perspectives on the Battle of the Little Bighorn*. Norman: University of Oklahoma Press, 1989.

Writer O. D. Wheeler interviewed Brave Wolf (left) and his wife about the Battle of the Little Bighorn on June 20, 1901, with Squint Eye translating. (L. A. Huffman, photographer, Montana Historical Society Photograph Archives, Helena)

Oral and Written Indian Perspectives on the Indian Wars

Margot Liberty

Historians and other scholars of the Indian wars are concerned with both oral and written accounts from Indian and white participants, on both sides of the conflict. All such reminiscences and interviews need careful evaluation and analysis. In dealing with these sources, the investigator needs to be aware of inherent problems and how best to understand and use information from them in research. What follows is a consideration of the value of such sources and what to look for in deciding their ultimate worth.

In general, soldier accounts were initially written, and most Indian accounts were initially obtained through interviews, then written down by the interviewer or someone else. Conventional wisdom holds that Indian accounts may be less reliable than soldier accounts because of their oral nature and because they have been transcribed by someone other than the original source. With the use of tape recorders, moreover, they are subject to mis-understandings in interpretation and translation, especially as translation may not occur until much later, thus losing authenticity with the passage of time. Indeed, such interviews must often be translated or augmented by the use of sign language, as in the work of Thomas Marquis and Frank Linderman, also known as "Sign Talker."[1] Although this distinction is not absolute—see the written account of the Sioux physician Charles Eastman concerning events at his hospital after Wounded Knee or the tape recording of old soldier accounts by Don Rickey, Jr.—it more or less holds.[2]

In addition, soldier accounts, especially those by highly educated officers, are credited with stressing the overall picture or grand scheme of events more than Indian accounts, which tend to focus on personal experience. Absolute accuracy was required of a warrior who recounted his deeds in battle, however, and verification was necessary if honors were to be won. Traditional Plains cultures had little concern for the wider view until outside pressures brought the need for different perspectives in later years. In all of this the nature of oral and written language plays a determining role. If Indian accounts are indeed to be counted less reliable but more detailed than soldier accounts, some reminders concerning oral and written language from the perspective of an anthropologist may help explain why that seems to be the case.[3]

Oral history is often linked conceptually to the invention of the tape recorder, although it actually originated with human speech itself and was relied upon for the vast majority of human experience prior to writing. It is limited by the extent of a single human memory, and it usually depends on face-to-face contact and personal transmission. Every language of the thousands known, whether written or not, is fully developed according to its own structures and principles and is able to incorporate changes through time as required. Each language is characterized by its own unique grammar as well as a particular selection of sounds from those possible to the human speech apparatus. Organizational principles vary widely but no language is "primitive," because each is a complete sophisticated system. Languages adapt quickly to express new ideas and information, but they are learned as total entities before six years of age; after that learning new languages becomes much more difficult.

At the time of Columbus, more than two hundred Indian languages, belonging to nine or ten stocks or major classifications, were spoken in native North America north of Mexico. None of these was written. In the Great Plains region in historic times— that is, following European contact—there were about thirty distinct languages belonging to six major linguistic stocks or divisions. Thus, the old question asked of frontier educational personnel, "Do you speak the Indian language?" indicated serious misunderstanding. An early teacher for the Bureau of Indian Affairs at Pine Ridge, who spent a good deal of time trying to learn Lakota, was astonished at its uselessness when he was transferred to the Southwest.[4] The linguistic diversity on the historic plains came about through the displacement of many native groups into the region from all directions after the arrival of horses and the adoption of buffalo hunting. The plains thus became a melting pot, or a linguistic Tower of Babel, in which unspoken sign language developed as a lingua franca—a form of communication Frank Linderman and Thomas Marquis, among others, made much use of.

Spoken language depends on the human speech apparatus, which is lacking in other species (including the great apes and sea mammals, whose thought processes may approach the sophistication of our own). Writing also depends upon the human upright bipedal posture that permits free use of the upper limbs and development of tool-using capacity by means of the oppositional thumb. Written language transcends space and time, as does speech, but because it can be passed from one human community and one human generation to the next, it is not dependent upon face-to-face contact (or by now, telephone or other mechanical transmission). Spoken language transcends space and time by the use of grammatical devices such as past and future tenses, and cognitive mapping, which distinguishes and names geographical localities, seasons, periods of time, and so on, but it cannot compare with the capacities of written language in this regard. Writing permits preservation and transmission of infinitely more material than spoken language, even with mnemonic devices such as winter counts or birchbark record rolls. As a device for cultural record keeping, writing is unique. It is amazing that it has existed for so short a time (five thousand to seven thousand years) in contrast to the whole of human experience (one million years at least). Before writing, everything we learned was transmitted by word of mouth.

Having suggested that any language can express anything, it should now be added that in a subtle conceptual sense this may not be true. If a work of literature "loses much in the translation" from Russian, say, to such a closely related language as English, we can be sure that the accurate translation of "exotic" languages is much more difficult, especially in the case of ideas and values with which the translator is not familiar. Most American Indian speakers of native languages by now have had to learn reading and writing in English. Many if not most members of older generations were uncomfortable with spoken English, and tended to go back to speaking their own languages once out of school, thus helping the native languages survive for another couple of generations. The more traditional people tended to be the least competent in English, an important factor in Indian wars research because those who had the most information often conveyed it the least well.

Very few Indian accounts of Indian fights were obtained in the informant's language. Most were derived from an interpreter or through the use of sign language, and sometimes both. Indian informants were often reluctant to cooperate fully or disclose everything they knew for fear of reprisal to themselves or to others they might tell about. Why else, an informant might reason, were these interrogators interested? As a result, answers to questions were often partial or incomplete. Questions could also be misunderstood. Indeed, problems of interpretation arose from inaccurate translation in both directions.

Differing agendas and abilities, moreover, affected various respondents. What was to be gained by telling these stories? A little money? Favors from a government agent if one cooperated? Penalties or loss of privilege if one did not? The wish to preserve such things in writing for future generations? The annoyance of (and possible punishment by) an informant's companions if he or she talked? How much did informants know directly through their own experiences, and what had they learned from others? How accurate were their memories, and which things were they unwilling or unable to tell?

Differing agendas and abilities affected interpreters as well. Was this part of their job? Whose side were they on? How fluent were they in each language? What things did they omit or withhold from translation, and why? Did they have special theories to prove or disprove? Were they after sensational details concerning "atrocities" or arguments to support a specific political agenda or individual reputation? How much time could they spend, or did they want to spend? Did they return to clarify ambivalent responses? Other limiting factors might be the circumstances of the interview—the physical discomfort, the presence of others, or the role of coercion. An example is the determination of Thomas Marquis, in *A Warrior Who Fought Custer* and *Save the Last Bullet for Yourself*, to prove that many Little Bighorn soldiers killed themselves in preference to facing what they believed was the inevitable torture of captives. Gathering much of his informant Woodenleg's information through sign language, Marquis derived a theory that few others have found acceptable.[5]

The desire for new Indian accounts is much greater among non-Indian historians or "Custer buffs," some of whom would give all they own for, say, new details concerning Custer's death. Surely some Indian family must know such things, they reason. Surely such details are to be found somewhere in yet undiscovered sources—someone's memory, a hidden ledger book, an untranslated tape recording, a clipping from some old trunk that offers a new interview account. Descendants of Indian participants, who tend to view the Custer fight in particular as a source of ethnic pride and, along with many other American citizens, something of a joke, have less fascination for such details. Often they are surprised at the continuing passion of whites for such knowledge—after all, they lost!

Requests for new Indian information from Indians these days are generally funneled through someone known as a tribal historian, who is informally selected in most cases for his or her interest in native history and culture, and because of his or her tolerance for and patience with inquisitive outsiders. Some of these people, such as Joe Medicine Crow, are real stars.[6] Some have had this duty thrust upon them and tend in the course of time to become irascible, especially with film crews. Investigations into tribal traditions also may be referred to officially appointed cultural committees for review and approval. (At Lame Deer, for example, each new film documentary is supposed to be authorized by the tribe.) The cultural committees change with each new tribal chairman, meet on an irregular basis (if ever), and are often difficult to find and convene. There is also concern for "intellectual property," along with the belief that the originators or owners of unwritten ideas should benefit from them. Among the Northern Cheyennes in recent years there has been a virtual "gag order" on descendants of certain tribal heroes who have access to accounts of such things as the Northern Cheyenne outbreak from Oklahoma. It is believed that any money derived from sharing such accounts should be distributed equally to all descendants, who may number in the hundreds. Often, the amount of money involved is overestimated. Nonetheless, individuals can get into trouble for "selling" information believed to be group property.

Money remains an important consideration in communities where many people live below the national poverty level. Although private film companies usually pay cash for interviews, public television guidelines for documentaries using oral history often prohibit payment of those interviewed on tape or camera. Funding agencies like the Montana Committee for the Humanities have similar guidelines. One tribal member interviewed for a major national series on western history said that she had traded her whole life for a box of candy.[7] Moreover, many interviews for use in documentaries wind up on the cutting room floor and never find their way into permanent archives. Elders selected for interviews because of their knowledge and experience may make less than dashing figures on screen and are thus excluded in the final cut. Such interviews are often the only material obtained from such elders, however, and they are vitally important to tribal history. An effort to gather and preserve such throwaways for future tribal use is urgently needed.

Before the advent of tape recorders, Indian and white accounts were gathered through face-to-face interviews sometimes for possible publication in little-known places, either at the time or subsequently. As a result, many accounts taken from old soldiers, or written by them or their relatives, have remained unknown for years, eventually surfacing in obscure newspapers such as the *Army and Navy Journal*, the *Army and Navy Register*, and the *National Tribune*, or in any one of thousands of small-circulation regional weeklies that may now be extinct. Despite their obscurity, such publications may offer accounts of whites interviewing Indians "on the spot" or close to it, for example, in early prison facilities.

Such accounts must be approached with caution. They may be so biased or sensational that they are of little historical use. Use of the term "Red Devil," for example, casts considerable doubt on the accuracy of the source.

Reminiscences by Indian participants often came down through several generations via oral tradition. How many reminiscences of authentic value have survived is a moot question; many now circulate as folklore. Examples include Cheyenne stories of the Cheyenne woman who killed Custer with her hatchet (he came to and sat up, having been earlier knocked out). We also hear of the warrior's son who broke an appointment with a historian because his friends, in jest, persuaded him he would be sent to jail for talking. There are also new speculations by Indians as well as whites. A Lakota pipe carrier told me in May 1994, for example, that Sitting Bull (p. 114) was not present at the Custer fight, having been so badly weakened by injuries resulting from his well-known sacrifice of one hundred pieces of flesh at the Rosebud Creek Sun Dance that he was unable to participate in the battle. The informant also said the body of Crazy Horse, cut into two pieces to help hide it, was demanded by the soldiers but saved for native burial by his relatives' substitution for the body of two bundles of old clothes!

To many tribal members, accounts that have come down through oral tradition in Indian families are today considered more authentic and less biased than written accounts of any kind, old or new, especially those by whites. I have been told of a loss of power, in an almost mystical sense, when such stories are written down.[8] Allowing for changes through time, and the overall limitations of human memory, it is unlikely that much new information will surface, but there always remains the chance of recovering that one telling detail.

My own experience with Indian oral history began four decades ago, when in 1954 I taught elementary school for the Bureau of Indian Affairs in the Northern Cheyenne Reservation community of Birney, Montana. Here I met the widely respected Cheyenne tribal historian John Stands in Timber, and we began the collaboration that was to become our book *Cheyenne Memories.*[9]

Born in 1884, John Stands in Timber worked at a time when research was easier because old-timers were still alive. Educated at

Haskell, Kansas, he spent much of his life collecting historical material from older members of his and other tribes. He served as an interpreter for such non-Indian researchers as J. W. Vaughn, Verne Dusenberry, and Peter Powell. His grandfather was the Cheyenne chief Lame White Man, killed at the Battle of the Little Bighorn. A cultural insider, he began gathering stories in 1900 when he was sixteen years old and continued doing so until his death in 1967 at age eighty-three. He visited and revisited chosen sources and gathered much information at intertribal events, such as fairs, powwows, and rodeos, consulting virtually anyone and everyone for additional details. He could write perfectly well in English, and several of his handwritten accounts and memoranda are in my possession. Like many tribal historians, however, he preferred to talk and listen.

Although his memory was amazing (we often filled several hours with a single story), Stands in Timber used written records in his work. He frequently checked tribal rolls to verify the ages of his informants, especially Little Bighorn battle participants. He would make certain calculations: "Let's see," he would say, "he was born in 1870 so he was six years old in 1876"; or, "She is seventy-five now and the census was in 1933, so she was forty-eight then." He also used written materials as reminders. A celebration program or banquet menu or some old clipping, while having nothing to do with the subject directly at hand, would spark his memory, and then he would be off like the Ancient Mariner. The stories remained in his head in living color, and he was always careful to cite his sources: Old Man Whitebird said this, but Dan Oldbull said something else.

Stands in Timber's original transcript, which I typed directly from the tape recordings made with him in 1958–1959, has been indexed recently, so that details not used in *Cheyenne Memories* are now retrievable.[10] Of interest are his comments on research experiences and methodology, as well as problems in achieving accurate translations. In his original narrative on the Horse Worship ceremony, for example, Stands In Timber commented that in "a lot of things, there's no word to compare the exact meaning with English." He reported that serious mistakes were sometimes made in the early days, as when some men smoked black gunpowder because the same English word, "powder," was used for kinnikinnick tobacco. In another instance, in an early baseball game, a player on his way to home ran through the cooking fire of his astonished wife after his teammates yelled to him in English: "Run Home! Run Home!" It was not uncommon for two men with varying proficiency in Cheyenne and English to talk back and forth in both languages. Stands in Timber recalled: "One talked Cheyenne and one talked English; they would sit there and talk and laugh. It sounded kind of funny." He also noted that sign language did not work well for all occasions, citing the case of Box Elder who married a Crow girl and had to talk in signs. "The marriage did not last very long," he said.[11]

More than most others of his generation, Stands In Timber investigated the Custer fight, which was remembered as a great triumph by his people. He held firmly in mind the locations of events important to the Cheyennes, and he hoped to see them marked for future generations. He succeeded with one—the death site of his grandfather, Lame White Man, on Custer Ridge, thanks to the efforts of research historian Don Rickey, Jr. It remains the only remembrance of an individual warrior found on the battlefield. As Rickey noted in 1961: "As you know I have been over parts of the Custer Battle with John Stands in Timber and he has pointed out several places where specific events occurred. Some of these are marked with small rock cairns. I made notes on some of his explanations, which should be in the research files."[12]

Other sites remained unmarked, however. In interviews with me in August 1961, when I was a seasonal ranger and historian at what was then Custer Battlefield National Monument, Stands In Timber told of some of these sites. Three are of particular interest: the story of a brother's suicide; the tale of a solitary escaping soldier; and the story of a Cheyenne coup counted with a cavalry guidon.[13]

In relating the story of the brother's suicide, Stands In Timber told of two large rocks at the Reno-Benteen battle site that may still be seen. The rocks, which are only partially exposed, lie near the east fence a short distance below the Thomas Meador marker, and indicate where a Sioux warrior and a small boy were shot by the soldiers. One of the rocks lies to the left of the draw, and one to the right. The one on the right is further down; the one on the left is closer to the soldier lines. The story given is this: A young Sioux boy had been captured by Indian scouts at the Battle of the Rosebud a week before the Custer fight. Presumably he was killed. The brother of this boy, also quite young (Stands In Timber's informant said they were boys, not yet men) was deeply grieved, and told his parents that he would die the same way. The Reno men were in siege position, and when an older Sioux warrior made a charge past the soldier lines, the boy followed him. The two of them galloped past from the north side (that is, from the left of the draw). The warrior swung down away from the soldiers but his horse was hit. When it fell, the warrior tried to run away but was killed. The boy, who did not see the line of soldiers, passed by them too closely and was killed as well, fulfilling his wish to die like his brother.

In the second story, Stands In Timber told of a solitary rider and speculated that he may have been the last man to die in the Custer fight. Stands In Timber got the story from Littlesun, a witness to the killing. Littlesun took Stands In Timber to the site in the vicinity of the Butler marker, not yet located on the field, when he visited the battlefield during the fiftieth anniversary celebration in 1926. Here, Littlesun said that he and Low Dog were on their way to join the fight against Custer and his immediate command when they met a solitary rider. "Low Dog and Littlesun were two warriors that went back and forth between the fights," Stands In Timber related.

> They were just leaving the Reno fight and going down toward Custer when a soldier on a fast horse broke from Custer's lines and galloped across towards Reno Hill. Low Dog and Littlesun met this rider, and tried to head him off but he got through them; then they turned and chased him. When they crossed the draw which the soldiers had come down in the first skirmish (Medicine Tail), Low Dog, who was a good shot, jumped off his horse and sat down to take good aim. He fired and knocked the rider off as he was going over a little knoll. Just then two or three Sioux came by and they took after the horse, but Littlesun said he could not see whether or not they caught it.[14]

Stands In Timber located the site where the rider fell about halfway up Medicine Tail Coulee, where a dim road used for scattering salt for range cattle runs below Weir Point and turns to pass through Cedar Coulee.[15]

At the third site, Stands In Timber said his informant told him of a warrior named Yellownose counting coup on a soldier with one of the troop guidons. The incident took place below and to the left of the Lame White Man marker, a place pointed out to Stands in Timber by Tallbull at the 1926 ceremonies, when Stands in Timber was taken over the field and also shown the death sites of Lame White Man and Noisy Walking. The soldier may have been among those of I Company. "Yellownose was in there close," Stands in Timber related.

> He saw two Indian horses run right into each other—the horses both fell and rolled, and he nearly ran into them himself but managed to turn aside. The dust was so thick he could hardly see. He swung his horse out and turned to charge back in again—it was close to the end of the fight— and suddenly the dust lifted away. He saw an American flag not far in front of him, where it had been set in the sagebrush. It was the only thing still standing, in that place, but over on the other side some soldiers were still fighting. So he galloped his horse past and picked the flag up, and rode on into the fight, and used it there to count coup on a soldier. He told that story many times, when they held those special dances where old men are used to start them that have done great things in battle. At camp gatherings of the Oklahoma Cheyennes the Dog Soldiers used to sing all night in front of different tepees along the village, and early in the morning when people started getting up they danced toward the center and any brave man could come before them on foot or on horseback and stop them, and tell what he had done. And Yellownose told that story then, too.[16]

An addendum to the Stands In Timber enterprise has recently come to light. In 1952, two years before my time at Birney, Stands In Timber participated in a project during which Northern Cheyenne tribal elder Dan Oldbull, one of the last of the traditional Cheyenne chiefs, met with anthropologist Robert Anderson, now deceased, to tape record some aspects of Northern Cheyenne culture. The material was made available to me by Anderson's widow in 1992. Oldbull lived at Birney, where four of his grandchildren attended school. As yet untranscribed and untranslated for lack of funding, these tapes include material on war customs among much else. Other such material will surely be found.

It is perhaps in the Oldbull tapes and other information like it, gathered previously by ethnologists, that more real Indian details of the Indian wars will be told. Not only will such data help us better understand existing Indian accounts, it will provide benchmarks to help authenticate or dismiss those that may be found in the future. But most important, they will help us understand and appreciate the ideas, practices, and beliefs the Plains Indians defended at the Little Bighorn in June 1876.

Notes

1. See Thomas B. Marquis, *A Warrior Who Fought Custer* (Minneapolis: Midwest Company, 1931); Thomas B. Marquis, *The Cheyennes of Montana*, ed. with introduction by Thomas D. Weist (Algonac, Mich.: Reference Publications, 1978); and Frank B. Linderman, *Plenty-Coups, Chief of the Crows* (1930; reprint, Lincoln: University of Nebraska Press, 1962).

2. See John D. McDermott, "Wounded Knee: Centennial Voices," *South Dakota History*, 20 (Winter 1990), 289-91; and Don Rickey, Jr., *Forty Miles a Day on Beans and Hay: The Enlisted Soldier Fighting the Indian Wars* (Norman: University of Oklahoma Press, 1963).

3. American anthropology combines four subfields: (1) cultural anthropology, including ethnology; (2) physical anthropology; (3) archaeology; and (4) linguistics. It has long been intimately entwined with study of these things in Native American culture, although much less today than a century ago. See Margot Liberty, ed., *American Indian Intellectuals: 1976 Proceedings of the American Ethnological Society* (St. Paul, Minn.: West Publishing, 1978).

4. Albert H. Kneale, *Indian Agent* (Caldwell, Idaho: Caxton Printers, 1950), 48-49.

5. Marquis, *A Warrior Who Fought Custer;* Thomas B. Marquis, *Keep the Last Bullet for Yourself: The True Story of Custer's Last Stand* (Algonac, Mich.: Reference Publications Inc., 1976).

6. Joseph Medicine Crow, *From the Heart of the Crow Country: The Crow Indians' Own Stories* (New York: Orion Books, 1992).

7. Personal communication to Margot Liberty, Summer 1994.

8. This sentiment is not uncommon during transitions from oral to written cultures. See for example typical sentiments in classical Greece described in Mary Renault's novel, *The Praise Singer:* "Men forget how to write upon the mind," says her protagonist Simonides. "To hear and to keep: that is our heritage from the Sons of Homer . . . The true songs are still in the minds of men." Mary Renault, *The Praise Singer: A Novel* (New York: Pantheon Books, 1978), 4-5.

9. John Stands in Timber and Margot Liberty, *Cheyenne Memories* (New Haven: Yale University Press, 1967), 3-10.

10. John Stands In Timber and Margot Liberty, original transcript of interviews of 1958–1959, 806 typed pages, 1959, in author's possession, indexed by John McDermott (hereafter transcript of interviews).

11. Ibid., 158.

12. Don Rickey, Jr., to Margot Liberty, August 15, 1961, Midwest Regional Office, National Park Service, Omaha, Nebraska, in author's possession.

13. Margot Liberty, "Sites of Indian Action on Custer Battlefield," typescript, August 20, 1961, in author's possession. I obtained this information from John Stands In Timber on August 19–20, 1961, and other dates.

14. Transcript of interviews, 357-58. George Bird Grinnell's account of this incident is as follows: "Just after the three companies had reached the gray horse company, a man riding a sorrel horse broke away from the soldiers, and rode back up the river and towards the hills, in the direction from which the soldiers had come. Some Indians followed him, but his horse was fast and long winded, and at last only three men were left in pursuit. A Sioux and two Cheyennes, Old Bear and Kills in the Night, both living in 1915, kept on, trying to overtake him. The Sioux fired at the man but missed him; then Old Bear fired, and a little later the man fell from his horse, and when they got to him they found that he had been shot in the back between the shoulders. It is conjectured that this was Lieutenant Harrington whose body was never identified." George Bird Grinnell, *The Fighting Cheyennes* (1915; reprint, Norman: University of Oklahoma Press, 1956), 353.

15. When he pointed out the site in 1961, Stands in Timber's vision was poor because of recent cataract operations. The place he indicated may not be precisely correct, but he was sure he was told "halfway to the head of Medicine Tail."

16. Transcript of interviews, 362-63. See also account in Grinnell, *Fighting Cheyennes*, 351.

West River History

The Indian Village on Little Bighorn River, June 25–26, 1876

Richard A. Fox, Jr.

On June 25, 1876, two battalions of the Seventh United States Cavalry attacked Sioux and Northern Cheyennes camped at Little Bighorn River. Strategic operations of Lieutenant Colonel George Custer's battalion were guided by village location and inhabitants' responses to attack. Yet researchers have scarcely paid attention to the Indian village, which consisted of numerous camps. Neglect is partly due to misguided distrust of the Indian record. That record indicates the village extended no farther north than abreast of Medicine Tail Coulee. Further, Indian testimony indicates most noncombatants raced away, some hurriedly breaking their camps. These developments suggest an alternative to the notion that warrior threats forced Custer's soldiers from village outskirts to killing field. Instead, Custer perceived a village on the run so he took his battalion northward out of Medicine Tail Coulee in an offensive pursuit.

The battle on Little Bighorn River, in what is now Montana, included three engagements between the Seventh United States Cavalry and Sioux and Northern Cheyennes—Major Marcus Reno's valley fight, Lieutenant Colonel George Custer's battle, and, about four miles away, the Reno/Benteen defense in which Reno and Captain Frederick Benteen participated. Many with

Reno's and Benteen's battalions survived; all in Custer's battalion died—some 210 men. The confrontation occurred over two days, June 25–26, 1876.[1] In June, two years later, Second Lieutenant Oscar Long, Fifth Infantry, visited the battlefield, evidently with Colonel Nelson Miles.[2] While there, he, like Miles, interviewed Little Bighorn battle warriors. Unlike Miles, Long named his informants—Hump, a Minneconjou Sioux, and two Northern Cheyennes, White Bull and Brave Wolf (p. 124). Long sent his interview in a letter to Lieutenant Frank Baldwin (also Fifth Infantry). In concluding, Long wrote, "The above disconnected facts, elicited from these Indians, are given as nearly verbatim as possible."[3]

"Disconnected facts," said Lieutenant Long. Since Long's observation, the "disconnected facts" gremlin has attended studies of the Little Bighorn fight. In 1962, historian Robert Utley commented on the historiographical nature of Indian accounts, noting numerous pitfalls, including cultural-linguistic differences between chronicler and informant, egocentric native males, falsehoods resulting from fear of reprisal, and others.[4]

Four decades before Utley's assessment, J. M. McCreight, who to his credit interviewed Little Bighorn battle warriors, decided Indian reports were not "entitled to any high degree of accuracy." Colonel W. A. Graham complained in 1953 that warrior stories of the battle are impossible to reconcile, largely because they were rendered in an alien tongue. Similarly, Stephen Longstreet hedged his Custer battle version, viewing Indian recollections as distorted. Hence for him, the story had "to be put together from bits and shards."[5]

Despite reservations, Longstreet did pay attention to the Indians. Similarly, Graham, although thoroughly vexed by them, published many Indian accounts, a commendable practice continued in the 1990s by Richard Hardorff and Jerome Greene.[6] These and other works recognize value in native testimony. Nonetheless, cautions such as Utley's have had an adverse net effect on Little Bighorn battle studies, recently to the extent that some authors have excluded the Sioux and Northern Cheyenne side of the story. Roger Darling, for example, avoided discussing the Custer battle in a 1990 book. In a *de facto* rejection of the Indian record, Darling explained that because no soldiers survived to tell the story, such attempts are futile.[7]

A year later, John Gray said much the same, although he did speculate at length about the fight. Gray, however, noted Northern Cheyenne and Sioux statements "reveal little more than [warrior] attitudes and fighting tactics."[8] He therefore dismissed altogether the many hundreds of recollections given by these people. Ironically, accounts compiled by some white chroniclers used by Gray came in part from Little Bighorn battle warriors.

For decades, white and Indian chroniclers went to great trouble to get the firsthand Indian story. For this reason alone, complete disregard for the Sioux and Northern Cheyenne legacies is deplorable. Yet this extreme position seems to be gaining acceptance, possibly, in part, because professionals active in Little Bighorn battle studies are far fewer than avocationals, some of whom are indeed talented. But whoever is involved, and whether resulting from extremism or more moderate views, philosophies that neglect the Indian record have had deleterious effects. For one, people burdened with such attitudes do not bother, except perhaps superficially, to become familiar with easily accessible information. As well, real or perceived difficulties in the Indian record have licensed authors to ignore wholesale that which is contrary to their notions while selecting that which is not.

Most damaging, though, aversion toward the Indian record has utterly stifled new discoveries. There is much out there still, either long-forgotten or unknown. As new materials surface, and they have lately, largely through the impetus of archaeology at the battlefield on Little Bighorn River, we will achieve a more complete historical perspective of events on June 25–26, 1876. The Little Bighorn story depends considerably on the Indian record— eyewitness relations, oral history, and oral tradition.

In this context, I propose to look at a rather narrow slice of the Indian record—the Indian village, a slice regularly ignored except incidentally, but certainly one critical for assessing the strategic nature of Custer's last battle. In examining the village, I consider some white accounts, which are, after all, also essential ingredients in Little Bighorn studies.

I believe that insights gained from archaeology furnish a reliable way to investigate history and that results derived from the methods of history *and* archaeology are more satisfying than those achieved by either discipline alone. Contrary to prevailing fatalistic interpretations of the Little Bighorn—Custer's battalion thrown on the defensive early and resisting to the last despite impossible odds—patterns in material remains have led me to suggest elsewhere that Custer's command maintained its offensive nearly to the end. Relying heavily on Indian recollections about the fighting, I found the archaeological story in the documentary record.[9]

I maintain similar views are available from Indian recollections recounting the village on Little Bighorn River and activities within it. Not incidentally, these accounts are for the most part straightforward. Why would a witness misrepresent the village location or gloss the reactions of inhabitants to an attack? Indeed, there are few reasons to label such accounts as suspect, except where ulterior motives drive results. The story, however, is one that must be pieced together. As a rule, white chroniclers were not much interested in the villagers and village, except for size, so they rarely asked. That story is mostly available only because Indians, when interviewed, exercised volition.

I first locate the village at the time of the battle on June 25, 1876, and then consider reactions of villagers to Reno's attack and Custer's subsequent appearance. To conclude, I argue this information prompts a plausible alternative to the popular fatalistic notions. Most materials cited here are in addition to those I have used elsewhere to support a similar but less inclusive argument.[10]

The Indian Village

Most people know the village on June 25 was located along the banks of Little Bighorn River on its west side (or south by some reckonings). The river typically is used as a reference landmark. Although in the battlefield vicinity the river actually flows northwesterly, researchers commonly refer to north, or northward. The nomadic village contained several Lakota Sioux bands, each arranged in its camp circle, and the Northern Cheyenne camp consisting of several bands. Indian accounts overwhelmingly agree that the Northern Cheyenne circle was northernmost and that a Lakota (hereafter Sioux) camp circle—the Hunkpapas—defined the southerly village limits. Between were other Sioux circles—

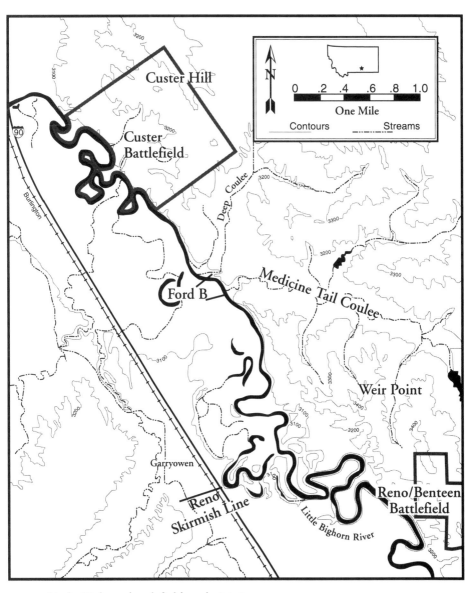

*Little Bighorn battlefield and vicinity
(Map by Richard A. Fox, Jr., and Kathryn Fehlig)*

Brulé, Oglala, Sans Arc, Minneconjou, and Blackfeet.

Occasionally people present from some other Sioux bands—Two Kettle, Yanktonai, Santee, and Lower Brulé—are assigned camp circles; more commonly they are placed with the above Sioux camps. As well, a handful of Arapahos and Southern Cheyennes were camped with the Northern Cheyennes (hereafter Cheyennes). Isolated accounts suggest people from a few other tribes were visiting, including some Arikaras, Gros Ventres (probably Hidatsas), and Assiniboines (perhaps referring to the Yanktonais).[11]

Others have considered village population. Here I do not intend to do so. Related to population, however, I will show that the village size on June 25 was no more than half of the more conservative estimates, or less than a quarter if outlandish claims such as Holmes Paulding's are entertained. Paulding, a surgeon who arrived on the scene on June 27 with Colonel John Gibbon, put the village at a whopping eight miles by two or three miles![12]

Nor will I present the case that the villagers were surprised by the Seventh Cavalry, although as a body they were indeed taken utterly by surprise, recovering only in time to prevent Reno from entering the village, if that is what he had in mind.[13] Not only that, Custer's later appearance farther north along the river, but on the side opposite Reno and the village, came as an eye-opener as well. Some of the accounts I use in portraying villager activities ought to make this clear.

Village Location

Locating the village requires a consideration of size, at least in general terms. Most white chroniclers portray an immense village extending from near Reno's valley skirmish line downriver to Custer's battlefield abreast of Custer Hill (see map, p. 143). This is a stretch of three miles, certainly not Paulding's eight or even Private Jacob Adams's (he fought with Reno) five miles.[14] Even a three-mile-long village is wrong. On June 25, after the Custer battle, inhabitants moved their encampment slightly downstream. Some explanations for relocation included avoidance of death lodges, avoidance of the stench from Custer's dead, and access to improved horse pasturage.[15]

Some of Walter Campbell's (a.k.a. Stanley Vestal) Sioux informants, and Wooden Leg, a Cheyenne, told of the move just downstream. So did Foolish Elk (Oglala), who said, "After the battle the whole camp moved northwest [downstream]." As well, Kill Assiniboine's wife, a Hunkpapa later known as Hattie Lawrence, said the camp moved "downriver [on the] afternoon of the battle."[16] Again situated west of Little Bighorn River, the north limits of the new village did indeed end at a point abreast of Custer Hill. Then, on June 26, with General Alfred Terry's column approaching from the north, the Sioux and Cheyennes trailed southward out of the valley, leaving two encampments—the prebattle and postbattle villages. With the Indians gone, military men inspected the site, and the two villages appeared to most observers as one.

Lieutenant Winfield Scott Edgerly was a rare exception.[17] Testifying at the Reno Court, an 1879 inquiry into Major Reno's conduct in the battle convened at his behest, Edgerly stated in relation to the river crossing at the mouth of Medicine Tail Coulee, identified as Ford B: "At first [the village] was higher upstream, after that it was moved out to the left and a little downstream [from Ford B]."[18] Edgerly likely had reason to know firsthand. After Benteen's battalion joined Reno, Captain Thomas Weir, one of Benteen's company commanders, moved out in Custer's direction, eventually reaching an elevation above the village now called Weir Point. As Weir's van, Edgerly likely reached vantage points that allowed him to closely observe the prebattle village.

Although an inflated size may have arisen innocently enough— two villages appearing as one—a huge encampment served a not-so-innocent purpose. Here was a convenient way to explain how "savages" bested a disciplined, "superior" army: a large, sprawling village with too many Indians. It was an "explanation" that implied the result would have been different in an even fight. Because a larger encampment meant more warriors, an inflated village has come down to us.

Indian accounts, considered momentarily, correctly size and place the village. But first some statements by non-Indians who were there. After the Indians left, Lieutenant Charles Roe came upon the Little Bighorn aftermath on June 27 with Terry's column (which included Gibbon). The lieutenant described the village site as a large circle adjoined by a "three-sided rectangle [sic]."[19] No doubt these were the "two divisions" of the encampment Captain Benteen saw and mapped.[20] Roe said Terry's engineers accurately measured this configuration at three miles.[21] What Roe (and Benteen) unwittingly described were the pre- and postbattle villages, together three miles in length.

One might then consider a prebattle village some one and a half miles in length. That is about what Fred Gerard, a civilian interpreter with the Seventh Cavalry, saw: a village about one and a half or two miles long.[22] When Reno abandoned the valley, Gerard was among those temporarily left behind, compelled to hide in the floodplain forest. There he undoubtedly gained an unanticipated close-up view of the prebattle village.

Compare these accounts with those of some of the inhabitants. Hump suggested a compact village, noting the lodges were close together all the way down. A newspaperman wrote that Kill Eagle (Blackfeet) said the lodges were put up "just as thick as they could be," although in context the reporter clearly was interested in describing a huge, densely populated village. Although quite general, Hump's and Kill Eagle's statements still accord well with Respects Nothing (Oglala), who said the encampment was situated on a plot about a square mile in size. Flying Hawk (Oglala) remembered the extreme length was a distance equivalent to about one and a half miles, although had the camp circles been arranged linearly, he thought, the village would have stretched for about three and a half miles.[23]

Both Respect Nothing's and Flying Hawk's are reasonable estimates. Relocation of encampments about this size puts the postbattle village within earshot of the Reno/Benteen field, where late into the night of June 25–26 defenders clearly heard village ceremonies.[24] As well, mile and one-and-a-half-mile lengths place an occupied postbattle village well away from the June 26 march up the Little Bighorn by General Terry's artillery, infantry, and cavalry, and particularly his scouts.

Relocation based on a prebattle size estimate attributed to Kill Eagle—a village six miles by one mile[25]—fails to meet these criteria, especially earshot—seven plus miles from the Reno/Benteen field.

Hence this claim is so absurd as to be attributable to the imagination of the interviewer (a newspaperman) and not that of Kill Eagle. Indeed, Terry would have had to march through part of the postbattle site on June 26, bivouacking either at its southern end or just short of the northern limits of the original site!

Crow King (Hunkpapa) pointed out a distance which his interviewer, also a reporter, thought meant a prebattle village "more than two and a half miles" long.[26] Perhaps Crow King spoke generally of the ground occupied during those few days in June. If so, his estimate fits nicely with the combined size of the pre- and postbattle villages. As a prebattle length, his estimate is difficult to accept. Acceptance means at its nearest the southern limit of the postbattle village lay some four and a half miles from the Reno/Benteen field, with high terrain intervening everywhere between, and therefore likely out of earshot, except perhaps for faint, intermittent sounds. Moreover, such a postbattle village, even if somewhat more crowded than the already compact original, would have stretched about three miles north of Custer's field—nearly adjacent to Terry's camp of June 26. Yet no one with Terry knew of the abandoned village until the next day.[27] So, acceptable recollections are those which describe a comparatively small prebattle village, and they are at odds with the huge, inflated village widely accepted today.

For an inflated village of any size, location obviously has to be in error. An error can be measured approximately or precisely. For my purposes, precise location, either of each camp circle or overall, is not important, and is probably unobtainable without archaeology, if then. Rather, I am concerned with the approximate location of the prebattle northern village limit in reference to Ford B at the mouth of Medicine Tail Coulee (see map, p. 143).

Over the years, some white chroniclers have avoided the error of an inflated village. For example, less than a decade after the affair, Philetus Norris, the second superintendent at Yellowstone National Park, correctly mapped the northern limit at Ford B. A 1906 map drawn by Edward Allison, who helped negotiate the surrender of the prominent Hunkpapa Sitting Bull (p. 114), shows tepee symbols running along the river. The far north symbol lies across from Medicine Tail Coulee. Edward Curtis interviewed

Cheyenne, Sioux, and Crow battle participants, publishing his story and map in 1908. His village, lacking camp circles, is also well sited. Charles Kuhlman, around 1940, drew the Cheyenne circle opposite Medicine Tail, probably using Thomas Marquis's interviews. More recently, Jerome Greene correctly mapped the encampment relative to Medicine Tail. Probably because these white authors relied on native testimony, their maps are today generally ignored—like the Indians who correctly positioned the village. One was Big Beaver, a Cheyenne who was there in 1876. About 1930 he sketched a panorama of the battlefield, placing the Cheyenne circle just upstream from Ford B.[28]

Brave Bear, a twenty-year-old Cheyenne in 1876, remembered his camp began opposite the mouth of Medicine Tail. He said (or the interviewer misunderstood him to say) that the Cheyenne circle extended north for two miles to a present-day bridge across Little Bighorn River.[29] The circle certainly did not extend this far, but the postbattle Cheyenne camp was indeed near the bridge.[30] In any case, Brave Bear recalled that he expected soldiers who came down Medicine Tail Coulee "to charge into the middle of our camp," that is, into the Cheyenne circle.[31]

Thomas Marquis, a Northern Cheyenne agency physician during the 1920s, interviewed Indian veterans of the Little Bighorn battle. Drawing from his informants, he on one occasion located the Cheyennes "at the ford opposite Medicine Tail coulee." Another time reckoning from the "present Garryowen railroad station," Marquis placed the Cheyennes less than a half mile downstream from the mouth of Medicine Tail Coulee. Elsewhere, Marquis's informants helped him map the prebattle and postbattle villages.[32] Sioux warriors, and other Cheyennes, also sketched or described a prebattle village extending northward to near or at the mouth of Medicine Tail.[33]

The Minneconjous were located along the river upstream from the Cheyennes, but near them in the compact village. In fact, Flying By, a Minneconjou, reported his camp was opposite Medicine Tail Coulee, which at its mouth is nearly a half mile wide. The river crossing there, at Ford B, is sometimes called the Minneconjou ford. The Sans Arcs, regularly described as between the Cheyennes and Minneconjous, were also situated along the river, likely near

Ford B. White Cow Bull (Oglala) said the camps "back from the ford" were Sans Arcs and Minneconjous, into which soldiers at Ford B may have fired. Red Hawk's (Oglala) village configuration is representative, although it probably should be more compact.[34]

Clearly the Cheyenne camp defined the downstream limit of the compact prebattle village, and it extended no farther north than the Ford B vicinity. Interestingly, Peter Thompson saw the lower end of this village. A private in C Company, one of the companies in Custer's battalion, Thompson said his horse played out near Medicine Tail Coulee, preventing him from keeping up with the command. He was with Private James Watson (C Company), whose horse also gave out. Thompson found his way into Medicine Tail Coulee before backtracking with Watson, both luckily making their way to Reno and Benteen. Years later, Thompson wrote a letter to *The Pathfinder*, excerpts of which appeared in a 1925 edition. The article recounts those moments after Thompson lost contact with Custer. "Both of us [Thompson and Watson] were on foot hiding in the brush *opposite the lower end of the village.*"[35]

Summarizing, reports of village size and location can be subsumed under two categories. In both, the southern village limit is near (about five hundred yards north-northeast of) Reno's skirmish line.[36] In one, the village stretches northward for miles to abreast of Custer Hill, or even extending beyond. In the second, a compact village extends in a northerly direction no farther than where Medicine Tail Coulee joins the Little Bighorn. In general, non-Indians created and have continued to nurture the first category; village inhabitants by and large the second. Differences between the two are measured not only in miles, but in accuracy, which applies only to the latter group.

Villager Reactions

I have argued elsewhere that Custer's battalion encountered a virtually vacant village.[37] Nearly every warrior rode out to meet Major Reno's threat at the southern, or upstream end. Women, children, and the aged responded to this attack by fleeing the village. Brave Bear remembered camp desertion was "pretty well along" before Custer, approaching Medicine Tail Coulee from the south, descended from the high bluffs into that drainage.[38] I also have argued that many other noncombatants joined the exodus when Custer appeared in Medicine Tail. Here I modify the argument by suggesting that the exodus included not only inhabitants but some unknown portion of the village as well, including tents and belongings.

Brave Bear recalled there was no time to take possessions; so did One Bull. On the other hand, Two Moons heard women were "leaving their clothing behind," and he told them "to remove all of such things with them." After disengaging from Reno, and while riding toward the Cheyenne camp, Two Moons stopped "squaws from carrying off lodges." Later, evidently after Custer's battalion appeared, Two Moons directed women to flee with their "goods."[39]

Moving Robe, a Hunkpapa woman, recalled a camp "in great commotion"; noncombatants, who just earlier had been instructed to "run for the hills in an opposite direction," that is, opposite Reno, were now "running away from the gunfire." A warrior later known as Charlie Corn remembered the commotion, during which women were moving "camp toward the little big horn."[40] Corn's letter is written in halting English, without punctuation, and is confusing. Seemingly he referred to women moving tents toward the river in the direction of "Custer camp"—that is, Medicine Tail Coulee—hoping to escape up that drainage from Reno's attack.[41] In any case, Corn evidently saw some folks striking lodges and moving out. Kate Bighead (Cheyenne) surely did. Her complete account is graphic—women were bringing in war horses, rapidly taking down tepees, loading pack horses, and fleeing with heavy burdens on their backs. Many took away nothing except children.[42]

Emily Standing Bear, an eight-year-old learning to swim when Reno appeared, reported that Crazy Horse gave instructions "to pack up and move away from the gunfire," and that her "camp" (Oglala) began moving south (west in conventional reckoning) away from Reno.[43] Presumably her people took tepees and possessions with them.

When she received the warning, Emily was in the river with other children who were bathing or learning to swim. One may

have been Sadie Whiteman, a thirteen-year-old Cheyenne, who
said she was bathing with women and children when the criers
came.[44] Another at the river was Four Women, an eleven-year-old
Hunkpapa, whom Walter Camp interviewed. She and her
playmates were told to hurry to the tepees.

Back in her camp, Four Women saw excited villagers. So did
Charlie Corn, who said women and children were crying. Sadie
Whiteman said, "all women and children very 'fraid . . . there was
much running and yelling in the camps." "Women and children
shrieked with terror," is the way Pretty White Buffalo Woman, a
Hunkpapa wife of Spotted Horn Bull put it. Four Women also
told of a difficult egress. Horses became unmanageable as soldiers
began firing. Travois carrying children broke loose. Finally her
party of about three hundred was on the move. After reaching
safety, men with Four Women returned to the village to bring
back horses, food, and lodges.[45]

Although it is difficult to determine how many Indians struck
their tepees or gathered possessions, certainly not everyone did.
Nonetheless, the combination of fleeing villagers, disappearing
lodges, and laden travois probably looked like a village on the move,
not just people. Indeed, two of the Seventh Cavalry's Arikara scouts,
Soldier and Strikes Two, saw precisely that—"[Sioux] tents going
down"—while peering into the village from the high bluffs above.[46]

That noncombatants did flee cannot be disputed, and in
multiple directions. Brave Bear thought some escaped toward the
Bighorn Mountains to the southwest. Indeed, Walks at Night, a
Cheyenne girl of twelve who was also swimming at the time, fled
with her mother to the Bighorns where later their menfolk joined
them.[47]

Many other fugitives scurried northward or westward. Some
Sioux informants told Doane Robinson, then director of the South
Dakota Historical Society, that they headed in the direction of
Bighorn River. Walter Camp arrived at the same conclusion from
his interviews with Cheyennes and Sioux.[48] Bighorn River lies north
and also west of Little Bighorn battlefield.

In 1877, the noted Oglala, Crazy Horse, spoke to a correspondent, who quoted him as saying, "the women, papooses,
children, and in fact all who were not fighters, made a stampede

in a northerly direction," the same direction remembered by Flying Hawk, "down the river."[49] Yellow Nose, a Ute raised with the Cheyennes, and Brave Bear recalled that noncombatants fled westward, where, in fact, many did go in order to retrieve the horse herds.[50]

As Charlie Corn intimated, noncombatants fleeing Reno's attack even escaped using Medicine Tail Coulee while, as Brave Bear recalled, "cotton from trees was flying as snow." Two Moons related that "considerable numbers of Sioux [noncombatants]" had spilled into Medicine Tail by the time Custer's battalion arrived. He said Custer's appearance caused them to disappear northward into ravines. One Bull (Hunkpapa) saw the soldiers coming down the coulee "toward the ford by the Minneconjou camp circle."[51]

Shave Elk, an Oglala later known as Thomas Disputed, also may have encountered Custer's battalion in Medicine Tail. According to Walter Camp, who interviewed him, Shave Elk rode into Medicine Tail intending to get toward Reno's rear. There he "discovered soldiers coming down [the] ravine." So Shave Elk retraced his route, returning to the village, where he spread the word.[52]

Clearly Custer's battalion came as a surprise. Gall, a Hunkpapa leader, recalled that when Reno attacked, women and children were told to go to the Cheyenne camp, where, in fact, Soldier Wolf, a Cheyenne, said many gathered.[53] Obviously Custer's presence was unknown when that happened. And others did not know. Red Feather (Oglala) was pestering some of Reno's men on the bluffs when word came that "another detachment" had appeared "east of the Cheyennes."[54]

Two Moons learned in a somewhat different manner. After helping to drive Reno's troops from the valley, and thinking victory was assured, he rode around the village "to quiet the camp" and to urge warriors into readiness for further action against Reno. Only then did word of the other soldiers come to him and others, news that renewed "much excitement" in the village.[55]

The other soldiers were Custer's and, as Red Feather said, they were east (across river) of the Cheyennes. In fact, their surprise appearance closed Medicine Tail Coulee to escapees from the lower village. Indeed, Mrs. Kill Assiniboine reported that she could not cross at Ford B because soldiers were coming. Kill Eagle, who remained in the village during the battle, recalled that eventually the upper camps lay deserted.[56] Undoubtedly many people were in the lower village when Custer arrived in Medicine Tail Coulee. His appearance there surely intensified the exodus.

There are other Indians who spoke of the exodus. The Oglala Shot in the Eye, for example, mentioned that noncombatants hurried away into the hills at Reno's assault. When Reno attacked, both of Thunder Hawk's wives fled. One of them, an Oglala woman later known as Julia Face, "went over on the hills with other squaws . . . and old men." Both wives returned to the village after Reno abandoned the valley, but with "the coming of Custer" one ran to the hills again (Julia Face stayed). Eagle Elk, an Oglala, speaking of Reno's attack, simply said the "older people ran away."[57]

Sitting Bull sometimes spoke of the noncombatants. On two occasions either he or the reporter described a premeditated ambush plan that included sending the noncombatants to safety well before the attack.[58] No such thing happened, but the noncombatants did flee from Reno's surprise attack, as Sitting Bull described elsewhere.[59] Interestingly, in one of the "ambush" accounts, Sitting Bull is said to have timed things so that Custer fired into empty tepees.[60]

In fact, Indian testimony suggests most standing tepees were empty when Custer's left wing arrived at the mouth of Medicine Tail.[61] An obscure person named James Park somehow nearly deduced this. In 1921, he wrote Walter Camp, saying, "Besides there was no Indian village for Reno to charge upon. The squaws and papooses was not there."[62] Actually, they were there when Reno attacked, but nearly all gone when Custer approached the Cheyenne circle. Equally important, Indian testimonies suggest that lodges were struck during the exodus and whisked away with camp goods. Perhaps that is another reason why the villagers relocated that afternoon.

Indeed, according to Kate Bighead, the inhabitants planned to remain in the village for only a night and move downstream the next day (June 25). She recalled that a "few women," preparing for the move, were striking lodges when the attack came. At that moment, said Eagle Bear (Oglala), the "women were cooking and packing their stores as we planned to break camp." Runs the Enemy (Two Kettle), a councilman, remembered the planned move, but said in the morning (June 25) elders decided to stay another day. Just after making the announcement around mid-morning, the soldiers came, according to Runs the Enemy.[63]

Conclusions

I have presented just a few Indian testimonies about their village. From them, and the several non-Indian accounts considered, I draw four points essential to an understanding of Seventh Cavalry strategic operations. First, Reno's ride toward the village drew virtually all warriors to him and initiated noncombatant flight. Second, many folks in the upper village, unaware of Custer's battalion, fled to the lower camp. Peter Thompson essentially saw this while still with Custer's battalion. He saw three parties of Indians, one riding toward the horse herd, another (warriors) "advancing" toward the upper camps (that is, toward Reno's attack), and a third (noncombatants) "charging" to the lower village.[64] Thus, it is at the lower village, with Custer's later appearance, that the exodus intensified.

Third, the exodus included not only people, but also goods and possessions, plus struck lodges, and perhaps many of them, particularly in the lower village where, between Reno's and Custer's appearances, villagers had time to break camp. Indeed, some families, in preparation for the planned move, were at least partially packed. Fourth, the village extended no farther north than near the confluence of Medicine Tail Coulee and Little Bighorn River. There lay the northernmost extremity, the Cheyenne circle. Therefore the exodus, largely west through northwest after Custer's appearance sealed the easterly exit, spilled essentially down and out of the valley.

This information alone, largely available from the Indians, should raise alternatives to the venerable fatalistic theme. Essentially, fatalists agree that Custer intended to strike across Ford B at the village center. Met by warrior throngs at the river, the offensive collapsed, and he was thrown back to Custer Ridge. In other variations, Custer anticipated an onslaught and thus left

Medicine Tail Coulee, making toward the northern village limit. But warrior hordes arrived at Custer's field first and quickly blunted the northerly move. In all variations, the general, surrounded on the ridge, found no choice but to organize and oversee a steadfast defense to the end.[65]

Reasoning from the village, one objection to the fatalist theme is obvious. Village center was not at the mouth of Medicine Tail, but the northern end was. Therefore, Custer did not leave Medicine Tail in favor of the northern village limit. Still, the soldiers could have been met by a large force as they sought to penetrate the village across Ford B. But noncombatants were using Medicine Tail as an escape route when Custer's soldiers appeared. Their presence caused escapees to alter their directions of flight. Odds seem slim that people redirected their flight in the presence of warrior throngs busy driving the soldiers away. But perhaps many warriors appeared somewhat later, in the nick of time so to speak, just as the soldiers were about to cross into the (nearly empty) village. Perhaps. But the point is, by understanding the village it becomes only one possibility requiring affirmation, certainly not a certainty, and particularly so if the village was not the target.

Indeed, based upon villager reactions, one may legitimately consider that however the encampment figured in strategic operations earlier in the day, it was not Custer's focus once he entered Medicine Tail Coulee. Clearly there was an exodus, and some part of the village proper was on the move, principally, I suspect, lodges comprising the lower camps, which is what Kill Eagle said.[66] Quite possibly what appeared as a rapidly disappearing village prompted Custer's battalion to draw northward out of Medicine Tail—not some massive attack or dire threat. Of course, such an idea is also in need of affirmation. In this context, one might fruitfully look at strategic responses to the cavalry attack and ideas some Indians had of what Custer's battalion was up to.

About 1901, Two Moons told Oliver Hanna, then a store owner near Lodge Grass, Montana, that the Indians did not want to fight. But when they saw Reno hurtling at them, the warriors went out to check the soldiers so noncombatants could get away. Eagle Elk observed precisely that: the warriors went right out to meet the soldiers, and "the older people ran away." So did Gall, who said the noncombatants "and camp out-fits were ordered to make their 'get away' . . . while the warriors went out to oppose Reno."[67] (Notice Gall mentioned "camp out-fits").

Brave Bear recalled a similar strategy. There was just enough time to "move out the women, children and old folks . . . while the men would engage in . . . a death struggle with the soldiers." And that is likely what Crazy Horse had in mind when he issued instructions to pack up and move away from the gunfire. Indeed, Crow King later said the intent was to hold Reno in check so the villagers could scatter.[68]

Certainly that is somewhat the way Doane Robinson saw it. An early investigator who interviewed Sioux who were there, Robinson concluded Custer mistook the noncombatant exodus for warriors in retreat, and that is why he went toward the north.[69] A variation of Robinson's view is attributed to Crazy Horse, who through a newspaper reporter supposedly said Custer mistook the exodus as the main body retreating; that is, noncombatants and many warriors.[70]

But Custer knew where the warriors were. So did Hump, who recalled, "it seemed, the way Custer came, that he started to cut off our retreat." Hump meant the village exodus, for that was the only retreat Indians made that day. As Iron Thunder was chasing Reno's men up the bluffs, word came to him of another group of soldiers—Custer's battalion. The report he got said these soldiers were "heading off the women and children from the way they were going." Flying Hawk heard the same while confronting Reno: "[Some] Indians rode up to us and said Custer was . . . heading off the women and children."[71] Certainly someone had noticed soldiers were following noncombatants.

That much was clear to Charlie Corn. In his 1909 letter to William O. Taylor, an early battle student and Reno survivor, Corn wrote, directly and poignantly: "You tried to get our children and wives so I was willing to die fighting for them that day." Corn told Taylor in a letter dated the next year that when the "big fight [the Custer battle] came off," he was the first to kill one of the soldiers "while they were fighting the women folks."[72] Nothing I have seen indicates Custer battalion troopers and noncombatants actually fought each other, but Corn's gist is clear. For him, Custer's soldiers were after Indian families, including his.

Indian perceptions of soldiers' motives need to be handled carefully. Nonetheless, Indian accounts of the prebattle village location, of instructions to flee, of fleeing villagers, of a village partially ready to move and in fact on the go, of the postbattle village, and of Custer chasing the noncombatants together provide an explanation for his battalion's presence far downriver. Such an explanation directly contradicts the core of fatalistic ideas, namely Indian testimonies that claim warriors threw Custer's soldiers on the defensive at the village outskirts and drove them to the killing field. Indeed, those accounts are themselves perceptions made in light of a grim aftermath; and they do not necessarily reflect the soldiers' understanding.[73]

An examination of the village demonstrates that attention to the Indian portion of the documentary record for the Battle of the Little Bighorn leads to an alternative view of the strategic nature of Custer's last battle. I suggest the same holds for whatever slice of this battle one wishes to investigate. In this study, a plausible, even strong alternative to the venerable, but problematic fatalistic theme arises from using Indian accounts. Maintaining the offense, Custer vacated Medicine Tail Coulee to chase after a rapidly disappearing village.

Independent data support this alternative, that Custer maintained his offensive until the end came, suddenly and unexpectedly.[74] Here I note simply that one way to maintain confidence in the fatalistic theory is to ignore the village. Similarly, fatalistic preconceptions are in large part why Indian testimonies seem anywhere from irreconcilable to tediously difficult. Shed such biases, and, although problems certainly do not evaporate, the task of interpretation becomes easier, including interpretation of the non-Indian record, which somehow is and absurdly has been perceived as less problematic and hence superior to Indian perspectives.

To deny that strategy hinges on the enemy's disposition and response seems fruitless. Yet, remarkably, in Little Bighorn studies the village and villagers have from the beginning received scant attention. Strategic actions by Custer's battalion were influenced by the lay of the prebattle village and activities within it. Equally important are reflections on the villagers' real-life experiences that day. Though I have not focused on that aspect, perhaps I have, even if but accidentally, provided some insight into the emotions, including those surrounding the deaths of women and children, that ran through the west river side on June 25, 1876—a side of the Little Bighorn battle about which we do not often hear.

Notes

James Brust, Thomas Buecker, Paul Harbaugh, Darrell Linthacum, Douglas McChristian, Michael Moore, Brian Pohanka, Christopher Summit, and probably others kindly provided information for this paper. Moore also furnished valuable comments on drafts. The paper is an outgrowth of work which began at the Little Bighorn Battlefield National Monument in 1983. Thanks are due to the Little Bighorn Battlefield National Monument staff from 1983 until now, the National Park Service, and the people above. The Custer Battlefield Historical and Museum Association and the University of Calgary funded much of the research from which I have drawn materials for this paper. I heard the term "west river history," or something like it, from someone else. I cannot recall who, but he or she used it as I do here. This paper was revised slightly from that read at the 1994 Little Bighorn Legacy Symposium and was submitted for publication on August 25, 1994.

1.   Custer at this time commanded the Seventh Cavalry, which was part of General Alfred Terry's command. On June 22, while on Yellowstone River, Custer left Terry, who expected to reunite with the Seventh somewhere in Little Bighorn valley. He did—with what was left—on June 27. Approaching the Indians on June 25 from east of the Little Bighorn, Custer sent Reno, his second in command, ahead. Reno soon crossed the river to its west side. Custer, staying on the east side, veered northward, eventually ending up at Custer battlefield. After crossing, Reno attacked northward down the valley. Facing a hurriedly organized but effective resistance, he elected to dismount his men and throw out a skirmish line. The skirmishers briefly advanced on foot before stopping short of what turned out to be a single, large Indian village. Somewhat later Reno retired to timber along Little Bighorn River, fighting there for about half an hour. The 130 or so men in Reno's battalion subsequently retreated, recrossing

the river before scrambling up the bluffs, suffering heavy casualties en route to the hilltop site known as the Reno/Benteen battlefield. There Reno fortuitously met Benteen's similarly sized battalion, which was attempting to join Custer after carrying out a reconnaissance upriver. The two battalions, later joined by the pack train (escorted by about 130 men), linked up, and were besieged for the rest of the day and much of the next. Between the time Reno first skirmished and his union with Benteen, Custer's men had ridden in a northerly direction into Medicine Tail Coulee, where they first engaged Indians, then out of it to the battlefield. About an hour after Reno and Benteen consolidated, Captain Thomas Weir led a movement northward along Custer's trail. He proceeded about one and a half miles before many Indians appeared, forcing a withdrawal. Although exact timing is controversial, Custer's men had perished by then.

2.   James Brust to author, July 20, 1994.

3.   Nelson A. Miles, *Personal Recollections and Observations of General Nelson A. Miles* (1897; reprint, New York: DaCapo Press, 1969), 286ff; Oscar F. Long to Frank Baldwin, June 27, 1878, box 1, BANC mss. C-B939, Oscar Long Collection, Bancroft Library, University of California, Berkeley.

4.   Robert M. Utley, *Custer and the Great Controversy: The Origin and Development of a Legend* (Pasadena, Calif.: Westernlore Press, 1962), 85-90.

5.   J. M. McCreight, "An Indian Chief's Version of Custer's Last Fight," Dearborn *Independent*, March 25, 1922; W. A. Graham, *The Custer Myth: A Source Book of Custeriana* (New York: Bonanza Books, 1953), 3-4; Stephen Longstreet, *War Cries on Horseback: The Story of the Indian Wars of the Great Plains* (Garden City, N.Y.: Doubleday, 1970), 227.

6.   Richard Hardorff, ed., *Lakota Recollections of the Custer Fight: New Sources of Indian-Military History* (Spokane, Wash.: Arthur H. Clark Co., 1991); Jerome A. Greene, ed., *Lakota and Cheyenne: Indian Views of the Great Sioux War, 1876–1877* (Norman: University of Oklahoma Press, 1994).

7.   Roger Darling, *A Sad and Terrible Blunder—Generals Terry and Custer at the Little Big Horn: New Discoveries* (Vienna, Va.: Potomac-Western Press, 1990), 215.

8.   John S. Gray, *Custer's Last Campaign: Mitch Boyer and the Little Bighorn Reconstructed* (Lincoln: University of Nebraska Press, 1991), 384.

9.   Richard Allan Fox, Jr., *Archaeology, History, and Custer's Last Battle: The Little Big Horn Reexamined* (Norman: University of Oklahoma Press, 1993).

10. Ibid.

11. For example, Graham, *The Custer Myth*, 89, 91; Thomas B. Marquis, *Wooden Leg: A Warrior Who Fought Custer* (1931; reprint, Lincoln: University of Nebraska Press, 1962), 208; Linda W. Slaughter, "Leaves from Northwestern History," *Collections of the State Historical Society of North Dakota*, 1 (1906), 277.

12. Thomas R. Buecker, ed., "A Surgeon at the Little Big Horn," *Montana The Magazine of Western History*, 32 (Autumn 1982), 42.

13. For this argument see Rod MacNeil, "The Indians Were Asleep in Their Tepees," *Research Review: The Journal of the Little Big Horn Associates*, 1 n.s. (December 1987), 13-15, 22.

14. Horace Ellis, "A Survivor's Story of the Custer Massacre," *Big Horn–Yellowstone Journal*, 2 (Spring 1993), 7.

15. Fox, *Archaeology, History, and Custer's Last Battle*, 372.

16. Wooden Leg quoted in ibid.; Fay Geiger, "In brief" recounting interview with Foolish Elk by C. A. Whitbeck and John S. Lockwood on June 12, 1926, n.d., Little Bighorn Battlefield National Monument, Crow Agency, Montana (hereafter LBNM); Hattie Lawrence in Kenneth Hammer, Camp Manuscript transcripts, n.d., p. 347, Manuscripts Department, Lilly Library, Indiana University at Bloomington (hereafter Camp Manuscripts, IU).

17. Captain Henry Freeman was another. See George A. Schneider, ed., *The Freeman Journal: The Infantry in the Sioux Campaign of 1876* (San Raphael, Calif.: Presidio Press, 1977), 64.

18. Ronald H. Nichols, ed., *Reno Court of Inquiry* (Crow Agency, Mont.: Custer Battlefield Historical and Museum Association, 1992), 455.

19. Charles Francis Roe, "General Roe's Narrative," in *Custer's Last Battle*, ed. Robert Bruce (New York: Office of the National Highway Association, 1927), 10.

20. Nichols, *Reno Court of Inquiry*, 408; W. A. Graham, *Abstract of the Proceedings of the Reno Court of Inquiry* (Harrisburg, Pa.: Stackpole Co., 1954), 305, end map.

21. Roe, "General Roe's Narrative," 10.

22. Nichols, *Reno Court of Inquiry*, 94.

23. Hump in Richard Upton, *The Custer Adventure: As Told by Its Participants* (El Segundo, Calif.: Upton and Sons, 1990), 83; Kill Eagle in Graham, *The Custer Myth*, 55; Respects Nothing, interview by Eli S. Ricker, November 9, 1906, pp. 2-4, series 2, box 6, tablet 29 (reel 5), Ricker Collection, Nebraska State Historical Society, Lincoln (hereafter Ricker Collection); Flying Hawk, interview by Eli S. Ricker, March 8, 1907, pp. 40-42, series 2, box 5, tablet 13 (reel 3), Ricker Collection.

24. See for example Private Charles Windolph, *I Fought with Custer: The Story of Sergeant Windolph, Last Survivor of the Battle of the Little Big Horn, as told to Frazier and Robert Hunt* (1947; reprint, Lincoln: University of Nebraska Press, 1987), 102.

25. Graham, *The Custer Myth*, 55.

26. Crow King quoted in ibid., 77.

27. Captain Henry Freeman noted in his journal that Terry's column, with which he marched, came upon the abandoned village (postbattle) three miles after breaking camp on the morning of June 27. Freeman also noted Reno's men were entrenched three and a half to four and a half miles from the point at which he came upon the village site. Schneider, *The Freeman Journal*, 58. The northern boundary fence of the Custer battlefield portion of the national monument is four and a half miles from the center of Reno's and Benteen's defense perimeter. This puts the downstream limit of the village site Freeman reported no farther north than the northern boundary fence. General Terry indicated the abandoned village lay three and a half to four miles from his June 26 camp. Alfred H. Terry, *The Field Diary of General Alfred H. Terry: The Yellowstone Expedition—1876* (Fort Collins, Colo.: Old Army Press, 1978), 24. Lieutenant Edward McClernand recalled stopping "soon" after an early start, and then traveling "a short distance" before reaching the village site. Edward J. McClernand, *On Time for Disaster: The Rescue of Custer's Command* (1969; reprint, Lincoln: University of Nebraska Press, 1989), 59. Surgeon Paulding said they traveled "but a few miles." Buecker, "A Surgeon at the Little Big Horn," 42. Darling locates Terry's June 26 campsite near the Crow Agency, Montana, sewage lagoon, which is three miles north of Custer's battlefield. Darling, *A Sad and Terrible Blunder*, 275.

28. Philetus W. Norris, *The Calumet of the Coteau, and Other Poetical Legends of the Border* (Philadelphia: J. B. Lippincott and Co., 1884), 37; Allison map, 1906, folder 30, box 2, mss. 8, Ricker Collection; Edward S. Curtis, *The North American Indians* (20 vols., 1907–1930; reprint, New York: Johnson Reprint Corporation, 1970), 3:44f; Charles Kuhlman, *General George A. Custer: A Lost Trail and the Gall Saga* (1940; reprint, Bellevue, Nebr.: Old Army Press, 1969), end map; Jerome A. Greene, *Evidence and the Custer Enigma: A Reconstruction of Indian-Military History* (Golden, Colo.: Outlook Books, 1986), 17; Drawing by Big Beaver, 1930, A-12, C1949, Thomas M. Marquis Collection, LBNM.

29. Robert Yellowtail (1957), "Accounts of Brave Bear, Whiteman Runs Him, and Walks at Night," n.d., unpublished, private collection, Darrell H. Linthacum, San Jose, California.

30. Marquis, *Wooden Leg*, 253, 387.

31. Yellowtail, "Accounts of Brave Bear, Whiteman Runs Him, and Walks at Night."

32. Billings, Montana, *Gazette*, August 13, 1933, p. 10, July 17, 1932, p. 12; Marquis, *Wooden Leg*, 387; Thomas Marquis, *Custer on the Little Bighorn* (1967; reprint, Algonac, Mich.: Reference Publications, 1986), 14.

33. See Fox, *Archaeology, History, and Custer's Last Battle*, 217, 299-303, 371-74.

34. Flying By in Hammer, p. 349, Camp Manuscripts, IU; Marquis, *Wooden Leg*, 209; White Cow Bull quoted in David Humphreys Miller, "Echoes of the Little Bighorn," *American Heritage*, 22 (June 1971), 33; Walter M. Camp, Statement of Thunder Hawk's squaw, June 1909, A312 C11402, Walter Camp Collection (hereafter Camp Collection), LBNM; Nick Buleau, interview by Eli S. Ricker [Red Hawk's testimony], November 20, 1906, p. 86, series 2, box 6, tablet 29 (reel 5), Ricker Collection; see also Fox, *Archaeology, History, and Custer's Last Battle*, 217.

35. *The Pathfinder*, August 8, 1925, emphasis added. In his published narrative, Thompson said the village center was near Ford B, which has been the common interpretation over the years. Daniel O. Magnussen, *Peter Thompson's Narrative of the Little Bighorn Campaign, 1876* (Glendale, Calif.: Arthur H. Clark Company, 1974), 165. Multiple independent lines of evidence, some related here and others elsewhere (Fox, *Archaeology, History, and Custer's Last Battle*), corroborate Thompson's 1925 statement in *The Pathfinder*. Though a story for another time, corroboration compels one to treat more seriously than usual other claims made by Thompson about his observations while stranded in Medicine Tail Coulee.

36. One period map, inaccurate in various aspects, shows a small group of tepee symbols labeled "Abandoned Lodges" a short distance behind (southeast of) Reno's skirmish line. Graham, *The Custer Myth*, 64. If an accurate aspect, it is not clear if the sketcher meant lodges abandoned as a result of Reno's attack, or if the symbols represent lodge sites or derelict lodges from an earlier camp. Either way, possibly eyewitnesses included them, if they existed, in village length estimates.

37. Fox, *Archaeology, History, and Custer's Last Battle*, 312-18.

38. Yellowtail, "Accounts of Brave Bear, Whiteman Runs Him, and Walks at Night."

39. Brave Bear in ibid.; One Bull in Miller, *Echoes of the Little Bighorn*, 30; Two Moons, interview by Eli S. Ricker, March 3-4, 1913, pp. 3, 6-7, 10, unnumbered tablet A, Ricker Collection (for this interview also see *Big Horn–Yellowstone Journal,* 2 (Winter 1993), 9-13; Graham, *The Custer Myth*, 102.

40. Walter S. Campbell, Story of Custer battle—by Tasina-mani-win [Moving Robe], n.d., folder 5, box 111, Walter S. Campbell Collection, Western History Collections, University of Oklahoma, Norman (hereafter

Campbell Collection, UO); Charlie Corn to William O. Taylor, April 23, 1910, folder 8, A312 C11405, Camp Collection, LBNM.

41. In his 1906 interview with Respects Nothing (note 23), Eli Ricker (Ricker Collection) explained the Oglalas referred to Medicine Tail Coulee by the name of Water Rat before the Little Bighorn fight, but afterwards, thinking for some reason Custer had camped on the drainage, they called it "Custer Camp Creek."

42. Kate Bighead in Marquis, *Custer on the Little Bighorn*, 84.

43. Emily Standing Bear in *Pute Tiyospaye (Lip's camp): The History and Culture of a Sioux Indian Village* (Albuquerque: Sloves-Bunnell, 1978), 43.

44. Carl L. Pearson, "Sadie and the Missing Custer Battle Papers," *Montana The Magazine of Western History*, 26 (Autumn, 1976), 14.

45. Four Women, interview by Walter M. Camp, May 21, 1909, box 3 (reel 3), mss. 57, Walter Mason Camp Papers, Harold B. Lee Library, Brigham Young University, Provo, Utah (hereafter Camp Papers, BYU); Charlie Corn to William O. Taylor, September 15, 1909, folder 8, A312 C11404, Camp Collection, LBNM; Pearson, "Sadie and the Missing Custer Battle Papers," 14; Mrs. Spotted Horn Bull (Pretty White Buffalo Woman), quoted in Graham, *The Custer Myth*, 84.

46. Orin G. Libby, *The Arikara Narrative of the Campaign against the Hostile Dakotas June, 1876* (New York: Sol Lewis, 1973), 117, 132.

47. Yellowtail, "Accounts of Brave Bear, Whiteman Runs Him, and Walks at Night."

48. Charles Edmund DeLand, "The Sioux Wars: Minnesota Outbreak; Red Cloud and Other Wars of 1867; Little Big Horn; Wounded Knee," *South Dakota Historical Collections*, 15 (1930), 716; Walter M. Camp to General E. S. Godfrey, September 18, 1918, box 1, Francis R. Hagner Papers, Manuscript and Archives Section, New York Public Library.

49. Crazy Horse quoted in "The Custer Fight: An Indian Version of the Massacre from the Lips of Crazy Horse Himself," Yankton *Daily Press and Dakotaian*, May 31, 1877; Flying Hawk quoted in Dearborn *Independent*, March 25, 1922.

50. "Yellow Nose Tells of Custer's Last Stand," *Big Horn–Yellowstone Journal*, 1 (Summer 1992), 15; Yellowtail, "Accounts of Brave Bear, Whiteman Runs Him, and Walks at Night."

51. Yellowtail, "Accounts of Brave Bear, Whiteman Runs Him, and Walks at Night"; Two Moon's story of the Custer fight given to Throssel in 1907, field notes folder 105, folder 9, box 6, mss. 57, Camp Papers, BYU; One Bull quoted in Miller, "Echoes of the Little Bighorn," 31.

52. Thomas Disputed, interview by Walter M. Camp, n.d., folder 20, box 1, Walter Camp Notes, Harbaugh Collection, Denver Public Library, Denver, Colorado (hereafter Camp Notes, DPL).

53. Walter M. Camp, handwritten copy of "Gall's account as told by Dr. H. R. Porter in Saint Louis *Globe-Democrat*, 4/18/189[3?]," folder 13, box 1, Camp Notes, DPL; Graham, *The Custer Myth*, 88; George B. Grinnell, "Cheyenne Notes (1898): Soldier Wolf as to the Custer Fight," folder 497, mss. 5, George Bird Grinnell Collection, Braun Research Library, Southwest Museum, Los Angeles, California.

54. He Dog, Red Feather, and Whirling, interview by Hugh Scott, 1920, box 4, no. 4525, Indian wars folder, Scott Collection, National Anthropological Archives, Smithsonian Institution, Washington, D.C.

55. Two Moons quoted in Hardorff, *Lakota Recollections of the Custer Fight*, 135-37. See also Graham, *The Custer Myth*, 102.

56. Mrs. Kill Assiniboine in Hammer, p. 347, Camp Manuscripts, IU; Kill Eagle in Graham, *The Custer Myth*, 55.

57. "The Custer Massacre: An Authentic Account of this Famous Tragedy as Told by Chief 'Shot-in-the-Eye' " in *Historical Biography and Libretto: Indian Congress* (Buffalo, N.Y.: Pan American Exposition, 1901), 21; Mrs. Thunder Hawk, interview by Sewell B. Weston, n.d., box 4 (reel 3), mss. 57, Camp Papers, BYU; Sewell B. Weston to Walter Camp, July 8, 1909, folder 5, A312 C13169, Camp Collection, LBNM; Eagle Elk, interview by John G. Neihardt, November 14, 1929, C3716–F431, Neihardt Papers, Western Historical Manuscript Collection, Ellis Library, University of Missouri–Columbia (hereafter Neihardt Papers).

58. Joseph K. Howard, *Montana Margins: A State Anthology* (New Haven: Yale University Press, 1946), 31; Linda W. Slaughter, "Leaves from Northwestern History: Sitting Bull's Account of the Battle of the Little Big Horn," *Sports Afield*, 32 (January 1904), 37; Slaughter, "Leaves from Northwestern History," *Collections of the State Historical Society of North Dakota*, 278.

59. See for example Graham, *The Custer Myth*, 70.

60. Howard, *Montana Margins*, 31.

61. When Custer arrived in Medicine Tail Coulee, he split his battalion into two wings. One, the two-company left wing plus the headquarters staff (about 85 men), went to Ford B. The other, some 125 men in three companies (right wing), stayed behind on an elevation just above the coulee. Later, the two wings joined at Custer battlefield. See Fox, *Archaeology, History, and Custer's Last Battle*, 275-322.

62. James Park to Walter Camp, July 24, 1921, folder 12 (reel 2), box 2, mss. 57, Camp .Papers, BYU.

63. Kate Bighead quoted in Marquis, *Custer on the Little Bighorn*, 83-84; Eagle Bear, "Massacre of Custer Retold as Indian Warrior Recalls Slaughter; Bloody Battle that Followed Described by 85-year-old Cavalryman," unattributed news clipping, dateline Pine Ridge, S.D., Sept. 25 [no year, probably 1937; probably by Frazier and/or Robert Hunt], folder 2, box 111, Campbell Collection, UO; Runs the Enemy quoted in Joseph K. Dixon, *The Vanishing Race: The Last Great Indian Council* (New York: Bonanza Books, 1913), 170-71.

64. Walter Camp to Peter Thompson, January 12, 1909, (Camp's questionnaire enclosed with letter, completed and returned by Thompson), A312 C11391, A312 C12471, A312 C12472, Camp Collection, LBNM.

65. See Fox, *Archaeology, History, and Custer's Last Battle*.

66. Kill Eagle in Graham, *The Custer Myth*, 55.

67. Two Moons in Oliver P. Hanna, *An Old-timer's Story of the Old Wild West: Being the Recollections of Oliver Perry Hanna—Pioneer, Indian Fighter, Frontiersman and First Settler in Sheridan County* (Casper, Wyo: Hawks Book Co., 1984), 92; Eagle Elk, interview by John G. Neihardt, November 14, 1929, C3716–F431, Neihardt Papers; Gall quoted in A. C. Huidekoper, *My Experience and Investment in the Bad Lands of Dakota and Some of the Men I Met There* (Baltimore: Wirth Brothers, 1947), 20.

68. Yellowtail, "Accounts of Brave Bear, Whiteman Runs Him, and Walks at Night"; Crow King in Judson Elliott Walker, *Campaigns of General Custer in the North-West and the Final Surrender of Sitting Bull* (1881; reprint, New York: Promontory Press, 1966), 102.

69. Doane Robinson to Joe L. Eastwood, August 14, 1929, folder 27, 3359-B, Doane Robinson Papers, South Dakota Historical Society, Pierre.

70. Crazy Horse in Graham, *The Custer Myth*, 63.

71. Hump and Iron Thunder quoted in Upton, *The Custer Adventure*, 81, 83; Flying Hawk quoted in Dearborn *Independent*, March 25, 1922.

72. Corn to Taylor, September 15, 1909; Camp to Taylor, April 23, 1910, Camp Collection, LBNM.

73. Fox, *Archaeology, History, and Custer's Last Battle*, 279.

74. Ibid., 312-18.

Archaeological investigation determined that most of the Custer battlefield markers placed in 1890, photographed here in 1898 by Fred E. Miller, were located correctly, but that the paired markers most likely mark only a single grave. (Montana Historical Society Photograph Archives, Helena)

Archaeological Perspectives on the Battle of the Little Bighorn

A Retrospective

Douglas D. Scott

The Little Bighorn battlefield range fire of 1983 was a significant event and, in a manner of speaking, heralded a decade of archaeological investigations at the battlefield. Several park managers had previously called for archaeological investigations, but only two were undertaken prior to the 1983 range fire. Since 1983 archaeological investigations have continued, in some form, to date. The 1994 Little Bighorn Legacy Symposium presented an opportunity to review the contributions of the archaeological investigations to the Little Bighorn story and to the fields of history and historical archaeology. This retrospective is not a rehash of the archaeological data recovered or their interpretation, but a review of the rather significant contributions made by the investigations to the fields of history and anthropology.

The principals involved in the archaeological project, which began in earnest in May 1984, were well aware that they were part of an innovative project, yet no one was fully cognizant of the wide-ranging impact the project would have on the National Park Service, the disciplines of history and historical archaeology, nor of the international recognition the project and its methodology would garner. Long disdained by most archaeologists, metal detecting has become widely accepted as another tool for archaeologists to investigate historic period sites since it was successfully used at the Little Bighorn battlefield. The difference between metal detecting to find objects and archaeological uses is the systematic manner in which archaeologists find and record the data located by detectors. In addition, the metal detecting inventory technique, associated with the standard archaeological procedure of artifact piece-plotting and the powerful interpretive tool of firearms identification as developed during the Little Bighorn archaeological investigations, has had application in recent international human rights investigations.

Metal Detectors and Archaeology

The concept of non-intrusive archaeology has become ingrained in the anthropological discipline of archaeology in the last two decades, and archaeologists are turning increasingly to methods of remote sensing as a means of site investigation.[1] The metal detector is now recognized as a legitimate archaeological tool because it is a simple and effective remote sensing research device.

The use of metal detectors in archaeological investigations is not new, but few reports on those investigations are published. One of the earliest documented uses of a metal detector on a military site is that of military historian Don Rickey.[2] Rickey used a metal detector to reveal firing lines at the Little Bighorn and Big Hole battlefields in Montana. Rickey also assisted archaeologist Robert Bray in using a detector to augment visual survey in mitigating the construction of a blacktop path at the Reno-Benteen defense site of the Battle of the Little Bighorn.[3] After Rickey, metal detectors essentially disappeared from the professional archaeological literature until an attempt was made to locate the 1846 Mexican War battlefield of Palo Alto, Texas.[4]

Use of detectors increased throughout the 1980s, with most archaeological uses of metal detectors concentrating on historic battlefields. A publicly visible use of detectors was achieved at the Little Bighorn battlefield.[5] Detectors have also been used on the Palo Alto battleground; at the Wagon Box Fight site in Wyoming; the K-H Butte site in Arizona; an 1880 Apache War battle site in New Mexico; an 1881 Apache War site in Arizona; and the Mine Creek Civil War battlefield in Kansas, among others.[6] Detectors have been used successfully at non-battle related sites in England, Canada, and at Fort Larned, Kansas.[7] Coupled with visual inventory, shovel probes, and test excavations (traditional archaeological techniques), metal detectors have proved themselves valuable tools to aid in establishing site boundaries, locating buried trash deposits, and potentially locating buried structural remains.[8]

Almost any historical archaeological site can benefit from the use of metal detectors. In inventory, they can be used to help determine horizontal site boundaries, and in excavation and testing they can be used to locate concentrations of artifacts. The detector can quickly and efficiently locate buried metallic debris associated with sites where no visible surface remains exist.[9] Metal detectors can locate construction debris associated with structural sites, thus aiding in defining the locations of structures and site boundaries. The metal detector is a tool to study metallic artifact distribution patterns across a site without resorting to expensive and time-consuming formal excavation units. Such an approach has proven of exceptional value in the study of battlefields. Detectors are now indispensable aids on many historic archaeological sites.

The method developed during the Little Bighorn battlefield inventories, subsequently improved at Big Hole National Battlefield and at the Civil War battlefield of Monroe Crossroads, North Carolina, is now the standard by which most archaeological metal detector inventories are judged.[10] The inventory consists of three sequential operations: metal detecting, recovery, and recording. During metal detecting, artifacts are located and marked. A recovery crew follows and carefully uncovers subsurface finds, leaving them in place. The recording team then plots individual artifact locations, assigns field specimen numbers, and collects the specimens. Visual inspection of the surface can be carried out concurrently with the metal detector survey utilizing traditional inventory techniques. A metal detector crew may consist of a crew chief, metal-detector operators, and visual inspectors who also pinflag the targets found by the detectors.

A systematic approach to site investigation is best under any circumstance. Detector operators walk in a line, following transects across the area to be inspected. While walking, the operators use a sweeping motion to examine the ground. Coils are held as close to the ground as possible to provide maximum vertical and horizontal coverage. Each operator can cover a sweep of roughly one and a half to two meters, depending on the individual's height and technique. Closer spacing obviously will gain more detailed coverage and more detailed information on the presence of metallic debris. However, the sweep of one and a half to two meters with a five-meter interval obtains a very respectable 35 percent sample of the study area (a more than adequate statistically valid scientific sampling of the metallic debris in the inventory area).[11] The metal detector operator can also cover a site in a series of closely spaced transects, so as to cover as close to 100 percent of the site as is humanly possible. A metal detector also may be used to obtain a statistically valid sample ranging from a random sample to a stratified random sample.[12]

Whether the goal is a random sample or near total coverage, the operators walk transects oriented to cardinal directions. When necessary, transect lines may be dictated by the orientation of topographic features. Either way, the operators need to maintain, as closely as possible, the designated intervals. Orientation and interval spacing are maintained by direction from the crew chief. A crew of five to eight operators is optimal for rapid areal coverage and supervision purposes, but investigations can be accomplished satisfactorily with only one detector and operator.

The pinflaggers follow behind the operators and flag the targets. It is difficult for the detector operator to pinpoint the target exactly while bending down with a flag. The pinflaggers can also examine the ground visually for surface artifacts, while the detector operators concentrate on their machines. When a target is located, it should be marked with a surveyor's pinflag or other suitable device. When the location is marked, the operator continues along the transect. Leaving the target undug may be the hardest part of the operation for the detector operator. However, if each operator stops to dig each target the transect lines quickly lose any semblance of order. The detector operators cannot dig their targets immediately if the detectors are to be kept on the transect line and evenly spaced. Of course, to every rule there is an exception, and sometimes a location may need to be excavated immediately to provide the operator with a check on machine performance. This is occasionally necessary because of the sophisticated nuances of interpreting machine functions, such as depth readings, metallic and object type-differentiation functions, object size interpretation, and pinpointing subsurface objects. The usual procedure, however, is to mark the location and leave it intact for the recovery crew.

In dense concentrations of metallic debris it may be necessary to recover the targets located and then re-detect the area multiple times to recover all the artifacts. The signal from larger metal objects may obscure the signal from other smaller or less dense targets unless the larger objects are removed from the detector field. Metal shafts of surveyor's pinflags can also obscure nearby buried targets, so that a dense field of surveyor's pins will affect the targets found.

The recovery crew excavates the artifact locations marked by the pinflags and then leaves the artifacts in place for recording. Traditional hand tools are used to dig or scrape the earth away from the artifact. No formal excavation unit is necessary, unless the goal of the recovery is to locate nonmetallic materials that may be associated with the target. If other objects are found associated with the metal object, the crew chief needs to decide whether to collect the object or mark it for later excavation. At the Little Bighorn battlefield, nonmetallic objects discovered in association with material found by the detectors included leather boots and animal and human bones. The types of objects likely to be located in association with the metal should be anticipated before the inventory and plans developed for dealing with them.

A recovery team should also include a metal detector to pinpoint the artifact. The detectors work best for this task when using a small coil that allows precise location of the object while still in the ground. Some detector operators can determine the object type and depth from the audible signal given out by the detector. Excavation time can be saved by using a small coil to pinpoint the artifact; otherwise, time may be wasted by digging a large area to recover a small object. Wire, nails, bolts, and other linear fasteners are notorious for giving ambiguous locational signals.

As with any archaeological investigation, provenance data for interpreting artifact patterns is paramount. Recording the data is crucial. In this example, the recording crew includes the rod person, the transit operator, and people to assign field-specimen numbers and bag the specimens. Artifacts are assigned sequential field-specimen numbers beginning at some appropriate alpha or numeric field catalog designator. The recording crew also needs to backfill the artifact holes so the area does not resemble a fairway after a poor golfer.

The projects at the Little Bighorn and Big Hole battlefields used total stations (combined transits and electronic distance meters) and electronic data collectors to record location and attribute data. Records were coded in the Sokkia SDR33 data collector, although a handwritten field catalog was also kept by a member of the recording crew as a backup. The electronic catalog was transferred from the SDR33 to a laptop computer on a daily basis. The Sokkia MAP program and Autodesk AutoCad programs were used for displaying the mapping data.

During the Big Hole battlefield inventory project, for example, each artifact located was piece-plotted as follows. The total station was set up at an established datum point. The rod person moved to the location of an artifact while another person filled out the bag for that artifact. The instrument operator read the distance and azimuth readings for each artifact location and these were recorded electronically. The machine electronically converted the distance and azimuth to coordinate data, which was also recorded electronically. The instrument operator transmitted this information to the recorders at the artifact location either by a portable two-way radio or by voice. A radio is useful if the distance involved is much greater than several meters; otherwise the instrument operator will be very hoarse in several hours. The recorders at the artifact entered the coordinate data, a note on the type of artifact, and the field specimen number into the handwritten field catalog. The rod person then radioed the artifact identification to the instrument operator, who entered the appropriate artifact code in the electronic data collector from a designated set of codes. Meanwhile, the artifact was bagged and the rod person moved on to the next artifact. Using this technique, with the electronic data collector and a four-person recording crew, it was usual for the crew at the Big Hole battlefield to piece-plot more than three hundred artifacts in an eight-hour day.

In an excavation, metal detectors can help find the areas of greatest artifact concentration within a site, thus helping to place excavation units in productive areas. During excavation, the detectors can help in determining vertical site boundaries in very homogenous soils. Such was the case at the Little Bighorn battlefield. After the archaeologist completed a unit level that appeared sterile, the unit was detected. Often this keyed the archaeologist to deeper buried material, and no unit was closed until the detectors were silent.

Metal detectors were invaluable tools at the Little Bighorn site. Little artifactual material would have been located using the traditional techniques of visual inventory, test excavations, or shovel probes. The detector, coupled with precise locational recording techniques, uncovered the patterned artifact distributions on the field. Without the detector, a radically biased view of the events would have unfolded.

Firearms Identification

During the archaeological investigations, the Little Bighorn battlefield was viewed as a crime scene. By using forensic techniques such as studies of firing pin marks on cartridge cases and rifling marks on bullets, it was possible to determine the variety of weapons used by the various participants. By combining crime lab methods with the archaeological constructs of spatial patterning and individual artifact analysis, it was possible to discover evidence for the movement of individual firearms over the field of battle, to verify cavalry positions, and to define previously unknown Indian fighting areas.

Firearms identification procedures applied to archaeological evidence are the same as those applied to a criminal investigation.[13] One archaeological specimen, termed the evidence cartridge case, is placed on one stage of a comparison microscope and another archaeological case of the same caliber is, in turn, placed on the adjacent stage and visually compared. Two types of characteristics are identified during the process: class characteristics and individual characteristics. Class characteristics indicate that a given case was fired in a specific firearm type. If the class characteristics match, then individual characteristics are examined. These include the depth of the firing pin mark, the size of the mark, breech face marks, manufacturing tool marks, and other features such as evidence of firing pin drag. Each firearm is unique in these characteristics; any case fired in a specific gun will retain microscopic evidence that is identical to another case fired in that gun. This technique of firearms identification has been used by law enforcement agencies since the early 1900s to prove a particular cartridge or bullet was fired from a particular gun.

The Little Bighorn firearms analysis identified forty-four different types of guns used by the Indian warriors. Another type of weapon found at the site was metal arrowheads, providing physical evidence that the stereotypical bow and arrow was also used. Indian arms included the army's Springfield carbine and Colt revolver, probably captured either in the Rosebud fight or the valley fight against Major Marcus Reno. In addition, some were taken from Custer's men during the battle. Muzzle-loading firearms were also well represented and included arms firing .44, .45, and .50 caliber balls; a .577 Enfield; a .36 caliber Colt Navy revolver; Colt .44 caliber revolvers; and Remington .44 caliber revolvers. Other firearms included a Maynard carbine, a Starr carbine, a Smith carbine, Remington and Colt .44 caliber rimfire conversions, shotguns, Ballards, Forehand and Wadsworths, Sharps .40, .45, and .50 calibers, and .50-70 caliber Springfield rifles.

The major Indian arms category, and ones with the largest numbers of individual firearms identified during analysis, included the .44 caliber Henry, .44 caliber Model 1866 Winchester, and the .44/.40 caliber Model 1873 Winchester, all repeating rifles. The army's single shot Springfield was simply not as fast as the repeating rifles, although it was more powerful and more accurate than a majority of the Indian arms.

By using modern firearms identification techniques it was possible to discover how many individual weapons were represented in the archaeological collection. This was accomplished by using techniques that entail microscopic comparison of each cartridge case against every other case of that type. The results have been nothing short of incredible. It is possible not only to identify the forty-four different firearms types noted above, but cartridge case and bullet analyses have demonstrated that there is evidence for the use of more than three hundred specific and individual firearms by the warriors at the battle. These figures are considered a minimum, as not all cartridge cases or bullets collected from the field of battle were available for comparison with the archaeological sample.

The use of forensic techniques provided new and stimulating information on the identification of individual weapons on the battlefield. Coupling this information with the spatial distribution of all artifacts, moreover, allowed for reconstruction of the movement of individual weapons during the battle. Combining historical information with the distribution of buttons, spurs, bullets, and cartridge cases allowed a detailed reconstruction of the battle to emerge.

This stimulating data also brought about, with assistance from a Kinnican Arms Chair Grant from the Winchester Gun Museum in Cody, Wyoming, an opportunity to search out and study actual firearms used in the battle.[14] The effort required finding well-documented battle-attributed firearms,[15] from which firing pin impressions were taken. More than 150 firearms were examined and firing pin impressions compared with the archaeological specimen cartridge cases. Fifteen firearms have now been documented as having seen service in the Battle of the Little Bighorn.

The Men with Custer: Developing Osteobiographies

Among the many legacies of the Battle of the Little Bighorn are the skeletal remains of those who died in the fight. In the intervening years some of those remains became exposed and were collected for reburial in the Custer National Cemetery (CNC), while others were discovered during the formal archaeological investigations. One element of the Little Bighorn archaeological investigations was to ascertain if the marble markers were accurately placed on the field in 1890. The archaeological investigations did determine that most markers are indeed correct, but that the paired markers most likely mark only a single interment. The recovery of human bone at many of the markers indicates the 1881 reburial team did a good but not complete job of recovering the dead.

Among the research questions raised during the archaeological studies were those related to the study of human remains. These research questions were designed to gather data from any available skeletal remains and to identify the remains with individual battle casualties, if possible, through proper and complete skeletal examination. The study also was intended to examine evidence that might add information on the health, status, wound trauma, and general lifestyle of the soldiers killed at the Little Bighorn.

Since 1877 there have been at least twenty documented discoveries of assemblages of human bone on the battlefield, exclusive of the formal archaeological investigations that were conducted there in recent years.[16] In four separate episodes at least ten skeletons were found on the battlefield and reburied in graves marked "Unknown" in the National Cemetery. None of the remains received any scientific analysis before they were reburied. Other collected specimens recently have been repatriated from private sources.

With that in mind Little Bighorn Battlefield National Monument managers determined that in addition to any remains recovered during the field inventories it would be appropriate to exhume the unanalyzed remains from the cemetery. This investigation was designed to undertake a formal forensic examination and add that information to the database on the men with Custer.[17]

Four possible identifications have been made from the bones recovered and from the limited descriptions available in the historical record.[18] While by no means an overwhelming number, these are significant given the limited data available. Particularly significant is the identification of Mitch Boyer. Controversy has reigned as to the location of Boyer's body. Private Peter Thompson stated he found the body on the left side of the river, and Sergeant Daniel Knipe noted that Boyer was buried in Deep Ravine. Whereas Colonel John Gibbon stated, "the body of our poor guide Mitch Boyer was found lying in the midst of the troopers slain, as the Sioux had several times reported they had slain him in battle."

And finally White Man Runs Him stated Boyer was found on a ridge.[19]

These recollections suggest that either Boyer's body was mistakenly identified by the various sources, or their memories had faded after so many years. Boyer was found at markers 33 and 34, just below the crest of a ridge that forms the north side of the primary drainage area of Deep Ravine. If this area was considered a part of Deep Ravine by the burial details, then this has important ramifications in reinterpreting the locations of those killed in or near Deep Ravine. However, it is possible that because of the crushed skull and the poor condition of the body Boyer was not properly identified. On the other hand, Boyer was one of few present not dressed in military attire and so his remains would have stood out from those of the soldiers. The identification of Mitch Boyer on the south skirmish line agrees more with John Gibbon's account that Boyer was found among the slain troopers. The importance of the findings, however, is that the archaeological data flatly contradict some common interpretations of the historical accounts. Either the accounts, or the common interpretations, are inaccurate. The question of inaccuracy has led Richard Fox to reassess the documentary records in light of the archaeological evidence.[20]

The human remains examined exhibited substantial evidence of perimortem trauma. The osteological data clearly demonstrate that some of the men were mutilated about the time of death. To what extent the bodies were mutilated cannot be precisely determined, but a relative impression of the type and extent of the injuries can be suggested based on the osteological material. The marker excavations yielded partial remains of twenty-one individuals, a 10 percent sample of the United States soldiers killed during the battle. The Custer National Cemetery exhumations yielded thirteen nearly complete skeletons.

In addition to the excavated remains, surface material found by the archaeological crew, visitors, and park staff yielded partial remains of another thirteen individuals. This provides a group of remains representing forty-seven of the soldiers who died at the Little Bighorn (roughly an 18 percent sample).

Many contemporary accounts of the June 27, 1876, burials note that mutilation was prevalent among the dead. The most common type of mutilation mentioned was the crushed skull. However, Lieutenant James Bradley claimed to have seen most of the dead, and he recalled little mutilation, mainly an occasional scalping.[21] Further, he believed that most of the disfigurement seen on the dead resulted from a blow with a hatchet, or war club, to kill a wounded man.

The archaeological evidence for incised or sharp force wounds, those made by knives, arrows, and hatchets, occurs in about 21 percent of the remains from the Custer battlefield and in only one case from the Reno-Benteen defense site. Wounds related to knives or arrows are seen in 11 percent of the Custer individuals, and hatchet-related injuries were noted in 10 percent of the Custer sample. It must be remembered that not all injuries are likely to have affected the bone; thus, the sample only reflects those injuries that cut to the bone. Nevertheless, it appears that a significant percentage of the soldiers killed must have been shot with arrows, cut with knives, or struck with hatchets about the time of death.

Blunt-instrument trauma to the skull appears as the most prevalent perimortem feature in the contemporary accounts, and the archaeological evidence supports this. There are fourteen cases in the Custer battlefield archaeological record where skull fragments are present. All cases exhibit blunt-instrument trauma. This group accounts for 41 percent of the Custer battlefield individuals represented archaeologically and all of those cases where skull fragments were present. This direct physical evidence suggests that blunt-force trauma to the skull was common.

The incomplete nature of the skeletal remains recovered limits the quantification of the amount of mutilation at the Custer battlefield site. Qualitatively, it is obvious from the archaeological evidence that mutilation was common. This is in concert with the historical record, although contrary to the recollections of Lieutenant Bradley.

That mutilation of the dead occurred is clearly evident in the historical and archaeological records. But the cause of mutilation must be placed in a cultural context. Most of our perspective of mutilation is derived from the Victorian view that mutilation is barbaric. That viewpoint has been perpetuated in much of the literature about Indian "atrocities."[22]

It is more appropriate, however, to view mutilation from the cultural context of the Sioux and Cheyenne, rather than Victorian whites. One of the most common themes in Indian explanations of mutilation is one that pervades human nature—a sense of rage and revenge. A sense of rage and revenge also contributed to the mutilation of the dead. White Necklace, Wolf Chief's wife, had found her niece decapitated after the Sand Creek massacre, and in revenge she decapitated a soldier at the Little Bighorn with her belt axe.[23] While revenge may have been the most obvious motivation for mutilation, there are also deeper cultural meanings ascribed to the practice. General Henry B. Carrington interviewed a member of Red Cloud's band as to the reason for the mutilation of the dead at the Fetterman fight.

Carrington reported the key to understanding the mutilation was an understanding of the Indians' own view of life after death. He noted:

> Their idea of the spirit land is that it is a physical paradise; but we enter upon its mysteries just in the condition we hold when we die. In the Indian paradise every physical taste or longing is promptly met. . . . In the light of this idea, those tortured bodies had a new significance. With the muscles of the arms cut out, the victim could not pull a bowstring or trigger; with other muscles gone, he could not put foot in a stirrup or stoop to drink; so that, while every sense was in agony for relief from hunger or thirst, there could be no relief at all.[24]

In this context, mutilation, in the view of the Sioux and Cheyenne participants, was a part of their culture. It must be viewed as a normal cultural expression of victory over a vanquished foe. That expression has two levels. The first level is the overt and obvious level of rage and revenge. The second level is symbolic or religious, a level where mutilation is a means to insure that an enemy cannot enjoy the afterlife in the fullness that the victor might anticipate. Thus, the mutilated dead at the Little Bighorn were symbols of victory to the Sioux and Cheyenne.

The men with Custer died more than one hundred years ago. But their bones tell a detailed story of their lives and deaths. Physical anthropologists have determined not only each one's age, stature, and probable cause of death, but have discovered new information on his lifestyle that cannot be garnered from the historical record alone. Perhaps most revealing is the harsh and rugged life led by these relatively young men as seen in the extent to which their lifestyle as cavalrymen on the frontier restructured and remodeled their bones. Clearly reflected in their bones is evidence of horseback riding and tobacco use. Equally important is correlation of the historical record with the physical anthropological data that has resulted in the probable identifications of Miles O'Hara, Edward Botzer, Vincent Charley, George Lell, and the possible identification of two other people. Facial approximations of other skulls have added potential likenesses of five as-yet-unidentified battle participants to the gallery of those who served in the Seventh Cavalry.

The tools of modern physical anthropology, while not solving every possible question of interest about the men, add to a growing historical and anthropological database. Of real significance is the identification of one set of remains as a Native American female, possibly a Crow. This elderly woman's remains were discovered in 1928, and without benefit of any analysis at that time, were buried in the Custer National Cemetery as an unknown soldier. Such an error underscores the value of thorough and complete scientific investigation of human remains found on the field of battle. Thus, it becomes apparent that researchers should not assume *a priori* that human remains found on or near the battlefield are those of a soldier. Other peoples have lived on and utilized the site for thousands of years. Our single-event focus at the Little Bighorn site requires expansion to appreciate the whole history of the place.

The remains of this Native American woman were returned to her people for proper disposition in accordance with the Native American Graves Protection and Repatriation Act of 1990. Those of the cavalrymen were reinterred in the National Cemetery.

Development of a Theory of Battlefield Archaeology

Archaeological investigations at Little Bighorn Battlefield National Monument provided a new perspective on the various elements of the Battle of the Little Bighorn. Those investigations led to the development of a post–Civil War battlefield model. The definition of a post–Civil War battlefield pattern is predicated upon an axiom basic to archaeological investigation. Human behavior is patterned. Behavioral patterns are expressed through individual behaviors constrained by the norms, values, sanctions, and statuses governing the group within which the individual operates. Among standing armies, military groups are rigidly defined and hierarchically ordered; they are less well defined among guerrilla forces, and individual behavioral roles are structured accordingly. Thus, in warfare, tactical operations (both defensive and offensive) precipitate individual behaviors that are carried out within and on behalf of the military unit to which the individual belongs. War tactics, which represent patterned behavior, include establishment of positions and the deployment and movement of combatants. The residues of tactics in warfare—artifacts, features and their contextual relationships—are also patterned and reflect details of battlefield behavior.[25]

That behavior is clearly reflected at the various battlefields investigated to date through archaeological techniques. The distribution of cartridge cases and bullets attests to the structured organization of the fighting groups. The archaeological data show that leaders employed their men according to prescribed tactics of the day or dictates of their culturally defined warfare behavior. Identification of individual patterns through firearms identification also provided the basis on which unit patterns were constructed. This involved tracing positions and movements but at the unit pattern level. In effect, the deployment of combat units was identified and traced archaeologically. Through archaeology, combatant positions have been identified, firearms identified and quantified, the sequence of events elucidated, history enhanced, and in some areas revised.

To reiterate, these data exist in a recognizable form in space on a field of battle, where organization is supposedly the least likely place to exist. In this case those organizations and culturally opposing forces are recognizable. The Little Bighorn battlefield archaeological investigations have led to other battlefield studies around the country, and these studies have become another step in defining the archaeological aspect of the anthropology of war.[26]

Applying Battlefield Investigation
Procedures in the Real World

The methods and theory of battlefield archaeology are being applied in more far-reaching modern conflict situations. The news media provide numerous stories of extrajudicial executions of persons all over the world, and the techniques of conflict investigation pioneered at the Little Bighorn battlefield are seeing duty in those situations today.

In most fields of scientific study, particularly in archaeological research, the interdisciplinary team concept is commonplace. This is also true in the field of human rights violation investigations. Those investigations routinely utilize personnel from law enforcement, document examiners, physicians, forensic pathologists, forensic anthropologists, and archaeologists.

Archaeologists bring to human rights investigations a unique set of qualifications garnered from years of field experience and site excavation. The skills include the proper excavation techniques and recovery of patterned data. Battlefield archaeology, due to its emphasis on conflict situations and precise recording techniques, has proven of exceptional value in several human rights investigations.

Investigative techniques developed or refined at the Little Bighorn, particularly associated with piece-plotting of evidence and the application of firearms identification, have been applied in three extrajudicial execution situations; Koreme, Iraq; El Mozote, El Salvador; and Packraca Poljana, Croatia.[27] In each of these situations, persons were killed and clandestinely buried.

The Koreme site involved the execution of over twenty-five male Kurds by Iraqi military personnel. During Saddam Hussein's Anfal campaign against the Kurds many of the male members of the village of Koreme were executed. Middle East Watch and Physicians for Human Rights recovered the remains and conducted autopsies to identify the dead. A part of the investigations entailed the recovery and analysis of cartridge cases associated with the event. The firearms identification process was able to ascertain the approximate number of shooters involved in the incident and the method of the execution. This information, coupled with various types of witness accounts, has aided the United Nations in bringing pressure to bear on the Iraqi government to cease its outright destruction of Kurdish villages and killing of inhabitants.

El Mozote, El Salvador, was a rural village that was destroyed by government troops during the recent civil war. According to witness accounts more than four hundred people were murdered and buried. The government denied the accusation, claiming that the deaths were all combat related, although some innocent victims had been caught in cross fire between government and rebel troops.

Excavation of one building known to have multiple burials proved to contain the remains of more than 136 children with an average age of seven years. Clusters of cartridge cases, all fired in M-16 United States–made weapons, were found near the door and window of the building. Analysis of the cartridge cases demonstrated the minimum number of shooters involved. This information coupled with the direct evidence of many gunshot wounds to the heads of the children argued for an execution instead of combat-related manner of death. The El Salvadoran government did concede the point and admitted that an excess of force had been used in the case of El Mozote. The information recovered during the forensic investigations was an important part of the evidence used by the United Nations to mediate an end to the civil war and bring about a reintegration of El Salvadoran society.

Another recent use of battlefield study techniques was in the war-torn areas of the former Yugoslavia. There forensic teams located, exhumed, and mapped graves and remains of people who had met violent death. Because this investigation, in the hands of a United Nations War Crimes Tribunal, is continuing, not all details are available to the public. It is known, however, that a combination of metal detecting and probing located nine clandestine graves containing the remains of nineteen individuals. Evidence associated with the remains included bullets, cartridge cases, jewelry, and a briefcase. All individuals bore evidence of traumatic death consistent with an extrajudicial execution.

Conclusions

Battlefield archaeology is a relatively new field of study. It has, however, demonstrated its utility in correcting errors in the historical record as well as in adding new information about battles and has proven itself useful in aiding human rights investigations.

Artifacts found on the field of battle and removed without context or provenance are still just relics. When the recovery of those artifacts is accomplished in a systematic manner, however, they become a valuable new source of information on the battle. Recovered battlefield artifacts constitute the physical evidence of the event and are useful for several purposes. As tangible evidence, they can be used in museums to interpret events. The data contained in an artifact in context also provide a new and independent evidence source for detailed analysis of specific battle elements, such as combatants' attire, armament, deployment, and movements. Most importantly, the artifact and its context represent the physical data needed to analyze and understand conflict situations in the broader context of the study of the anthropology of war.

Notes

1.   Douglas D. Scott and Paul R. Nickens, "Nonintrusive Site Evaluation and Stabilization Technologies for Archaeological Resources," *Public Historian,* 13 (Summer 1991), 85-96.

2.   Don Rickey, Administrative History of Custer Battlefield National Monument, Crow Agency, Montana, 1958, manuscript, Little Bighorn Battlefield National Monument, Crow Agency, Montana.

3.   Robert Bray, A Report of Archaeological Investigations at the Reno-Benteen Site, Custer Battlefield National Monument, June 2 to July 1, 1958, manuscript, Midwest Archeological Center, National Park Service, Lincoln, Nebraska (hereafter MAC).

4.   Edward P. Baxter and Kay L. Killen, *A Study of the Palo Alto Battleground Cameron County, Texas,* Report 33 (College Station: Texas A and M University, 1976).

5.   Douglas D. Scott and Richard A. Fox, Jr., *Archaeological Insights into the Custer Battle: An Assessment of the 1984 Field Season* (Norman: University of Oklahoma Press, 1989); Douglas D. Scott, Richard A. Fox,

Jr., Melissa A. Connor, and Dick Harmon, *Archaeological Perspectives on the Battle of the Little Bighorn* (Norman: University of Oklahoma Press, 1989); Douglas D. Scott, "Archeological Investigations at the Reno-Benteen Equipment Disposal Site," in *Papers on Little Bighorn Battlefield Archaeology*, Reprints in Anthropology, vol. 42 (Lincoln: J and L Reprint Co., 1991), 1-183.

6.   Charles Hacker, *A Thunder of Cannon: Archeology of the Mexican American War Battlefield of Palo Alto* (Santa Fe: Division of Anthropology, Branch of Cultural Resources, Southwest Regional Office, 1994); David Reiss and Skylar S. Scott, "Archaeological and Historical Investigations at the Wagon Box Fight, Sheridan County, Wyoming," *Wyoming Archaeologist*, 27 (Fall 1984), 57-78; Karl Lambach and Robert Burton, "Apache Archaeology of Hembrillo Canyon, White Sands Missile Range, New Mexico," n.d., manuscript in author's possession; Larry L. Ludwig and James L. Stute, *The Battle at K-H Butte: Apache Outbreak–1881: Arizona Territory* (Tucson: Western Lore Press, 1993); William B. Lees, "When the Shooting Stopped the War Began" in *Look to the Earth: Historical Archaeology and the American Civil War*, ed. Clarence R. Geier, Jr., and Susan E. Winter (Knoxville: University of Tennessee Press, 1994), 59-89.

7.   T. Gregory and J. G. Rogerson, "Metal-detecting in Archaeological Excavation," *Antiquity*, 58 (no. 224, 1984), 179-84; K. David McLeod, "Metal Detecting and Archaeology: An Example from EbLf-12," *Manitoba Archaeological Quarterly*, 9 (Spring 1985), 20-31; William B. Lees, "Results of an Archeological Evaluation of a Proposed Maintenance Building Location, Fort Larned National Historic Site, Pawnee County, Kansas," 1984, Lawrence Office of Archeological Research, Museum of Anthropology, University of Kansas.

8.   William Hampton Adams and Keith Garnett, "The Historical Geography of Fort Yamhill," in *Fort Yamhill: Preliminary Historical Archaeological Research Concerning the 1856–1866 Military Post*, ed. William Hampton Adams (Corvallis: Department of Anthropology, University of Oregon, 1991), 35-38.

9.   William P. Dowdy, "A Spatial Distribution Study in the Fort Jefferson Research Area, with an Assessment of the Utility of a Metal Detector as a Research Tool," (honors thesis, Murray State University, Murray, Ky., 1994).

10.   Douglas D. Scott, *A Sharp Little Affair: The Archeology of Big Hole Battlefield*, Reprints in Anthropology, vol. 45 (Lincoln, Nebr.: J and L Reprint Co., 1994).

11.   Scott et al., *Archaeological Perspectives*, 24-35.

12.   Hacker, *A Thunder of Cannon*.

13. Douglas Scott, "Firearms Identification for the Archeologist," in *From Chaco to Chaco: Papers in Honor of Robert H. Lister and Florence C. Lister,* ed. Meliha S. Duran and David T. Kirkpatrick, Bulletin of the Archaeological Society of New Mexico, no. 15 (Albuquerque: Archaeological Society of New Mexico, 1989), 141-51.

14. Douglas Scott and Dick Harmon, "A Sharps Rifle from the Battle of the Little Bighorn," *Man at Arms,* 10 (Winter 1988), 12-15.

15. Douglas Scott and Dick Harmon, "General Nelson Miles' List of Surrendered Sioux War Guns," *Man at Arms,* 15 (Winter 1993), 31, 34-36.

16. Jerome A. Greene, *Evidence and the Custer Enigma: A Reconstruction of Indian-Military History* (Reno, Nev.: Outbooks, 1986), 59.

17. P. Willey, "Osteological Analysis of Human Skeletons Excavated from the Custer Battlefield National Cemetery," Technical Report, forthcoming, MAC.

18. Scott et al., *Archaeological Perspectives,* 73-74; Willey, "Osteological Analysis"; Douglas Scott, Melissa Connor, and Clyde Snow, "Nameless Faces of the Little Bighorn," *Greasy Grass,* 4 (May 1988), 2-4; Douglas D. Scott and Clyde Collins Snow, "Archeology and Forensic Anthropology of Human Remains from the Reno Retreat Crossing," in *Papers on Little Bighorn Battlefield Archeology: The Equipment Dump, Marker 7, and the Reno Crossing,* ed. Douglas D. Scott, Reprints in Anthropology, vol. 42 (Lincoln: J and L Reprint Co., 1991), 207-36; Clyde Collins Snow and John Fitzpatrick, "Human Osteological Remains from the Battle of the Little Bighorn," in Scott et al., *Archaeological Perspectives,* 243-82.

19. Richard G. Hardorff, *The Custer Battle Casualties* (El Segundo, Calif.: Upton and Sons, 1989), 20-130.

20. Richard Allan Fox, Jr., *Archaeology, History, and Custer's Last Battle: The Little Big Horn Reexamined* (Norman, University of Oklahoma Press, 1993).

21. E. A. Brininstool, *Troopers with Custer: Historic Incidents of the Battle of the Little Big Horn* (Harrisburg, Penn.: Stackpole, 1952), 258-60.

22. Frederick M. Hans, *The Great Sioux Nation* (Chicago: M. A. Donahue and Co., 1907), 15-98.

23. Peter J. Powell, *Sweet Medicine: The Continuing Role of the Sacred Arrows, the Sun Dance, and the Sacred Buffalo Hat in Northern Cheyenne History* (2 vols., Norman: University of Oklahoma Press, 1969), 2:40-150.

24. Henry B. Carrington, *The Indian Question* (1884; reprint, New York, Sol Lewis, 1973).

25. Richard A. Fox, Jr., and Douglas D. Scott, "The Post–Civil War Battlefield Pattern," *Historical Archaeology*, 25 (no. 2, 1991), 92-103.

26. Scott, *A Sharp Little Affair;* Hacker, *A Thunder of Cannon.*

27. Douglas Scott, "Firearms Identification at the Koreme Execution Site," appendix 3, in Kenneth Anderson, *The Anfal Campaign in Iraqi Kurdistan: The Destruction of Koreme* (New York: Middle East Watch and Physicians for Human Rights, 1993); Clyde Collins Snow, Robert H. Kirschner, Douglas D. Scott, and John F. Fitzpatrick, "El Mozote: Informe de la Investigacion Forense," in Anexo Tomo I, *From Madness to Hope: The 12-Year War in El Salvador* (New York: Informe de la Comision de la Verdad Para El Salvador, United Nations, 1993), 1-3; Douglas D. Scott, "Identificacion de Arms de Fuego en el Sito de Ejecucion de El Mozote," in ibid., 7-9.

Photographer Fred E. Miller recorded the Seventh Cavalry's visit to the Custer monument in 1901. (Montana Historical Society Photograph Archives, Helena)

"Holy Ground"
The United States Army Embraces Custer's Battlefield

Paul L. Hedren

T he harrowing sight of the dead bodies crowning the height
on which Custer fell . . . will remain vividly in my memory
until death." Major Marcus Reno penned these words on
July 5, 1876, as he concluded his official report on the Battle of the
Little Bighorn. However historians subsequently judge Reno's
conduct in the most calamitous affair of the Great Sioux War, one
cannot help but sense a curious compassion and anguish in his
words. Reno was stigmatized by the Little Bighorn catastrophe for
the remainder of his life.[1]

In truth, the horrors of the Little Bighorn battlefield were neither
Reno's nor the Seventh Cavalry's to bear alone, but were
tribulations befalling the entire American army. The heart of a
cavalry regiment was destroyed at the Little Bighorn. But as with
the great phoenix of legend, from that tragedy came both
extraordinary charity for the regiment's survivors and a veneration
for a battlefield that soon became a metaphor and ultimately a
memorial for the Seventh Cavalry's and the United States Army's
role in the settlement of the American West.

In the wake of the battle, the Little Bighorn survivors had no
time to mourn. The burials on June 28 were cursory at best,
"respectful gestures" opined one historian. In the harsh realities of
the moment, only the Seventh's fallen officers received even a

semblance of interment, and the enlisted casualties were barely covered with scattered dirt and sagebrush as the field was hurriedly abandoned in the press of the summer campaign.[2]

The Seventh's haste was understandable. The survivors nursed fifty-two wounded comrades desperate for proper medical care. And inwardly perhaps they and the relief force feared tangling again with the massive coalition of Lakotas and Northern Cheyennes that had so thoroughly decimated the Seventh's ranks. As well, most of the soldiers were keenly aware of Colonel Joseph Reynolds's inglorious fight on the Powder River three months earlier, and while they had not yet learned of Brigadier General George Crook's disastrous fight at Rosebud Creek, they unwittingly bore the sting of its consequences at Little Bighorn. If there was comfort at the moment in Alfred Terry's and John Gibbon's camp, it only came in their ability to get away from what one witness called a "pestilence-laden atmosphere."[3]

Predictably, reverberations from the Little Bighorn rippled swiftly through the army's world. Picture Elizabeth Custer learning of the tragedy from Captain William McCaskey at Fort Abraham Lincoln on the evening of July 5. "From that time the life went out of the hearts of the 'women who weep'," she wrote.[4] Picture, as well, other army dependents like Elizabeth Burt, whose husband marched with General Crook. "We at Fort Laramie were a profoundly depressed collection of women," she wrote after learning of Custer's defeat. "You can well imagine how hard and sorrow-breeding it was to sit and think and think and imagine all kinds of disasters. Truly, wives of soldiers and sailors have mixed with their happiness, very many anxieties unknown to other wives."[5]

Mrs. Custer observed how the Little Bighorn battle "wrecked the lives of twenty-six women at Fort Lincoln," but in truth its impacts reached well beyond the Dakota and Wyoming frontier to touch virtually every segment of the closely knit Regular Army. The late-nineteenth-century American army was a peculiar community possessed of a culture borne of custom and the isolation of the post–Civil War frontier. In a country of some forty million people, the army's size was inordinately small, a reflection of the nation's traditional disdain for a standing force. But nearly all of its 2,150 officers and 25,000 enlisted men nurtured a distinct sense of family, particularly in the environment of their garrison homes. As one officer put it, "companionship begot friendship and affection. To have lived a season together in a frontier post weaves a bond that is never loosened."[6]

Perhaps that unity of family was strongest among the officer corps, nearly all of whom upheld a very strict and inflexible code of honor. By and large, these were men quite well educated for their time who saw themselves as a chivalrous elite—gentlemen and professionals with a high sense of responsibility and soldier duty. Forget divisive squabbles during Custer's tenure with the Seventh Cavalry. Forget the stratification separating officers, wives and children, relatives, servants, and enlisted men. Disaster unified the classes. And never in the nation's entire westering experience did tragedy seem greater than the human toll paid manifest destiny at the Little Bighorn in the Great Sioux War.[7]

One of the hallmarks of a close-knit community is the concern and compassion expressed for its own, and barely had the shock of the Little Bighorn been realized when that quality emerged. There appeared in the July 29, 1876, issue of the *Army and Navy Journal* a letter reporting on the sorrow and suffering afflicting the widows and orphans of the Seventh Cavalry. The writer noted that these bereaved were still months from the receipt of a small pension and were nearing the end of such charity as could be bestowed by the quartermasters and commissaries at their respective posts. With a warm endorsement, the *Journal's* editor, William Church, concluded that "such sudden and unexpected bereavement never before fell to the lot of one regiment and we are sure that every officer and soldier who reads . . . [this] . . . will gladly alleviate to the best of his ability the deep distress of the helpless ones."[8]

Church's appeal netted prompt results. Within two weeks more than $900 was received, with some of the money sent immediately to Lieutenant General Philip Sheridan for distribution to the cases of greatest need. For many weeks thereafter the *Journal* reported a torrent of donations, some coming singly, most coming in the names of regiments and posts. By mid-September the fund topped $5,000, and the *Journal* printed a letter from an officer's widow thanking the contributors for their remembrances and expressing the desire of three bereaved ladies that "their share of the fund . . . be given to the widows and orphans of the enlisted men." Quite likely the letter writer was Maggie Calhoun, wife of the Seventh Cavalry's First Lieutenant James Calhoun and George Custer's sister.[9]

By November's end donations topped $10,000 and procedures were established to distribute the receipts. While generally the allotments would conform to rates accorded rank by the existing pension laws, the *Journal* deemed it fitting that monies raised from enlisted men go to the wives and families of enlisted men. The Seventh Cavalry counted fourteen such widows and twenty-five children who by January received checks varying from $193 to $365. The monthly enlisted pension rate was $8, so easily these checks were significant.[10]

Counted among the deceased officers of the Seventh were eight widows and seven children who subsequently received disbursements varying from $510 to $1,050. The campaign eventually netted more than $14,000, of which some $7,500 was paid to the widows and orphans of officers, and $5,800 paid to enlisted families. In its June 30, 1877, issue, *Journal* editor Church commented on the satisfactions of the relief campaign. The widows, one and all, request "that we should make known to the contributors how deeply they have been touched by the kindness shown them in this expression of comradeship, which is one of the noblest features of Army life."[11]

The Great Sioux War, of course, was prosecuted to an end, a final battle occurring May 7, 1877, on a small tributary of Rosebud Creek. But for several Seventh Infantry and Crow Indian couriers passing the Little Bighorn battlefield in late July 1876, it was events occurring outside the war and not the conflict itself that intensified an interest in that blood-soaked field. Doubtless, the success of Frederick Whittaker's controversial book, *A Complete Life of Gen. George A. Custer*, appearing in November 1876, fanned America's emotions. Although Whittaker had neither the way nor the inclination to visit the Little Bighorn battlefield as he prepared his work, by placing blame for Custer's defeat on President U. S. Grant, Major Reno, and Captain Frederick Benteen, he brought vivid notice to the dead.[12]

But so, too, did the grieving widows, families, and friends of the Seventh Cavalry, who wished for reburials of their deceased in "some less lonely spot." More than any other senior officer, General Sheridan engaged in an extensive correspondence with the survivors. "I have been much pressed by the friends of the officers who fell with Custer . . . to bring in their bodies. I have assured them that we would do all we could to accómplish this purpose," Sheridan wrote General Terry in late March 1877. Quickly he asked General William Sherman, the army's commander in chief, whether the secretary of war had sufficient incidental funding for this purpose, and although the War Department vacillated at first, contingency funding was quickly found.[13]

General Sheridan assigned the delicate task of disinterment and reburial to his brother Michael, who served in division headquarters as an aide-de-camp with the rank of lieutenant colonel. From Major Reno came preliminary information on the original burials at the Little Bighorn. Generally, those officers who died with Custer were interred by order of rank, he reported, but Myles Keogh, John Crittenden, and James Calhoun were buried separately, as were Donald McIntosh and James DeWolf. First Lieutenant Henry Nowlan, in 1876 the Seventh's quartermaster, had marked the graves and would be able to point them out, but Reno predicted that "it will . . . be a labor to recover the bodies."[14]

News of the proposed 1877 Little Bighorn expedition spread quickly and correspondence with the families intensified. Some expressed wishes for private burials in hometown plots, but most were content with a suggested reburial in the national cemetery at Fort Leavenworth, Kansas. Colonel Thomas Crittenden of the Seventeenth Infantry, alone, expressed the wish that his son John be left on the field where he fell.[15]

After traveling the Northern Pacific Railroad to Bismarck and the steamboat *John C. Fletcher* to the mouth of the Little Bighorn River, Michael Sheridan reached the battlefield on July 2, 1877. As he passed the fledgling Bighorn Post, soon to be named Fort Custer, Sheridan rendezvoused with Captain Nowlan and Company I of the Seventh Cavalry. Nowlan assisted with the original burials and now bore a sketch-map to aid in verifying locations and identifications. Sheridan and Nowlan crossed onto the field at the

Medicine Tail Coulee and soon encountered soldier graves, and then those of officers. Nowlan readily identified the burials on Custer Hill, a task greatly simplified by cedar stake markers surviving from 1876. The delicate exhumations commenced on July 3, and the remains of ten officers were carefully transferred to pine boxes specifically constructed for this purpose at Bighorn Post. Crittenden's body was the single exception. In accordance with his father's wishes, the lieutenant's remains were enclosed in a coffin and reburied on the field.[16]

Nowlan's subaltern, Second Lieutenant Hugh Scott, superintended the general reburials on the battlefield. The men of Company I scoured the prairie in every direction. "There was no time to dig deep graves," Scott later recounted, but the remains were neatly covered and marked with cedar stakes. In his report, Mike Sheridan foreshadowed a looming wish for the field. One day the stakes would help in collecting the remains, he wrote, before being "buried in a cemetery, if one be declared there." Indeed, that the battlefield should become a national cemetery soon became a crusade for General Sheridan and the entire American army, as they increasingly came to revere that "holy ground."[17]

Lieutenant Colonel Sheridan's expedition finished its work on July 4 after thoroughly exploring the village site and valley south to Reno's crossing. Convinced that his mission was complete, despite not locating the remains of several officers, Sheridan departed for Bighorn Post. There the remains were put under guard in the first and yet only building standing at the new fort. On July 7 the pine boxes were transferred to the steamer *Fletcher* and conveyed to Fort Abraham Lincoln, arriving there on July 12. Although he was later challenged on the thoroughness of the exhumations and identifications, young Sheridan defended his work emphatically and provided little reason to doubt either his intent or success.[18]

At Fort Abraham Lincoln, Major Joseph Tilford superintended the transfer of the officers' remains to metallic burial caskets, and on July 27 consigned them to the railroad express agent in Bismarck for delivery to their places of final interment. Sheridan's month-long expedition received extensive national newspaper coverage, as did the principal reburials at Fort Leavenworth on August 4,

1877, and George Custer's at the United States Military Academy on October 10.[19]

While Michael Sheridan labored on the Little Bighorn battlefield, his brother Philip embarked on his own western odyssey that soon brought him to the very same ground. The lieutenant general gloried in visiting places of high drama. Twice during the summer of 1876 he had traveled to Fort Laramie and Camp Robinson to confer with his senior commanders and scope the Sioux War landscape. Here now was his chance to examine the most dramatic of this war's battlefields. Sheridan's party arrived at the Little Bighorn on July 21 after having crossed the plains of southern Wyoming and the Bighorn Mountains. Michael's policing efforts were plainly evident, yet a certain ghoulishness still lingered on the field.[20]

Among Sheridan's party was General Crook and Crook's chief lieutenant, John Bourke. A meticulous diarist, Bourke penned evocative sketches of the relic-strewn battlefield. The officers explored in small groups, and in one instance Bourke's party stumbled onto four human skulls in close proximity, with a fifth nearby, and yet a sixth under an adjacent bush. On some portions of the field, Bourke noted that "it was hard to go ten yards in any direction without stepping on portions of the human anatomy." Referring to the hill upon which Custer was presumed to have perished, Bourke called that knoll "'holy ground', where our poor men died like sheep in the shambles."[21]

The conditions on the battlefield were such that a second survey for human remains was ordered, this one organized by Lieutenant Colonel George Forsyth, Sheridan's military secretary. Three detachments of Fifth Cavalrymen from Sheridan's escort, each commanded by a commissioned officer, combed the battlefield and buried or reburied every human bone encountered. In his report to Sheridan, Forsyth expressed the belief that his effort was entirely successful, but he cautioned that the spring rains would again expose skeletons.[22]

Ever the pragmatist, Sheridan found satisfaction in Forsyth's careful policing, which left the graves "nicely raised as in cemeteries inside of civilization." But the general worried about the army's ability to provide long-term care for this vast graveyard. In reflection several months later, he wrote Sherman that he wanted the site set off as a national cemetery, to be cared for by the garrison at Fort Custer. And if that was impractical, Sheridan would have the remains transferred to the Fort Custer cemetery. That national cemeteries provided perpetual care for the nation's military dead was by then a well-established practice in civilized America, and Sheridan saw it as proper and fitting in southeastern Montana as well.[23]

As Sheridan continued on to Bighorn Post and a rendezvous with General Sherman, he swelled with the satisfactions of having tamed the vast landscape that had once been Lakota country. "The valley of the Little Horn . . . was almost a continuous meadow," he wrote, "with grass nearly high enough to tie the tops from each side across a horse's back. This was the country of the buffalo and hostile Sioux only last year. There are no signs of either now; but in their places we found prospectors . . . [and] . . . emigrants."[24]

Sheridan's subsequent report intimated personal feelings about the Little Bighorn battlefield. The creation of a national cemetery there was the rightful way to honor these dead, he thought. Since 1862 an elaborate array of eastern national cemeteries had been founded, in part as a testimonial to the human toll in saving the Union. In a similar way, a Custer national cemetery would honor the valiant Seventh Cavalrymen whose blood in 1876 secured Indian country so that it might one day be a range for cattle or farmland for corn and wheat. As Antietam, Gettysburg, Arlington, and other great cemeteries commemorated the Union cause during the Civil War, Custer's battlefield would memorialize the costs borne by the army in winning the West.[25]

On July 23 the nation's senior army commanders, Sherman and Sheridan, rendezvoused aboard the steamboat *Rosebud* on the Bighorn River a few miles below Post No. 2. Sheridan had just completed his inspection of the burgeoning new fort and doubtless voiced satisfactions about it and the actions taken at the Little Bighorn battlefield. As well, he brimmed with pride over the visible wealth of Lakota country. Sherman was on his own inspection tour and shared fully Sheridan's enthusiasm for the opening of the Yellowstone and Powder river country. In reporting on his visit, Sherman wrote Secretary of War George McCrary that Post No. 2

and its mate, Post No. 1, located at the mouth of Tongue River, were occupied now by strong, enterprising garrisons, and as a result the "Sioux Indians can never again regain this country."[26]

Although particulars are lacking, it seems probable that Sherman visited the Custer battlefield during his day-long pause at Bighorn Post, joining photographer John Fouch and Nelson Miles of the Fifth Infantry as among the first of a host of visits by notables to the site in the late 1870s. These visits typically netted two observations. One had to do with continuing embarrassing conditions on the field. The natural elements worked against the preservation of the graves, and it seems that visitors were always detecting human remains. While Sheridan doubtless winced as he learned of these reports, surely he was canny enough to see them as bolstering his call for the expanded protection of the battlefield.[27]

Another consequence of these early visits was the alarming evidence of relic hunting. As early as Sheridan's inspection in late July the general decried the desecration of battlefield graves, believing some of it the handiwork of "curiosity hunters in the shape of human coyotes." Similarly, when the gold prospector Herman Bischoff visited the battlefield on August 17 he recorded how he took tin plates and canteens as souvenirs. Likewise, one of Bischoff's travel mates, William Allen, boasted of collecting cartridge cases on the field.[28]

Perhaps the worst example of relic hunting occurred in late August 1878 when officials at Fort Custer learned that a station keeper of the Rock Creek stage line possessed human remains. That unnamed operator of the way stop opposite the Little Bighorn battlefield received a severe admonishment from First Lieutenant William Rawolle, adjutant at Fort Custer, as he surrendered a "trophy" skull collected on the battlefield and destined for one of the stage company proprietors. Clearly, the collecting of artifacts on this and other Indian wars battlefields, a serious contemporary issue, has deep historical roots.[29]

Repeated reports of exposed human remains on the Little Bighorn battlefield led to orders in late October 1878 to Lieutenant Colonel George Buell, the founder and commanding officer of Fort Custer, to collect the bones and inter them in a general grave. Buell was also directed to erect a stone pyramid atop the burial to shield it from future depredation. The order came as winter set in and was not discharged until the following spring when Lieutenant Colonel Albert Brackett, Buell's successor, detailed Captain George Sanderson and Company C of the Eleventh Infantry to thoroughly police the battlefield.[30]

Sanderson spent the first week of April combing for human remains, which he buried in a common grave atop Custer Hill. Convinced that horse bones had much to do with inciting visitor emotions over exposed remains, Sanderson's infantrymen gathered those, as well, and placed them in the center of a cordwood monument erected atop the common grave. The remaining burials were all remounded. In his report Sanderson urged that they, too, be consolidated in a mass grave topped with stone, or that individual headstones be placed at the scattered grave sites. In due course, both actions were realized.[31]

As Sheridan grappled with evolving obligations to the preservation and memorialization of the Little Bighorn battlefield, an even thornier issue gained such momentum in the late 1870s that the army could avoid it no longer. A well-entrenched institution like the army was a living paradox. While it could exhibit an extraordinary kindness like its successful campaign on behalf of its widows and orphans, the army could also be an obstinate guardian of its own. Except for the courts-martial of Henry Noyes, Alexander Moore, and Joseph Reynolds in the wake of the Powder River debacle of March 17, 1876, the army demonstrated little enthusiasm for assessing blame for its Little Bighorn defeat or any other failing of the Great Sioux War. But Frederick Whittaker's ceaseless attacks on Marcus Reno, whom he brandished as the man most responsible for the death of Custer, became impossible to avoid.[32]

The deaths of 268 officers and men of the Seventh Cavalry weighed heavily enough on the regiment in the years after the battle without Whittaker's vitriol. Whittaker's best-selling biography showered blame for the Custer disaster on Grant, Reno, and Benteen, but as the months waned the abuse was redirected to Reno, whom Whittaker vilified as a coward. Exhausted by these relentless attacks, Reno, too, joined the call for a court of inquiry to investigate formally his conduct at the Little Bighorn.[33]

The Reno Court of Inquiry convened on January 13, 1879, at the Palmer House in Chicago. The reviewing panel consisted of three respected senior officers, Colonel Wesley Merritt of the Fifth Cavalry, Lieutenant Colonel William Royall of the Third Cavalry, both of whom were veterans of the Great Sioux War, and Colonel John King of the Ninth Infantry, who served as president. Yet another veteran of the war, First Lieutenant Jesse Lee, regimental adjutant of the Ninth Infantry, served as recorder, the military equivalent of prosecutor. Reno was defended by civilian counsel, Lyman Gilbert of Pennsylvania.

The inquiry lasted four weeks with testimony taken daily except Sundays. Twenty-three witnesses were called, including Reno, but the evidence generated proved inconclusive and often conflicting. Typically the officers either endorsed Reno's actions or showed a reluctance to criticize him. The civilian witnesses were far less hesitant in their attacks and depicted states of confusion, demoralization, and even drunkenness at the Little Bighorn. But to every charge, Gilbert mounted an effective countercharge. And in a lengthy summary he crafted a hypothetical statement from Custer that seemed to capture the sentiment of the court. Having returned from the grave to meet Major Reno, Gilbert was sure that Custer would say: "Our efforts failed to be mutual supports because of overwhelming force that confronted each of us, and your honor takes no stain."[34]

Recorder Lee concluded the proceedings on February 11 with a statement summarizing the charges and evidence against Reno. Lee's words were steady and lacked hostility. "It is for the Court to decide . . . whether Major Reno is in any way responsible for the defeat of the 7th Cavalry and the massacre of General Custer," he counseled. In a closed session lasting the remainder of that afternoon, King, Merritt, and Royall deliberated the findings and declared: "The conduct of the officers throughout was excellent, and while subordinates, in some instances, did more for the safety of the command by brilliant displays of courage than did Major Reno, there was nothing in his conduct which requires animadversion from this Court."[35] From the army's perspective, the case for culpability at the Little Bighorn was properly and publicly investigated and officially closed.

On October 16, 1878, the army's quartermaster general, Montgomery Meigs, recommended that a suitable monument be erected on the battlefield and that all remains be interred in a common grave. Secretary of War George McCrary concurred on January 29, 1879, and ordered the establishment of a national cemetery of the fourth class. Within a month the quartermaster department awarded a contract to the Mount Auburn Marble and Granite Works of Cambridge, Massachusetts, for the granite obelisk that soon became the enduring symbol of the battlefield.[36]

Meanwhile, the Custer Battlefield National Cemetery was announced by General Orders No. 78, issued by the headquarters of the army on August 1, 1879. Fronting the Little Bighorn River and eventually encompassing a square mile of land focused on Custer Hill, Sheridan had at last attained his vision for the preservation and memorialization of that "holy ground."

By then the Little Bighorn battlefield had become something of a pleasuring ground for an increasing number of summer tourists. Thomas Leforge, a well-known interpreter at Fort Custer, guided battlefield visits with such frequency that he often camped on site to relieve himself of consuming travel to and from the fort. The discovery of human remains by Leforge and others lingered as a curiosity. The sight of bones troubled Granville Stuart enough when he visited the battlefield in May 1880 that he called the place a "ghastly sight." He did not hesitate to collect souvenir bullets and shell casings, however.[37]

A final policing of the Little Bighorn battlefield occurred in July 1881 when First Lieutenant Charles Roe led Company C of the Second Cavalry from Fort Custer to the field. The great stone monument provided by the quartermaster department was nearly twenty-four months traveling from its Massachusetts quarry to Fort Custer and the battlefield, and Roe's first duty was to erect that three-piece, thirty-six-thousand-pound obelisk atop Custer Hill. The monument was girded by a large stone and mortar foundation, and the Second Cavalrymen fashioned a derrick crane from ash timbers cut along the river to lift the stones into position.[38]

Once raised, Roe's men then cut a deep trench around the base and reinterred the individual graves that dotted the field, including those from Reno's entrenchments and the valley. "I took great pains in gathering together all the remains . . . , giving it my personal attention," Roe reported. By the standards of his day, the reburials were thorough, although the world has since developed a new appreciation for the recovery of major and minor human bones from a battleground as vast as this. The single conscious exception to the reburial of 1881 was John Crittenden's grave, which remained undisturbed on the field.[39]

Ironically, as Roe completed his epic work some five years after the great battle, the distinguished Hunkpapa Lakota leader Sitting Bull (p. 114) led 187 followers into Fort Buford, Dakota Territory, just 240 miles northeast, where he surrendered after a fitful exile in Canada.[40] By every measure, the Great Sioux War was concluded. The last of the protagonists had submitted to reservation life. The northern transcontinental railroad was again advancing westward. The cattle empire was spreading its tentacles into the valleys of the Yellowstone Basin. And the United States Army had created a monument to its sacrifices in empire building.

At Sheridan's initiation, the Little Bighorn battlefield had truly emerged as a memorial to the men in blue. Indeed, that this landscape was bloodied by white *and* red warriors was never forgotten by the army or its successors. But from the moment of the initial interments on June 28, 1876, this was the Seventh Cavalry's graveyard, alone. In the shame of the army's most humiliating defeat during the Indian wars came a shrine to the greater successes of that conflict. This was thankless and controversial duty, to be sure. But while few might remember Beaver Creek, Kansas; Infernal Caverns, California; Davidson's Canyon, Arizona; Grace Creek, Nebraska; Richard Creek, Wyoming; or the hundreds of other places where soldiers were killed in Indian combat, the Little Bighorn battlefield would survive to remind the United States Army and the nation of the price they paid for manifest destiny.[41]

Notes

1. "Report of Major M. A. Reno," July 5, 1876, in *Report of the Secretary of War, 1876* (Washington, D.C.: Government Printing Office, 1876), 479.

2. Edgar I. Stewart, *Custer's Luck* (Norman: University of Oklahoma Press, 1955), 469-75; Richard G. Hardorff, *The Custer Battle Casualties: Burials, Exhumations, and Reinterments* (El Segundo, Calif.: Upton and Sons, 1989), 23-36.

3. For a synopsis of the war, see Paul L. Hedren, "The Great Sioux War: An Introduction," *The Great Sioux War, 1876–77:* The Best From Montana The Magazine of Western History (Helena: Montana Historical Society Press, 1991), 1-21. John S. Gray, "Captain Clifford's Story of the Sioux War of 1876," part 2, (Chicago) *Westerners Brand Book*, 26 (January 1970), 83.

4. Elizabeth B. Custer, *"Boots and Saddles," or, Life in Dakota with General Custer* (New York: Harper and Brothers, 1885), 269; Shirley A. Leckie, *Elizabeth Bacon Custer and the Making of a Myth* (Norman: University of Oklahoma Press, 1993), 190-91.

5. Merrill J. Mattes, *Indians, Infants and Infantry: Andrew and Elizabeth Burt on the Frontier* (Denver: Old West Publishing Company, 1960), 230. For other reactions, see Paul L. Hedren, *Fort Laramie in 1876: Chronicle of a Frontier Post at War* (Lincoln: University of Nebraska Press, 1988), 131.

6. Custer, *Boots and Saddles*, 268. Concepts of the army as family are discussed in Oliver Knight, *Life and Manners in the Frontier Army* (Norman: University of Oklahoma Press, 1978), 110-62. The quote is from George A. Forsyth, *The Story of the Soldier* (New York: D. Appleton and Company, 1900), 109.

7. On concepts of professionalism and the code of honor see Knight, *Life and Manners*, 4-6; Paul Andrew Hutton, *Phil Sheridan and His Army* (Lincoln: University of Nebraska Press, 1985), 142-43; Sherry L. Smith, *The View from Officers' Row: Army Perceptions of Western Indians* (Tucson: University of Arizona Press, 1990), 6-7.

8. Edgar I. Stewart, "The Custer Battle and Widow's Weeds," *Montana The Magazine of Western History*, 22 (January 1972), 53-54; William C. Church to M. V. Sheridan, November 17, 1876, microfilm reel 8, MSS 19,308, Philip H. Sheridan Papers, Library of Congress, Washington, D.C. (hereafter Sheridan Papers).

9. Stewart, "The Custer Battle," 54-55.

10. Ibid., 56-57; *Army and Navy Journal*, November 4, 1876; "List of Widows of Enlisted Men, 7th U.S. Cavalry," microfilm reel 9, Sheridan Papers, which is a correct list of enlisted recipients. Stewart's list is improperly transcribed.

11. Stewart, "The Custer Battle," 57-59.

12. Jerome A. Greene, *Yellowstone Command: Colonel Nelson A. Miles and the Great Sioux War, 1876–1877* (Lincoln: University of Nebraska Press, 1991), 201-18; Paul L. Hedren, "'three cool, determined men': The Sioux War Heroism of Privates Evans, Stewart, and Bell," *Montana The Magazine of Western History*, 41 (Winter 1991), 26; Frederick Whittaker, *A Complete Life of Gen. George A. Custer* (New York: Sheldon and Company, 1876), 594-606.

13. St. Paul and Minneapolis *Pioneer Press*, May 24, 1877; Sheridan to A. H. Terry, March 26, 1877, Sheridan to Sherman, April 4, 1877, E. D. Townsend to Sheridan, April 18, 1877, E. D. Townsend to Sheridan, April 28, 1877; microfilm reel 8, Sheridan Papers.

14. Special Orders No. 40, Military Division of the Missouri, May 16, 1877, Little Bighorn Battlefield National Monument, Crow Agency, Montana (hereafter LBNM); Reno to James W. Forsyth, April 29, 1877, P. H. Sheridan to M. V. Sheridan, May 16, 1877, microfilm reel 8, Sheridan Papers.

15. Crittenden to Sheridan, May 10, 1877, microfilm reel 8, Sheridan Papers. The Fort Leavenworth National Cemetery was designated in 1862 as an expansion of the post burial ground. See Dean W. Holt, *American Military Cemeteries: A Comprehensive Illustrated Guide to the Hallowed Grounds of the United States, Including Cemeteries Overseas* (Jefferson, N.C.: McFarland and Company, 1992), 133, 136.

16. "Colonel Sheridan's Report," in *The Custer Myth: A Source Book of Custeriana*, ed. William A. Graham (New York: Bonanza Books, 1953), 374-75 (reproducing Nowlan's map on p. 374); Special Orders No. 63, Department of Dakota, May 22, 1877, Record Group 393, Records of United States Army Continental Commands, 1821–1920, National Archives, Washington, D.C. (hereafter NA).

17. Hugh Lenox Scott, *Some Memories of a Soldier* (New York: Century Co., 1928), 48; "Colonel Sheridan's Report," 374-75. The name "holy ground" was bestowed by John G. Bourke. See John G. Bourke diary, July 21, 1877, microfilm edition of original at the United States Military Academy, Nebraska State Historical Society, Lincoln.

18. "Colonel Sheridan's Report," 375. These remains were conveyed to Fort Abraham Lincoln: Cooke, Keogh, T. Custer, Riley, Smith, Calhoun, G. Custer, Yates, DeWolf, and McIntosh. Crittenden was reburied on the field, and Harrington, Lord, Porter, Sturgis, and Hodgson were not located.

"Remains of Officers taken up on Custer's battle-ground," July 12, 1877, Office of the Quartermaster General, Cemeterial Branch, Interments in Fort Lincoln, Dakota Territory, LBNM. In 1913 Walter Camp received a letter from Henry P. Jones reporting gossip from James P. McNally of Nowlan's company. According to McNally, the identification of Custer's remains was disputed and Michael Sheridan is alleged to have stated: "Nail the box up; it's all right as long as the people think so." Camp Collection, Western History Department, Denver Public Library, Colorado. The delicacy and thoroughness of the exhumations was challenged by the Chicago *Tribune* on July 30, 1877, and Sheridan responded by calling all allegations "lies." Nowlan's identifications were precise, Sheridan contended, and the remains were disinterred as carefully as possible. M. V. Sheridan to Chicago *Tribune*, July 30, 1877, microfilm reel 8, Sheridan Papers. See also Sandy Barnard, "Custer Burial Revisited—West Point, October 1877," *6th Annual Symposium, Custer Battlefield Historical and Museum Assn., Inc., held at Hardin, Montana on June 26, 1992* ([Crow Agency, Mont.: Custer Battlefield Historical and Museum Association], 1992), 66-74. The concept of thoroughness in burial and exhumation is given new meaning, however, by Douglas D. Scott et al. in *Archaeological Perspectives on the Battle of the Little Bighorn* (Norman: University of Oklahoma Press, 1989), 243-82.

19. St. Paul and Minneapolis *Pioneer Press*, August 4, 1877; Cheyenne *Daily Leader*, August 4, 1877; Minnie Dubbs Millbrook, "A Monument to Custer," *Montana The Magazine of Western History*, 24 (Spring 1974), 24-25. Hardorff provides an overview of the specific officer disinterments, transfers, and reburials in *The Custer Battle Casualties*, 37-42.

20. Hedren, *Fort Laramie in 1876*, 111-12, 166; "Lieutenant-General Sheridan's Report of a Reconnaissance of the Bighorn Mountains and the Valleys of the Bighorn and Yellowstone under His Personal Supervision during the Month of July, 1877," in *Reports of Inspection Made in the Summer of 1877 by Generals P. H. Sheridan and W. T. Sherman of Country North of the Union Pacific Railroad* (Washington, D.C.: Government Printing Office, 1878), 10.

21. John G. Bourke diary, July 21, 1877.

22. Sheridan to Sherman, April 8, 1878, G. W. Forsyth to Sheridan, April 8, 1878, microfilm reel 9, Sheridan Papers; Paul L. Hedren, ed., "Eben Swift's Army Service on the Plains, 1876–1879," *Annals of Wyoming*, 50 (Spring 1978), 148.

23. Sheridan to Sherman, April 8, 1878, microfilm reel 9, Sheridan Papers.

24. *Reports of Inspection Made in the Summer of 1877*, 5. Sheridan's role as an agent of western expansion is thoughtfully explored by Hutton in *Phil Sheridan and His Army*, 302-30; and Paul Andrew Hutton, "Phil

Sheridan's Frontier," *Montana The Magazine of Western History,* 38 (Winter 1988), 17-31.

25. Holt, *American Military Cemeteries,* 2-3; Karl Decker and Angus McSween, *Historic Arlington* (Washington, D.C.: Decker and McSween Publishing Company, 1892), 68-71.

26. "Report of Col. O. M. Poe," in *Reports of Inspection Made in the Summer of 1877,* 64-65; Sherman to McCrary, July 25, 1877, in ibid., 29.

27. On photographer John Fouch, see James S. Brust, "John H. Fouch, First Photographer at Fort Keogh," *Montana The Magazine of Western History,* 44 (Spring 1994), 7. Regarding bones on the Little Bighorn battlefield, see Thomas B. Marquis, *Memoirs of a White Crow Indian (Thomas H. Leforge)* (New York: Century Co., 1928), 311-12; A. F. Mulford, *Fighting Indians in the 7th United States Cavalry* (Corning, N.Y.: Paul Lindsley Mulford [1878]), 148-49; Hardorff, *The Custer Battlefield Casualties,* 65-67; and John S. Gray, "Nightmares to Daydreams," *By Valor and Arms,* 1 (Summer 1975), 36-37. Hardorff makes a compelling case that Mulford's description was pirated from a New York *Sun* article appearing July 25, 1877, but the young trooper did visit the field and was capable of the observation.

28. Sheridan to Sherman, April 8, 1878, microfilm reel 9, Sheridan Papers; Edna LaMoore Waldo, trans., "Deadwood to the Big Horns, 1877: A Diary Kept in German by the Late Herman Bischoff of Deadwood, South Dakota in 1877," *Annals of Wyoming,* 9 (April 1933–January 1935), 27; William A. Allen, *Adventures with Indians and Game, or Twenty Years in the Rocky Mountains* (Chicago: A. W. Bowen and Co., 1903), 68, 71.

29. Rawolle to Keeper Stage Station, Rock Creek Line, Custer's Battlefield, Fort Custer Letters Sent, August 30, 1878, LBNM; name and date corrected by Fort Custer Post Return, August 1878, microcopy 617, roll 277, NA. See also Billings *Gazette,* March 23, 1994.

30. Assistant Adjutant General, Department of Dakota, to Buell, October 29, 1878, LBNM; Fort Custer Post Return, April 1879, NA; Gray, "Nightmares to Daydreams," 37.

31. Sanderson to Post Adjutant, Fort Custer, April 7, 1879, LBNM.

32. J. W. Vaughn, *The Reynolds Campaign on Powder River* (Norman: University of Oklahoma Press, 1961), 166-90; Hedren, *Fort Laramie in 1876,* 80-82, 216-17; Zenobia Self, "Court-Martial of J. J. Reynolds," *Military Affairs,* 37 (April 1973), 52-56.

33. Leckie, *Elizabeth Bacon Custer,* 221-22; Robert M. Utley, *Custer and the Great Controversy: The Origin and Development of a Legend* (Pasadena, Calif.: Westernlore Press, 1980), 53-57.

34. Utley, *Custer and the Great Controversy*, 57-60; Ronald H. Nichols, ed., *Reno Court of Inquiry: Proceedings of a Court of Inquiry in the Case of Major Marcus A. Reno* (Crow Agency, Mont.: Custer Battlefield Historical and Museum Association, [1992]), reproducing the official transcript. The quote appears on 611.

35. Nichols, ed., *Reno Court of Inquiry*, 624, 629; General Orders No. 17, Headquarters of the Army, Adjutant General's Office, March 11, 1879, RG 393, NA.

36. Meigs to McCrary, October 16, 1878, LBNM; Don Rickey, Jr., *History of Custer Battlefield* ([Crow Agency, Mont.]: Custer Battlefield Historical and Museum Association, 1967), 29, 60-61. As with creation of the national cemetery, the monumenting of the Little Bighorn battlefield was in keeping with contemporary actions on many Civil War battlefields, where memorials recalled and affirmed the tragedies and sacrifices of war. See Richard West Sellars, "Vigil of Silence: The Civil War Memorials," *History News*, (July–August 1986), 19-21.

37. Marquis, *Memoirs of a White Crow Indian*, 311; Paul C. Phillips, ed., *Forty Years on the Frontier as Seen in the Journals and Reminiscences of Granville Stuart* (Glendale, Calif.: Arthur H. Clark Company, 1957), 120-21.

38. Roe to Assistant Adjutant General, Department of Dakota, August 6, 1881, LBNM; Rickey, *History of Custer Battlefield*, 60-63.

39. Roe to Assistant Adjutant General, August 6, 1881, LBNM; "Custer Battlefield Monument," *Army and Navy Journal*, September 17, 1881; Kenneth Hammer, ed., *Custer in '76: Walter Camp's Notes on the Custer Fight* (Provo: Brigham Young University Press, 1976), 250; Scott et al., *Archaeological Perspectives on the Battle of the Little Bighorn*, 281-82.

40. Paul L. Hedren, "Sitting Bull's Surrender at Fort Buford: An Episode in American History," *North Dakota History*, 62 (Fall 1995), 2-15.

41. On the larger role of the army in the settlement of the American West, see for example, Hutton, *Phil Sheridan and His Army*; Robert G. Athearn, *William Tecumseh Sherman and the Settlement of the West* (Norman: University of Oklahoma Press, 1956); and Robert Wooster, *The Military and United States Indian Policy, 1865–1903* (New Haven: Yale University Press, 1988).

PART III
The Myth

Custer at Aldie, *by Alfred R. Waud, from Frederick Whittaker,*
A Complete Life of Gen. George A. Custer *(New York: Sheldon
and Co., 1876) (Courtesy Brian W. Dippie)*

"What Valor Is"

Artists and the Mythic Moment

Brian W. Dippie

Elizabeth B. Custer, widowed at thirty-four, could never bring herself to directly contemplate the general's final moments. She twice tried to view John Mulvany's gargantuan painting *Custer's Last Rally* (1881, fig. 27) when it was exhibited in Chicago in 1882, but her head spun and she grew faint, so vivid was the impression it created.[1] William F. "Buffalo Bill" Cody requested her presence at a reenactment of the Last Stand in 1886, and, on stationery bordered in black, she refused, explaining, "I cannot even think of what you suggest to me with calmness. . . . Though I am physically well my nerves have been so shattered by the tragedy of my sad life I cannot endure a tax upon them. . . . I beg you to believe that to do anything for so loyal a friend of General Custer would be a great pleasure to me and I regret my inability."[2] Even *"Boots and Saddles"* (1885), her reminiscence of "life in Dakota with General Custer," stopped short of recounting his death on the Little Bighorn ("God knows even those few last pages were written in blood").[3] But though she might not address Custer's Last Stand herself, Elizabeth Custer never doubted for a moment what it represented.

In 1888 a Boston company approached her with plans to paint and exhibit a fifty-by-four-hundred-foot cyclorama (a circular panorama) called *Battle of the Little Big Horn*. Her cooperation in such matters was deemed essential, but she was too busy at the time to help and the project moved ahead without her. The Cyclorama's manager and chief artist visited the Custer battlefield that summer and acquired battle relics, Crow and Sioux artifacts, and photographic portraits of the leading participants from David F. Barry. The gigantic painting was finished by the end of the year, and Mrs. Custer was now invited to contribute a short account of the general's last battle to the exhibition program. She refused the request, as always, but asked Captain Edward S. Godfrey to contribute in her stead, noting that there was a particular urgency to comply. The proprietors of the Cyclorama had already received letters from Major Marcus Reno and Captain Frederick Benteen and were "shrewd enough" to recognize "that an account from two enemies of General Custer (still bitter and untruthful) would not be exactly the thing to insert in a book describing a fight which, though unfortunate in its ending, left an undying proof of what valor is."[4]

Elizabeth Custer was unable to visit the Cyclorama—"I cannot summon the courage"—but she knew what it honored and, because of the work of artists, we can *see* what she meant.[5] We can conjure up the image of a man at bay, standing erect in his buckskins, the center of a whirling vortex of charging Indians and fallen soldiers, fearless and proud as he defies death itself. The artists *created* this image—indeed, it is fair to say that they created Custer's Last Stand. They gave it instantly recognizable form and planted it in our heads. How it came about was left to others. What matters is that fixed image of doomed heroism, that "undying proof of what valor is."[6]

Newspapers fought over its implications. They found in Custer's Last Stand betrayal, cowardice, impetuosity, disobedience, and heroic self-sacrifice—controversy galore. Poets found a higher lesson in defeat, and told the world of courage that transcended controversy. "Thou of the sunny, flowing hair, in battle," Walt Whitman intoned,

> I erewhile saw, with erect head, pressing ever in front,
>   bearing a bright sword in thy hand,
> Now ending well the splendid fever of thy deeds,
> (I bring no dirge for it or thee—I bring a glad, triumphal
>   sonnet;)

> There in the far northwest, in struggle, charge, and saber-
> smite,
> Desperate and glorious—aye, in defeat most desperate,
> most glorious,
> After thy many battles, in which, never yielding up a gun
> or a color,
> Leaving behind thee a memory sweet to soldiers,
> Thou yieldest up thyself.[7]

Writers have woven Custer and the Last Stand into a couple of hundred different novels and stories, if only a handful of plots, and moviemakers have doted on Custer's stirring grand finale since the earliest days of Hollywood.[8]

Even sole survivors, those ubiquitous poseurs who entertained the public with their improbable tales through the 1930s, incorporated the geography of one famous Last Stand painting into the landscapes of their personal adventures. Not surprisingly, it was the Anheuser-Busch advertising print, *Custer's Last Fight* (1896, fig. 30), that figured so prominently in their accounts. Willard J. Carlyle, for example, told the story several times of how, as a sixteen-year-old Montana Ranger, he was wounded in the mouth, captured by the Sioux, and held prisoner in the camp on the Little Bighorn when Custer attacked. Usually he told journalists that he was closely guarded but able to catch "occasional glimpses" of the battle.[9] Custer was the last to fall, and when Carlyle inspected his body a few minutes later, still gripped his sword in one hand and his pistol in the other. In a letter to Mrs. Custer in 1926, Carlyle expanded his claims. Now he was in "full sight . . . [of] the terrible battle":

> Those of the red-skins who had lost their horses, closed in on foot and slowly but surely they picked off the white men, one by one, until at last only the brave General Custer was left with his comrades dead around him.
> One sweep of his saber and an Indians head was split in two, one flash of his revolver, his last shot, and a red-skin got the bullet between the eyes, then he fell with a bullet in the breast, the last of that brave band.[10]

Carlyle supposedly saw all this from a nearby hill; we can safely assume he actually saw it over a few Buds at a nearby bar.

"Silent Smith," the most garrulous old-timer Stuart Holbrook ever met, did not spectate from a safe distance. He survived the Last Stand by lying under a horse for "two whole days" and was armed with official documents, medals and thirty-eight guns to prove his story. Pressed for details by Holbrook during an interview over beers, Smith rose, marched briskly up to a copy of the Anheuser-Busch print on the saloon wall, and with his cane indicated a dead horse in the foreground: "I was right there— right there under *that* hoss."[11]

But no sole survivor was more explicit than Ben McIntosh, a slick con man who in the years 1914–1919 masqueraded as Curley (p. 75), Custer's genuine Crow Indian scout. (It is testament to the intricate interplay between fact and fiction in the Custer myth that the real Curley played himself in a reenactment of Custer's Last Battle staged by the Great Rocky Mountain Show in Milwaukee on July 4, 1884, just eight years after the actual battle was fought. Reporters found the reenactment "very exciting," noting that a crowd of thousands "warmly applauded" Curley's escape from the field where "the yellow-haired chief met his doom."[12])

Popular legend had Curley fleeing for his life draped in a Sioux blanket; Ben McIntosh embroidered it. In one version, he fought back-to-back with Custer at the Last Stand as the Sioux and Cheyennes closed in, making good his escape only after the general refused the offer of the blanket for himself.[13] Better was the version McIntosh came up with in Chicago in January 1914. Having dined with Rain in the Face in the Sioux camp the night before the battle, he was late arriving at the Last Stand, he told a reporter, but was in time for the final charge immortalized in the print of *Custer's Last Fight*. It featured a prominent Indian "pushing his way toward Custer as he falls." "Well," McIntosh declared dramatically, "I am that Indian. I reached Custer's side and held his head as he fell back dead"—shot through the heart, his saber still in hand, just as the picture showed it. Not that the Budweiser print was *entirely* accurate. "There was no scalping and no mutilation," McIntosh insisted, and the artist was wrong in portraying it. "Four hundred and seventy-three officers and soldiers were killed but not a mark was found on them except those made by bullets."[14] It took some gall to criticize mistakes in an entirely imaginary work of art introduced to support your own prevarications. But sole survivors commonly established their veracity by challenging another's. And McIntosh's criticism of *Custer's Last Fight* does nicely illustrate the artists' achievement in creating a reality of their own.

Poseurs aside, the fact that there were no survivors of Custer's Last Stand freed up the artists. They could draw on their imaginations: Who *knew* for sure what the Last Stand looked like? The Indians, of course. They were the victors, after all, and left vivid pictographic records honoring their individual feats.[15] But Custer's Last Stand is a white mythic construct, responsive to white American concerns. Thus the first artists to depict the battle offered personal interpretations of a cultural ideal—self-sacrificing heroism—and artists ever since have been at liberty to "see" Custer's Last Stand as they choose. Some have imposed factual constraints on themselves—topographical accuracy, fidelity to dress, weaponry, and the like. Some have ventured beyond visual realism to psychological realism, capturing the horror of the end as morale collapses, despair sets in, and hopelessness haunts the faces of the doomed soldiers. Eric von Schmidt's fascinating *Here Fell Custer* (1976, fig. 11) is a case in point.[16] But most artists have been faithful to the higher truth of heroism on the grand scale perfectly expressed by Eric's father Harold von Schmidt in his painting *Custer's Last Stand* (fig. 12), reproduced in *Esquire* magazine in 1950. "Three-quarters of a century after his death on a stark bitter hill in Montana the Custer legend stands invincible, immutable," the accompanying text noted. "Seven decades of critical attack has failed to dent it. Custer's Last Stand is a hallowed immortality."[17] And so the myth.

The first portrayal of Custer's Last Stand appeared in the New York *Daily Graphic* on July 19, two weeks after receipt of the news of disaster out west. William M. Cary's *The Battle on the Little Big Horn River—The Death Struggle of General Custer* (fig. 13) showed unflinching courage in the face of overwhelming odds—white civilization surrounded, indeed stormed, by red savagery. The Indians will kill that man standing there at the center of the storm, but his spirit is indomitable. What he stands for, literally and figuratively, must, as Walt Whitman argued, "triumph" in the end. There seems an aura of inevitability about it all. Could artists have shown Custer's defeat in any other way?

In fact, the artists fumbled around in 1876. Criticism of Custer abounded at the time. Certain high officials called him vainglorious and rash. Dark accusations circulated that he had recklessly thrown away the lives of his entire command to salve a wounded ego and redeem his own tarnished reputation. Political controversy swirled around his defeat in a presidential election year. In 1876, it was *not* at all inevitable that Custer would be made a hero.[18] In his poem published on July 10 Whitman had written:

> Continues yet the old, old legend of our race!
> The loftiest of life upheld by death!
> The ancient banner perfectly maintained!
> (O lesson opportune—O how I welcome thee!)[19]

Three days later, and almost a week before Cary's representation of the Last Stand, the very first depiction of Custer's death appeared in the *Illustrated Police News.* Titled *The Indian War—Death of General George A. Custer at the Battle of the Little Big Horn River, Montana Territory, June 25* (fig. 14), it showed Custer among the first to fall. Where was the "lesson opportune" in that? It would never do.

Other artists thought in terms of a last charge. J. O. Davidson provided a cover drawing for the New York *Illustrated Weekly* that August showing Custer in his buckskins, a solid wall of soldiers riding behind him, waving his hat as he gallops over a dead Indian. This confuses the narrative line: Who is winning—and who is losing? A poem by Edgar Fawcett shared space with Davidson's drawing and struck the appropriate note:

> So from thy sorrowing country thou shalt win
> Rank beside all her loyalest and her best,
> Thou new Leonidas, with thy noble kin,
> Slain in that wild Thermopylae of the West![20]

But Davidson's illustration in and of itself failed to convey the mythic essence of doomed finality. Last charges lack the Last Stand's visceral appeal. How do we even know they are *last* charges? An illustration by Alfred R. Waud of *Custer at Aldie* (1876, p. 208) equates with another by an artist named Kelly of *Custer's Last Charge* (1878, fig. 15). There is nothing to choose between them. Waud illustrated a legendary event in Custer's Civil War career; Kelly, a poem by Captain Jack Crawford—and only Crawford's verse gave point to Kelly's image:

> Charge, comrades, charge! see young Custer ahead!
> His charger leaps forth, almost flying;
> One volley! and half of his comrades are dead—
> The other half fighting and dying![21]

No ambiguity clouds a Custer's Last Stand. The visuals express, unequivocally, Whitman's "lesson opportune." Dismounted cavalrymen, their horses dead around them. Flight cut off, escape impossible. Grounded and doomed. How the soldiers face certain death—bravely, carelessly, defiantly—is what matters: "Desperate and glorious—aye, in defeat most desperate, most glorious." Custer must literally *stand* and meet his fate head on, proving worthy of the mythic end that life had scripted for him. Heroism is palpable in J. Steeple Davis's *Custer's Last Fight* (1897, fig. 16), O. Reich's *Custer's Last Stand and Death* (1898), an anonymous artist's *Custer's Last Rally on the Little Big Horn* (1900, fig. 1), and almost every Last Stand since.

William Cary had set the standard in July 1876; Alfred Waud perfected it that fall. His *Custer's Last Fight* (fig. 17), like his *Custer at Aldie*, illustrated Frederick Whittaker's fulsome instant biography *A Complete Life of Gen. George A. Custer* and served as a visual equivalent to Whittaker's breathless prose. "Truth and sincerity, honor and bravery, tenderness and sympathy, unassuming piety and temperance, were the mainsprings of Custer, the man," Whittaker wrote. "As a soldier there is no spot on his armor, as a man no taint on his honor."[22] Waud, who knew the difference between a last charge and a last stand, showed Custer in just this way at the end—cool, amidst a raging chaos, sturdy and unmovable, his head the apex of a triangle, his men its slopes, his light-colored buckskin suit set off by their dark uniforms, in all, the epitome of perfect heroism, of "grace under pressure." That central triangle has an elemental appeal, at once simple and powerful, and Waud's influence is everywhere in Last Stand art. His Custer, for example, reappeared early, in an 1878 lithograph by Henry Steinegger notable for offering two Custers for the price of one. Titled *General Custer's Death Struggle. The Battle of the Little Big Horn* (fig. 18), it featured *both* Cary's uniformed general and Waud's buckskin-clad hero.

Thus was Custer's Last Stand conceived by William Cary and Alfred Waud in the very year Custer died. In time it became the defining event of America's Indian wars. The ironies are immense. Custer's Last Stand was a victory for the Sioux and their allies that hurried their defeat. It was a defeat for Anglo-Americans that ensured their more rapid victory. And it was, in its own time, understood as a *moral* victory, proving the superiority of white civilization over red savagery. Once established, the Last Stand was perpetuated through repetition. Its imagery is incestuous. The same basic elements reappear in picture after picture, repeated, recycled, and renewed. Eventually the core image of Custer's Last Stand was entrenched in the American mind. We can understand the process by turning again to Cary and Waud.

William Cary did a second Last Stand in 1884 that was published as *Battle of the Big Horn.—Death of Custer* (fig. 19). The most obvious change would seem to be its vertical format, although Cary's original sketch (fig. 20) was actually horizontal, as before. The page design of the school reader in which it appeared dictated the vertical design. Spin-offs have restored its horizontal composition: Kurz and Allison's 1889 lithograph *Battle of the Big Horn*, for example, and a poster for the "Greatest Motion Picture Ever Conceived or Constructed," that 1909 epic of "Massacre and Mutilation," *Custer's Last Stand* (fig. 2).

Waud, in turn, revisited the Little Bighorn in an 1892 illustration titled *Custer's Last Stand* (fig. 21). The pyramidical arrangement of figures survived the intervening years, but Waud's new version was genuinely vertical in composition. The viewer is placed at Custer's feet, gazing up at the hero. He towers over us. The very perspective is mythic. A source, interestingly, would seem to be a generic *Last Stand* (fig. 22) painted by Frederic Remington in 1890 and published as a double-page spread in *Harper's Weekly* on

January 10, 1891. Waud's adaptation of Remington completes a circle that confirms the incestuous nature of Last Stand art. In a drawing made about 1877 at the impressionable age of fifteen, Remington had relied on Waud's 1876 illustration to create his own *Custer's Last Fight* (fig. 23); in his reprise of the subject sixteen years later, Waud relied on a Remington painting that remained indebted to the first Waud version. And Waud's original pyramid of troopers with Custer at its center is still visible in another Remington, *Custer's Last Fight* (fig. 24), published in 1903. Thus image feeds on image.

The movies are a case in point. Hollywood has borrowed from Waud's 1876 *Custer's Last Fight* time and again for the Last Stand scenes in films that are favorable to Custer (*The Scarlet West*, 1925, fig. 25) as well as those that are not (*Sitting Bull*, 1954), suggesting the adaptability of the core image to any narrative end. In *Little Big Man* (1970, p. 260), for example, Custer is a raving lunatic at the end—the quintessential Vietnam-era military madman striking poses out of Waud and others in parody of the heroic conventions of the Last Stand myth. As an artistic construct Custer's Last Stand is inherently cinematic. Artists have provided everything from establishing shots (Gayle P. Hoskins's *Custer's Last Fight*, 1953) to close-ups (the Kinneys' *The Last Stand*, 1914), and the movies, of course, have done the same. The climactic sequence in *They Died with Their Boots On* (1941, fig. 37) mixes overhead shots with close-ups of Errol Flynn's Custer. The camera does the work of the eye, always seeking out and isolating that figure at the center of things who makes the action visually and emotionally coherent—not just another Indian battle, but *Custer's* Last Stand.

Well before the invention of moving pictures, showmen set the static image of Custer's Last Stand into motion. In 1886, to mark the tenth anniversary of the Battle of the Little Bighorn, and to capitalize on his own involvement in the Great Sioux War as well as the recent success of Elizabeth Custer's reminiscence *"Boots and Saddles,"* Buffalo Bill Cody decided to reenact the Last Stand. On August 13 he wrote Mrs. Custer noting that he would stage the reenactment that winter and "shall spare no expense to do credit to our exhibition and deepen the lustre of your glorious husband's reputation as a soldier and a man. May I hope that you will give your sanction to the plan and by your presence endorse my effort to perpetuate his memory."[23] As we have seen, Mrs. Custer turned Cody down, but perhaps she relented. That November, the Wild West moved into Madison Square Garden for the winter season, staging *The Drama of Civilization*, a "motion-spectacle, or dramatic pageant, of American pioneer life." The director's son recalled watching "the gigantic scenic preparations and the early rehearsals, at which the widow of General Custer herself was present in conference with my father, while he directed the tragic mock-fight with the Indians, in which long-haired 'Buck Taylor,' as Custer, was the last to fall among the dead."[24] "The Last Charge of Custer" was not included in the opening performance of *The Drama of Civilization* on November 27 but was introduced within a week and proved popular enough to be repeated in Manchester in 1887–1888 and Glasgow in 1891–1892. The Custer battle was added to the Wild West itself midway through the 1893 season.[25] "Not a single white man was left to tell the tale of this terrible conflict, the most dreadful in all the annals of savage warfare," a program sold at the show in 1898 explained,

> and it heroically demonstrated the fact that, even when certain death called for the performance of duty, the American soldier could eclipse the charge of the Six Hundred at Balaklava, and rival the patriotic sacrifice of the Greeks under Leonidas at Thermopylae. . . . It is a reproduction which wounds and death alone could emphasize. . . . Words can no more do it justice than they could enhance the noble character and sacrifice of those whose memory it perpetuates; erecting to them, as it were, a daily monument, in addition to the storm-beaten one, marking the spot where the American Murat fell, face to the foe.[26]

Although the actual reenactment was essentially a last charge, as a photograph (fig. 26) of a performance in Brooklyn in 1894 confirms, the Wild West's posters nevertheless borrowed from other artists to nail down the Last Stand imagery.

A 1904 poster, *Custer's Last Stand as Presented by Buffalo Bill's Wild West* (fig. 3), is loosely based on the gargantuan 1881 painting by John Mulvany, *Custer's Last Rally* (fig. 27). At eleven by twenty feet it overwhelmed Walt Whitman when he saw it in New York. Here was the "lesson opportune" writ large! "Nothing in the books like it," Whitman enthused, "nothing in Homer, nothing in Shakespeare; more grim and sublime than either, all native, all our own, and all a fact."[27] Equally interesting is an earlier Buffalo Bill poster (fig. 4) issued around 1896. It uses Mulvany's title, *Custer's Last Rally*, but borrows freely from a different work, the most famous Last Stand of them all, beloved of Willard Carlyle, Silent Smith, Ben McIntosh/Curley/Hicks, and generations of beer-drinkers, the Anheuser-Busch lithograph *Custer's Last Fight* (fig. 30).

Custer's Last Fight reached back a decade to a huge oil of the same title by a relatively obscure St. Louis artist, Cassilly Adams. At nine and a half by sixteen and a half feet, independent of two end panels that accompanied it, Adams's *Custer's Last Fight* (fig. 28) easily rivaled Mulvany's *Custer's Last Rally* in size; indeed, publicity claimed that the total work was thirty-two feet long.[28] Adams was not the artist Mulvany was. His figures were awkward and stiff, his background dull. Still, the end panels were an arresting touch: one (fig. 29) showed George Custer as a child playing soldier, the other (fig. 5), dead in his buckskins on the field of battle, the sun setting behind him.[29] Readers of Cormac McCarthy's contemporary classic *Blood Meridian; or the Evening Redness in the West* (1985) will find much to ponder in the second image. But it is this secular triptych's centerpiece that draws the eye, and its central grouping that commands attention. For at almost the exact center of the composition is Custer lunging at an Indian with his saber, his empty pistol clubbed in his left hand, still fiercely resisting the inevitable as the savage hordes close in upon him. Others did better paintings than Cassilly Adams, but no one better captured the Last Stand's heroic essence. His *Custer's Last Fight*, substantially reworked by a Milwaukee lithographer named Otto Becker, was the prototype for an American icon.[30]

Since it was first distributed by the Anheuser-Busch Brewing Association in 1896, Becker's *Custer's Last Fight* has been continually reprinted, reinterpreted, and revered in nostalgic recollection. John Erlichman, one of Richard Nixon's White House advisers, recalled the pleasure he took in studying Frederic Remington's oil *The Charge of the Rough Riders* (1899) whenever meetings in the Roosevelt Room dragged and his mind wandered, but it was, he said, no match for *Custer's Last Fight*:

> When I was three years old, my mother used to take me to a barber shop run by a Mr. Sapp. He had placed the huge Anheuser-Busch print of *Custer's Last Fight* where I could raptly study it as he cut my hair. Cavalrymen and Sioux were locked in bloody hand-to-hand combat all over the barber shop, it seemed, and I could hardly wait to go back to Mr. Sapp's to see more of the battle of Little Big Horn. Remington's *Rough Riders* is less interesting.[31]

Who could resist a barber with a sense of humor?

Anheuser-Busch's *Custer's Last Fight* has a noble pedigree: by Becker out of Adams, with a weather eye to Zulu War exoticism (the crushing defeat of British forces at Isandhlwana in 1879, fig. 31) and a concern for topographical accuracy that elevates its weirdness to sheer perfection.[32] Becker also drew on a Gustave Doré illustration (fig. 32) for *Dante's Inferno* for the artistic and symbolic flourish in the lower right corner of *Custer's Last Fight*, the naked soldiers writhing in their death agonies.[33] It is a flourish that makes no sense in terms of the picture's narrative (Who on earth undressed these men?), but good sense as a tribute to Becker's countryman (Becker emigrated from Germany at nineteen) and as a symbolic comment on the earthly inferno that was the Little Bighorn. Becker cribbed from that giant of western illustration, Frederic Remington, for another compelling note—the real-looking Indians charging head-on through the smoke and dust towards Custer above the waves of all-purpose savages (with their Zulu cowhide shields, stabbing spears, and knobbed wooden clubs) rushing in from front and side. Reading from left to right, three Remingtons make cameo appearances: *Kiowa Buck Starting a Race* (*Century Magazine*, July 1889, fig. 33), *Unhorsed* (*Century Magazine*, January 1892, fig. 34), and *Indian Horse-Race—Coming over the Scratch* (*Century Magazine*, July 1889, fig. 35).

Evident in Becker's decision to incorporate a factual setting and Remington Indians into *Custer's Last Fight* is a central tenet of historical (and western) art: accuracy of detail—*verisimilitude*—equals *authenticity* or *truth*, no matter how implausible the overall conception. To this day, artists offer up new Custer's Last Stands, each touted as more accurate than its predecessors, and most equally committed to a nineteenth-century concept of doomed heroism. H. Charles McBarron's *Custer's Last Stand—1876* (1962, fig. 6), Joe Grandee's *A Day of Legend—When Courage and Destiny Meet* (1982), Mort Kunstler's *Custer's Last Stand* (ca. 1986), Michael Gentry's *Long Hair's Last Sun* (1992), and Michael Schreck's *Command Hill* (1993, fig. 7) come to mind.[34]

This quest for historical accuracy is an old game in Custer art, and a revealing one. Both William Cary and Alfred R. Waud in 1876 brought firsthand western experience to their Custer's Last Stands, and Waud had impressive Civil War credentials as well. John Mulvany, Cassilly Adams, and even the proprietors of the 1889 Cyclorama all gathered artifacts and portraits, interviewed participants, and did their bit to assure viewers that what they saw before them was as authentic in its particulars as it was heroic in its overall impression. By Mulvany's own account, he toured the Custer battlefield in 1879, made sketches on the spot, visited the Sioux reservation, studied the dress and equipment of the soldiers, secured portraits of Custer and his officers, and even consulted with officers at Fort Leavenworth as he worked on the painting in his Kansas City studio. "Whenever nature is to be represented it should be nature itself, and not somebody's guess," he explained. "I made myself acquainted with every detail of my work, the gay caparisoning of the Indian ponies, the dress of the Indian chiefs and braves; in fact, everything that could bear upon the work."[35] His contemporaries were persuaded. "The artist has brought to this subject deep and careful study, and it has cost him three years of hard labor," the Louisville *Commercial* reported. "All this has been done with a love of country and a burning desire to portray one of the most illustrious deeds in its history. His genius enables him to bring all into one great picture."[36]

Cassilly Adams, like Mulvany a Civil War veteran ("it is this fact which gives to his work so much of the realism of terrible fighting," Mulvany's publicity noted), painted his *Custer's Last Fight* for two St. Louis businessmen.[37] Following Mulvany's lead they hoped to make money exhibiting the painting in the Midwest. Adams's son recalled his father's working for a year on the oil, with real Sioux Indians in their war paint and cavalrymen in their uniforms posing for him in his studio. As for the Cyclorama, its program noted that it was painted in "the studio of E. Pierpoint of New York":

> Mr. Pierpoint obtained his photographs and sketches on the field, and from survivors of the Reno part, scouts and citizens who were in the fight or on the field directly after, he secured much accurate and important data. Also from the official reports in the War Department at Washington. From various sources, photographs of the officers and men were also collected.[38]

The prize for accuracy, according to its own publicity, however, went to Edgar S. Paxson's six-by-nine-foot *Custer's Last Stand* (1899, fig. 8).[39] "Several other pictures of Custer's Last Battle have been painted," a promotional brochure noted, "but none like this. The others are full of anachronisms and absurdities which show the authors of them were unfamiliar with the details of the subject, and which cannot stand the test of historical criticism. . . . Mr. Paxson's great painting is faithful to history and that is a *sine qua non* in a historical painting. . . . The moral grandeur of the American Thermopylae is at last before us."[40] Paxson's devoted research over (he claimed) twenty years included interviews with the Cheyenne Two Moon, the Sioux Gall, and the Crow Curley, contacts with ninety-six officers and enlisted men associated with the battle, revealing correspondence with Edward S. Godfrey in 1896, and repeated visits to the battlefield.

Paxson spent about four years actually painting *Custer's Last Stand*.[41] He finished in December 1899 and, mindful of precedents and hopeful that the Spanish-American War had roused the country's patriotic ardor, toured his gigantic picture. A Montana poet extended her good wishes:

> Yes, Remington has tried it; Mulvaney, too, as well;
> But none so true has pictured, how gallant Custer fell!
> See, that picture of the Battle and the after awful hush!
> No need is there of asking; for Paxson held the brush.[42]

A friendly critic praised Paxson's artistry: "No one can stand before this picture unmoved. . . . There is so much suggested—the calm bearing in the face of hopeless despair evinced by the true soldier, and the fanatic and triumphant joy of the savage. It is almost a moment of breathless hush on the part of the soldier, as if gathering force for the final blow, while the air is affrighted with the murderous yell of the fierce, overpowering foe."[43]

Paxson did organize some two hundred figures along parallel diagonals, and there is a pyramid buried in the composition. But he stuffed it so full of *things* that it feels claustrophobic: it is as though every curio in his studio collection found its way into the finished work. Despite its capacious size, and the hushed air of expectancy his contemporaries perceived, there is not a breath of air in it. It is the ultimate painting as compendium, and the ultimate example of the documentary fallacy entrenched in Last Stand art. Factual particulars do *not* a larger fact make. Nevertheless, tradition has it that Elizabeth Custer wept upon viewing Paxson's painting.[44] And that was why realism mattered so much in Custer art. It validated the Last Stand's heroic premise. Thus, Mrs. Custer swooned at the sight of Mulvany's *Custer's Last Rally*, and could not "summon the courage" to visit the Cyclorama. *Too real to bear*—that was the intended reaction, and all grist for the publicity mill when these gargantuan paintings went on exhibition before the public for a dime or a half dollar.

Few artists have cared to follow Paxson's lead. The tangled confusion of his *Custer's Last Stand* defies easy imitation, although some have repeated a Paxson figure or pose—and one painter has tackled the tangle itself. Fritz Scholder, an influential native artist with an interest in "Indian kitsch" and an ironic touch in sending up prime specimens, has paid Paxson homage in *The Last Stand* (1976). Heroic-sized itself at five and two-thirds by eight feet, Scholder's painting reduces Paxson's to its basic elements—the anonymous many lost in the purpled shadows of time, and the Boy General, golden in his buckskins, the glowing center of an enduring American myth. Earlier, in 1969, Scholder had taken this mythic distillation a step further. In a spoof of the very first Last Stand, he showed William Cary's heroic Custer posed alone against a field of black, slashed with scarlet. Perfectly titled *Custer*

& 20,000 Indians (fig. 9), it dispensed with the Indians entirely to get at the essence of all the Last Stand paintings.

Custer owes the artists a king's ransom. By making his Last Stand "an undying proof of what valor is," they have made him immortal.

Notes

1.   Lawrence A. Frost, *General Custer's Libbie* (Seattle: Superior Publishing Company, 1976), 256, citing the Detroit *Evening Journal.*

2.   Elizabeth B. Custer to William F. Cody, August 17 [1886], William C. Garlow Collection, Buffalo Bill Historical Center, Cody, Wyoming (hereafter BBHC).

3.   Elizabeth B. Custer to Edward S. Godfrey, December 6 [1885], typescript, Don Russell Collection, BBHC (hereafter Russell Collection).

4.   Elizabeth B. Custer to Godfrey, January 8, 1889, typescript, Russell Collection. Godfrey had only two weeks to prepare a sketch of the battle, but it seems likely he was responsible for the text that appears in the Cyclorama program. Mrs. Custer had been especially agitated by Frederick Benteen's letter to the Cyclorama Company in which, she told Godfrey, he "even accuses those splendid soldiers with my husband of retreating in great disorder." The account actually published in the program was entirely different. Benteen and Marcus Reno were indicted for failing to support Custer's attack, precipitating the Last Stand where fell, "fearless, and fighting to the last, the noble Custer, surrounded by brothers and friends." See A. J. Donnelle, Manager, *Cyclorama of Gen. Custer's Last Fight against Sioux Indians, or the Battle of the Little Big Horn, with Grand Musée of Indian Curios* (Boston: Boston Cyclorama Co., 1889), 8-9, 11. As late as February 19 Mrs. Custer wrote to a Mr. Brown that she was still "preparing material" for the Cyclorama's guidebook. E. L. Reedstrom, "The Red Cravat," *Little Big Horn Associates Newsletter*, 3 (Fall 1969), 17.

5.   Elizabeth B. Custer to Proprietors of the Boston Cyclorama Co., January 25, 1889, in Donnelle, *Cyclorama of Gen. Custer's Last Fight*, 13.

6.   The standard work on Last Stand art is Don Russell, *Custer's Last; or, The Battle of the Little Big Horn in Picturesque Perspective* (Fort Worth: Amon Carter Museum of Western Art, 1968). Russell wrote one of the two pioneering works on Last Stand art, "Sixty Years in Bar Rooms; or 'Custer's Last Fight'," (Chicago) *Westerners Brand Book*, 3 (November 1946), 61-63, 65-68, and thereafter maintained a lively interest in the subject. His article included a preliminary checklist of known Last Stands, subsequently expanded into *Custer's List: A Checklist of Pictures Relating*

to the Battle of the Little Big Horn (Fort Worth: Amon Carter Museum of Western Art, 1969), and supplemented by "Custer's List—Continued," *Garry Owen 1976: Annual of the Little Big Horn Associates,* ed. Paul A. Hutton (Seattle: Little Big Horn Associates, 1977), 196-215. Also see Russell's "What really happened at Custer's Last Stand?" *ARTnews,* 77 (December 1978), 63-65, 68, 70. Interest in the Last Stand art, like the art itself, continues to thrive. See, for example, Judy Henry, "A Centennial Commemoration of the Custer Battle," *Southwest Art,* 5 (May 1976), 70-81; James S. Hutchins, "Still Dodging Arrows," *Gateway Heritage,* 1 (Winter 1980), 18-29; Christopher M. Summitt, "Apologia Pro 'Custer's Last Stand,'" *Greasy Grass,* 5 (May 1989), 20-29; and Gregory Lalire, "Custer's Art Stand," *Wild West,* 6 (April 1994), 54-62, 94.

7.   Walt Whitman, "A Death-Sonnet for Custer," New York *Tribune,* July 10, 1876; reprinted with many other Custer poems in Brian W. Dippie, comp. (in collaboration with John M. Carroll), *Bards of the Little Big Horn* (Bryan, Texas: Guidon Press, 1978), 23. Whitman's poem is better known under its later title, "From Far Dakota's Cañons."

8.   For bibliographies of Custer in fiction, see Brian W. Dippie, *Custer's Last Stand: The Anatomy of an American Myth* (1976; reprint, University of Nebraska Press, 1994), 193-201, supplemented by Dippie and Paul Andrew Hutton, "Custer in Pop Culture, An Update," in *Custer and His Times: Book Three,* ed. Gregory J. W. Urwin and Roberta E. Fagan (Conway: University of Central Arkansas Press and Little Big Horn Associates, 1987), 261-71, which includes a listing of comic book stories supplementing, in turn, Brian W. Dippie and Paul Andrew Hutton, *The Comic Book Custer: A Bibliography of Custeriana in Comic Books and Comic Strips,* pub. no. 4 (Bryan, Texas: Brazos Corral of the Westerners, [1983]). The literature on Custer in the movies is now substantial; for a comprehensive, up-to-date treatment see Hutton's essay in this volume.

9.   "Eyewitness of Custer Massacre Questions All Previous Accounts," Boston *Sunday Post,* August 6, 1922; "Indian Fighter, Last to See Gen. Custer Alive, Found on Boulevard/Was Prisoner of Sitting Bull; Saw Custer Die," Lynn, Massachusetts, *Daily Evening Item,* May 6, 1924.

10.   Willard J. Carlyle to Elizabeth B. Custer, July 4, 1926, in William A. Graham, comp., *The Custer Myth: A Source Book of Custeriana* (Harrisburg, Pa.: Stackpole Company, 1953), 355.

11.   Stewart H. Holbrook, "Phonies of the Old West," *American Mercury,* 68 (February 1949), 235.

12.   Milwaukee *Sentinel,* July 5, 1884; Milwaukee *Journal,* July 5, 1884. The Great Rocky Mountain Show, composed of cowboys and Indians from Montana, played in Janesville, Wisconsin, on July 3 with Curley identified as "the scout and the only survivor of the Custer massacre."

Janesville *Gazette*, July 2, 1884. It performed in Milwaukee twice daily, July 4–6 (Milwaukee *Sentinel*, July 4, 1884), and went bust shortly after. The Livingston, Montana, *Daily Enterprise* on August 8, 1884, reported the return of the Crow Indian contingent to their reservation, thus terminating Curley's fascinating entry into show business. I am indebted to Professor James D. McLaird, Dakota Wesleyan University, Mitchell, South Dakota, for these references.

13. Ken Canfield, "How Curley Conned Topeka," *Hoofprints*, 6 (Spring–Summer 1976), 18-19, utilizing accounts from the Topeka *Daily Capital*, 1916.

14. The New York *Sun*, January 18, 1914, reported William E. Morris's reactions to McIntosh, who in effect had assumed the real Curley's identity. In the 1916 version of his story, McIntosh was the son of a Scotch-Irish Canadian father and a Crow Indian mother, raised by Cheyennes and four other tribes over an eighteen-year period, and was also known by the name of Bloody Knife. In the 1914 version, he was the son of a Scotsman and was kidnapped as an infant by Comanches, Kiowas, and Apaches who raised him until he was twenty-four. McIntosh loved aliases. When he reemerged with an entirely new story in the 1920s, he was now the son of a Scotsman and the sister of Chief Gall and had been known as "Bat" and "Little Bat" since he was kidnapped at the age of five and raised by the Comanches. By the time he returned home at seventeen he was fluent in thirty-six Indian languages. McIntosh no longer claimed to be a participant in the Custer battle but "only a spectator," and he vigorously denounced the supposed survivors as imposters. "Several," he said, "are serving time at Leavenworth now for that very thing"—a coy reference to the year and a day he actually spent in Leavenworth in 1916–1917 as a convicted swindler. Butte *Daily Post*, March 24, 1921.

McIntosh's final transmogrification appears to have taken place later that same decade when he became Colonel Washosa (Braveman) Hicks, known to the Indians as Wasose or Chief Brave Man, and to whites as Buffalo Bill Cody's first "Captain Jack," an expert pistol shot trained by Wild Bill Hickok himself, and later as Captain W. B. (Curley) Hicks, renowned Indian scout. He was born W. B. McAlpin, the son of a Scotch-Irish man (sometimes identified as a Philadelphia millionaire) and Quanah Parker's sister (or was it Quanah Parker and Cynthia Ann Parker's daughter?—he could not decide, though this arrangement would certainly raise a few eyebrows!), and married Nanetah (or Qualatah), Geronimo's daughter, after she rescued him from being burned at the stake. Ernestine Breisch, "Death of Custer Described by Indian Scout Now Living at National Military Home," Dayton, Ohio, *Journal*, February 17, 1929, along with a note in Hicks's hand, container 23, folder 15, William J. Ghent Papers, Library of Congress, Washington, D.C. Hicks got lots of attention in the press. In some accounts he was Custer's last messenger, just fifty paces from the general when he was mortally wounded and able to escape death himself by using two Indian bodies as shields while he rode through the enemy lines. See "Indian Scout Claims Close Association with Custer," unidentified clipping [ca. 1930]; also "Days of Wild West Are Recounted by Scout, Who Saw Gen. Custer Killed," Dayton, Ohio, *Daily News* [ca. February 1929]. (Hicks now denounced the Budweiser print as inauthentic for showing Custer with a sword in his hand when he carried only a pistol at the end and admitted to serving three years at Leavenworth for killing six Mexicans in a fight); and Amy Porter, "Captain Hicks Has Been Busy 88 Years," unidentified clipping [Cincinnati, ca. February 1929], in E. A. Brininstool, comp., "Liars, Fakers and Alleged 'Sole Survivors' of the Battle of the Little Big Horn June 25–26, 1876," scrapbook (1933), Gilcrease Museum, Tulsa, Oklahoma. Also see Bruce A. Rosenberg, *Custer and the Epic of Defeat* (University Park: Pennsylvania State University Press, 1974), 75. I give so much detail because I believe that outrageous liars like Carlyle and "Silent Smith" and Curley/McAlpine/Hicks are neglected heroes of Custer's Last Stand—the myth, that is. Like the artists who gave it form, they helped keep it alive in the popular press through a cross-fertilization with the dime novels, the Wild West shows, and the earliest movies. In their own way they inspired an earlier generation of Custer scholars (just as films and paintings and other aspects of popular culture have inspired a later generation) to seek the truth behind the fiction.

15. See Leslie Tillett, ed., *Wind on the Buffalo Grass: The Indians' Own Account of the Battle at the Little Big Horn River, and the Death of Their Life on the Plains* (New York: Thomas Y. Crowell Company, 1976), for its examples of native art on the Custer theme, not for its text.

16. See Eric von Schmidt, "Custer, Dying Again at that Last Stand, is in a New Painting," *Smithsonian*, 7 (June 1976), 58-65; and, for the story behind the painting, his "Sunday at the Little Bighorn with George," *Montana The Magazine of Western History*, 42 (Spring 1992), 50-61.

17. Stewart H. Holbrook, "There Was a Man: Custer, Fighting General," *Esquire*, 34 (September 1950), 52, facing a fold-out reproduction of Von Schmidt's painting. Eric von Schmidt, "Custer, Dying Again," 62, noted that his father considered Custer "a glory-hunting ass, and it is ironic that his painting is now considered a somewhat romantic interpretation." *Somewhat?*

18. See, for example, Robert M. Utley, *Custer and the Great Controversy: The Origin and Development of a Legend* (Los Angeles: Westernlore Press, 1962); Brian W. Dippie, "'What Will Congress Do About It?': The Congressional Reaction to the Little Big Horn Disaster," *North Dakota History*, 37 (Summer 1970), 161-89; and Dippie, "The Southern Response

to Custer's Last Stand," *Montana The Magazine of Western History*, 21 (Spring 1971), 18-31.

19. Whitman, "A Death-Sonnet for Custer," 23.

20. Edgar Fawcett, "Custer," New York *Illustrated Weekly* (mon. ed.), 2 (August 1876), front cover.

21. Captain Jack [John Wallace] Crawford, "Wild Bill's Grave," *The Poet Scout: A Book of Song and Story* (New York: Funk and Wagnalls, 1886), 50-51.

22. Frederick Whittaker, *A Complete Life of Gen. George A. Custer* (New York: Sheldon and Company, 1876), 628.

23. William F. Cody to Elizabeth B. Custer, August 13, 1886, in Frost, *General Custer's Libbie*, 261.

24. Percy MacKaye, *Epoch: The Life of Steele MacKaye, Genius of the Theatre, in Relation to His Times and Contemporaries* (2 vols., New York: Boni and Liveright, 1927), 2:76, 90. It is possible that Mrs. Custer attended a performance of Cody's show—see Frost, *General Custer's Libbie*, 261. It is more likely that she approved the scene-painting (by Matt Morgan) without ever watching the reenactment itself, since the New York *Sun* for October 31, 1886, noted that "Mrs. Custer will be announced as superintending the picture of the spot where her husband was killed." MacKaye, *Epoch*, 2:80. When the Custers' erstwhile maid visited Mrs. Custer in New York in the autumn of 1886, she was sent by herself to see Cody's show. Elizabeth B. Custer, *Tenting on the Plains; or, General Custer in Kansas and Texas* (New York: Charles L. Webster, 1887), 46.

25. Paul Fees to the author, June 15, 1988; also see Sarah J. Blackstone, "Custer Joins the Wild West Show," in *Custer and His Times*, ed. Urwin and Fagan, 250-54.

26. *Buffalo Bill's Wild West and Congress of Rough Riders of the World* (New York: J. A. Rudolf, 1898), 9, 23.

27. New York *Tribune*, August 15, 1881; portion on *Custer's Last Rally* reprinted in *Press Comments on John Mulvany's Great Painting of Custer's Last Rally* (n.p., [ca. 1883]), 1.

28. *Custer's Last Fight: Painted by Cassilly Adams—Representing the Last Grand Indian Battle that Will Be Fought on This Continent* (1886), cited in Robert Taft, *Artists and Illustrators of the Old West, 1850–1900* (New York: Charles Scribner's Sons, 1953), 335 n. 48.

29. Don Russell, "Those Long-Lost Custer Panels," *Pacific Historian*, 11 (Fall 1967), 28-35. The end panels are all that is left of the painting they accompanied, which was destroyed by fire in 1946. For the appearance of the triptych with panels in place, see Brian W. Dippie, "Brush, Palette and the Custer Battle: A Second Look," *Montana The Magazine of Western History*, 24 (Winter 1974), 56.

30. Inspired by the destruction of Adams's *Custer's Last Fight*, two pioneering works on the painting and print appeared in 1946: Russell, "Sixty Years in Bar Rooms; or 'Custer's Last Fight'"; and Robert Taft, "The Pictorial Record of the Old West, IV: Custer's Last Stand—John Mulvany, Cassilly Adams and Otto Becker," *Kansas Historical Quarterly*, 14 (November 1946), 361-90, which reappeared slightly revised as a chapter in his *Artists and Illustrators of the Old West*.

31. John Erlichman, "Art in the Nixon White House," *ARTnews*, 81 (May 1982), 76-77.

32. The Little Bighorn–Isandhlwana comparison has become a modern favorite, intelligently treated in James O. Gump's *The Dust Rose Like Smoke: The Subjugation of the Zulu and the Sioux* (Lincoln: University of Nebraska Press, 1994). For the Zulu elements in Becker's *Custer's Last Fight*, see Angus McBride, *The Zulu War* (London: Osprey Publishing Limited, 1976).

33. The Becker-Doré link was first noted by Brian Pohanka—see John M. Carroll, "Anheuser-Busch and Custer's Last Stand," *Greasy Grass*, 3 (May 1987), 26.

34. The paintings mentioned have all appeared in color on the cover of *Greasy Grass,* the annual of the Custer Battlefield Historical and Museum Association. See also Frank McCarthy's *The Last Stand: Little Big Horn* (1989) and John Hull's *Custer's Last Stand* (1991). Also revealing is the artist E. Lisle Reedstrom's "Custer Paintings and Historical Accuracy," *Roundup Magazine*, 2 (September–October 1994), 16-19, which defines historical accuracy as attention to detail.

35. Kansas City *Daily Journal*, March 2, 1881, quoted in Taft, *Artists and Illustrators of the Old West*, 135.

36. Louisville *Commercial*, December 17, 1882, in *Press Comments on John Mulvany's Great Painting of Custer's Last Rally*, 4.

37. "The Artist," ibid., 8.

38. Donnelle, *Cyclorama of Gen. Custer's Last Fight*, 11.

39. Paxson copyrighted his painting in 1900 as *Custer's Last Fight*, but his grandson insisted it be called *Custer's Last Stand* on the basis of family tradition that his grandfather preferred that title. W. E. Paxson, " 'Custer's Last Stand': The Painting and the Artist," *True West*, 11 (September-October 1963), 14-16; 52-53; William Edgar Paxson to the author, November 5, 1963; William Edgar Paxson to Don Russell, February 28, 1965, Russell Collection; William Edgar Paxson, Jr., *E. S. Paxson: Frontier Artist* (Boulder, Colo.: Pruett Publishing Co., 1984), 115 n. 1. In fact, in a letter to his friend Frank Linderman dated February 8, 1914, Paxson wrote: "The [Montana State] Legislators beside many friends are very much interested in the 'Custers Last Fight' and want to secure it for the

state, can you help me in the matter?" Frank Bird Linderman Collection, Archives, Maureen and Mike Mansfield Library, University of Montana, Missoula. The copyrighted title should be restored.

40. *Custer's Last Battle on the Little Big Horn in Montana June 25, 1876/ Paxson's Great Historical Painting* (Peoria, Ill.: Frank and Sons Print, [ca. 1900]), 16.

41. Press accounts claiming that Paxson spent twenty years on *Custer's Last Stand* usually stated that the painting itself took seven or eight years. See, for example, Antoinette E. Simons, "Worked Twenty Years on One Picture," *American Magazine*, 80 (July 1915), 50. Paxson's interest in the subject may well have developed over twenty years. But he began work on the painting in 1895 (Paxson, *E. S. Paxson*, 47), and since he was still actively gathering information about the battle at the beginning of 1896, it is reasonable to say that *Custer's Last Stand* took him four years, not twenty, to paint.

42. Joanna S. Grigg, quoted in Marian A. White, "A Group of Clever and Original Painters in Montana," *Fine Arts Journal*, 16 (February 1905), 81.

43. Ibid., 79, 81.

44. See Paxson, *E. S. Paxson*, 47. Given her consistent stance, it is highly unlikely that Mrs. Custer viewed Paxson's painting several times.

Fig. 1. Custer's Last Rally on the Little Big Horn, *from D. M. Kelsey,* Our Pioneer Heroes and Their Daring Deeds *(Chicago: Thompson and Thomas, 1900). All images courtesy Brian W. Dippie unless otherwise noted.*

Fig. 2. Custer's Last Stand, American Show Print Co., Milwaukee, Wisconsin, 1909 *(Buffalo Bill Historical Center, Cody, Wyoming)*

Fig. 3. Custer's Last Stand as Presented by Buffalo Bill's Wild West, *Courier Co., Buffalo, New York, circa 1904 (Buffalo Bill Historical Center, Cody, Wyoming)*

Fig. 4. Custer's Last Rally, *A. Hoen and Co., circa 1896 (Buffalo Bill Historical Center, Cody, Wyoming, gift of Mr. William J. B. Burger)*

Fig. 5. Revered Even by His Savage Foes, *by Cassilly Adams, 1886 (Arizona Historical Society, Tucson)*

Fig. 6. Custer's Last Stand—1876, *by H. Charles McBarron, 1962*
(Montana Historical Society Museum, Helena)

Fig. 7. Command Hill, *by Michael Schreck, 1993*
(© Michael Schreck, courtesy of the artist)

Fig. 8. Custer's Last Stand, by Edgar S. Paxson, 1899 (Buffalo Bill Historical Center, Cody, Wyoming)

Fig. 9. Custer & 20,000 Indians, *by Fritz Scholder, 1969*
(© Fritz Scholder, courtesy Wiley T. Buchanan III)

Fig. 10. Fort Apache, *lobby card (RKO, 1948)*
(Courtesy Paul Andrew Hutton)

Fig. 11. Here Fell Custer, *by Eric von Schmidt, 1976 (detail)*
(© 1976/Eric von Schmidt, 1986/Minglewood Press)

Fig. 12. Custer's Last Stand, *by Harold von Schmidt, 1950*
(First appeared in Esquire, *September 1950, Hearst Corporation, New York)*

Fig. 13. The Battle on the Little Big Horn River—The Death
Struggle of General Custer, *by William M. Cary, from the New York
Daily Graphic, July 19, 1876 (Library of Congress, Washington, D.C.)*

Fig. 14. (Right) The Indian War—Death of General George A. Custe[r]
at the Battle of the Little Big Horn River, Montana Territory, June 25
from Illustrated Police News, *July 13, 1876 (Courtesy John M. Carroll an[d]
Buffalo Bill Historical Center, Cody, Wyoming[)]*

THE ILLUSTRATED POLICE NEWS
LAW-COURTS AND WEEKLY RECORD

VOL. 20—NO. 507.   FOR THE WEEK ENDING THURSDAY, JULY 13, 1876.   PRICE TEN CENTS.

THE INDIAN WAR—DEATH OF GENERAL GEORGE A. CUSTER, AT THE BATTLE JUNE BIG HORN RIVER, MONTANA TERRITORY.

Fig. 15. Custer's Last Charge, *by [James E.?] Kelly, 1878, from Captain Jack Crawford,* The Poet Scout: A Book of Song and Story *(New York: Funk and Wagnalls, 1886)*

Fig. 16. Custer's Last Fight, *by J. Steeple Davis, 1897, from Edward S. Ellis,* Ellis's History of the United States *(Cleveland: Helman-Taylor Co., 1899)*

Fig. 17. Custer's Last Fight, *by Alfred R. Waud, from Frederick Whittaker,* A Complete Life of Gen. George A. Custer *(New York: Sheldon and Co., 1876)*

Fig. 18. (Above) General Custer Death Struggle. The Battle of the Little Big Horn, by Henry Steinegger, Pacific Art Co., San Francisco, 1878 (Library of Congress, Washington, D.C.)

Fig. 19. (Left) Battle of the Big Horn.—Death of Custer, by William M. Cary, from Charles J. Barnes and J. Marsha Hawkes, Barnes New National Fifth Reader (New York: American Book Co., 1884)

Fig. 20. Untitled sketch of Custer's Last Stand, by William M. Cary
(Gilcrease Museum, Tulsa, Oklahoma)

ig. 21. (Right) Custer's Last
d, by Alfred R. Waud, from
dward S. Ellis, Indian Wars
the United States (Chicago:
J. D. Kenyon, 1892)

Fig. 22. Last Stand, *by Frederic Remington, 1890, from* Harper's Weekly, *January 10, 1891*

Fig. 23. Custer's Last Fight, *by Frederic Remington, circa 1877 (The R. W. Norton Art Gallery, Shreveport, Louisiana)*

Fig. 24. Custer's Last Fight, *by Frederic Remington, 1903*
(Bradford Brinton Memorial, Big Horn, Wyoming)

Fig. 25. Scene from The Scarlet West *(First National, 1925)*

Fig. 26. "Custer's Last Charge," Buffalo Bill's Wild West show, Brooklyn, 1894
(Denver Public Library, Western History Collection)

Fig. 27. Custer's Last Rally, *by John Mulvany, 1881*
(Library of Congress, Washington, D.C.)

Fig. 28. Custer's Last Fight, *by Cassilly Adams, 1886*
(Library of Congress, Washington, D.C.)

Fig. 29. Coming Events Cast
Their Shadows Before,
by Cassilly Adams, 1886
(Arizona Historical Society,
Tucson)

Fig. 30. Custer's Last Fight, *by Otto Becker, Milwaukee Litho. Co., 1896*

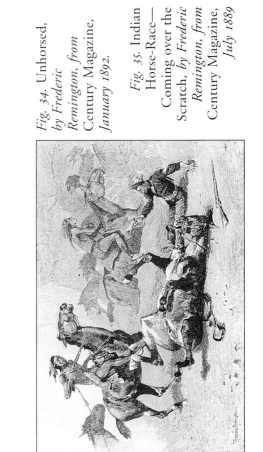

Fig. 33. Kiowa Buck Starting a Race, by
Frederic Remington, from Century
Magazine, July 1889.

Fig. 32. The Gluttons—Ciacco, by Gustave
Doré, circa 1861 from Dante Alighieri's
Gottliche Komodie (Berlin: W. Moeser, n.d.)

Fig. 31. The final stand of the British soldiers
against the Zulus at Isandhlwana, from the
London Graphic, March 15, 1879

Fig. 34. Unhorsed,
by Frederic
Remington, from
Century Magazine,
January 1892.

Fig. 35. Indian
Horse-Race—
Coming over the
Scratch, by Frederic
Remington, from
Century Magazine,
July 1889

Fig. 36. Charles Dudley, Custer, with William S. Hart in Wild Bill Hick◌ *(Paramount, 1923) (Courtesy Paul Andrew Hutton)*

Fig. 37. They Died with Their Boots On, *lobby card (Warner Brothers, 1941) (Courtesy Paul Andrew Hutton)*

Fig. 38. James Millican as Custer in Warpath *(Paramount, 1951) (Courtesy Paul Andrew Hutton)*

Fig. 39. Britt Lomond as Custer in Tonka *(Walt Disney Productions, 1958) (Courtesy Paul Andrew Hutton)*

Fig. 40. (above)
Custer of the West,
poster (Cinerama, 1968)
(Courtesy Paul Andrew
Hutton)

Fig. 41. (right)
Gary Cole, left, as Custer and
Dean Stockwell as Sheridan
in the television miniseries,
Son of the Morning Star
(ABC, 1990–1991)
(Courtesy Paul Andrew
Hutton)

"Correct in Every Detail"
General Custer in Hollywood

Paul Andrew Hutton

At the conclusion of John Ford's classic film *Fort Apache* (1948, fig. 10), a group of newspaper reporters questions Lieutenant Colonel Kirby York (John Wayne) about his forthcoming campaign against Geronimo, while also reflecting on the glorious reputation of his regiment. That glory is chiefly derived from the last stand of the regiment's previous commander, Lieutenant Colonel Owen Thursday (Henry Fonda). Colonel York despised Thursday, who had in reality sacrificed the regiment to racial arrogance, vainglorious pride, and wounded vanity. The last stand had in fact been a near-rout in which Thursday had played little part except to initiate disaster. "No man died more gallantly," York responds to a reporter's praise of Thursday, his voice sad and dripping with irony, "nor won more honor for his regiment." Asked if he has seen the grand painting of "Thursday's Charge" now hanging in the nation's capitol, the colonel answers affirmatively.

"That was a magnificent work," declares an enthusiastic reporter. "There were these massed columns of Apaches in their warpaint and feathered bonnets, and here was Thursday leading his men in that heroic charge."

"Correct in every detail," the colonel responds.

Of course, as Colonel York and the film's audience know only too well, not a single detail of the painting was correct. But York has come to understand that if the sacrifice of his regiment is to have any value it must be as myth. That myth, even if mostly false, can still provide an ideal of courage and sacrifice that will give the new regiment (and the new nation) strength, pride, and a sense of identity.

Director Ford and screenwriter Frank S. Nugent understood that the importance of heroes is not to be found in the often mundane or sordid reality of their lives, but rather in what society makes of them. Ford, who based *Fort Apache* loosely on the Custer story, had no problem in revealing the incompetence, hypocrisy, and brutality of the frontier army or in displaying the honor, dignity, and heroism of the Native Americans twenty years before it became fashionable to do so.

Some critics, who often castigate Ford as a chauvinistic celebrationist, are puzzled by the conclusion of *Fort Apache*. They fail to comprehend its subtlety, which goes, of course, to the heart of understanding and accepting our most cherished national myths for what they actually are. Ford had no problem with the ending.

Critic and filmmaker Peter Bogdanovich questioned Ford about the ending of *Fort Apache* in a 1967 interview, rightly pointing out that it foreshadowed the conclusion of an even darker Ford portrayal of frontier myth in *The Man Who Shot Liberty Valance* (1962):

> Bogdanovich: The end of *Fort Apache* anticipates the newspaper editor's line in *Liberty Valance*, "when the legend becomes a fact, print the legend." Do you agree with that?
> Ford: Yes—because I think it's good for the country. We've had a lot of people who were supposed to be great heroes, and you know damn well they weren't. But it's good for the country to have heroes to look up to. Like Custer—a great hero. Well, he wasn't. Not that he was a stupid man—but he did a stupid job that day.[1]

Despite Ford's belief that myth was "good for the country," his artistic vision is dedicated in both *Fort Apache* and *The Man Who Shot Liberty Valance* to the explanation of a truth about the past that was lost to most of his Hollywood peers and to many historians as well: that good men, with noble motives, can do evil. His truthful fiction of the Custer battle, *Fort Apache*, remains the best of over forty celluloid portrayals of America's most flamboyant military failure, George Armstrong Custer.[2]

The trick, of course, in reviewing the checkered cinematic career of the enigmatic General Custer is to find a film that is correct in *any* detail, much less one correct in *every* detail. Much like John Wayne's Colonel York in *Fort Apache* we, as the audience viewing these films, must search for a higher correctness in them than a mere adherence to fact—and that can prove a daunting task indeed.

Custer's dead troopers had yet to receive a proper burial before the redoubtable William F. "Buffalo Bill" Cody was amazing eastern audiences with his *The Red Right Hand; or Buffalo Bill's First Scalp for Custer*. Now, you had to admire Cody's grit, for in the summer of 1876 he had abandoned the eastern stage (where he had been doing good box-office business since 1872) to rejoin his old regiment on the plains. Everyone from General Phil Sheridan on down believed this would be the last great Indian war, and Cody was not about to miss it.

Having heard the shocking news about Custer, the Fifth Regiment was scouting the rolling hills along Warbonnet Creek, Nebraska, on July 17, 1876, when an advance party of Little Wolf's Cheyennes, on their way north to join Sitting Bull (p. 114), clashed with a small party of soldiers led by Cody. The long-haired scout, garbed in one of his stage costumes of black velvet trimmed with silver buttons and lace, brought down the only casualty in the skirmish, an unfortunately bold Cheyenne warrior with the ironic name of Yellow Hair (the name was in recognition of a blond scalp he had taken). Cody promptly lifted the fellow's hair, proclaiming his grisly trophy as "the first scalp for Custer." The soldiers then chased the Indians back to the Red Cloud Agency in one of the army's few victories of the Great Sioux War.[3]

Within five weeks Cody left the army, heading eastward where the opportunities for glory before the footlights were far greater than on the plains. The new play, according to Buffalo Bill, was a five-act monstrosity "without head or tail . . . a noisy, rattling, gunpowder entertainment." It was Cody's most successful play.[4]

After Warbonnet Creek it became increasingly difficult to tell if art were imitating life or vice versa. Cody had dressed the morning of July 17, 1876, in his Mexican vaquero stage outfit in anticipation of a battle with the Indians. He was anxious to later tell his eastern audiences that his colorful costume was authentic, for he wanted to shed the drab buckskins he had always worn. Dressed properly for the part he ventured forth and boldly killed an Indian in a frontier ritual that immediately reaffirmed his hero status. He then hurried east, scalp in tow, to exploit this act before audiences hungry for a look at a "real Wild West" as fresh as the morning headlines, but already anachronistic to an increasingly urban, industrial society. It was as if the frontier West was providing them with living, breathing entertainment. After his premier performance at Warbonnet Creek (and it certainly was a more daunting act than Errol Flynn or John Wayne ever had to perform), Cody simply took the show on the road in *The Red Right Hand*, and the profits were indeed impressive.

When Cody initiated his famous Wild West show in 1883 he continued his personal identification with the Custer story. Sitting Bull toured for a season with the company, and Custer's Last Stand was often reenacted as the climax of the program (fig. 26). As time passed Cody updated the historical pageants, so that the Last Stand rotated with scenes from the Spanish-American War or the Boxer Rebellion, but Cody's first scalp for Custer remained standard fare throughout the show's long run.[5]

Cody was naturally attracted to the new medium of moving pictures. As early as 1894 his Wild West company was filmed by the Edison Kinetoscope for the peep-show circuit. It was financial disaster, however, that brought Cody into the film business. Fred Bonfils and Harry Tammen, the buccaneering capitalists who owned the Denver *Post*, forced Cody into bankruptcy in 1913 and then used him to form, in collaboration with the Essanay Company, the Colonel W. F. Cody (Buffalo Bill) Historical Pictures Company in September 1913.

The company was to film a historical epic of the Indian wars using many of the actual participants, including Cody, retired Lieutenant General Nelson Miles, Frank Baldwin, Charles King, Dewey Beard, Iron Tail, Short Bull, and Running Hawk. The scenario for *Buffalo Bill's Indian Wars* was by Charles King, a former Fifth Cavalry officer who had been with Cody at Warbonnet Creek and had since become a famous novelist. It included the Battle of Summit Springs, Cody's first scalp for Custer, the death of Sitting Bull, and was climaxed with a re-creation of the tragedy at Wounded Knee. Denver *Post* reporter Courtney Ryley Cooper, who would later ghostwrite the autobiography of Cody's wife and write a 1923 Custer novel, *The Last Frontier*, that would be twice filmed by Hollywood, reported that the picture, thanks to Cody and General Miles, "was historically correct in every detail and that not a feature was forgotten."[6]

The government, having provided six hundred cavalrymen for the film, may have been unhappy with Cody's determination to portray the massacre at Wounded Knee truthfully. Cody and Miles quarreled bitterly during the filming and their long friendship came to a stormy end.

The government delayed release of the film for almost a year. When it finally played in New York and Denver, Cody and several Sioux appeared on stage to introduce it. The film was rereleased in 1917 after Cody's death but was never widely distributed. "My object of desire," declared Buffalo Bill before his death, "has been to preserve history by the aid of the camera with as many living participants in the closing Indian wars of North America as could be procured."[7] Perhaps in his final foray into show business, Buffalo Bill had, for once, been too truthful. Ben Black Elk, whose father was in the film, claimed that the Interior Department banned it and later destroyed it. No copy is known to exist today.

Even before Cody's film was completed in October 1913, the Custer story had already been told at least four times on film. William Selig's 1909 one-reeler, *Custer's Last Stand or On the Little Bighorn*, used a reenactment of the battle on the actual site by the Montana National Guard as the centerpiece of its story. More ambitious was Thomas Ince's 1912 three-reeler, *Custer's Last Fight*. Starring as well as directed by Francis Ford, the brother of John Ford, the movie centered on the old tale that Rain in the Face had stalked Custer at the Little Bighorn to avenge his earlier arrest. The film ranks as one of the few Custer movies to treat Indians as vicious savages, leaving no doubt that the Sioux must be swept aside to make way for the greater civilization that Ford's Custer represents. Sitting Bull is portrayed as a coward while Custer appears as a wise, experienced commander. Ford's heroic portrayal of Custer set a pattern unbroken in film until his brother made *Fort Apache* in 1948.[8]

Like *Fort Apache*, D. W. Griffith's 1912 film, *The Massacre*, presented an impressionistic interpretation of the Custer fight far removed from the penchant for historical detail found in the Ince film. The battle is secondary to the primary story of a pioneer family moving West and of the heroic scout who silently loves the pioneer's wife. Unlike the Ince film, the Griffith film treats the Indians heroically. An attractive Indian family is presented in parallel to the pioneer family, but their happy lives are destroyed in a Washita-like massacre led by a long-haired, Custer-like cavalry officer. The Indian father escapes, but his wife and child are slain, and he swears dark revenge. When the Indian leads his warriors against the wagon train, now escorted by the same cavalry troopers who had killed his family, the soldiers and settlers form a ring around the young pioneer's wife and infant. One by one the whites perish—gambler and priest, general and scout—falling side by side. When the young pioneer arrives with a rescue column he finds wife and child alive under the pile of corpses, the men having made human shields of themselves.

Custer is identifiable as the leader of the cavalry, but was not named in the film—possibly because such liberties were taken with the facts of Little Bighorn and possibly because the Ince film was released at the same time. Nevertheless, *The Massacre* clearly presents the essence of the early Custer myth, both in print and on film: the heroic self-sacrifice of Custer and his men to protect the pioneers and expand civilization's borders.

Bison Films, the releasing company for the Ince film, also released *Campaigning with Custer* in 1913 and *Custer's Last Scout* in 1915. Successful novels were the basis of two more Custer films of that era: Vitagraph's 1916 four-part serial, *Britton of the Seventh*, featuring Ned Finley as Custer, based on Cyrus Townsend Brady's 1914 novel; and Marshall Neilan's *Bob Hampton of Placer* (1921), starring Dwight Crittenden as Custer and based on Randall Parrish's 1910 book. Both films dealt with the theme of a disgraced officer who redeems himself at the Little Bighorn. This plot device became commonplace in Custer fiction and films. Custer appeared briefly in Clifford Smith's *Wild Bill Hickok* (1923, fig. 36), where he persuades William S. Hart as Wild Bill to strap back on his pistols to bring law and order to the frontier. Custer made another cameo in Metropolitan's *The Last Frontier* (1926), this time assisting Wild Bill and Buffalo Bill in a film based on Courtney Ryley Cooper's 1923 novel. RKO remade the film as a serial in 1932 with William Desmond as Custer.[9]

Several Custer films were released to coincide with the fiftieth anniversary of the Last Stand. The first was J. G. Adophe's 1925 nine-reeler, *The Scarlet West* (fig. 25), which used the unusual plot device of an Indian hero. Robert Frazier portrayed Cardelanche, the educated son of a Sioux chief who attempts to lead his people over to white culture. Frustrated in his efforts, he leaves the Sioux and accepts a commission in the cavalry. He soon falls in love with the post commander's daughter, played by Clara Bow, but the gulf between them proves too great and he returns to his own people after they wipe out Custer's command. Such an involved plot was not allowed to slow the action in Anthony J. Xydias' *With General Custer at Little Bighorn*, released the following year as part of a series of films on American history by Sunset Pictures.[10]

Universal's 1926 film, *The Flaming Frontier*, was the best publicized of the rash of Custer films, billed as "the supreme achievement in western epics."[11] Again the story involved a disgraced soldier who wins redemption at Little Bighorn. In this case the soldier was former pony express rider Bob Langdon, played by Hoot Gibson, who is unjustly expelled from West Point. He quite naturally heads West and promptly finds employment as a scout for Custer, played by Dustin Farnum. Corruption on the frontier and ineptitude in Washington undermine the efforts of the heroic Custer to keep peace with the cheated Indians who are finally driven to the warpath. At the last moment, Custer sends scout Langdon for reinforcements, and although he is unable to save the Seventh, Langdon does defeat the white villain, rescue the heroine, and get reinstated to West Point.

The Last Stand was elaborately staged with Farnum, who came out of retirement to portray Custer, giving his role the ultimate hero treatment. One ad for the film simply ran a portrait of Farnum as Custer over the banner—"see his sublime courage in *The Flaming*

Frontier."[12] The critic for the New York *Times* was unimpressed, however, noting that Farnum "was in one of his lax moods while impersonating General Custer."[13]

When the film premiered at New York's Colony Theater on April 4, 1926, General Edward S. Godfrey was a special guest of honor.[14] He had distinguished himself as a young lieutenant in Captain Frederick Benteen's detachment at Little Bighorn, and his 1892 article in *Century* magazine had often been praised as the best account of the battle by a participant. He received a standing ovation from the crowd and then settled in to watch the great tragedy of his youth distorted into fanciful entertainment for a people completely divorced from frontier times. One wonders if Custer's widow, Elizabeth, who then lived in New York City, could bring herself to visit Colony Theater.

The Flaming Frontier proved to be the last major silent film on Custer, although the general briefly rode again in Tim McCoy's *Spoilers of the West* in 1927. After the rash of commemorative Custer films, the story was neglected for a decade, had a brief revival of interest in the years just before World War II, then vanished again as a Hollywood subject until 1948.

By the time filmmakers returned to his story, Custer's heroic image was under assault from a variety of sources. Most notable of these was Frederic F. Van de Water's highly successful 1934 biography, *Glory-Hunter*. For fifty-eight years no one had dared to chip away at the hallowed image of Custer, created by the popular press in the decade after Little Bighorn and then carefully nurtured by Elizabeth Custer in a trilogy of best-selling memoirs. Biographies by Frederick Whittaker, Frederick Dallenbaugh, and Frazier Hunt were wildly hagiographic, while for those whose tastes were not literary in nature the Anheuser-Busch Company had more than 150,000 copies of Otto Becker's *Custer's Last Fight* (fig. 30) distributed as a standard prop of saloon decor. This gaudy print, as close to both history and art as many turn-of-the-century Americans ever got, earnestly reinforced the message of Custer's heroic sacrifice. Custer's critics, and there were many both inside and outside the military, held their tongues so long as his widow lived. But she outlived them all, not dying until 1933.[15]

Van de Water, well known in eastern literary circles as an editor, critic, poet, and novelist, was heavily influenced in his writing by the debunking spirit of the 1920s, best exemplified by Lytton Strachey's pioneering *Eminent Victorians* (1918). Many other writers had followed Strachey's lead, and all were deeply touched by the cynicism growing out of World War I, by a rising spirit of antimilitarism, by the work of Sigmund Freud, and by a new emphasis on social forces at the expense of the previous celebration of the individual. Many heroes besides Custer were reinterpreted to suit the times, but while other reputations survived the attacks, Custer's did not.

Few books have had so immediate and dramatic an impact on both historical interpretation and the popular mind as did Van de Water's *Glory-Hunter.* The biography is simply the most influential book ever written on Custer. Van de Water created a compelling portrait of a man consumed by ambition, driven by demons of his own creation, and finally destroyed by his own hubris. Gone forever was the marble hero of the past.

Within a few years the glory-hunter interpretation became the standard portrayal of Custer in the popular press and fiction. It set the tone for novels such as Harry Sinclair Drago's *Montana Road* (1935), Ernest Haycox's *Bugles in the Afternoon* (1944), Will Henry's *No Survivors* (1950), Frank Gruber's *Bugles West* (1954), Thomas Berger's *Little Big Man* (1964), and Lewis B. Patten's *The Red Sabbath* (1968).[16]

Films were changing as well, and at first it seemed as if Hollywood might follow the cynical lead of the literary elites. Adapting to the revolutionary changes wrought by the coming of sound, films such as *The Dawn Patrol* (1930) and *All Quiet on the Western Front* (1930) exposed the insanity of war; while *Little Caesar* (1930), *The Public Enemy* (1931), and *Scarface* (1931) condemned the power of the underworld while linking it to societal indifference and poverty. Meanwhile, *The Front Page* (1931), *I Am a Fugitive from a Chain Gang* (1932), and *The Dark Horse* (1932) made it clear that corruption was not confined to the mobsters.

As social commentaries such films, combined as they were with a more daring approach to sexuality and violence, enraged conservative segments of the American public. These groups found their voice with the 1933 formation of the Legion of Decency. Will

Hays, who had been appointed twelve years earlier by the major film companies to insure the decency of Hollywood's product, now found a powerful ally in the legion. His job had proved futile until the church-backed legion gave him the clout to clean up Hollywood. Gone was the sex and violence, but a successful attack was also launched against the cynical irreverence and negative tone of the social commentary films. Censorship triumphed so that the slum problems that produced the gangsters were replaced by the agonies of young Andy Hardy as he learned the social graces, and the corruptions endemic in political life were drowned out by the spirited songs and high-stepping dancers of Busby Berkeley musicals. The only truly serious topics touched upon were in celluloid versions of classic literature, and even they were cleaned up. Thus was the American cinema made safe for every sheltered twelve year old in the country.[17]

In such a stifling atmosphere no film was about to attack a national hero like Custer. Furthermore, the very forces in the late twenties that had led to the social commentary films had also left the Western in disrepute as simple-minded entertainment for the masses. With the 1929 stock market crash the studios retrenched and proved unwilling to finance films of the magnitude necessary to tell Custer's story. This trend was exacerbated by the coming of sound, for the bulky and expensive sound equipment made outdoor action dramas more difficult and costly to film.

Prestige Westerns continued to be made throughout the 1930s, with *Cimarron* in 1931 becoming the first of three Westerns to date to win the Academy Award for Best Picture, but they were limited to only one or two a year. Instead the genre was dominated by the budget, or B, Western. Led by Republic Studio, many independent production companies now rushed to fill the entertainment gap created by the desertion of the Western by the majors. Stories became increasingly simple minded and action oriented, with the singing cowboy emerging as a Hollywood staple. Gone was the stark western realism pioneered by silent star William S. Hart. In its place came the entertaining froth of Ken Maynard, Buck Jones, Hoot Gibson, and Gene Autry. Not until the commercial and critical success of John Ford's *Stagecoach* in 1939, which also rescued John Wayne from the Republic Bs, was interest in serious, prestige Westerns renewed.[18]

Custer thus turned up in only five films in the decade, with three of them low-budget serials for the Saturday-matinee crowd: RKO's 1932 remake of *The Last Frontier* with William Desmond as Custer; the fifteen-episode *Custer's Last Stand* in 1936 with Frank McGlynn, Jr., as a rather elderly-looking Custer (the serial was cut and rereleased as a feature a decade later); and the 1939 Johnny Mack Brown vehicle *The Oregon Trail,* with Roy Barcroft as Custer. Clay Clement had a cameo as Custer in *The World Changes* (1933), a dark tale of the rise of a meat-packing magnate starring Paul Muni. Custer appears only long enough to inform Muni's isolated Dakota family that the Civil War is at last over, but they never knew it started. Finally, Custer is featured in the splashiest epic Western of the decade, Cecil B. DeMille's 1937 celebration of manifest destiny, *The Plainsman.*

DeMille's film once again brought Custer (John Miljan) together with Wild Bill (Gary Cooper) and Buffalo Bill (James Ellison), this time with a glamorous Calamity Jane (Jean Arthur) thrown in for good measure, in a wild tale remarkable for its fidelity to minute historical detail (the statue on Custer's desk is correct) and its absolute disregard for the broad outlines of the historical record.

Custer appears as something of a domineering father figure to the other characters—scolding, rescuing, ordering. The Last Stand is briefly depicted in a dream sequence narrated by Anthony Quinn as an Indian warrior captured by Hickok and Cody. Rarely has the usually subtle connection between nineteenth-century artwork and twentieth-century film been so blatantly displayed as in the tableau vivant of the Alfred Waud drawing (fig. 17) from Whittaker's biography that composes the Last Stand sequence in the film. When an Indian bullet finally pierces his ever-so-noble heart, Custer clutches onto the flag he has gallantly defended and slowly sinks from view. The uncharitably correct critic for the New York *Times,* a paper which had long since committed itself to the debunked Custer of the Van de Water camp, noted that "Custer rated no more than he received: a brief fadeout."[19]

Custer was back twice in 1940. First in the person of Paul Kelly in MGM's *Wyoming,* a light but entertaining Wallace Beery

Western filmed in Jackson Hole, Wyoming. Beery plays his patented good-badman role, helping Custer clean up a crooked town in a film best remembered as the initial teaming of the affable star with Marjorie Main. More impressive was Warner Brothers' *Santa Fe Trail*, directed by Michael Curtiz and purporting to tell the story of how young Jeb Stuart (Errol Flynn) and George Custer (Ronald Reagan) frustrate John Brown in Kansas, then capture him at Harpers Ferry. Raymond Massey's portrayal of Brown as a mad Old Testament prophet steals the show, despite the film's pro-Southern posture.

Not the least of the film's inaccuracies was that the real Custer was but sixteen at the time of Brown's Kansas raids. The Robert Buckner script also had Reagan's Custer as thoughtful and introspective, given to furrowing his brow and actually thinking that slavery just might be wrong—none of which characteristics was in keeping with the real Custer. Even Reagan, who had just finished his role as George Gipp in *Knute Rockne—All American*, noticed that the plot was not following his childhood history lessons. "I discovered I would again be playing a biographical role," he noted, "but with less attention to the truth this time."[20] The New York *Times*, later to be at odds with Reagan so often, was in complete agreement this time: "For anyone who has the slightest regard for the spirit—not to mention the facts—of American history, it will prove exceedingly annoying."[21] But while *Santa Fe Trail* may have flunked as history, it got an A as rousing entertainment.

There was no slackening of Custer's celluloid appearances in 1941. As the nation warily confronted a world consumed by war, and hesitatingly prepared for its own inevitable entry into conflagration, military heroes became quite popular again. Alfred Green's *Badlands of Dakota* for Universal featured Addison Richards as Custer in yet another horse opera reuniting him with Wild Bill (Richard Dix) and Calamity Jane (Frances Farmer). Robert Stack, then a young contract actor appearing in only his fourth film, remembered it as "one of the most forgettable westerns ever made."[22]

Two powerful Hollywood tycoons clashed early in 1941 over Custer films. Both Jack Warner and Sam Goldwyn developed prestige Westerns on Custer, and then argued bitterly over just who had priority rights to the story. Custer belongs to the public domain, of course, so neither possessed exclusive "rights," but Warner triumphed and Goldwyn eventually gave up on his film. He had envisioned *Seventh Cavalry* as a surefire box-office winner to follow the success of his 1940 hit *The Westerner* with Gary Cooper and Walter Brennan. Goldwyn planned to reunite these two stars in *Seventh Cavalry*, with Brennan (who had won an Academy Award for his Judge Roy Bean portrayal in *The Westerner*) as a villainous Custer and Cooper as a Captain Benteen–like officer.

It was Warner Brothers' *They Died with Their Boots On* (fig. 37) that went into production. The title was from Thomas Ripley's 1935 popular history of western gunfighters, a property purchased by Warner but never developed. It was a major film for Warners, with $1,357,000 eventually budgeted for the production. Michael Curtiz, the director of swashbuckling adventure films such as *Captain Blood*, *The Charge of the Light Brigade*, and *The Adventures of Robin Hood*, was scheduled to direct the film but was replaced by Raoul Walsh once Errol Flynn was cast as the lead. Flynn and Curtiz had clashed on previous films and would not work together again. Walsh, also a master of the adventure film, with such classics as *What Price Glory?* and *High Sierra* to his credit, was just as importantly a great drinking buddy of Flynn.[23]

The original script by Wally Kline and Aeneas Mackenzie clearly was influenced by the Van de Water biography, but the studio decided to rewrite the script to better fit the Flynn persona. Associate producer Robert Fellows properly characterized it as a "fairy tale, with no attempt at adherence to historical fact." Still, screenwriter Lenore Coffee, called in to punch up the romantic scenes between George and Elizabeth, was horrified by "really shocking inaccuracies" in the script. She was ignored and, despite her major contribution to the final script, denied screen credit.[24] Warner Brothers had firmly decided to treat General Custer in the same swashbuckling manner in which they had handled Robin Hood in 1938. The tenor of the times influenced the decision. "In preparing this scenario," screenwriter Mackenzie assured producer Hal Wallis, "all possible consideration was given the construction of a story which would have the best effect upon public morale in these present days of national crisis."[25] While *Life* magazine lamented that the film "glorifies a rash general," and the New York *Times* accused "writers in warbonnets" of scalping history, the only critics that Warner Brothers cared about lined up in droves to see *They Died with Their Boots On*. It was a huge success at the box-office.[26]

The impressive action sequences in the film were particularly difficult to shoot. Because of the excessive number of injuries to horses caused by the use of the "Running W" in Warners' *The Charge of the Light Brigade* (1936) the American Humane Association had successfully sued the studio to stop the cruel practice.[27] To the increased difficulty in portraying horse falls were added new Screen Extras' Guild rules preventing directors from hiring only experienced riders. Many old cowboys had drifted into the employ of the studios in the silent era and for years they formed a reliable cadre of cheap talent for riding scenes in Westerns. Walsh and other directors had been able to hire specific cowboys for action scenes in their films, but the new union rules changed all that.[28]

In the opening days of filming the cavalry charges, more than eighty of the inexperienced riders were injured. Three men were killed. As the buses carrying the extras left the studio for the Lasky Ranch in Agoura, where the battle scenes were shot, they were followed by an ambulance. One day Anthony Quinn hired a hearse to follow the ambulance, which panicked the extras and sent them scurrying back to the studio. Eventually Walsh got the experienced riders he wanted.[29]

The film follows Custer from West Point to Little Bighorn, and only in the opening sequences is the harder edge of the original script still evident. But Custer's vain buffoonery and rashness in the West Point and Civil War sections of the film quickly give way to thoughtful heroism once he reaches the frontier.

Flynn brought his usual charm and elan to the Custer role, of course, and was ably supported by Olivia de Havilland, who had been teamed with him seven times before, as Elizabeth Custer. This is the only film to deal with the relationship of the Custers at great length, with the script displaying a great reliance on Elizabeth's books as source material.[30] Stanley Ridges played Romulus Taipe, the villainous soldier turned politician, who is obviously based on

Grant's venal secretary of war, William W. Belknap. John Litel portrayed Custer's mentor, General Phil Sheridan, while Charley Grapewin was along for comedy relief as a crusty California Joe. G. P. Huntley portrayed Custer's British adjutant, who is called Lieutenant Butler in the film, although named Cooke in the original script. The character is obviously based on Custer's true adjutant, William W. Cooke, who was a Canadian known as "Queen's Own," the same nickname given to the Butler character in the film. Having faced recent lawsuits over historical films, the studios often changed the names of real characters to avoid possible litigation.

The film is one of the few Westerns to make the important connection between the Civil War and national expansion. After the Gettysburg sequence, where the inexplicable plot device of an accidental promotion thrusts Custer into high command so that he can save the Union by turning back the rebel cavalry, the war is told through a series of effective montages. The new national hero returns home to Michigan to wed Elizabeth and settle into civilian life. He is approached by Taipe to lend his name to a shady stock deal but angrily rejects the offer, proclaiming: "I'll gamble with anything, my money, my sword and even my life. But there's one thing I won't gamble with, and that is my good name!"

Recalled to active service through the influence of his wife, he quickly organizes the Seventh Cavalry from a band of misfits and outcasts into a crack regiment that breaks the power of the hostile tribes. Custer pledges to Crazy Horse (Anthony Quinn) that in exchange for peace he will guard the sacred Black Hills from white intrusion. In another bow to western art, the scene between Flynn and Quinn is based on Charles Schreyvogel's painting *Custer's Demand*.

This interferes with the railroad-building scheme of Taipe and his accomplice, Ned Sharp (Arthur Kennedy), and they conspire to have Custer recalled to Washington while they plant false rumors of gold in the Black Hills. Custer's attempts to expose their conspiracy before Congress is ruled as hearsay, admissible only as a dying declaration. Frustrated, Custer is finally able to convince President Grant (Joseph Crehan) to restore him to his command. Realizing that the Seventh Cavalry will have to be sacrificed to give General Sheridan more time to mobilize troops to defeat the enraged and betrayed Indians, Custer marches toward Little Bighorn.

The night before the battle Custer writes a letter exposing Taipe which, as a dying declaration, will be admissible as evidence. He asks his adjutant to carry it back to the fort, explaining that he does not wish a foreigner sacrificed in such a "dirty deal" as the coming battle. Butler indignantly refuses, reminding Custer that the only real Americans present are in the Little Bighorn valley waiting for the Seventh.

Custer then knowingly leads the Seventh Cavalry to its doom. And what a glorious doom it is—enacted against a powerful Max Steiner sound track countering "Garry Owen" against a rhythmic, ragged Indian theme. With his troopers all dead around him, his pistols empty, his long hair dancing in the western breeze, Custer draws his saber and falls from a shot from Crazy Horse's rifle as a charge of mounted warriors rides over him.

The final victory, of course, belongs to Custer. Elizabeth and Sheridan use his final letter to force Taipe's resignation and to receive a pledge from Grant to return the Black Hills to the Sioux. As Sheridan comforts Elizabeth with the assurance that her husband "won his last battle—after all," Custer and his regiment march off into a celluloid sunset to the strains of "Garry Owen."

If only historical reality could have been so sublime. Novelist and screenwriter George MacDonald Fraser, in his marvelous book *The Hollywood History of the World*, dismisses *They Died with Their Boots On* as "typical Hollywood dream-rubbish of the worst kind," a viewpoint echoed by other critics at the time the film was released and ever since.[31]

The historical errors in this particular film are legion: Custer was not promoted to general by mistake; he was not a civilian after the Civil War; he was more than willing to engage in shady business deals reflective of the Gilded Age in which he lived; he did not organize the Seventh in Dakota, but rather in Kansas; he did not protect the Black Hills but rather opened them up; he was not the enemy of the railroad capitalists but their best friend on the northern plains; he was not a defender of Indian rights; he did not knowingly sacrifice his regiment at Little Bighorn to save others;

Custer's hair was cut short at the time of the battle, and he did not carry a saber, nor did any of his men; the Sioux were not protected in their rights to the Black Hills as a result of his sacrifice; and on and on and on. But who is truly surprised by that? It is simply ridiculous to expect films to be true to the facts of history. They are works of fiction. If, by chance, they use a story to tell us a greater truth about ourselves and our past then they have succeeded as art. If they give us a momentary diversion and make us smile or tug at our heart, then they have succeeded admirably at what they are—popular entertainment.

They Died with Their Boots On is wonderful entertainment—a rousing adventure reflective of our dreams of how we wish our past might have been. But there is a veneer of truth—Custer was a dashing, romantic soldier; he and Elizabeth did have a storybook marriage; the Sioux were a terribly wronged people; and the Last Stand was indeed the result of events set in motion by venal capitalists and inept, corrupt politicians. Perhaps the film's greatest artistic triumph is in cutting to the essence of the American love affair with Custer—that the golden-haired soldier was the best his nation had to offer as the people's sacrifice to somehow atone for the ghastly treatment of the Native Americans. Vine Deloria, Jr., hammered home the same message again in the title to his 1970 best-seller: *Custer Died for Your Sins.*

By chance, the film's release in late November 1941 coincided with American entry into World War II. As the people reeled from the news of Pearl Harbor, Wake Island, and Bataan, they could clearly identify with the heroic self-sacrifice of Custer and the Seventh Cavalry. The greedy capitalists, crooked politicians, and gallant soldiers of *They Died with Their Boots On* made perfect sense to a people marching out of economic depression and into war.

There were dramatic changes in the western film genre during the war years. The major filmmakers tended to produce fewer prestige Westerns, lavishing budgets instead on escapist fare (this was the heyday of the MGM musical) or on films concerned with the war effort. The independents, of course, continued to crank out formula Westerns at a prodigious rate, with Roy Rogers overtaking Gene Autry in 1943 as the top Western money-making star. Several of the prestige Westerns that were made foreshadowed the trend toward social and psychological films that followed the war. Most notable among these were William Wellman's *The Ox-Bow Incident* (1942) with its bleak vision of the frontier's moral code; Howard Hughes's *The Outlaw* (1943) and King Vidor's *Duel in the Sun* (1946) with their preoccupation with eroticism; and Raoul Walsh's *Pursued* (1947), perhaps the first Freudian-inspired Western.[32]

While none of these themes is explicit in the first postwar Custer film, John Ford's *Fort Apache* (1948), it is nevertheless clear that much of the glossy veneer that surrounded Custer's image in the past had been worn away. While high courage and self-sacrifice are major themes in Ford's film, just as they were in *They Died with Their Boots On*, this time Custer was not to be the hero.

Unrecognized as such by film critics at the time, *Fort Apache* is a fictionalized telling of the Custer story with the locale shifted to the Southwest to make use of Ford's beloved Monument Valley. By changing the historical setting to the stark moral universe of Monument Valley, by fictionalizing his story line, and by freeing himself from the shackles of historical detail, Ford saved himself from the kind of factual criticism leveled at the Walsh film and allowed his artistic vision full rein. The result is a masterpiece of this peculiarly American art form that comes closer than any other Custer film to explaining the great contradictions of the protagonist's life, death, and legend.[33]

"A legend is more interesting than the actual facts," Ford once said in commenting on Custer.[34] In *Fort Apache* he does not celebrate that legend, but rather explains it. Henry Fonda's Lieutenant Colonel Owen Thursday is a textbook soldier bitter over his postwar reduction in rank from general and anxious to escape from his new frontier assignment by some glorious deed. His rigidity antagonizes his subordinates, and none more so than John Wayne's Captain Kirby York. When the corrupt practices of Indian agent Silas Meacham (Grant Withers) force Cochise (Miguel Inclan) to bolt the reservation, Thursday sees his chance. Through York's efforts the Apaches are persuaded to return from Mexico to meet with Thursday. But the colonel disregards York's promises to Cochise and prepares to attack. Protesting this duplicity, York is accused of cowardice by Thursday and ordered to the rear to protect the pack train. The troops then follow Thursday into Cochise's ambush, with the colonel unhorsed early in the charge. The wounded Thursday ignores York's offer of escape and rejoins his doomed command.

Thursday's tragic flaw, like that of the real Custer, is that he is unable to restrain an individuality bordering on megalomania. A martinet when it comes to enforcing military regulations, he cannot himself abide by the rules of his community, the cavalry. His every action is directed by personal desires, not community needs or moral values. His contempt for ritual is made apparent in his reluctance to fulfill his duty by dancing with the sergeant-major's wife at the NCO Ball, and by his refusal to engage in courtly discussion with Cochise. In the end he disregards better advice and leads his men into a deadly trap. ("They outnumber us four to one. Do we talk or fight?" asks York just before the battle. "You seem easily impressed by numbers, Captain," Thursday responds.) His soldiers follow Thursday because they are solidly members of the community—he leads them into slaughter because he is not. Yet Thursday, for all his faults, is a leader, and so he ignores escape and rejoins his command.[35]

The Indians remain tangential to the main theme of *Fort Apache*. Cochise is presented as a wise leader who wishes to avoid war while his Apaches are an honorable, cheated people. Unlike other celluloid last stands where the men die spread out as individuals, in *Fort Apache* the little band of soldiers forms a tight knot. Thursday stands with them, finally a member of the community he disdained. A distant rumble of hooves builds to a crescendo as the Apaches suddenly burst onto the scene, ride over the soldiers, and just as quickly vanish into the swirling dust. Their appearance is only fleeting as they claim their victory and affirm both Thursday's dishonor and his heroism.[36]

The Indian victory in *Fort Apache* is turned into a spiritual victory for the defeated soldiers, just as Custer's Last Stand achieved a power as legend far greater than any victory Custer might have won at Little Bighorn. Just as John Wayne's York reaffirms the importance of Thursday's sacrifice at the conclusion of *Fort Apache*, so did soldiers of Custer's generation protect his reputation. General

William T. Sherman noted in an 1876 letter that Custer had made several tactical mistakes at Little Bighorn, "but his gallant fight and death spread the mantle of oblivion over such trivial errors."[37] Similar views were expressed by Captain Frederick Benteen, who had commanded a wing of the Seventh at Little Bighorn and who might well have been the model for the York character in *Fort Apache*. Observing that Custer had been enshrined with a monument at West Point, Benteen noted that despite his own contempt for the dead man, Custer's example was good for the cadets: "if it makes better soldiers and men of them, why the necessity of knocking the paste eye out of their idol?"[38] Sherman, Benteen, and many others in the army participated in a quiet cover-up of Custer's folly so that the army and the nation might have a glowing myth. Although Ford exposed the truth behind the Custer myth in *Fort Apache* he was not attacking it. On the contrary, he reaffirmed its usefulness.

Ford made no apologies for his treatment of the Indians in his films. He was hardly a romantic in his approach to the Indian wars, often comparing the plight of the Indians to that of the Irish. "Let's face it," Ford told Peter Bogdanovich, "we've treated them very badly—it's a blot on our shield; we've cheated and robbed, killed, murdered, massacred and everything else, but they kill one white man and, God, out come the troops."[39]

Still, Ford approached the plight of the Indians with a balanced perspective. "The Indians are very dear to my heart," Ford declared. "There is truth in the accusation that the Indian has not been painted with justice in the Western, but that is a false generalization. The Indian did not like the white man, and he was no diplomat. We were enemies and we fought each other. The struggle against the Indian was fundamental in the history of the Far West."[40]

Of the major Custer films before *Fort Apache*, only the Ince and DeMille features had dealt insultingly with the Indians, while *The Massacre*, *The Scarlet West*, and *They Died with Their Boots On* had all treated them sympathetically. Hollywood tended to follow the general dichotomy of American literature that alternated between images of the Indian as nature's nobleman and as debased savage. While Westerns had long been populated by noble red men (often as trusty sidekicks), crooked Indian agents, whiskey traders, and various types of Indian haters, the vast majority of films in the genre treated the natives as part of a harsh environment that was to be conquered. Few films attempted to develop the basic humanity of Indian characters adequately.[41]

The 1950 box-office success of Delmer Daves's *Broken Arrow* forever altered the Hollywood approach to Indians, however, and resulted in a long string of films with Indian heroes (invariably portrayed by whites).[42] The Western was simply following a trend toward social commentary that began immediately following World War II with films like *Lost Weekend* (1945), *The Best Years of Our Lives* (1946), and *The Snake Pit* (1948). Films concerned with racial justice were especially popular, as evidenced by *Gentleman's Agreement* (1948), *Home of the Brave* (1949), *Pinky* (1949), and *No Way Out* (1950). While such message films quickly vanished in the early 1950s as race became a more divisive national issue, the trend toward racial-justice Westerns continued throughout the decade. Because Indian people were neither a visible nor politically organized minority at the time, and because the "Indian problem" had already been settled by conquest, little controversy resulted from such films.[43]

It was only natural for Hollywood to demythologize Custer, ever the symbol of the Indian wars and the cavalry, and use him as an evil counter to the new Indian heroes. As such, the moviemakers finally got to the point their literary cousins had reached in the 1930s. With rather monotonous regularity Custer was portrayed in both films and novels throughout the 1950s and 1960s as a vain racist in search of personal glory at the expense of innocent, usually quite peace-loving, natives. This new Custer image was so all-pervasive by 1971 that *Life* magazine labeled the Custer Battlefield National Monument in Montana "a sore from America's past" and suggested its elimination.[44]

The Custer films of the 1950s aided in dramatically altering public perceptions of the Indian wars. The first three Custer films of the decade, however, were quite traditional. Both *Warpath* (1951, fig. 38) and *Bugles in the Afternoon* (1952) used the Little Bighorn battle as a convenient backdrop for conventional revenge sagas. Custer was not an important character in either film. James Millican in *Warpath* portrayed Custer as arrogant and contemptuous of his

Indian foe, while Sheb Wooley in *Bugles in the Afternoon* gave no hint of Custer's personal characteristics (even though Custer was a central, and negative, character in the Ernest Haycox novel upon which the film was based). *Little Big Horn* (1951), despite the clever use of Otto Becker's barroom print as an advertising motif, did not portray Custer or his last battle. Instead, the film, produced by Charles Marquis Warren, western novelist turned scriptwriter and director, is a variant on the horror movie in which every member of the cast stupidly goes one by one down into the basement. In this case it is a squad of soldiers, led by feuding officers Lloyd Bridges and John Ireland, who ride off to warn Custer only to meet horrible fates one by one.

John Ford returned to Custer twice in this period. *She Wore a Yellow Ribbon* (1949) begins with a Seventh Cavalry guidon whipping in the wind as a voice-over narrator informs the audience: "Custer is dead. And around the bloody guidon of the immortal Seventh Cavalry lie two hundred and twelve officers and men." That fact dictates the action that follows in this splendid technicolor Western scripted by Frank Nugent and Laurence Stallings and based on the James Warner Bellah short story, "War Party." In Ford's *The Searchers* (1956), again scripted by Nugent, the aftermath of a Washita-like massacre is depicted. Custer's cavalry is seen herding captive women and children through the snow into an army post, while "Garry Owen" plays on the sound track. In a scene cut from the final release print, John Wayne as antihero Ethan Edwards confronts Peter Ortiz as an arrogant Custer about the massacre. Only a publicity still and the original script remain to remind us of Custer's fleeting appearance in the single greatest Western ever made.

In *Sitting Bull* (1954) a glory-hunting, racist Custer played by Douglas Kennedy manages to frustrate the efforts of Dale Robertson as an army officer and J. Carrol Naish as an incredibly noble Sitting Bull to prevent war. The Sidney Salkow and Jack DeWitt script then has Custer disobeying his orders in a headlong rush to destroy the Sioux. After the Last Stand President Grant comes west to save Robertson from a firing squad and make peace with Sitting Bull. This history rewrite was too much for the New York *Times* film critic, who noted that "Grant was an optimist toward Indians, but he wasn't an absolute fool: and that is apparently what some scriptwriters take the poor public to be."[45] Naish, an Irish-American who had portrayed General Phil Sheridan in *Rio Grande* in 1950 and was to play General Santa Anna in *Last Command* in 1955, seemed to be every casting director's favorite historical character. This was his second outing as Sitting Bull, having played the role in the 1950 musical, *Annie Get Your Gun*.

Crazy Horse is given credit for wiping out the Seventh in the 1955 film, *Chief Crazy Horse*, although the battle is not depicted. Victor Mature, terribly miscast as the mystical Sioux warrior, does the best he can. The Franklin Coen and Gerald Adams script was at least fairly faithful to history. More interesting today is the behind-the-scenes tragedy that accompanied the making of the film. Twenty-three-year-old Susan Ball, who plays Crazy Horse's wife, went ahead with her role despite having just had a leg amputated because of cancer. She died soon after the film was completed.

Columbia's *Seventh Cavalry*, released the next year, was based on a Glendon Swarthout story about a cavalry officer accused of cowardice for missing Little Bighorn but who redeems himself by leading a suicide mission to bury Custer's dead. Randolph Scott plays the officer who constantly defends Custer's reputation against the aspersions cast by Major Marcus Reno and others. Such a defense of Custer was already a Hollywood rarity.

Custer, as portrayed by Britt Lomond, was particularly sadistic and racist in Walt Disney's *Tonka* (1958, fig. 39). Lomond played the villain in the successful Disney *Zorro* television series, and he brought the same graceful snarl to his Custer role.

Based on David Appel's novel, *Comanche*, the film purported to tell the story of the only cavalry mount to survive Custer's Last Stand and of the young Indian boy who cared for him. Sal Mineo played the Sioux youth, White Bull, whose love for the stallion, Tonka, causes his banishment when he frees the horse to prevent its mistreatment by a rival brave. The horse eventually becomes the mount of Captain Myles Keogh (Philip Carey), who previously appeared as a particularly vibrant memory in Ford's *She Wore a Yellow Ribbon*. Custer's maniacal hatred of the Indians brings on war, and at Little Bighorn the kindly and heroic Keogh is killed by White Bull's rival. When the Indian attempts to scalp the fallen officer he is trampled to death by the enraged horse. White Bull fights with the Sioux in the battle and is terribly wounded. Found on the battlefield with his horse, they are both nursed back to health by the soldiers. The army seems to hold no grudges in this Disney version of history, for the horse becomes the mascot of the cavalry with White Bull as his uniformed stable attendant.

The battle in *Tonka* is among the best ever filmed, with the terrain fairly correct and troop movements following the sketchy details that are available. Custer does not even get his standard gallant death scene, being shot early in the battle as he huddles behind a dead horse. Of the Custer films to date only *Tonka* and *Little Big Man,* (p. 260) have deviated from the stereotypical last stand image.

Philip Carey, who portrayed Captain Keogh in *Tonka,* was promoted to the role of Custer in *The Great Sioux Massacre.* This 1965 Columbia film also marked a return to familiar territory for director Sidney Salkow, who had directed *Sitting Bull.* Also starring in the film was Cherokee actor Iron Eyes Cody, another alumnus from *Sitting Bull,* where he had portrayed Crazy Horse. Cody began his career in pictures in 1912 in Griffith's *The Massacre,* and later appeared in *The Plainsman, They Died with Their Boots On,* and *Fort Apache,* certainly a record for appearances in Custer films.[46]

Carey's Custer begins the film by sympathizing with the plight of the Indians, but his head is soon turned by the blandishments of a conniving politician. Believing that a great victory over the Indians will be his ticket to the White House, Custer disregards the advice of Major Reno (Joseph Cotton) and Captain Benteen (Darren McGavin) and leads the Seventh to its doom. The most interesting aspect of the battle is the ludicrous juxtaposition of long shots of mountain scenery borrowed from *Sitting Bull* with Sonoran desert close-ups filmed near Tucson.

Also released in 1965 was Arnold Laven's *The Glory Guys.* Sam Peckinpah's script, based on Hoffman Birney's 1956 novel, *The Dice of God,* has something of the raw realism and violent action that he would bring to the Western as a director by decade's end, but for the most part the film remains a pedestrian retelling of the Little Bighorn story. Andrew Duggan's General McCabe is yet another Indian-hating racist blinded by personal ambition who finally gets just what he deserves.

The most impressive Custer film of this period was never made. Wendell Mayes wrote a marvelous script for Twentieth-Century Fox, titled "The Day Custer Fell," and Fred Zinnemann, of *High Noon* fame, was set to direct it. Richard Zanuck approached Charlton Heston to take the Custer part but Heston declined, saying, "I don't see how you can make a serious film about a man who seems to have been not only egocentric, but muddleheaded. He was neither a very good soldier nor a very valuable man."[47] The eighteen-million-dollar project eventually collapsed as a result of the financial debacle that crippled Fox in the wake of the studio's production of *Cleopatra*.

Leslie Nielsen had a cameo as Custer in the 1966 Universal remake of *The Plainsman*, while the Little Bighorn was used as a prelude to the action in *Red Tomahawk*, released by Paramount that same year. The latter has the distinction of being the last of a series of A. C. Lyles's B-Westerns, marking the final gasp of that particular film type. Despite this rash of Custer films, the western genre was reaching the end of the celluloid trail, at least temporarily.

The Western had thrived during the 1950s, reaching a new maturity and attracting Hollywood's top talents. Major stars appeared regularly in prestige Westerns throughout the decade, with the genre accounting for nearly 30 percent of the major studios' total feature production. Yet, just as for the Sioux at Little Bighorn, at the Western's moment of greatest triumph the seeds of doom were already sown.[48]

Early television was desperate for programming, and old budget Westerns filled the bill. Features starring Tim McCoy, Hoot Gibson, and Bob Steele became standard fare while serials such as *Custer's Last Stand* from 1936 fit particularly well into television time slots. It was William Boyd, however, who proved just how lucrative television could be. He stopped making Hopalong Cassidy films in 1948 and promptly licensed the rights to his sixty-six films to television. By 1950 Boyd oversaw a Hoppy industry estimated at $200 million as the incredible success of his television Westerns promoted a wide array of merchandising. Gene Autry went over to television in 1950, followed soon after by Roy Rogers. Their products, and a host of other television Westerns, employed the conventions of the B-Western and aimed for the same juvenile audience. The impact on the small independent production companies was devastating. Although they had enjoyed a boom by selling their products to television in the late 1940s, they were now consumed by the very medium they had nurtured. In 1958, the greatest of the independents, Republic, went under.

Walt Disney broke with the major film studios in 1954 and began producing programs for the fledgling ABC network. His *Disneyland* television program revolutionized the neophyte medium with a three-part series on the life of Davy Crockett. By the time the last episode of the trilogy aired on February 23, 1955, a national craze of unprecedented proportions was underway. Soon every moppet in America had a coonskin cap and every network a stable of horse operas. These new television Westerns, like the Davy Crockett programs, emphasized high production values and aimed for an audience beyond the kindergarten crowd. In the fall of 1955 ABC launched Hugh O'Brien in *The Life and Legend of Wyatt Earp*. CBS countered with James Arness in *Gunsmoke*, and the TV adult Western was born. By the 1958–1959 season six of the top seven programs on television were Westerns, with forty-eight western series galloping across the airwaves by 1959.[49]

The overexposure caused by television, a loss of faith in old conventions, and the death or retirement of major stars all contributed to a stark decline of the Western in the 1960s. While 130 western feature films had been released in 1950, and sixty-eight in 1955, only twenty-eight were released in 1960, down to twenty-two by 1965. Much of what was made simply parodied the genre, such as *Cat Ballou* in 1965 or *Waterhole No. 3* in 1967, or played off the new conventions of violence imported with the Italian Westerns of Sergio Leone and others. Other filmmakers became obsessed with the death of the frontier, usually tinged with a romantic nostalgia for what was lost. *Lonely Are the Brave* (1962), *The Man Who Shot Liberty Valance* (1962), *Ride the High Country* (1962), and *Butch Cassidy and the Sundance Kid* (1969) all used this theme, but it was Sam Peckinpah's violent 1969 masterpiece *The Wild Bunch* that most fully realized its potential. The Westerns that followed *The Wild Bunch* became so focused on the closing of the West that they helped close out the Western.[50]

The dark tragedy and explicit violence of the Westerns of the late sixties and early seventies clearly reflected the times in which they were made. While the decade began with a burst of optimism and bright promise with the election of John F. Kennedy and the unveiling of his "New Frontier" assault on poverty and racism, it ended with dark alienation dominating a nation torn asunder by domestic unrest and foreign war. Political assassination, continuing racism, and resultant black militancy, the self-serving deception of the people by two presidential administrations, and above all the frustrating and divisive Vietnam War all tore at the social fabric and undercut national identity. The ecology movement led to a new view of wilderness conquerors as ecological exploiters. Indian civil rights organizations rose to prominence, pointing out that their ancestors had lived in harmony with the land. Many now came to view Indian culture as a more rational, natural way of life. No group was more affected by these new views than the young, who were, of course, also the main patrons of motion pictures.

The new Westerns reflected this growing disenchantment with both the present and the past. Heroism and self-sacrifice gave way to greed and self-interest in films like *Hombre* (1967) and *McCabe and Mrs. Miller* (1971). Those who could not adjust to an increasingly corrupt society were destroyed by it, as in *Billy Jack* (1971), *The Life and Times of Judge Roy Bean* (1972), and *Tom Horn* (1980). Racism continued as a major theme, but the triumph of justice that had marked the endings of *Broken Arrow* and *Cheyenne Autumn* was replaced with tragedy, as in *Tell Them Willie Boy Is Here* (1969), or genocide, as in *Soldier Blue* (1970). Finally, western heroes were regularly debunked: Wyatt Earp in *Hour of the Gun* (1967) and *Doc* (1971); Jesse James in *The Great Northfield, Minnesota Raid* (1971) and *The Long Riders* (1980); Buffalo Bill Cody in *Buffalo Bill and the Indians* (1976); Billy the Kid in *Dirty Little Billy* (1972); and Pat Garrett in *Pat Garrett and Billy the Kid* (1973). Custer made perfect grist for the mill of the celluloid debunker.

ABC Television, in attempting to exploit the youth fixation of the 1960s, presented a heroic Custer in a 1967 series starring Wayne Maunder. Titled *Custer*, the program's advertising emphasized that its hero was "long-haired, headstrong, flamboyant, and a maverick."

Despite the haircut, America's youth did not warm to the program, while Indian groups got rather heatedly outraged. The National Congress of the American Indian demanded equal time to respond to the premiere episode, declaring that "glamorizing Custer is like glamorizing Billy the Kid" because he "endorsed a policy of genocide and massacred village after village of Indians."[51] *Newsweek* criticized the show, pointing out that Custer was not a suitable hero because he "was court-martialed twice, once left his men to die, discarded a son squired through Indian wenching, and had a reputation for cruelty."[52] It was disinterest, however, that finished off Custer in midseason—the ratings were abysmal. Long-haired maverick or not, a heroic Custer was a tough sell in the sixties.

Television had dealt often with the Custer story, most especially during the 1950s western craze. Custer had proven the basis of particularly compelling episodes of *The Twilight Zone, Cheyenne, Gunsmoke, Time Tunnel,* and *Branded.* But after ABC's debacle with Custer, the general lost his popularity with producers. When he did appear again, in the 1977 NBC *Hallmark Hall of Fame* teleplay of "The Court-Martial of George Armstrong Custer," it would be as a near-raving lunatic. James Olsen's unhinged Custer was derived from Douglas C. Jones's best-selling fantasy novel in which Custer is the only survivor of Little Bighorn.[53]

Two trends of the dying western genre—the European Western and the end-of-the-frontier Western—were combined with the gimmickry of cinerama in *Custer of the West* (1968, fig. 40). Filmed in Spain and starring English actor Robert Shaw as the title character, the film made a sincere if misguided effort to deal with the complexities of frontier expansion and the Indian wars. Custer is a hell-for-leather soldier who loves a fight for the sake of a fight, but who finds the one-sided warfare with the Indians troubling. He is even more worried by the onrushing industrial revolution and the impersonal impact it will have on combat. "Trains, steel, guns that kill by thousands—our kind of fighting is done," he tells visiting Indians. In destroying the Indians this Custer is also destroying the only warriors left who are just like himself. Shaw postures, broods, and agonizes until he finally rushes purposefully to his doom at Little Bighorn. Custer is the last man alive on the stricken field, and the Indians pull back to allow him to leave.

Unwilling to face life in a corrupt, changing world, Custer places a single bullet in his pistol and shouts the charge.

Custer of the West was a bust at the box office, and critical reviews attacked its semi-positive view of its protagonist. Charles Reno, a grandnephew of Major Marcus Reno, sued the film's producers, claiming his ancestor was slandered by Ty Hardin's portrayal of him in the film. The New York State Supreme Court dismissed the case in Custer's only victory during the sixties.[54]

The 1960s also witnessed a revitalization of interest in the plight of the American Indian, both past and present. Ironically, much of this new sensitivity to past injustice was a direct result of the Vietnam War. The Indian was often used as a vehicle by literary artists to attack American involvement in Vietnam. Arthur Kopit's critically acclaimed play, *Indians* (filmed in 1976 by Robert Altman as *Buffalo Bill and the Indians*) and Ralph Nelson's *Soldier Blue* (1970) use an Indian wars theme to attack the Vietnam War. Indian civil rights groups became increasingly active during this period, encouraged by the national reception of Vine Deloria's best-selling manifesto, *Custer Died for Your Sins*, in 1969. Indian topics became all the rage among eastern publishers, especially after the enormous success of Dee Brown's *Bury My Heart at Wounded Knee* in 1971.

Arthur Penn's 1970 film, *Little Big Man*, fit perfectly into its times, proving to be the second-highest grossing movie of the year. Based on Thomas Berger's deeply ironic novel, the film follows the travail of Jack Crabb (Dustin Hoffman) as he aimlessly moves back and forth between the worlds of the Indians and the whites. Crabb gradually comes to recognize the purity of the simpler Cheyenne way over the decadence of the white world. The leader of the whites is, of course, Custer—bloodthirsty, opportunistic, arrogant, and finally stark raving mad.

Director Penn and screenwriter Calder Willingham made no pretense at objectivity. Penn used his film as a vehicle to attack the arrogant, wrong-headed brand of leadership that prolonged the fighting in Vietnam rather than admit a mistake. Custer, Penn felt, was "so infatuated with his capacity to win, so racially assured that he belonged to a superior breed," that he led his men into a hopeless battle, and thus made the perfect historical metaphor. "Although I am focusing on history," Penn explained in a press

Richard Mulligan as Custer in Little Big Man
(Cinema Center Films, 1970) (Courtesy Brian W. Dippie)

release, "I believe that the film is contemporary because . . . history does repeat itself."[55]

The detailed, and fairly accurate, depiction of Custer's attack on Black Kettle's village on the Washita is used as an obvious parallel to the My Lai Massacre, even to the casting of oriental actress Amy Eccles as Crabb's Indian wife killed in the slaughter. Sound bytes as if from the Vietnam-era six-o'clock news appear, as when Custer defends the Washita massacre to a shocked subordinate: "This is a legal action, lieutenant. The men are under strict orders not to shoot the women—unless, of course, they refuse to surrender. History will confirm the larger moral right is ours."

At Little Bighorn Custer is trapped by his own arrogance, ignoring evidence of a trap rather than "change a Custer decision." The battle is a rout, with no lines of defense or order. Custer, entirely unhinged, wanders about ranting until struck down by arrows just before he can kill Crabb. This time there is to be no glory, no heroism, no redemptive sacrifice—just a well-deserved and ignoble death.

This harshly ideological portrait, while containing some elements of truth, is ultimately even more wildly inaccurate than *They Died with Their Boots On*. Richard Mulligan's Custer is a preening buffoon who cannot be taken seriously. He is all conceit and bluster, failing entirely as menacing devil or as a particularly dangerous opponent. The sense of irony that marked Thomas Berger's novel, where Custer is always larger than life, is gone entirely from the film version. Finally, the great Indian victory at Little Bighorn is trivialized, for there can be no honor in defeating such a cowardly band of soldiers led by such a complete idiot.

Little Big Man is a disturbing tragedy clothed in the conventions of broad farce. It fed on the conventions of the western genre, holding them up to ridicule and sometimes turning them upside down. Custer, that most famous of all frontier warriors—the hero, the martyr, the sacrifice of his race—was now exposed as a clown dressed up in a soldier suit. *Little Big Man* struck a responsive chord with audiences and for two decades had the final word on General Custer and his celebrated Last Stand.

Hollywood may have finished with Custer after *Little Big Man*, but he returned in the 1974 French film *Touche pas la femme blanche*. Marcello Mastroianni's Custer was a "milksop braggart and dandy infatuated with his own success." The Last Stand was filmed in a Paris excavation pit with Vietnamese refugees playing the Sioux. Director Marco Ferreri found it "laughable" that "the conquerors are eventually wiped out too. That's what happened at Little Big Horn and what will happen tomorrow, I hope, everywhere." But Ferreri's Marxist vision of Little Bighorn was never released in the United States.[56]

Hollywood appeared to be finished with the Custer story, and perhaps with the western genre as well. A new, darker vision of the past had settled on a torn and divided nation. Guilt and self-doubt had replaced pride and optimism. The Westerns of the 1970s reflected this national malaise, finally cannibalizing themselves and parodying the genre out of existence. At the same time, the old masters left the scene. *Gunsmoke*, the last great television Western, was canceled in 1975. John Ford died in 1973, Howard Hawks in 1977, John Wayne in 1979, Raoul Walsh in 1981, and Sam Peckinpah in 1984. No one stepped forward to take their places. By 1980 only six Westerns were released by the studios. Finally, in 1980, the *coup de grace* was applied to the genre by the collapse of United Artists studio after the critical and commercial failure of Michael Cimino's *Heaven's Gate*.

Custer's celluloid career rose and fell with the fortunes of western film. He persisted as a heroic figure on film far longer than he did in print, but in all cases he proved a remarkably resilient and flexible historical figure. From a symbol of heroic self-sacrifice in the winning of the West, Custer gradually evolved into a symbol of white arrogance and brutality in the conquest and exploitation of the West. As the popular perception of the military, the environment, the Indians, and the West changed, a new Custer myth emerged in place of the old. But always, the fascination with this dashing if misguided soldier held firm—at least so long as the western film prospered.

These Custer films have been like glass windows—sometimes opening up a pathway to an understanding of the past, as in *Fort Apache*—and other times staying shut to mirror the times in which they were made, as with *They Died with Their Boots On* and *Little Big Man*. We can never hope to discern the facts of history from them, but the best of them can effect a truthful fiction well worth contemplation and perhaps tell us something about ourselves.

The video cassette revolution of the 1980s has given a new life to many of these old features. Major films such as *The Plainsman*, *They Died with Their Boots On*, *Fort Apache*, and *Little Big Man* are all now easily accessible on videotape. Even minor titles, such as *Little Big Horn*, *Bugles in the Afternoon*, and *Seventh Cavalry*, are reaching entirely new audiences as a result of video sales and rental outlets. This, of course, has remarkably increased the audience and influence of older films, so that the impact of a film will no longer be tied only to the generation of its release period. Errol Flynn's Custer can now compete with Richard Mulligan's Custer for the hearts and minds of a vast video audience, both now and far into the future.

We may assume that Hollywood is not done with General Custer either. The enormous success of *Lonesome Dove* on television, coupled with the recent triumph of Kevin Costner's *Dances with Wolves* at the movie theaters, has heralded to many the return of the Western. These two features approached our western heritage from decidedly different points of view, but both dealt with their subjects on a grand scale, treating their material seriously and recreating a compelling past for their audiences.

At the same time there has been a remarkable revival of interest in Custer. Evan S. Connell's freewheeling exploration of Custer and his singular, epic moment at Little Bighorn, *Son of the Morning Star*, was the surprise best-seller of 1984. *Time* listed it as one of the top books of the decade. Connell's portrait of Custer as a brave, experienced, but driven soldier full of compelling contradictions did much to rehabilitate his reputation. That was followed in 1988 by Robert M. Utley's definitive biography, *Cavalier in Buckskin: George Armstrong Custer and the Western Military Frontier*, which gave an even more positive portrait of its protagonist.

Son of the Morning Star (fig. 41) was promptly developed as a television miniseries. Scripted by Melissa Mathison (who wrote *E.T.*), the production initially had Kevin Costner signed to portray Custer. NBC, not feeling that Costner was a big enough star, passed on the project. Costner went on to superstardom and the miniseries finally found a home at ABC. It aired in 1991 with Gary Cole as Custer, Rosanna Arquette as Elizabeth, Dean Stockwell as Sheridan, and Rodney Grant (who is also featured in *Dances with Wolves*) as Crazy Horse.

Despite impressive production values and a careful reconstruction of Custer's last battle, *Son of the Morning Star* was not particularly successful in either a commercial or dramatic sense. Cole and Arquette were terribly miscast as the leads. As written, this Custer was a far more positive presentation than the dangerous buffoon of *Little Big Man*, but Cole failed to infuse any charm or basic decency into his portrayal. His Custer seemed petulant, spoiled, and totally self-absorbed. It is difficult to care about his romance with Arquette's Elizabeth or his ultimate fate. As military spectacle *Son of the Morning Star* had its moments, but it utterly failed as grand human tragedy.

Custer remained a popular figure during the television western revival of the 1990s. Ever the colorful symbol of the military frontier, although straitjacketed in negative caricatures, he was a handy historical character. Most notable was the reoccurring Custer of the popular CBS series *Doctor Quinn, Medicine Woman*. He was played as the relentlessly evil foil to Quinn and her ever-so-noble friend Black Kettle. Custer also appeared as not quite so villainous on the short-lived 1995 series *Legend* on UPN, and as a preening and murderous villain in a nicely done 1996 episode of the syndicated series *The Lazarus Man*. Nineteen ninety-six also brought a flurry of publicity over the multimillion dollar purchase by New Line Cinema of a new Custer feature film script by *Dances with Wolves* author Michael Blake.

The interest in Blake's script is reflective of Hollywood's continuing fascination with Custer and his last battle. As a captivating symbol of the Indian wars, Custer will continue to be interpreted and reinterpreted by creative artists. It is indeed too powerful a tale to be ignored for long. Custer, dying again, and again, and again will ever provide audiences with lessons about the past, the present, and the future. But, of course, he never really died. Ultimately, that bold young American warrior achieved his greatest ambition—immortality.

Notes

1. Peter Bogdanovich, *John Ford* (Berkeley: University of California Press, 1968), 86.

2. When John Ford approached Frank Nugent to write the screenplay Ford gave Nugent a list of some fifty books to read on the Indian wars. Later Ford sent him to Arizona to get a feel for the landscape. "When I got back," Nugent recalled, "Ford asked me if I thought I had enough research. I said yes. 'Good,' he said, 'Now just forget everything you've

read, and we'll start writing a movie.'" So much for the impact of scholarship on film. Lindsay Anderson, *About John Ford* (New York: McGraw-Hill Book Co., 1981), 77-79. *Fort Apache*, like the other two films in Ford's cavalry trilogy, *She Wore a Yellow Ribbon* (1949) and *Rio Grande* (1950), was based on a James Warner Bellah short story. Bellah later wrote the scripts for Ford's tale of the buffalo soldiers, *Sergeant Rutledge* (1960) and *The Man Who Shot Liberty Valance* (1962). His cavalry short stories, most of them originally published in the *Saturday Evening Post* in the late 1940s, appeared as James Warner Bellah, *Reveille* (Greenwich, Conn.: Fawcett Gold Medal, 1962).

3. Paul L. Hedren, *First Scalp for Custer: The Skirmish at Warbonnet Creek, Nebraska, July 17, 1876* (Glendale: Arthur H. Clark Co., 1980).

4. William F. Cody, *The Life of Hon. William F. Cody, Known as Buffalo Bill* (Lincoln: University of Nebraska Press, 1978), 360; Don Russell, *The Lives and Legends of Buffalo Bill* (Norman: University of Oklahoma Press, 1960), 253-57.

5. The evolution of Cody's show is fully and ably discussed in Don Russell, *The Wild West or, A History of the Wild West Shows* (Fort Worth: Amon Carter Museum of Western Art, 1970).

6. Kevin Brownlow, *The War, the West and the Wilderness* (New York: Alfred A. Knopf, 1979), 232.

7. Ibid., 228. See also Russell, *Buffalo Bill*, 457-58, and William Judson, "The Movies," in *Buffalo Bill and the Wild West* (Pittsburgh: University of Pittsburgh Press, 1981), 68-75.

8. Vincent A. Heier, Jr., "Thomas H. Ince's *Custer's Last Fight*: Reflections on the Making of the Custer Legend in Film," [St. Louis Westerners] *Westward*, 5 (May 1976), 21-26; Brownlow, *The War, the West and the Wilderness*, 257-60.

9. Data on silent Custer films is in Kenneth W. Munden, ed., *The American Film Institute Catalog of Motion Pictures Produced in the United States: Feature Films 1921–1930* (New York: AFI, 1971); Edward Buscombe, ed., *The BFI Companion to the Western* (New York: Atheneum, 1988); and Allen Eyles, *The Western* (New York: A. S. Barnes, 1975). *Camping with Custer*, released in 1913, is most likely a variant release title of *Campaigning with Custer* of the same year. Most certainly the 1912 film *Custer's Last Raid* is the same film as Ince's *Custer's Last Fight*. The Ince film is one of the few of these films to have survived; almost all of them have been lost.

10. Munden, ed., *American Film Institute Catalog*, 284, 420, 687; Indianapolis *Star*, December 20, 1925.

11. Indianapolis *Star*, September 26, 1926.

12. Ibid., September 23, 1926.

13. New York *Times*, April 11, 1926.

14. Ibid., April 5, 1926. Despite the epic qualities and enormous budget of *The Flaming Frontier*, no copy of the film is known to exist today.

15. For the evolution of the Custer myth see Paul A. Hutton, "From Little Big Horn to Little Big Man: The Changing Image of a Western Hero in Popular Culture," *Western Historical Quarterly*, 7 (January 1976), 19-45; Brian W. Dippie, *Custer's Last Stand: The Anatomy of an American Myth* (Missoula: University of Montana, 1976); Robert M. Utley, *Custer and the Great Controversy: The Origin and Development of a Legend* (Los Angeles: Westernlore Press, 1962); Bruce A. Rosenberg, *Custer and the Epic of Defeat* (University Park: Pennsylvania University Press, 1974); Kent Ladd Steckmesser, *The Western Hero in History and Legend* (Norman: University of Oklahoma Press, 1965); Edward Tabor Linenthal, *Changing Images of the Warrior Hero in America: A History of Popular Symbolism* (New York: Edwin Mellen Press, 1982) and Richard Slotkin, *The Fatal Environment: The Myth of the Frontier in the Age of Industrialization, 1800–1890* (New York: Atheneum, 1985).

16. For Custer fiction see Brian W. Dippie, "Jack Crabb and the Sole Survivors of Custer's Last Stand," *Western American Literature*, 4 (Fall 1969), 189-202.

17. Robert Sklar, *Movie-Made America: A Cultural History of American Movies* (New York: Random House, 1975), 173-94. So powerful and so attentive to detail did the censorship groups become, that by 1943 they could pressure Producers Releasing Corporation to change the name of the main character of the highly successful Billy the Kid film series from the historical Billy Bonney to the fictional Billy Carson. Thus, matinee-crowd moppets were rescued from the glorification of western outlaws. Paul Andrew Hutton, "Dreamscape Desperado," *New Mexico Magazine*, 68 (June 1990), 44-57.

18. Two invaluable guides to the western genre are Buscombe, ed., *BFI Companion to the Western*, and Phil Hardy, *The Western* (New York: William Morrow and Co., 1983). Highly opinionated but delightful, is Brian Garfield, *Western Films: A Complete Guide* (New York: Rawson Associates, 1982), while an equally personal but more anecdotal overview is in Jon Tuska, *The Filming of the West* (Garden City, N.Y.: Doubleday, 1976). The standard history remains George N. Fenin and William K. Everson, *The Western: from Silents to the Seventies* (New York: Grossman Publishers, 1973), while two useful anthologies are Jack Nachbar, ed., *Focus on the Western* (Englewood Cliffs, N.J.: Prentice-Hall, 1974) and Richard W. Etulain, "Recent Interpretations of the Western Film: A Bibliographical Essay," *Journal of the West*, 22 (October 1983), 72-81.

19. New York *Times*, January 17, 1937.

20. Michael E. Welsh, "Western Film, Ronald Reagan, and the Western Metaphor," in *Shooting Stars: Heroes and Heroines of Western Film,* ed. Archie P. McDonald (Bloomington: Indiana University Press, 1987), 153. See also Tony Thomas, *The Films of Ronald Reagan* (Secaucus, N.J.: Citadel Press, 1980), 109-14; Ronald Reagan with Richard G. Hubler, *Where's the Rest of Me?* (New York: Duell, Sloan and Pearce, 1965), 95-96; Ronald W. Reagan, "Looking Back at *Santa Fe Trail,*" *Greasy Grass,* 6 (May 1990), 2-5.

21. New York *Times,* December 21, 1940.

22. Robert Stack and Mark Evans, *Straight Shooting* (New York: Macmillan, 1980), 63.

23. Rudy Behlmer, *Inside Warner Bros. (1935–1951)* (New York: Viking, 1985), 173-74.

24. Tony Thomas, Rudy Behlmer, and Clifford McCarty, *The Films of Errol Flynn* (New York: Citadel Press, 1969), 106-11. See also Kingsley Canham, *The Hollywood Professionals: Michael Curtiz, Raoul Walsh, Henry Hathaway* (New York: A. S. Barnes, 1973), and Peter Valenti, *Errol Flynn: A Bio-Bibliography* (Westport: Greenwood Press, 1984), 30-31, 72-73.

25. Behlmer, *Inside Warner Bros.,* 175-78; John E. O'Connor, *The Hollywood Indian: Stereotypes of Native Americans in Films* (Trenton: New Jersey State Museum, 1980), 42.

26. *Life,* December 8, 1941, 75-78; New York *Times,* November 30, 1941.

27. Fine wires were attached to leg bands on a horse's front legs, with the other ends tied to logs buried in the ground. Slack between the horse and log allowed a strong gallop before the horse's front legs were suddenly jerked from under him. Dramatic scenes of horses plunging forward or turning somersaults were the result. Neither horse nor rider had to be trained for such stunts. Many horses were killed in the fall or had to be destroyed because of broken legs. Anthony Amaral, *Movie Horses: Their Treatment and Training* (Indianapolis: Bobbs-Merrill, 1967), 9-20.

28. Among the old westerners who gravitated to Hollywood were Wyatt Earp, Charlie Siringo, Al Jennings, Emmett Dalton, and Bill Tilghman. For more on the cowboys who provided the essential cadre of rough riders for the movies see Dianna Serra Cary, *The Hollywood Posse: The Story of the Gallant Band of Horsemen Who Made Movie History* (Boston: Houghton Mifflin, 1975).

29. Richard Schickel, *The Men Who Made the Movies* (New York: Atheneum, 1975), 47-48; Buster Wiles, *My Days with Errol Flynn: The Autobiography of a Stuntman* (Santa Monica: Roundtable Publishing, 1988), 97-100; William R. Meyer, *The Making of the Great Westerns* (New Rochelle, N.Y.: Arlington House, 1979), 108-21.

30. Tony Thomas, *The Films of Olivia de Havilland* (Secaucus, N.J.: Citadel, 1983), 181-87.

31. George MacDonald Fraser, *The Hollywood History of the World: from One Million Years B.C. to Apocalypse Now* (New York: William Morrow, 1988), 200. Fraser is the author of several screenplays as well as the successful Flashman series of novels. That series includes one of the best available Custer novels, *Flashman and the Redskins* (New York: Alfred A. Knopf, 1982). Two other critical discussions of the relationship of western films to western history are Jon Tuska, *The American West in Film: Critical Approaches to the Western* (Westport: Greenwood Press, 1985), and Wayne Michael Sarf, *God Bless You, Buffalo Bill: A Layman's Guide to History and the Western Film* (Rutherford, N.J.: Fairleigh Dickinson University Press, 1983). Also see Mark C. Carnes, ed., *Past Imperfect: History According to the Movies* (New York: Henry Holt, 1995).

32. Buscombe, ed., *BFI Companion to the Western*, 42-45, 426-28. For more on the postwar Western see Philip French, *Westerns* (New York: Oxford University Press, 1977); and Jim Kitses, *Horizons West: Anthony Mann, Budd Buetticher, Sam Peckinpah: Studies of Authorship within the Western* (Bloomington: Indiana University Press, 1969).

33. Few filmmakers have been as discussed as Ford, arguably the greatest director in the history of film. For studies that consider *Fort Apache* in some detail see Tag Gallagher, *John Ford: The Man and His Films* (Berkeley: University of California Press, 1986); Anderson, *About John Ford*; J. A. Place, *The Western Films of John Ford* (New York: Citadel Press, 1974); Andrew Sarris, *The John Ford Movie Mystery* (Bloomington: Indiana University Press, 1975); Joseph McBride and Michael Wilmington, *John Ford* (New York: DaCapo Press, 1975); John Baxter, *The Cinema of John Ford* (New York: A. S. Barnes, 1971); Peter Stowell, *John Ford* (Boston: Twayne, 1986); and two more biographical works, Andrew Sinclair, *John Ford* (New York: Dial Press, 1979); Dan Ford, *Pappy: The Life of John Ford* (Englewood Cliffs, N.J.: Prentice-Hall, 1979). Ford's impressive body of cinematic work on the American frontier experience and on American history in general obviously had a dramatic impact on the nation's collective imagination concerning its past. His work is well worth study as art, cultural artifact, and a lesson on popular history.

34. Sinclair, *John Ford*, 142.

35. For more on *Fort Apache* see Russell Campbell, "Fort Apache," *The Velvet Light Trap*, 17 (Winter 1977), 8-12; William T. Pilkington, "Fort Apache (1948)," in *Western Movies*, ed. William T. Pilkington and Don Graham (Albuquerque: University of New Mexico Press, 1979), 40-49; Tony Thomas, *The West That Never Was* (Secaucus, N.J.: Citadel Press, 1989), 104-11.

36. In the original James Warner Bellah short story Thursday arrives on the stricken battlefield after the massacre and commits suicide. James Warner Bellah, "Massacre," *Saturday Evening Post*, 219 (February 27, 1947), 18-19, 140-46.

37. Robert M. Utley, ed., "Sherman on Custer at Little Big Horn," *Little Big Horn Associates Newsletter*, 9 (October 1975), 9.

38. W. A. Graham, *The Custer Myth: A Source Book of Custeriana* (Harrisburg, Pa.: Stackpole Books, 1953), 325.

39. Bogdanovich, *John Ford*, 104.

40. Sinclair, *John Ford*, 149.

41. For the image of Indians in film see Gretchen M. Bataille and Charles L. P. Silet, eds., *The Pretend Indians: Images of Native Americans in the Movies* (Ames: Iowa State University Press, 1980); Ralph E. Friar and Natasha A. Friar, *The Only Good Indian . . . The Hollywood Gospel* (New York: Drama Book Specialists, 1972). For the broader context see Brian W. Dippie, *The Vanishing American: White Attitudes and U.S. Indian Policy* (Middletown, Conn.: Wesleyan University Press, 1982); Robert F. Berkhofer, Jr., *The White Man's Indian: Images of the American Indian from Columbus to the Present* (New York: Alfred A. Knopf, 1978); Roy Harvey Pearce, *Savagism and Civilization: A Study of the Indian and the American Mind* (Baltimore: Johns Hopkins Press, 1965); Raymond William Stedman, *Shadows of the Indian: Stereotypes in American Culture* (Norman: University of Oklahoma Press, 1982); Richard Slotkin, *Regeneration through Violence: The Mythology of the American Frontier, 1600–1860* (Middletown, Conn.: Wesleyan University Press, 1973).

42. Some examples include *Battle at Apache Pass* (1952), *Hiawatha* (1952), *Conquest of Cochise* (1953), *Apache* (1954), *Taza, Son of Cochise* (1954), *Broken Lance* (1954), *White Feather* (1955), *The Indian Fighter* (1955), and *The Savage* (1953) which, although based on L. L. Foreman's 1942 Custer novel, *The Renegade*, altered the story and dropped Custer from the film.

43. Sklar, *Movie-Made America*, 279-80.

44. Alvin Josephy, "The Custer Myth," *Life*, July 2, 1971, 55.

45. New York *Times*, November 28, 1954.

46. Iron Eyes Cody and Collin Perry, *Iron Eyes: My Life as a Hollywood Indian* (New York: Everest House, 1982).

47. Charlton Heston, *The Actor's Life: Journals 1956–1976* (New York: E. P. Dalton, 1976); Wendell Mayes, "The Day Custer Fell" (unpublished screenplay, 1964).

48. John H. Lenihan, *Showdown: Confronting Modern America in the Western Film* (Urbana: University of Illinois Press, 1980); Buscombe, ed., *BFI Companion to the Western*, 45-48.

49. J. Fred MacDonald, *Who Shot the Sheriff? The Rise and Fall of the Television Western* (New York: Praeger, 1987), 15-85; Paul Andrew Hutton, "Davy Crockett: An Exposition on Hero Worship," in *Crockett at Two Hundred: New Perspectives on the Man and the Myth*, ed. Michael A. Lofaro and Joe Cummings (Knoxville: University of Tennessee Press, 1989), 20-41.

50. For the films of this period see Nachbar, ed., *Focus on the Western*, 101-28; French, *Westerns*, 135-67; Hardy, *The Western*, 274-363; Tuska, *Filming of the West*, 559-84; and Buscombe, ed., *BFI Companion to the Western*, 48-54.

51. Friar and Friar, *The Only Good Indian*, 274-75.

52. *Newsweek*, August 7, 1967, 51; New York *Times*, September 7, 1967; P. M. Clepper, "He's Our George," *TV Guide*, September 23, 1967, 32-34. In an effort to recoup some of their losses, the producers combined several episodes of the television show and released it in Europe as a feature, titled *The Legend of Custer*. The same had been done with the Custer episodes of the Cheyenne television show.

53. Paul A. Hutton, "Custer's Last Stand: Background," *TV Guide*, November 26, 1977, 39-42. See also John P. Langellier, "Movie Massacre: The Custer Myth in Motion Pictures and Television," *Research Review: The Journal of the Little Big Horn Associates*, 3 (June 1989), 20-31, and Dan Gagliasso, "Custer's Last Stand on Celluloid," *Persimmon Hill*, 19 (Spring 1991), 4–12. Custer appeared again in the 1979 television movie *The Legend of the Golden Gun*, where Keir Dullea portrayed him as a General MacArthur clone complete with sunglasses and pipe. Another television movie, *The Legend of Walks Far Woman* in 1982, features the Little Bighorn but does not portray Custer.

54. New York *Times*, October 2, 1968, March 18, 1960.

55. Gerald Astar, "The Good Guys Wear War Paint," *Look*, December 1, 1970, 60; *Little Big Man* (Cinema Center Films Pressbook, 1971), 4. See also John W. Turner, "Little Big Man (1970)," in Pilkington and Graham, eds., *Western Movies*, 109-21.

56. Brian W. Dippie, "Popcorn and Indians: Custer on the Screen," *Cultures*, 2 (no. 1, 1974), 162-63. Custer returned to the screen in a 1976 spoof of early Hollywood, *Won Ton Ton the Dog Who Saved Hollywood*, where Ron Leibman plays the actor Rudy Montague, who portrays Custer in the film within the film; the overblown 1981 Western, *The Legend of the Lone Ranger*, where Lincoln Tate had a cameo as a rather foolish Custer; and in the 1984 comedy *Teachers*, in which Richard Mulligan reprised his Custer role while portraying an escaped mental patient who dressed up as historical characters. By the 1980s Hollywood viewed the Custer story only as comic relief.

Contemporary Perspectives on the Little Bighorn

John P. Hart

I f the Custer story and the Battle of the Little Bighorn is fertile
ground for the historian, it is for the communication theorist
as well. The historical context involves intercultural
communication as one examines misunderstandings between
cultures both past and present. The Montana battle was the result
of problems in interpersonal relationships and communication as
much, if not more, than strategic military errors. To understand
the evolution of the Custer persona, especially after his death, is
not so much to study historical facts as it is to study symbols,
myth, and rhetoric. This essay attempts to provide an overview of
some of the issues communication theory can illuminate about
the legacy of Little Bighorn. Specifically, it addresses the symbolism
involved in naming the site and how that symbolism affects the
site's mythic value. It also suggests some rhetorical responses to
dealing with that symbolism.

Richard Slotkin has written three massive volumes that comprise
a history of myth in America. Slotkin concludes that the most
important myth to American culture is the myth of the frontier,
and he believes that the most important part of the frontier myth
is the last stand.[1] Insofar as the last stand has been personalized
into Custer's Last Stand, by extension, given Slotkin's conclusions,
the most important mythic figure in American culture is not

Abraham Lincoln or George Washington but George Armstrong Custer. Perhaps this explains the length and ferocity of what Edward Linenthal terms the ideological struggle over the battle site.[2]

The most significant symbolic act in the contemporary history of the battlefield was probably the changing of its name in 1991 from Custer Battlefield National Monument to Little Bighorn Battlefield National Monument. The official rationale for the change was that the original name was unique and did not fit with National Park Service (NPS) criteria for naming parks.[3] The new name is problematic in that it is the *only* battlefield in the park system to be called a monument, rather than a military park, a memorial, or simply a battlefield. By contrast at least, the original name shared personification with Perry's Victory and International Peace Park, which commemorates the victory of Oliver Perry at the Battle of Lake Erie.

In the case of the Little Bighorn, there was no move to make the new name consistent with NPS procedure because bureaucratic consistency was *not* the primary motive for the original name change. Although supporters of the name-change legislation, House Resolution 848, specifically denied it, textual analysis betrays other reasons for the name change. Statements such as "the time has come . . . to cease 'honoring' Custer," "Custer symbolizes . . . a U.S. government bent toward genocidal policies with regard to American Indians," and "it would be a very small gesture of atonement for past U.S. policies to change the name of the park" suggest other motivations.[4] Rhetoricians observe that the intent of the speaker is largely irrelevant; what matters is the perception of the audience. Custer would still seem to be dying for our sins.

There is a problem with taking Custer's name off the monument if Custer is viewed as a hero, but what about the many who do not view Custer as a hero? They, too, should be concerned because of the symbolic power and detrimental effects of scapegoating. Taking Custer's name off the battlefield in effect allows society to sweep its treatment of Indian peoples under the rug.

Philosopher Kenneth Burke argues that in the plot of human drama, we resolve guilt by either scapegoating others or blaming ourselves.[5] Removing Custer's name from the battlefield can only be construed as dishonoring the soldier. This reinforces the popular post-Vietnam view that genocidal generals are responsible for the government's poor handling of its relationships with Native Americans. Scapegoating individuals removes the blame from society as a whole. By shifting the blame from society to Custer, we make it right and have no need for further action. This absolves white society today of any guilt towards Indian peoples. By blaming one ancestor, we remove ourselves from the legacy of guilt. Now we can all watch *Dances with Wolves* and cheer for the same side. This is tragic, both because it ignores the lessons of history and because it does not resolve America's responsibility toward wronged minorities.

Among its various observable effects, scapegoating, because it drew the greater attention, obscured the drive for an Indian memorial. For many Indian people, the memorial was the primary concern, not the name change.[6] As former battlefield superintendent Barbara Sutteer (née Booher), a supporter of the name change, later remarked privately:

> What saddens me is that the name change came to overshadow the memorial. Indian people wanted the memorial, yet it got lost in the hysteria over the Custer name. For example, we were to have a ceremony at the Battlefield on the Fourth of July 1992 to present the legislation for the memorial, but the media focused instead on the name change and described the event as a rededication of the battlefield.[7]

Scapegoating also encouraged injurious rhetorical counterstrategies. The rhetoric of the Custerphiles often resembles what communication scholar Theodore Windt calls a diatribe, the "last resort for protest," the rhetorical equivalent of the primal scream.[8] One need look no further than the ad hominem attacks on various members of the National Park Service to find evidence of this.[9] While the diatribe may be cathartic to the rhetor, it is what communication scholar David Berlo would term "consummatory," rhetoric for its own sake or for the enjoyment of the speaker, as opposed to "instrumental" communication, or rhetoric for the purpose of effect (although consummatory communication can be persuasive if the audience identifies with the rhetor).[10] Custerphiles appear to be willing to make a last stand over everything from a Black Elk quotation on the wall of the visitor center at the battlefield to the color of the sidewalks at the Reno-Benteen site.[11]

Although the furor over the North Shields Venture proposal to create a historical theme park next to the battlefield demonstrated that they are still capable of rising to the occasion, Custerphiles show all signs of "leaving the field" in terms of the battle site itself. This is a shame because their recent rhetoric, judging from their organizational literature, shows signs of moderation.[12] That the remaining Custerphiles' one cry seems to be for fairness should indicate to the NPS a need to make sure agency personnel are doing their job of balancing sides, so that neither side wins Linenthal's symbolic battle for the site.

The myth-revisionist pendulum cycle, meanwhile, has not resulted in truth; it has merely swung back to reveal a new myth. What Kenneth Burke describes as an "Iron Law of History" seems illustrative. Burke's view of history as human drama describes a cycle of order, sin, guilt, victimization (scapegoating or mortification), and redemption.[13] The drama, however, is not linear as it has no finite beginning or definite end. Rather, it is circular—redemption restores order and the cycle/drama resumes again.

At its most general level the myth today is that of viewing Indian peoples as "noble savages." This myth is hardly a new one. An earlier example of its propagation was James Fenimore Cooper's "Leatherstocking" series of novels of the early 1800s. The images of the "noble" and "barbaric" savage have represented the two major competing myths in America's view of Indians. Ironically, a stated purpose of Custer's *My Life on the Plains* was to dispel the "noble savage" myth.[14] Custer's position was that not either but both views—noble and barbaric—were true. History shows that the occasional predominance of the noble savage myth has not prevented tragedy. For example, it has not prevented the loss of tribal land. In fact, this countermyth has had negative consequences. Even Slotkin, a critic of the frontier savage myth, concludes: "This counter-myth has its own internal contradictions and destructive fallacies. Carried to its logical extreme, it . . . suggest[s] that to recover one's proper role in the myth of regenerative violence we must actually or implicitly identify with the enemy and see him as an embodiment of those virtues we once claimed as our own."[15]

Rotten with perfection, the countermyth to white America still labels the Indian as the "other." This is the first tragedy. The second tragedy is, as Slotkin explains, that "in the real world of American politics, it [the countermyth] produced aberrant and extreme forms of protest . . . identification with or participation in, 'guerrilla warfare' or terrorism within the United States—which ultimately discredited the counter-myth and its proponents."[16]

That is, the denigration of Custer does not give us a new myth with new values. Instead, it reaffirms the core values of the original myth, what Slotkin calls regeneration through violence. "What has been lost is not the underlying myth but a particular set of historical references that tied a scenario of heroic action to a particular version of American national history," Slotkin writes. He adds: "The passing of the Western may mark a significant revision of the surface signs and referents of our mythology, but it does not necessarily mark a change in the underlying system of ideology, which is still structured . . . through savage war."[17] The myth cycle then, fits Burke's "Iron Law of History." It is circular.

Slotkin reasons that the original myth brought many good things, including successful movements for democratic reform, such as abolition, labor and welfare legislation, and renewed concern for civil rights. He cautions, however, that, although an old myth is dying there is no new myth to replace it. (He accepts the idea that demystification leads to new myth).[18]

There are a number of reasons Indian peoples should consider whether they wish to destroy the Last Stand myth. The first, discussed previously, is because it encourages scapegoating. Burke's law of history shows us that to absolve sin we achieve redemption through either scapegoating (blaming others) or mortification (blaming ourselves). Scapegoating Custer allows white America to achieve redemption by blaming Custer for the shoddy treatment of the Indian peoples. If we do not scapegoat, Burke believes the only option is mortification. Blaming society in general rather than

Custer the General is not only closer to the historical truth but would probably be more productive for public policy advances for Indian peoples. The noble savage countermyth has historically been shown not to work.

Additionally, without the Last Stand there is no platform for contention. If the soldiers were "bunched together in helpless clusters, shooting wildly in all directions," then there is nothing glorious in the Indians' last stand in defense of their way of life.[19] Victory is not glorious without a worthy opponent. If the last stand is not glorious, by definition, it ceases to be a last stand—for whites or Indians. Are Indian peoples willing to live without honoring their own past, even while they destroy Custer's?

Besides the dangers inherent in scapegoating, degrading Custer raises the specter of rhetoric divorced from reality. We honor soldiers from wars of the present for serving their country while stripping honors from soldiers of past wars. We claim not to dishonor these soldiers while we call their actions "atrocities." We then substitute "victory" for "neutrality" once we have won. In an age where United States presidents and vice presidents openly acknowledge with a wink that they do not mean the words they say, each misstatement, each lie, leads us toward the platonic nightmare of "pure sophistry." When, as is the case today, "rhetoric" is often a derogatory term and "mere rhetoric" is a synonym for doing nothing, we are on the brink of words becoming meaningless. Words are enactments of a symbolic nature. When we are willing to change symbols not because it is right but because it is easier and cheaper than giving money or land, we come dangerously close to a world in which spin and doublespeak not only exist but rule.

The way out of the tragedy of history, according to Burke, is the comic. The vehicle of the comic form is rhetoric and when rhetoric ceases to mean anything we are doomed to Santyana's prophecy of repeated history. At an even larger level—insofar as one subscribes to Burke's view that language makes us human—when language becomes meaningless, it follows that humanity becomes meaningless as well. Is there a way out from the myth and the countermyth? The myth has been satirized to the saturation point—Custer, for example, makes a regular appearance in Gary

Custer Monument, 1916, fortieth anniversary celebration. Custer has been both revered and reviled in the 120 years since his famous Last Stand. (L. A. Huffman, photographer, Montana Historical Society Photograph Archives, Helena)

Larson's *The Far Side.* Whether Indian peoples are willing to let the countermyth undergo similar revision is an open question. Possibly the pain of the original tragedy is too near to allow for satire. Only time will provide such answers.

Why has the Custer myth had trouble surviving? Historians note that Custer has to be viewed in terms of the Last Stand. This should not imply, however, that Custer would not have been famous without the Last Stand (although without it, he undoubtedly would be less infamous). Had Custer not already been a noted Civil War hero, the Last Stand would not have been remembered. Who remembers Arthur St. Clair, William Fetterman, or Francis Dade (despite the fact that the latter has a government-owned battlefield named after him)? It is the mythic power of the Last Stand, combined with political and press reaction in the political context of the times, that forms what might be called the act/agent ratio.[20] In other words, the legacy of the Last Stand (the act) has come to subsume the persona of Custer (the agent). The political context of Custer's Last Stand was the Belknap scandal, in which Custer lost command of the 1876 expedition because he testified before Congress to the government's poor handling of both Indians and soldiers. Viewing the Last Stand in this context, one shifts from the aforementioned act/agent ratio to a scene/act ratio.[21] In this case, the overall historical context (the scene) subsumes the Last Stand (the act). Making this shift helps demystify the role of the agent (Custer) by reducing the emphasis on the act (the Last Stand), with its past and present mythic baggage.

Custer's character has been examined to the point of overkill. One needs only to refer to bibliographies of works on Custer and the Little Bighorn to so conclude. The closest contemporary parallel we have is the media examination of presidential candidates or the coverage of entertainment stars in such outlets as *National Enquirer* and *Hard Copy*. The microscope the presidential candidate goes under need not be explained, but Custer has been undergoing this kind of scrutiny for more than one hundred years. In the larger scheme of things, what real difference to the legacy should it make that Custer may not have been faithful to his spouse? Many are not. What difference does it make if he held hopes of being president one day (although not in 1876)? Many do. Unlike Gary Hart, Custer's personal life was not a matter of public record. Should Franklin Delano Roosevelt be considered less of a president because of his extramarital affair with Lucy Mercer?

Much of this has to do with America's preoccupation with what one communication scholar terms "glory figure ethos."[22] Glory figure ethos exists when the individual's credibility transcends his or her field so that he or she is considered expert in all things. The circumstances surrounding Adolph Hitler and Joseph Stalin are examples of glory figure ethos. So is the aura of certain contemporary entertainers when elements of society believe what they say on matters of public policy. Basketball star Charles Barkley, defying the trend, recently made news when a commercial aired with his statement: "I am not a role model. . . . Parents should be role models. Because I dunk a basketball doesn't mean I should raise your kids."[23]

A healthy society, some argue, should move towards an agent ethos, in which the individual is not superhuman but rather has credibility because of accomplishing specific acts in a field of expertise. Both the Custer myth and the anti-Custer myth are based on the glory figure type. Attempting to move away from a glory figure ethos towards an agent ethos is to engage in demythology. Perhaps when we can judge historical figures like Custer for their competency as a specified agent, in this case as a soldier, then maybe we will observe, as one commentator put it, "the harbinger of an era when all our heroes needn't be perfect, nor desire our emulation."[24]

Folklorist Bruce Rosenberg detailed the primal nature of last stand myths, and Custer's certainly fits his category.[25] Rosenberg noted the lack of a literary masterpiece that would permanently ingrain the Custer Last Stand myth. Brian Dippie notes that many of the values the Custer myth stands for—individualism, self-sacrifice, etc.—are no longer important in contemporary America.[26] But the difficulty of maintaining the Custer myth may run deeper. Of all the last stands Rosenberg discusses, only in the case of Custer's are the antagonists who were involved now part of a single political unit. Leonidas's Last Stand at Thermopylae endures because the antagonists, the Greeks and Persians, are still perceived as separate groups and as enemies. Masada is still an important symbol to an Israel surrounded by hostile enemies, just as the Masada garrison was surrounded by Roman soldiers. Today, however, Indian peoples and non–Native Americans are all Americans with some common goals.

Whether a last stand myth—inherently a conflict between cultures—can survive now that the antagonists are not only friendly but viewed by some as one political unit is doubtful. The cognitive dissonance in mythologizing an enemy who is now a friend, combined with a collective guilt over the methods non–Native Americans used to win domination over the land, is probably too much for the American psyche to bear.

Whether a last stand myth favorable to Custer can survive is also doubtful, but can a positive Custer myth survive, especially without the Last Stand? The road to "redemption" would obviously seem to lie outside of the last stand myth, but extracting the Custer persona from the Last Stand has been difficult. Although some have sought "salvation" for Custer as a Civil War hero, most public perceptions of Custer remain unaltered.[27] Why?

One reason is the continuing influence of Frederic Van de Water's 1934 Custer biography, *Glory-Hunter*.[28] Although historians often point to Jay Monaghan's or Robert Utley's books as the best modern Custer biographies, the anti-Custer view is pervasive because of the Van de Water volume.[29] Why? Probably because, as a psychobiography, it helps "explain" Custer—it paints a portrait by describing motivation. In any event Van de Water's portrayal will likely have continued influence on the Custer myth and continue to insure anti-Custer works, just as Frederick Whittaker's *A Complete Life of Gen. George A. Custer* encouraged pro-Custer works a century earlier.[30] The only way to counter Van de Water would seem a pro-Custer biography to supplant him. Such a biography, combined with the freeing of the Custer persona from the Last Stand, might allow Custer to reemerge in the public mind as a positive cultural icon, this time as a Civil War hero. Whether Indian peoples would want this is an open question. Whether they would be able to stop it is also open. As the countermyth dismantles the last stand myth, it dismantles Custer as mythic figure, both as a hero and as an antihero. This may be the silver lining for Custerphiles. For only in the symbolic death of the "Last Stand Custer" can a "Civil War Custer" arise, phoenix-like, from the ashes of cultural memory. Maybe.

But can Custer survive as a mythic hero in the meantime? Rosenberg notes that virtually all western cultures have last stand myths, and he believes the Custer myth can transcend its racist ideology. He writes: "The myth of Custer's Last Stand may also suggest to us something more than a sacrifice to manifest destiny; if that were all this legend would have died with the ethos." To Rosenberg, Custer is Camus's "existential man," someone "who rises slightly above the inevitability of his life and of his death, by bravely fighting his miserable fate to his last breath." The portrayal, he notes, has literary parallels. "He is Sisyphus, smiling as his boulder crashes down the slope of the hill once again," Rosenberg writes, adding: "[H]e is Macbeth knowing that he must soon die, yet resolving to die with the dignity of a Scottish king."[31]

Camus's "existential man," according to Rosenberg, also has historical parallels. "Like Roland, Leonidas, Saul or the alleged last message from Wake Island to 'send us more Japs,'" he argues, "Custer is the embodiment of our defiance—against those people, societal forces and coercions, institutions, obligations, and destinal traps that seem to envelop and at least partially smother the lives of those of us who live in modern, urban society." One recalls that Sitting Buffalo, who referred to Custer as a human being, described Custer's death this way: "He killed a man when he fell. He laughed. He had fired his last shot." As Rosenberg notes: "Custer on the hilltop, waving his sword defiantly at the . . . faces of the enemy who he knows in his heart will eventually overwhelm him, is that part of all of us which resists capitulation, and it is that part of us that defies, or wants to defy, our society, our surroundings, our situation in life."[32]

Thus, the Custer of myth would seem to have transcendence, even beyond the death of the frontier myth: "Such a Custer is of course one of America's greatest heroes," Rosenberg concludes, "and despite renewed . . . assaults, this time upon his memory and fame, he will remain heroic to most of white America." Rosenberg adds: "When we denigrate Custer we sacrifice some idea within ourselves."[33]

Which myth is symbolic of Custer—Rosenberg's fallen hero of the Last Stand? Slotkin's regeneration through violence? Camus's existential man? The answer is all of the above—the myths are not mutually exclusive. Slotkin claims regeneration through violence is a uniquely American myth, akin to what some term a cultural myth. Rosenberg and Camus are dealing with transcultural values. Communication scholar Janice Rushing terms them archetypal myths.[34] Certainly Slotkin's violence is a necessary component in Rosenberg's martyred warrior. That Custer fits more than one archetype helps explain his drawing power. Perhaps Custer fits other archetypes as well. At one time Custer functioned as a Christ figure—white America's sacrifice to manifest destiny. Does he survive today as a Moses figure? He leads the people to the promised land—the fabled West, but he has sinned (the Washita Battle, Black Hills invasion, whatever) and therefore cannot enter it. So he dies within view of paradise, in 1876, when the country is on the verge of "civilization." The example has explanatory power in dealing with white America's guilt.

What rhetorical stances can possibly help us break the tragedy of the legacy of the Little Bighorn? Indian people should contemplate whether they have won the second Battle of the Little Bighorn. Many changes at the battlefield—Indian administrative personnel, the monument name change, authorization for an Indian memorial—have all come to pass. Regardless, Indian people should consider whether the use of Custer as a devil symbol, which Alvin Josephy tells us was a deliberate strategy, continues to be productive.[35] Would it have helped civil rights efforts for blacks to focus on Robert E. Lee?

What can Custerphiles do? The rhetoric of the diatribe, as justified as it might be, as cathartic as it might be, will not change things. Preaching to the choir with the rhetoric of the true believer will not bring about policy changes if the choir is small.

What options does the National Park Service have? As with Indian peoples, perhaps it is time to declare victory and move from what Linenthal describes as a corrective stance, to a neutral one.[36] The theme of the Indian memorial—"Peace through Unity"— provides a clue, a rhetoric of reconciliation.[37] Both sides want equal time and honor. This will not be accomplished until each side understands that the other has different cultural values. But we can start with the use of symbolic transformation—words. If so, we should avoid the use of words like "hostile" and "squaw" just as we should not use "racist," "rednecks," or "nuts" to describe Custerphiles.[38] An interest in Custer does not automatically translate into a dislike for Indian people. For their part, Custerphiles should remember that the Battle of the Little Bighorn for many Indian people is not a hobby but a part of their lives that effects them even today. References, such as playing cowboys (or cavalry) and Indians, no matter how humorously intended, only serve to reinforce the views of Indians who regard whites as bigots.[39]

Why do these groups need to reconcile? Because long after the politicians have found another cause, the media another story, government officials another job, and academicians another book, they are the ones who remain at this site. As George A. Custer IV recently noted: "Ideally some day we can all, Red or White, citizen or bureaucrat, review the battle and its participants on its own terms free from all the clutter and confusion of social ideology and government ineptitude. A little bit of respect for others and a LOT more listening might make that day come a little bit sooner."[40]

If reconciliation fails, we risk the tragedy of eternal struggle. "As a Nation, we diminish ourselves when we sway with political winds and bury the lessons of history," Wyoming Senator Malcolm Wallop wrote in dissenting to the bill to change the name of the battlefield. "It should be possible to separate the courage and sacrifice of individuals, both Indian and non-Indian, from the decisions of their leaders and the policies and politics which brought the combatants to that windblown plain in southern Montana. The emotional reaction to Custer's Last Stand is a lesson we ignore at our peril."[41]

Indeed.

Notes

1.   Richard Slotkin, *The Fatal Environment: The Myth of the Frontier in the Age of Industrialization 1800–1890* (New York: Atheneum, 1985), 14-15.

2.   Edward T. Linenthal, *Sacred Ground: Americans and Their Battlefields* (Urbana: University of Illinois Press, 1991), 127-71.

3.   U.S. Senate, Committee on Energy and Natural Resources, "Little Bighorn National Monument," Senate Repts. 102–173, October 3, 1991 (Washington, D.C.: Government Printing Office, 1992), 2 (hereafter Senate Repts).

4.   Gay Kingman, "Miscellaneous National Parks Legislation," Senate, Hearing before the Subcommittee on Public Lands, National Parks and Forests of the Committee on Energy and Natural Resources, July 25, 1991 (Washington, D.C.: Government Printing Office, 1992), 100-101 (hereafter Parks Hearing). See also Herman J. Viola, *Ben Nighthorse Campbell: An American Warrior* (New York: Orion Books, 1993), 47.

5.   Kenneth Burke, *The Rhetoric of Religion: Studies in Logology* (Berkeley: University of California Press, 1973), 191-221.

6.   Conrad Burns, Parks Hearing, 76.

7.   Viola, *Ben Nighthorse Campbell*, 276.

8.   Theodore Windt, Jr., "The Diatribe: Last Resort for Protest," *Quarterly Journal of Speech*, 58 (February 1972), 1-14.

9.   Viola, *Ben Nighthorse Campbell*, 277. See also *Custer/Little Bighorn Battlefield Advocate*, 1 (Winter 1994), 14.

10. David Berlo, *The Process of Communication: An Introduction to Theory and Practice* (New York: Holt, Rinehart and Winston, 1960), 17-20. See also Northrop Frye, "Archetypal Criticism: Theory of Myths," in *Anatomy of Criticism: Four Essays* (Princeton: Princeton University Press, 1957).

11. Linenthal, *Sacred Ground*, 130-31, 215-16.

12. *Custer/Little Bighorn Battlefield Advocate.*

13. Burke, *Rhetoric of Religion*, 191-221.

14. George A. Custer, *My Life on the Plains* (1874; reprint, Lincoln: University of Nebraska Press, 1971), 21-24.

15. Richard Slotkin, *Gunfighter Nation: The Myth of the Frontier in Twentieth Century America* (New York: Atheneum, 1992), 591.

16. Ibid., 630, 591.

17. Ibid., 642-43.

18. Ibid., 654, 655.

19. James Welch with Paul Steckler, *Killing Custer* (New York: W. W. Norton and Co., 1994), 169. Steckler and Welch made the film shown to visitors at the battlefield; as such, it functions as the official position of the park service.

20. Kenneth Burke, *A Grammar of Motives* (Berkeley: University of California Press, 1969), xv, 15-20.

21. John P. Hart, "The Custer Myth: Some Modern Implications," presentation, April 1992, Southern Speech Communication Association, San Antonio, Texas; John P. Hart, "Custer and the Tragedy of Myth" (doctoral diss., University of Kansas, 1994).

22. Otis M. Walter, *Speaking to Inform and Persuade* (New York: Macmillan, 1982), 115-27.

23. Vern E. Smith and Aric Press, "Who You Calling Hero?" *Newsweek,* May 24, 1993, 64.

24. Ibid.

25. Bruce Rosenberg, *Custer and the Epic of Defeat* (University Park: Pennsylvania State University Press, 1974), 1-3.

26. Brian W. Dippie, *Custer's Last Stand: The Anatomy of an American Myth* (Missoula: University of Montana Publications in History, 1976), 134-44.

27. Gregory J. W. Urwin, *Custer Victorious: The Civil War Battles of General George Armstrong Custer* (London: Associated University Presses, 1983).

28. Frederic F. Van de Water, *Glory-Hunter: A Life of General Custer* (Indianapolis: Bobbs-Merrill, 1934).

29. Jay Monaghan, *Custer: The Life of General George Armstrong Custer* (Boston: Little and Brown, 1959); Robert M. Utley, *Cavalier in Buckskin: George Armstrong Custer and the Western Military Frontier* (Norman: University of Oklahoma Press, 1988), 210-11.

30. Frederick Whittaker, *A Complete Life of Gen. George A. Custer* (New York: Sheldon and Company, 1876).

31. Rosenberg, *Custer and the Epic of Defeat*, 282.

32. Ibid., 282; W. A. Graham, *The Custer Myth: A Source Book of Custeriana* (Lincoln: University of Nebraska Press, 1986), 73.

33. Rosenberg, *Custer and the Epic of Defeat*, 282, 284.

34. Janice Hocker Rushing, "On Saving Mythic Criticism—A Reply to Rowland," *Communication Studies*, 41 (Summer 1990), 143.

35. Alvin Josephy, "The Custer Myth," *Life,* July 2, 1971, 48-59. In 1987 *National Geographic* noted that the site was "the only national memorial to soldiers who gave their lives for the U.S. during the Indian Wars of the last century" (April 1987, p. 413). The official brochure the NPS currently distributes at the monument states in its first sentence: "Little Bighorn Battlefield National Monument memorializes one of the last armed efforts of the Northern Plains Indians to preserve their ancestral way of life." Note the Custer/Seventh Cavalry omission. See National Park Service, "Little Bighorn Battlefield," pamphlet number 1994-301-085/80115 (Washington, D.C.: Government Printing Office, 1994).

36. Linenthal, *Sacred Ground*, 131, 168.

37. Ibid., 163.

38. Viola, *Ben Nighthorse Campbell*, 274. See also Linenthal, *Sacred Ground*, 155.

39. *USA Today*, July 21, 1992, 11A.

40. *Custer/Little Bighorn Battlefield Advocate.*

41. Malcolm Wallop, Senate Repts., 9.

American Indian Movement demonstrators carry the U.S. flag upside down "as a symbol of the distress of the American Indian" during the centennial celebration at Custer Battlefield, June 25, 1976. (R. N. Wathen, Jr., photographer, courtesy Hal Stearns)

Signifying on the Little Bighorn

Richard S. Slotkin

Here we are, 120 years after the Battle of the Little Bighorn, still talking about Custer and Sitting Bull (p. 114), Reno and Crazy Horse. Still asking what happened, and why? Was all that blood shed for nothing? Was it shed in sacrifice—and if so, sacrifice for objectives that were worthy or unworthy? Was the Sioux War of 1876 justified or unjustified? Inevitable or avoidable? If we had it to do over again—what would we do? Negotiate? Surrender? Take the Gatling guns? Unite the Seventh Cavalry's three battalions before ordering Reno to charge the village? We keep going over all of it, from the great questions of historical significance and moral principle to the little questions about what Benteen thought he was doing, how long L Troop held back the hostiles, and where Crazy Horse was.

And who is this "we" anyway, the "we" who keeps worrying and worrying these "Custer questions" generation after generation? Who just cannot leave Custer alone?

For most of the last 120 years, the battle was known as Custer's Last Stand. And the "we" who worried about its facts and its meanings were United States citizens, mostly white, of colonial and European ancestry, for whom "Custer's Last Stand" was a classic American myth, a defining moment in American history. And the "America" it defined was one symbolized by a small band of white and Euramerican soldiers, representatives of a progressive and democratic order, standing to the last against the overwhelming might of dark-skinned, anti-progressive people, who represented barbarism and savagery. When the republic decided to memorialize permanently the event by dedicating its hallowed ground as a national military park, it was the most natural thing in the world to name it "Custer Battlefield." For "us" the battle was about Custer.

"Us" in this case has included just about every sort of American, except—until very recently—Native Americans. Of course the Battle of the Little Bighorn figures in tribal memory, history, and myth; and Indians have been engaged in the Custer debates since Curley's deposition was taken back in 1876. But I have never heard of any association of tribal historians calling a conference just to talk about this single event. The best recorded and, for most of the last century, the most typical form of Indian engagement with the "Custer questions" has been as respondent to questions posed by white interlocutors: how did the Custer battalion maneuver, who killed the Long-haired Chief? It was not until long after the battle that most of the participants learned who it was they had been fighting, and even then, Custer was a particularly significant figure only to the Southern Cheyennes, who owed him a grudge for the battle of the Washita and the broken pledges of the Medicine Lodge "treaty." It is my impression that the stories told for themselves, by those peoples whose ancestors participated in the battle— Cheyennes, Lakotas, Arapahos, Arikaras, and Crows—have private meanings and a set of emphases and priorities that are very different from those that have dominated the national public discourse on Little Bighorn. For them the battle is an episode in Sitting Bull's or Crazy Horse's story, the story of some particular ancestor—or, as in Black Elk's retelling, an episode in the unfolding of a particular spiritual vision. At a conference of the advisory board for Paul Stekler's film documentary, *Battle at the Little Bighorn,* two years ago, William Tall Bull, tribal historian of the Northern Cheyennes, spoke powerfully about the Custer battle. He did so in response to a direct question: was the battle a "myth," did the battle have special meaning for his people? But he did so with great, palpable reluctance; and although I will not repeat the story he told in response, I will say that the questions he was asking were radically different from those we had thought most important.

Yet in the end, he did respond to our question.

If, over the years, Custer has become a significant figure for Native Americans, that is in part an artifact of the structure Euramerican culture has imposed on the intercultural conversation. Indian writers and political leaders—from all tribes, not just the original participants—recognize the significance Custer has for their Euramerican interlocutors, and talk Little Bighorn in order to make themselves intelligible to "us"—so that they, too, can effectively participate in the national, public debate over values and policies: as, for example, in the title of Vine Deloria's book, *Custer Died for Your Sins.* They may speak of Custer (as Jim Welch does) as a way of symbolizing a historical experience that unites Native Americans, whether their ancestors fought Custer or not, and despite the differences in their cultures, histories, and geographical homelands—the experience of defeat, subjugation, and exclusion by Euramerican society: by "us." This Indian usage of "Custer" also reflects the emergence, through years of cultural struggle, litigation, and wrangling with federal bureaucracies, of a pan-Indian ethnic or political consciousness. Yet if Native American writers, polemicists, and historians bring a different valuation to their invocation of Custer, it is nonetheless true that in entering the mainstream of national public discourse they too find Custer a figure of inescapable significance, the man who must be talked about, figured out, understood.

Not that we have always agreed on how Custer was to be understood. Like all heroes, Custer is the symbolic center for major conflicts of value and belief. He has been variously represented as a Christlike martyr who died for the sins of a corrupt society and as a glory-hunting megalomaniac; as a skilled tactician betrayed by cowardly subordinates and as "a gallant idiot who could lead a charge supremely well but do very little else"; as a friend of the Indian, who said that if he were an Indian he should prefer dying with Crazy Horse and the hostiles to slow death and moral decay on a reservation, and as the most cruel and cynical agent of imperial racism, perpetrator of a massacre at the Washita, instigator of the Black Hills gold rush and of the Sioux War of 1876–1877, in which he perished. When "we" feel good about our history, about our cultural symbols and the republic for which they stand, we tend to play Custer as Errol Flynn and heroic sacrifice; when we are feeling critical or dubious, we pit a vicious Custer against a "Noble Red Man" version of Sitting Bull or Crazy Horse. Custer is our myth. He signifies to us; he speaks of our potential for good and evil. So we cannot leave him alone, and whenever we start to tell the story of the Little Bighorn and the Plains Indian wars, Custer and his Last Stand always appear at the center of the story.

As a result, a relatively minor military engagement and a man of marginal historical importance have acquired a disproportionate weight and presence in our culture. "Custer's Last Stand" is practically an American idiom, part of the language, a perennial reference for comedians, cartoonists, politicians, poets, and novelists. Don Russell's exhaustive study of last stand illustrations led him to conclude that the Battle of the Little Bighorn is the most frequently depicted event in all of American history. He cataloged one thousand different depictions, many of which have been reproduced thousands and hundreds of thousands of times—paintings, line cuts, lithographs, posters, bumper stickers, bubblegum cards, T-shirt logos, cereal boxes, comic book covers. The famous "Budweiser lithograph" (fig. 30) became an icon of popular illustration and has been prominently displayed in saloons and diners since 1885. In 1942 the War Department struck off two thousand copies and distributed them to army camps around the country: the image of slaughter was supposed to inspire the troops with a spirit of heroic sacrifice. It was the Budweiser poster that introduced me to Custer at the age of six, when I saw it hanging above the corned beef and pastrami at Cousin's Deli on Avenue D in Brooklyn.

And then there are the movies: dozens of films in which the Last Stand is the central catastrophe, from Thomas Ince's silent *Custer's Last Fight* in 1912 to *Little Big Man* (p. 260) in 1970. And hundreds more films and television programs (war films as well as Westerns) in which Custer's Last Stand is an explicit or implicit reference point—ranging from classics like John Ford's *She Wore a Yellow Ribbon* to that episode of *Twilight Zone*, in which a National Guard tank crew, on summer maneuvers, gets caught in a time warp and ends up trying to get their tank to the Little

Bighorn in time to rescue Custer.

As if it were worth traveling back in time for that purpose alone.

Why Custer? Of all the important events of that time—Reconstruction, the building of the railroads, the emergence of big business, the sudden and almost catastrophic modernization of American business and politics—why is it the Last Stand that we choose to remember?

I think it is because, from its moment of origin, the Custer story has served a vital cultural and political function: to symbolize the cultural crisis of modernization, of America's transition from an agrarian republic to an industrial and imperial nation-state. The Custer story draws on the imagery of the nation's oldest mythology—the myth of the frontier—but modifies that myth to serve the ideological needs of a modern, post-frontier, metropolitan society.

The myth of the frontier recasts the history of American development as a heroic legend, in which a powerful, progressive, prosperous, and democratic nation emerges out of the perennial struggle of pioneers to defeat the Indians and develop the virgin wilderness. The myth combines two ideological themes into a single coherent fable: the themes of "bonanza economics" and "savage war." The first is an economic mythology, an American mystification of capitalist development, which sees the discovery and conquest of new lands and resources as the basis of our great national wealth. According to the myth, the Old World lives by an economics of scarcity and can develop only through the disciplines of forced savings and class exploitation. America's is an economy of abundance, where the existence of limitless free land and unappropriated natural resources means that money may be said to grow on trees and gold (as Custer once said) is to be found among the roots of the grass. Where the European commoner hopes at best to subsist, the American looks forward to something like wealth—a "bonanza" of surplus cash or production, the product of the land's excessive richness or of speculation. The only problem is that of gaining access to the land, and that was the central tenet of democratic politics from the colonial period on. It is critical to the myth that the New World, the virgin lands of the West and their wealth, come to us as if out of nowhere: unlooked-for, a windfall. Nature, not labor, gives such resources their value, and hence they come to us free of the social costs that burden development in metropolitan Europe.

But access to the virgin land can only be gained through "savage warfare": persistent battle against the natives of the American wilderness and others of "primitive" racial or ethnic endowment— Indians, Africans, Mexicans, Filipinos, Asians, and peasants from Ireland or southern and eastern Europe—peoples who symbolize the recalcitrance of Nature and the resistance of human nature to civilization and its disciplines and discontents.

Like the virgin land and bonanza myths, the myth of savage war is also rooted in historical fact. Every stage of westward expansion, from Jamestown on, was marked by Indian wars. Moreover, to exploit the cheap land frontier to the west, Americans exploited cheap labor frontiers to the east and south: at least half of the land seized from the Indians before 1850 was exploited by means of slave labor; and the railroad frontier of the Gilded Age was built by cheap immigrant labor from Europe and Asia.

The "savage war" theme mystifies politics in a way that complements the mystification of economics in the virgin land/ bonanza theme. In the Old World (so the story goes), social violence is directed inward, deployed by one class to subjugate or overthrow another in the struggle for scarce resources, with the result that Europe is both unstable and resistant to genuine democracy. But in America, the social costs of development are externalized—in effect, symbolically exorcised. Social violence is projected outward against "them that are not a People" (as the Puritans liked to say)— against tribes of alien race and culture, living beyond the geographical borders of civilization (in the case of Indians and Africans) or beyond the margins of civil society (in the case of domestic slaves and other, non-naturalized immigrants).

As the virgin land/bonanza myth sanctifies the territorial boundaries of national society, the savage war myth defines and sanctifies a concept of national identity and character. In each stage of its development, the myth of the frontier represents progress as achieved through a scenario of regeneration through violence: a heroic departure from the limits of existing society; purification through a regression to a more primitive or "natural" state; and redemption, through triumph over the wilderness and its native people, which makes the West safe for civilization (symbolized by white women).

But the ideological core of the savage war myth is its rationalization of the subordination of one class of human beings to another. Any class that can be likened to the mythic savage as an enemy to civilization and progress becomes eligible for treatment according to the savage war scenario and becomes a candidate for subjugation, segregation, or even extermination, becomes the legitimate object of violent, perhaps military coercion, rather than a fellow subject and citizen of the democratic polity.

This implication of the myth became fully manifest between 1873 and 1893, a period of social and political crisis that saw the defeat of Reconstruction, the opening and closing of the last land frontier in the contiguous United States, and the modernization of the American economy—the rapid development of large-scale industrialization and corporate concentration.

The period began with the catastrophic bank panic of 1873, which ended the long cycle of American economic expansion. The panic produced the worst depression in American history, and it was followed by twenty years of chronic economic difficulty.[1] As a result, the modernization of American society was marked by a rising tide of social violence. Workingmen and farmers turned to radical politics in reaction to an experience of "degradation" in the workplace and victimization in the marketplace; managers and landlords defended their interests with escalating levels of force and violence. In the South these national crises merged with battles over the ending of Reconstruction and the establishment of the "Jim Crow" regime; and the violence of labor/management, tenant/ landlord conflicts was complicated by racial violence and the terror campaigns mounted by white supremacist organizations. The crisis of politics and values that attended this social and economic disruption was given added force by the demographic revolution that was going on at the same time: millions of new immigrants were arriving from Europe and Asia; and there was a massive out-migration of African Americans from the South.

The economic crisis of the 1870s produced a major transformation in American mythology, which I have described in some detail elsewhere.[2] The most important agents of that transformation were the proprietors, editors, and journalists of the great urban newspapers and journals, which had developed (since 1850) into a medium for the nationwide circulation of information and opinion. They addressed three simultaneous crises, which they saw as organically related: the urban "class warfare" that began with the Tompkins Square "riot" of 1874; the breakdown of Reconstruction in the South and the threat of a "race war" in the region; and the failure of federal policy in the opening of western lands—specifically, by sponsoring a discredited scheme of railroad development, and failing to solve the "Indian question."

All three stories would reach a violent climax in 1876–1877—a two-year period that also saw the celebration of the centennial of American independence and a hotly contested presidential election which ended in a tie—and was "stolen" in a back room deal between Democratic and Republican conservatives. During those two years Reconstruction would collapse in a last wave of race riots and Ku Klux outbreaks; labor unrest would culminate in the Great Strike of 1877, which seemed a foretaste of proletarian revolution; and the failure of western development would culminate in the outbreak of the Sioux War of 1876 and the catastrophe of Custer's Last Stand. For several crucial months in the summer of 1876, during the confusion and furor of the presidential campaign, the Last Stand story provided the most dramatic, appealing, and coherent story line; and imagery drawn from that story was used by the great daily newspapers to interpret events simultaneously occurring in the presidential canvass, the South, the Mollie Maguire trials, and labor disorders in the mean streets.

In addition to their temporal coincidence, these crises—the South, the Indian war, labor troubles, and the election—were seen to have a structural kinship. In each, a conflict had arisen between the will and desires of a "lower" human order or class (Indians, black and immigrant laborers, urban wageworkers) and the imperative requirements of the new industrial system as defined by its owners and managers. Workers, Indians, and freed slaves had asserted in their different ways their desire to control the conditions and terms of their labor and/or the land from which they gained subsistence. The Republican administration was identified (inaccurately) with a "philanthropic" (in our terms, "liberal") ideology, which followed the pre–Civil War doctrines of "free labor": political authority was to be vested in "the people" rather than an elite; and the acquisition of both economic competence and political self-control was to be made universally available. But such a wide diffusion of political and economic power seemed incompatible with the requirements of a modern industrial order, whose prosperity depended on the expert management of large and complexly interlocking systems of capitalization, production, and distribution. The health of the new corporate order seemed to require the willing subordination of worker to manager and of private ambition to corporate necessity. But this was an ideology logically at odds with the traditional values of self-government, freedom of opportunity, and the political ideology of "free labor" for whose vindication the Civil War had been fought, and which the newspapermen shared (or were afraid to openly contradict).[3]

The contradiction was evaded by an act of ideological sleight of hand: the use of race-war symbolism, drawn from the myth of the frontier, to interpret the class warfare of workers and managers. The Indian war was at once a current event and a symbol of the primal and genetic strife from which the nation was born. The events of the Sioux War of 1876, culminating in Custer's Last Stand, were treated as a paradigm of the disaster that might overtake "civilization as we know it" if moral authority and political power were conceded to a class of people whose natural gifts were like those of "redskin savages."

The basic link between white workers, blacks, and Indians was their common resistance to the managerial disciplines of industrial labor; and to the Malthusian discipline of the labor marketplace, which required men to "work or starve," and to accept starvation wages when the market decreed them. But equally significant was the determination of these groups to use the political power of the national government to defeat the managers and the marketplace. According to the newspapers, Indians "used" the Indian Bureau and powerful lobbies of Radicals and "philanthropists" to "monopolize" and keep from development lands that could better be used by white farmers or railroads. Blacks used the Freedmen's Bureau and the same "philanthropic" or Radical lobbyists to obtain federal funds and troops to sustain their political "monopoly" of

Reconstruction legislatures. Workers demanded government support for strikes, subsidized rents, and soup kitchens to feed the unemployed during the depression. Finally, each of these groups appeared to threaten society with violence "from below": the Indians were already on the warpath; southern elections and labor disputes were already marked by racial violence; and labor demonstrations in the cities raised for the newspapermen "The Red Spectre of the Commune."

The newspapers' account of the politics of Indian affairs and Reconstruction policy was distorted, and to some extent fabricated, to suit the polemical needs of the managerial ideology which the editors supported. Their primary objective was to weaken the capacity of organized workers and farmers (and their allies among the "philanthropic" elite) to use the instruments of democratic politics for advantage in their struggle with landlords, employers, and managers. By framing the class conflict as a choice of "racial" identification between "savagism" and civilization, these editorialists hoped to deprive the embattled workers/freedmen/ Indians (and their Radical Republican allies) of the sympathy they had hitherto received from the "middle class": that putative majority of farmers and city dwellers who had not yet become either proletarians or members of a corporate hierarchy.[4]

The representation of the working classes as "white savages" was facilitated by the large and growing presence of immigrants in American society. As early as 1869, Charles Francis Adams had predicted that the American laboring classes would soon be reduced to three racially defined "proletariats"—Celtic in the North, African in the South, and Oriental in the Far West. Because (in Adams's view) these races were incapable of properly exercising the responsibilities of self-governing citizens, Americans would have to consider restricting their access to voting and other political rights.[5]

Custer's Last Stand, and the events leading up to it, offered the most dramatic and broadly appealing approach to the development of a new, "managerial" version of the frontier myth. In 1874, when the economic depression was at its depth—while the Mollie Maguires were striking in the coal fields, while black Union Leaguers and white Ku Klux Klansmen battled in the South, while the unemployed "rioted" in New York's Tompkins Square—Custer was leading an exploratory expedition into the Black Hills: a long-anticipated and controversial move to open up the Sioux reservation, widely covered in the press. The major papers sent correspondents to accompany Custer, and the New York *World* made an arrangement with Custer himself to get early news if any gold was discovered. The bankrupt Northern Pacific Railroad and its anxious creditors were also intensely interested: the instigation of a gold rush or the opening of the Black Hills to settlement would raise the value of the railroad's land-grant collateral. The railroad had engaged Custer as a publicist the previous year and counted on his giving their lands a good write-up. He gave them their money's worth. On August 16, 1874, the *World's* front-page lead story was headlined: "THE BLACK HILLS / General Custer's Official Report / The Reports of Surface Gold . . . Fully Confirmed / A March Amidst Flowers of Exquisite Color and Perfume / The Garden of America Discovered."[6]

Custer's enthusiastic report painted the Black Hills as both a new El Dorado and a Garden of Eden, paradise for the lion and the lamb, the goldbug and the Granger. Custer combined these two versions of frontier wealth in a single image with his assertion that the miners had found "gold among the roots of the grass."

Eastern newspapers greeted Custer's discovery as renewed proof that the virgin resources of the frontier could still rescue America from the scarcity and social warfare of Europe. The Chicago *Inter-Ocean* editorialized:

> There could hardly be a more fortunate event for the country . . . [Opening the Black Hills] would give occupation to thousands who, from the dull condition of business, are now without work, and stimulate trade and enterprise in every direction. . . . The sequence is obvious. There was a crisis in 1848–9; California was opened and helped us out. There was a crisis in 1857; in 1858 Colorado was opened and helped us out. There is a crisis in 1873, from the effects of which we have not yet recovered; the Black Hills will be opened and pull us through.[7]

The problem was that the Indians, and their liberal or "philanthropic" supporters among the Radical Republicans, resisted the opening of the Black Hills on the ground that it would violate our treaty with the Lakotas and provoke a war. The Radicals. They were the same people who believed in enfranchising southern blacks and coddling angry workingmen and giving votes to women. Radicals and savages stood between an America in crisis and the new frontier that would save it. Obviously, both must go and the sooner the better. Indians and strikers must learn that to stand in the way of progress—trade, industry, development—is the unpardonable crime. On the front pages of the *World*, the *Tribune*, the *Herald* in New York, words initially belonging to headlines about the Indian war began to migrate to headlines about labor and Reconstruction. "Redskins" or "Reds" meaning Indians reappeared as references to "Red" strikers. Blacks in the South were accused of "savagery," of inaugurating a "War of Races"—a phrase also associated with the Indian wars. Editorialists in these papers addressed Indians, striking workers, and protesting freedmen with the same message: they must learn the essential discipline of an industrial society, which is that one cannot "withdraw one's labor" at will—a complex society and economy could not survive were that permitted. Rather, each of these "savage" classes must learn to "work or starve." Here is one example (from the New York *Daily Graphic*) of many I could cite, in which condemnation of Indian rights to the Black Hills segues without break into animadversions on strikers:

> The Indian is no such creature as he has been represented to our sympathy and imagination. He is a degraded relic of a decayed race, and it is a serious question whether he is worth civilizing, even if he is capable of civilization. . . . Were the money and effort wasted in trying to civilize the Indian wisely expended in reclaiming and educating the savages in our cities the world would be vastly better off in the end. The globe is none too large for the civilized races to occupy, and all others are doomed by a law that is irrevocable and is folly to resist.[8]

But if the lower classes of the city are also "savages," are they too a "decayed race" doomed to extinction or subjugation?

When—against all expectation—the "decayed" Lakotas, Cheyennes, and Arapahos wiped out Custer and his command on the Little Bighorn, the whole mythic substructure of American ideology was suddenly called in question. If the Indians could win, perhaps progress could be successfully resisted; perhaps the nation would not be rescued from its economic follies by a Black Hills bonanza. And if the red savages could defeat Custer, perhaps black savages could reclaim the South, and white savages revolutionize the great industrial cities. Here is E. L. Godkin of the *Nation* magazine on the Last Stand and its implications for the social crisis of the metropolis:

> [The Custer tragedy has produced] a loud demand for [the] "extermination" [of the Indians]—a course for which there is something to be said, if by extermination is meant their rapid slaughter. But if they are to be exterminated, why any longer pauperize them [i.e., by maintaining them on the reservations] and then arm them? What would be said if the city of New York, after lodging its thousand tramps in comfortable idleness during the winter, were to arm them on leaving the alms house with a good revolver and knife [for hunting]. But why should it be worse to do this thing to savage whites than to savage Indians?[9]

Godkin's editorial question was prophetic. Custer's Last Stand was followed one year later by the outbreak of the Great Strike of 1877, which temporarily stopped railroad traffic across the country and produced what seemed like revolutionary insurrections in most major cities of the East and middle west. Following the logic of the metaphor that equates Indians, strikers, and blacks, Godkin demands an end to the liberalization of political and economic life, even an end to talk of human rights:

> [Philanthropists] must exercise . . . greater watchfulness over their tongues, in devising schemes of social improvement, and in affecting to treat all things as open to discussion, and every question as having two sides, for purposes of legislation as well as speculation. Some of the talk about the laborer and his rights that we have listened

> to . . . such as the South Carolina field hand, to reason
> upon and even manage the interests of a great community,
> has been enough, considering the sort of ears on which it
> now falls, to . . . put our very civilization in peril. . . . Vast
> additions have been made to our population . . . to whom
> American political and social ideals appeal but faintly, if at
> all, and who carry in their very blood traditions which give
> universal suffrage an air of menace to many of the things
> which civilized men hold most dear.10

Here, it seems to me, we have the essence of the Custer myth and the secret of its longevity in the twentieth century.

Its symbols provide a uniquely American figuration of the perils and potentials of modernization. In Custer and his men the heroic traits of preindustrial pioneers—Boone, Crockett, Frémont, Carson—are merged with the virtues of the managerial elite that rules the world of corporations and bureaucracies: professional and commanding men at the head, disciplined subordinates serving obediently below. Against them stand all the forces that resist modernization and incorporation: primitive ethnicities, alien races, renegade individuals who cannot accept discipline or subordination.

In the Custer figuration, we define ourselves against an irreducible, irredeemable Other. As issues and times change, the identity of that Other also changes: sometimes the Other represents wild impossible freedom, a fantasy counterculture of play and/or rebellion which opposes, point for point, the values of discipline, hierarchy, and self-denial that inform middle-class society; and sometimes the Other is just the Other, an implacable racial and ideological enemy who cannot be negotiated with, only destroyed, like the Japanese in 1941–1945 or the Vietcong in 1961–1973; or perhaps, on the contemporary scene, Muslim fundamentalists (especially Shiites); and, closer to home, the Crips and the Bloods. But the primal exclusion of our history is the exclusion of the Native American. The symbolic basis of our concept of the Other, the first and foremost of our excluded classes, is the Native American.

Usually the "Indian" character of the "Other" is implicit, but sometimes the equation is embarrassingly plain. For example: From

1886 to 1898, Buffalo Bill's Wild West celebrated the conquest of the frontier by reenacting the history of conquest, and the climactic act of the performance was a reenactment of Custer's Last Stand (fig. 26), featuring cowboys in uniform, Seventh Cavalry veterans, and genuine Lakota performers—some of them veterans of the Little Bighorn. The frontier was declared closed in 1890, and by 1898 the United States had found a new frontier overseas in the Caribbean, the Philippines, and China. In 1898 Buffalo Bill replaced Custer's Last Stand with a reenactment of Teddy Roosevelt's charge up San Juan Hill; in 1900 he displayed scenes from the Filipino Insurrection against the American takeover; and in 1901, a scene from the American intervention in the Boxer Rebellion. In each of these reenactments, the part of the enemy—whether Spaniard, Filipino, or Chinese—was played by the show's Indian performers.

The myth of exclusion that began with the Indian is, of course, not restricted in application to the Indian. As my account of the newspaper wars of 1876 may suggest, the myth of Indian exclusion undergirds a whole complex of social and political exclusions. Some of these affect domestic constituencies—Jim Crow segregation, Oriental exclusion acts, no Jews or dogs allowed, no Irish need apply. Some serve to identify a foreign enemy: the savage Hun of 1917; the Yellow Peril, embodied first by the Japanese, then the Red Chinese, and finally the Vietnamese. The Indian war formula makes each group eligible for segregation or violent assault by identifying it as racially or culturally alien and unassimilable, primitive, barbarous, carrying in its nature, in its very blood, principles opposed to democracy and progress. Ambassador Maxwell Taylor, testifying on Vietnam before Congress in 1966, complained that "it is very hard to plant corn outside the stockade when the Indians are still around. We have to get the Indians away . . . to make good progress."[11] One combat soldier said that this war was fought according to "The Indian idea . . . the only good gook is a dead gook."[12] He was, of course, paraphrasing—and attributing to the Indians—an anti-Indian sarcasm historically attributed to General Philip Sheridan, to the effect that "the only good Indians he ever saw were dead," a remark that, given its source, had at the time some seriously genocidal implications. But the combat soldier in Vietnam does not know the source; this is folk wisdom he is speaking, and in folk wisdom, genocide is never our intention, but the wish of the savage Other. Which is why we've got to do it to them—before they can do it to us.

But my favorite Vietnam quote is this from Senator Russell Long, complaining about his liberal colleagues' antiwar sentiments. If their attitude had prevailed among the pioneers, he says there would have been no United States. "If the men who came on the Mayflower were frightened to helplessness the first time they had to fight Indians, they would have gone back to England. . . . But they fought the Indians and won, meanwhile losing some fine Americans, until this Nation became great."[13]

It is easy to laugh at Russell Long. Just who was the real American when Miles Standish and Massasoit faced off in the Massachusetts woods? But we laugh at Long because he is so bumptiously ingenuous in repeating—without saving qualifications and obfuscations—what has always been the core belief of our national identity: that to be a real American is to be the real or spiritual descendant, not of Massasoit or Sitting Bull, but of what Theodore Roosevelt called "the army of fighting pioneers" who carved a new nation out of a savage wilderness.

This confusion over who and what is American is critical to our fate as a nation. The question is between us now, as it was between Standish and Massasoit, William Harrison and Tecumseh, Governor John Floyd and Nat Turner, Abraham Lincoln and Frederick Douglass, and, yes, Custer and Sitting Bull. Will we continue to base our national identity on a mythology of exclusion—or reimagine our myths as fables of inclusion? In passing on to new generations our national memory, or history, will we require everyone—black, white, brown, yellow, red—to see the Battle of the Little Bighorn as Custer's Last Stand? Or is there a perspective from which we can see that, in the Indian wars no less than in the Civil War, in every one of our battles we did indeed lose some fine Americans. That in the struggles that have shaped our society—Indian wars, labor wars, racial conflicts, the Winning of the West, the industrial and postindustrial revolutions—every American victory has also been an American defeat.

We cannot go back and do it again. We cannot save Custer by time-traveling to warn him—take those Gatlings, Autie, don't trust

Major Reno, and listen to your goddamn scouts. Nor can we help Sitting Bull and Crazy Horse by saving the buffalo, keeping all those broken promises, firing all those crooked agents, and preventing the century of physical and cultural deprivation that would follow the Indians' surrender and return to the reservations.

About the past, all we can do is try to understand all of it, and remember it properly—get not just the facts but the spirit right. We can write histories that are not mere celebrations or justifications of the victors; histories that identify as much with the defeated as the triumphant, histories that fully include the historically excluded. As Adrienne Rich says, we honor our past not only by sharing pride in our achievements but by acknowledging and mourning our crimes and failures by saying: "This we have done, to our sorrow."[14] And after celebration and mourning, we will still have to decide how we can best go about coping with the legacies of the Little Bighorn—coping with the world bequeathed to us by our common history and doing justice in our own place and time.

We have at least, at last, renamed the battlefield, calling it by the name of its river: Little Bighorn Battlefield National Monument. Not Custer's battlefield, not Sitting Bull's, but the river's—and the nation's. A small gesture, but to my way of thinking not at all insignificant.

Notes

1. Richard Slotkin, *The Fatal Environment: The Myth of the Frontier in the Age of Industrialization, 1800–1890* (1985; reprint, New York: Harper-Collins, 1992), chap. 15; Michael Denning, *Mechanic Accents: Dime Novels and Working-Class Culture in America* (New York: Routledge, Chapman and Hall, 1987), 55-57; David Gordon, Richard Edwards, and Michael Reich, *Segmented Work, Divided Workers: The Historical Transformation of Labor in the United States* (Cambridge: Cambridge University Press, 1982), 50, 52.

2. Slotkin, *Fatal Environment*, chaps. 15, 18, 19.

3. Ibid., chap. 13; Richard P. Adelstein, " 'The Nation as an Economic Unit': Keynes, Roosevelt, and the Managerial Ideal," *Journal of American History*, 78 (June 1991), 160-87; Reinhard Bendix, *Work and Authority in Industry: Ideologies of Management in the Course of Industrialization* (Berkeley: University of California Press, 1956), 1-20, 99-116, 198-274; Alfred D. Chandler, *The Visible Hand: The Managerial Revolution in American Business* (Cambridge: Belknap Press of Harvard University Press, 1977); Morton Keller, *Affairs of State: Public Life in Late Nineteenth Century America* (Cambridge: Belknap Press of Harvard University Press, 1977); Jeffrey G. Williamson and Peter Lindert, *American Inequality: A Macroeconomic History* (New York: Academic Press, 1980); Thomas C. Cochran, *Business in American Life: A History* (New York: McGraw-Hill, 1972), chaps. 14-16; Robert H. Wiebe, *The Search for Order, 1877–1920* (New York: Hill and Wang, 1967), chaps. 1-5. On the response of workers to the new industrial order see E. P. Thompson, *The Making of the English Working Class* (New York: Vintage Books, 1966); Melvyn Dubofsky, *Industrialism and the American Worker, 1865–1920* (New York: Thomas Y. Crowell, 1975); Herbert G. Gutman, *Work, Culture, and Society in Industrializing America: Essays in American Working Class and Social History* (New York: Alfred A. Knopf, 1976); David Montgomery, *Beyond Equality: Labor and the Radical Republicans, 1862–1872* (New York: Vintage Books, 1967); David Montgomery, *The Fall of the House of Labor: The Workplace, the State, and American Labor Activism, 1865–1925* (New York: Cambridge University Press, 1989); and Daniel T. Rodgers, *The Work Ethic in Industrial America, 1850–1920* (Chicago: University of Chicago Press, 1980).

4. Slotkin, *Fatal Environment*, chaps. 15, 18, 19; Denning, *Mechanic Accents*, chap. 4.

5. Charles F. Adams, Jr., "The Protection of the Ballot in National Elections," *Journal of Social Science*, 1 (June 1869), 91-111; E. L. Godkin, "The Late Riots," *Nation*, 631 (August 2, 1877), 68-70; E. L. Godkin, "Our Indian Wards," *Nation*, 576 (July 13, 1876), 21-22; Richard L. McCormick, *The Party Period and Public Policy: American Politics from the Age of Jackson to the Progressive Era* (New York: Oxford University Press, 1988), pt. 3; Slotkin, *Fatal Environment*, chap. 19.

6. New York *World*, August 16, 1874.

7. Chicago *Inter-Ocean*, August 1, 1874.

8. New York *Daily Graphic*, July 10, 1876.

9. Godkin, "Our Indian Wards," 21-22.

10. Godkin, "The Late Riots," 68-70.

11. Maxwell Taylor, quoted in Richard Drinnen, *Facing West: The Metaphysics of Indian-Hating and Empire Building* (Minneapolis: University of Minnesota Press, 1980), 369.

12. Quoted in Robert J. Lifton, *Home from the War: Vietnam Veterans Neither Victims Nor Executioners* (New York: Simon and Schuster, 1973), 42-43, 48-51, 53-55.

13. Russell Long, quoted in *The Viet-Nam Reader*, ed. Marcus G. Raskin and Bernard B. Fall (New York: Vintage Books, 1967), 386.

14. Adrienne Rich, "An Atlas of the Difficult World," in *An Atlas of the Difficult World: Poems 1988–1991* (New York: W. W. Norton, 1991), 22-23.

F. Jay Haynes photographed the Little Bighorn battlefield in 1894 with the soldiers' markers snaking across the landscape to the Custer Monument on the distant hilltop. (Montana Historical Society Photograph Archives, Helena)

From Shrine
to Historic Site

The Little Bighorn Battlefield National Monument

Edward T. Linenthal

At a conference several years ago, I said that from my perspective elements of the nation's patriotic landscape—battlefields in particular—were every bit as sacred as Jerusalem, Rome, or Mecca. This scandalized several people in the audience, one of whom announced that he was amazed that anyone could make such a ludicrous statement. Feeling somewhat cranky myself, I did not help matters, saying only that I was "amazed that he was amazed." (This exchange, of course, could have gone on for sometime.) Someone else, trying to resolve all of this, said that perhaps Jerusalem was a "really" sacred place, and the Little Bighorn or Gettysburg were "sort of" sacred. What does it mean to call a place sacred? Sacred places are products of human work. They become meaningful sites through acts of interpretation and often contested sites as different groups vie for ownership of the site's meaning and legacy. There is then, no "really" sacred space that exists apart from human attempts to consecrate a place, to make it sacred. And, cultural analyst David Chidester reminds us, "sacred space is not merely discovered, or founded, or constructed; it is claimed, owned, and operated by people advancing specific interests."[1]

The cultural ownership of sacred sites will often be at stake, often intensely contested. Far from being a placid sacred site, for example, the Temple Mount in Jerusalem has been "repeatedly contested within and between the Jewish and Muslim communities."[2] Anyone who needs convincing that battlefields and other places on the American memorial landscape register as sacred, as places where meaning and ownership are constantly up for grabs, need only think of contemporary issues: the escalating preservation controversies swirling around Civil War sites, or the arguments about locating the United States Holocaust Memorial Museum adjacent to the Washington Mall.

There is no more contested site in the nation than the Little Bighorn battlefield. There is no better place to examine the layers of memory that make up the biography of a place, a biography that offers a revealing window into cultural change. There is no better example of the National Park Service's attempt to turn a shrine into a historic site. There is no better illustration of the fact that Americans are ready and willing to struggle with complex versions of history, to listen and learn from formerly hidden stories that shake the soothing comfort of traditional heroic narratives that for so long defined the meaning of the Little Bighorn. It is at that powerful, evocative, and haunting place that we witness a most interesting and hopeful sign in the continuing attempts to understand the collected identities that define us. In contrast to the raucous voices in the cultural battles arguing about the vices and virtues of multiculturalism, or screaming about revisionist history in the National Museum of American Art's exhibition "The West as America," interpretation at the Little Bighorn has successfully opened the site to various voices, various stories, and made it a place where, ideally, *any* American can be at home: from those Custerphiles who worship their hero to Custerphobes who hate him. All are drawn to raise their voices, present their cases, and leave their imprint on the sacred ground of the Little Bighorn.

For a century, of course, this was not the case. Custer and the men of the Seventh Cavalry were celebrated as Christlike figures, who through their blood sacrifice opened the West for the advance of civilization. America, created through the Revolutionary War, reborn in the baptism of blood that was the Civil War, was now reshaped again through the redemptive sacrifice of war and warriors. Commemorative events served to classify Native Americans in the white mind. Patriotic rhetoric offered token praise to the skilled but barbaric enemy who was being led from his savage state to "ways of pleasantness" by the power of white ideals.[3]

By 1976, Native Americans and other minority groups in America were no longer willing to be defined by the master narrative of the culture. And, by 1976, the National Park Service was painfully aware of the fact that it was managing what many perceived to be—for better or worse—a shrine to Custer. The well-known controversies that erupted during the centennial (p. 286) make sense if we think about the Little Bighorn as sacred ground. Like Protestants during the Reformation, Native American protesters engaged in symbolic guerrilla warfare at a sacred center, a place where their voices would disrupt the ritual inattention of a previous century. In response to Robert Utley's thoughtful centennial speech, in which he asked that the battle and the participants not be used "artificially to serve contemporary needs and ends, however laudable," the actions of Native Americans showed that they were attacking the *first* culturally constructed, hence "artificial" interpretation of the meaning of the battle. Often, initial interpretations quickly become seen as part of the nature of things, rather than as interpretive readings of an event.[4] Pronouncements about the significance of the Battle of the Little Bighorn in the late nineteenth century emerged out of that period's concerns and needs as do our current attempts. This is part of the continuing dynamism of historical interpretation. No generation can rest assured that it has scaled the mountain to gaze with serenity over the "facts" down below. Recall literary scholar Hayden White's important insight that a fact is an "event under description."[5]

From 1976 to the present, a sea change in interpretation has taken place at the Little Bighorn: no longer do white voices proclaim, as they had in 1926, that the battle was a "temporary victory of the Red man's savagery," and that this "vengeance only hastened the doom that awaited." Instead, for example, in 1986, Native Americans and white Americans took part in the reburial of the remains of troopers from the Seventh Cavalry uncovered during the archaeological excavations in 1984 and 1985. Enos Poor Bear, a former chief of the Oglala Sioux, reminded Native Americans that the battlefield was not alien land, for there was "no spot on earth more steeped with Indian tradition and pride," and he asked Native American listeners to "emulate the virtues" exhibited by their ancestors to "fashion . . . a better day and brighter future."[6]

Beyond the interpretive changes in National Park Service programs—among them the recognition that where one stands determines what one sees, resulting in an expansion of interpretive programs to the site of the Indian village—the National Park Service worked to transform the battlefield from a shrine to Custer into a historic site where different groups of Americans had a voice in the construction and alteration of memory. Some of this change was quite controversial, the name change, for example. The planning for an Indian memorial, on the other hand, was somewhat less controversial. It is to these issues I now turn.

Beginning in the early 1970s, there was sporadic uneasiness within the National Park Service over the name Custer Battlefield National Monument. In 1975, however, Robert Utley warned those championing the virtues of a name change that "few undertakings are more perilous than tampering with established nomenclature." The Little Big Horn Associates (LBHA) rose in vigorous opposition to the idea, and there was no more serious discussion of it until 1987, when in response to various proposals for renaming the site as a part of the park service's plan to standardize the names of battle sites, National Park Service Chief Historian Edwin Bearss commented, "we in the History Division are somewhat ambivalent about the merits of 'Little Bighorn' in lieu of 'Custer.'" "So much of the public fascination with the battle," he wrote, "has stemmed from its association with the colorful, controversial character of Custer . . . there is something to be said for retaining his name in the site's title. If there is one battlefield that deserves to be personalized in this fashion, this is surely the one."[7]

Largely because of her enthusiastic support of the name change and the Indian memorial, former superintendent Barbara Booher— of Ute and Cherokee ancestry—incurred the wrath of some Custerphiles. Catapulted into the public eye in 1990 when *People* magazine ran a story titled "General Custer Loses at Little Big Horn Again as Indian Activist Becomes Keeper of His Legend," Booher was the object of particularly harsh attack. Through her appointment, the park service sent a clear message that the interpretive momentum sparked by the centennial would continue. The public trust, it said, did not require that the site's superintendent be fixated on Custer, or be a military historian, or even be a white male. Yet for some Custerphiles, Booher was an intruder into the inner sanctum. Those who refused to see nineteenth-century Native Americans as Americans, but saw them instead as "enemies," now saw a descendant of the enemy within and found it intolerable.

Hearings on the name change were held in Billings on June 10, 1991. Former superintendent James Court argued that General Alfred Terry's field engineer had used the name "Custer's Battlefield" on a map prepared for the annual report to the secretary of war in 1877. Court, aware that no other National Park Service battle site was named for a person, argued that this made the battlefield unique. He also utilized arguments that had become standard with opponents: removing Custer's name would be an inappropriate act of scapegoating, making Custer guilty for the sins of Indian policy in the nineteenth century; and renaming the battlefield smacked of historical revisionism, that is, "changing the name to suit a current political or social cause." The Custer Battlefield Historical and Museum Association worried that the site would not be popular if renamed—thereby endangering an "already economically depressed area"—and the city council of Hardin, Montana, was concerned about absorbing the cost for reprinting promotional material and about the cost to the state for changing road maps and signs.[8]

During congressional deliberations, Senator Malcolm Wallop of Wyoming objected to the name change, arguing that it was an attempt to "alter history," and did "damage to the historical context" of the battle, although he took great pains to point out that he was not trying to glorify Custer or denigrate park service interpretation. Wallop argued that the site was famous *only* because Custer died there, an argument not greatly different from one made by Chief Historian Bearss in 1987.[9]

Supporters of the name change reiterated the fact that National Park Service battle sites are not named for individuals and that the change would be an appropriate act of interpretive balance. Robert

Utley offered congressional testimony supporting the legislation. Speaking at the Montana History Conference on October 25, 1991, Utley said that no change should be made to "appease a sentiment that may be only a fad." Nevertheless, he observed, the Custer name was as offensive to many Native Americans as was the Confederate flag to many African Americans, and usage of both "should be sharply examined and limited as necessary to remove the offense. The time has come," he said, "to embrace the more neutral, and the more accepted usage in naming battlefields."[10]

Responding to the accusation that changing the name would be a blatant disregard of the *intent* of an earlier generation of military men who named the site, Douglas McChristian, the park service's chief historian at the battlefield, argued that there was "compelling historical evidence to support the name change." Although General Terry's field engineer had used Custer's name on a map, McChristian noted that an earlier report filed by Terry did not name the site, nor did the field engineer's earlier maps. In fact, these earlier maps revealed that the engineer "considered the whole area fought over as the Little Bighorn battlefield." Custer's name was used on the 1877 map, said McChristian, largely for political purposes, as General Terry "had his own reasons . . . for focusing as much attention as possible upon the late Custer and away from himself and other officers." There were, McChristian said, various names assigned to different sites *within* the area where the "Battle of the Little Big Horn" had been fought.[11]

It is difficult to take seriously the argument that the new name— the Little Bighorn Battlefield National Monument—will hurt visitation to the battlefield or seriously damage area tourism. Montana's *Regional Tour Guide* for that part of the state is subtitled "Custer Country." National forest lands within the state are named after Custer, stores and motels carry his name, and his face adorns a variety of tourist brochures. In short, Custer remains a powerful symbolic presence in southeastern Montana.

Crow tribal member Barney Old Coyote offered a different reading of the land in his testimony at the name change hearings in Billings. "The fact is," he said, "that this has always been, is now, and always will remain Crow Country. . . . Custer lived here less than 36 hours! His remains have been removed to West

Point. . . . The remains of Crow Indians through the ages are still here, hence our position that this is Crow Country, not Custer Country."[12]

Both those who supported a name change and those who opposed it shared the conviction that these acts are significant revisions of memory. They recognize that the naming of a place is an act of ownership, an act of interpretive dominance. Unlike Custerphiles, however, those who questioned not only the name of the battlefield but the dominant symbol of "Custer Country" see the changes as acts of *corrective* memory, undoing a dominant cultural construction that had, in their opinion, endured far too long. They did not see the changes as heretical alterations of a sacred narrative.

For many Native Americans, the monument on Custer Hill was a part of an alien landscape. Charlie Black Wolf, a Cheyenne, declared, "There should be a monument there [to] Cheyennes, Arapahos, Sioux, there should be a monument there for the people." Interest in erecting an Indian monument at the battlefield has been sporadic. Early evidence includes a letter from the daughter of a Cheyenne warrior killed in the battle to the superintendent on July 27, 1925. There were men living, she said, who knew where her father fell, and "we would be glad if you could help us get the places marked, so [they] might be remembered on the next anniversary." In January 1971, Governor William L. Guy of North Dakota argued that it was time to "memorialize the Indian Americans in their struggles in a way at least equal to the memorials already lavished on the white Americans of Indian war fame." The park service responded to this and other calls for an Indian memorial with a claim that the battlefield was a "historical area designed to interpret a major event in American history and not a memorial to either the white man or the Indian." Although technically correct, it was also quite beside the point. The battlefield *and* the monument on Custer Hill were generally understood as memorials to Custer and his men. Indeed, how could that not be the case, since the remains of the dead troopers are buried beneath the monument, their names are inscribed on it, and the monument is dedicated to them.[13]

The controversy simmered until 1988. On the 112th anniversary following a prayer service held on the battlefield, American Indian Movement leader Russell Means—whose visceral hatred of Custer had been apparent in several well-publicized confrontations with the park service at the battlefield—led a group that removed sod from the grave of the enlisted men and "poured a frame of pre-mix cement onto which they laid [a] plaque" (p. 102). The inscription read: "In honor of our Indian patriots who fought and defeated the U.S. Calvary [sic]. In order to save our women and children from mass-murder. In doing so, preserving rights to our Homelands, Treaties, and sovereignty."[14]

Clearly, Means and his group understood that such a provocative act of defilement would gain public attention. They had escalated symbolic guerrilla warfare beyond protest at centennial events to physical intrusion at a patriotic gravesite. Most visitors, reported superintendent Dennis Ditmanson, were "generally supportive of the idea of an Indian monument while finding both the location, and the wording, of the plaque inappropriate." Some Custerphiles expressed their outrage at this act of defilement but supported the idea of an Indian memorial. Some were opposed to a memorial, and used inappropriate historical analogies to argue their case. One said an Indian memorial was tantamount to Jews erecting a monument to Nazis, or Armenians erecting a monument to Turks. This breathtaking logic, that Native Americans were somehow comparable to political regimes that put into practice modern forms of genocide, did not pass unnoticed. One respondent wrote: "Custer and his men were no innocent victims of a massacre; they were soldiers who went looking for a fight and got more than they bargained for."[15]

The plaque was subsequently removed from the gravesite, on September 6, 1988, and placed in the visitors center where, Ditmanson wrote, it would serve as a "temporary symbol of our intent to develop a memorial that will represent the shared perspectives of the tribes involved in the battle. It also [would serve] to represent certain contemporary Native American attitudes about the National Monument." The park service had responded creatively to the plaque controversy. By putting it on display, they allowed it, and the attitudes it stood for, to become a visible part of the history of the site. Visitors would realize that they were at a dynamic site of American history, whose meaning was contested, a place that mattered.[16]

Opposition continued as legislation designed to establish an Indian memorial was introduced in April 1990 during the 101st Congress by Montana representative Ron Marlenee. It was cosponsored by Colorado congressman Ben Nighthorse Campbell, a Northern Cheyenne whose great grandfather fought in the battle, and Montana congressman Pat Williams. The legislation died unexpectedly when, shortly before Congress adjourned, Representative Williams tried to attach a name change provision to the bill. Representative Marlenee was opposed to the name change and refused to accept Williams's amendment, calling instead for public hearings. Opposition continued. One LBHA member asked "What's next? Do we build a monument to the Japanese at Pearl Harbor and to the Mexicans who died at the Alamo?" George Armstrong Custer IV, while not opposed in principle, argued that "no memorials to past enemies of the United States have ever been financed by the Federal Government," overlooking, of course, that Civil War national military parks, including Gettysburg, Vicksburg, Chickamauga-Chattanooga, Shiloh, and Antietam, are federally funded, and both Union and Confederate lines of battle are marked.[17]

Numerous letters to Superintendent Booher recall interest in the commemorative balance so eagerly sought at Civil War battlefields as a precedent for evaluating the appropriateness of an Indian memorial. For example, a Missourian wrote, "we respect and honor Confederate generals . . . fighting for slavery and/or states sovereignty. This is palatable. However, are native Americans who fell in defense of *their* freedom, *their* way of life and *their* ancient homeland less worthy of respect given by fair historical treatment?" Letters of support came also from those connected with the Seventh Cavalry. Proud of the fact that his father served with the Seventh in Mexico and then in France during World War I, a Bostonian wrote the letter he believed his father "would have written were he alive today. . . . I wish you a monument as wide as the prairies and as tall as the Rockies."[18]

After much debate, legislation sponsored by Representative Campbell passed both houses during the 102d Congress, and on

December 10, 1991, Public Law 102-201 was enacted. It not only changed the name of the battlefield but also established an advisory committee—only recently named—to advise the Secretary of the Interior regarding an appropriate memorial.

Neither resolution of the Indian memorial issue nor the name change nor more balanced programs at the battlefield will transform the site into a placid memorial environment, for Custerphiles and Custerphobes—having perhaps given up frontal assaults on the park service—still seek to call attention to their interpretation of the site through ritual incursion. On June 11-14, 1992, for example, Russell Means held a Sun Dance on Crow land immediately adjacent to the battlefield after Superintendent Booher rejected his request to hold it *on* the battlefield. Despite the fact that the ceremonial site was readily visible from the road to the Reno-Benteen site, Means was reportedly "offended" by visitors who stopped to photograph the ceremony. He arranged to have the road closed, claiming his right to religious privacy under the American Indian Religious Freedom Act. Booher decided that it was in the public's best interest to avoid conflict. Consequently, she decided that the park service would take charge of the road closure to avoid violence.

Her judgment was bitterly attacked in the LBHA newsletter as yet another example of the park service's attitude of appeasement. Clearly, Means's actions were designed to embarrass Booher and the park service. Could it be that a more inclusive message at the battlefield posed strategic problems for Native American activists who needed Custer and the Little Bighorn as a symbol of evil? Or was this simply a tactical irritant, a way of staking claim to the site? Or, more alarming, was it an attempt to force the park service into potentially violent enforcement of its right to keep the road open, which could lead to a well-publicized confrontation from which Native American activists could gain political capital?

The ceremonies to receive formally the Indian memorial and name change legislation were held on Veterans' Day, November 11, 1992. On a cold, snowy day, approximately one thousand spectators gathered at the battlefield. Among them were Delores Mills, a descendant of Crazy Horse; Emmanuel Red Bear, Jr., great-grandson of Sitting Bull (p. 114); and Claudia Iron Hawk, whose grandfather fought in the battle. That evening, Senator-elect Campbell, who spoke at a buffalo meat dinner provided by the Oglala Sioux, declared that the name change was an act of inclusion, "to give our people equal time . . . so that our part in history could be written for the first time." Now, said Campbell, "I feel I'm welcome."[19]

Custerphiles have also held ceremonies at the battlefield. Before Barbara Booher became superintendent, a small group that called itself "The Committee of American Traditions" was regularly allowed on the battlefield at midnight to conduct a ceremony at Custer Hill to honor the Reno-Benteen water carriers—men who made the perilous trip down the bluffs from their defensive position to bring water to their comrades. Booher angered Custerphiles by insisting that the ceremony take place during regular park hours. Reluctantly, they agreed.

Personal memorial expressions also give shape to this contested landscape. For example, Brian Pohanka, an LBHA member and senior researcher for Time-Life's multivolume history of the Civil War, as well as a consultant for the film "Glory," wrote to Booher in November 1990 describing acts that reveal the intimate relationship between person and place. Pohanka noted that there were already three stone markers at places where Indian warriors fell during the battle. "Many times I have walked down to them with other students of the battle, and rebuilt the little piles of stone so these important sites are not lost to history."[20]

For a century, an important part of the Little Bighorn story was, indeed, "lost to history," and the events I have discussed are best understood as attempts to restore, to recover, to excavate, to remember what had been for so long forgotten in the dominant narratives. All of us who care about the cultural significance and continued preservation of the Little Bighorn battlefield should look forward to the dedication of the Indian memorial, for monument dedications are opportunities for intense and focused remembering and opportunities as well for acts of ritual reconciliation, moments of healing in the ongoing negotiations over the meaning of the Little Bighorn.

Notes

This essay was adopted from my book, *Sacred Ground: Americans and Their Battlefields* (Champaign: University of Illinois Press, 1993), and is published here with permission from the University of Illinois Press.

1. David Chidester and Edward T. Linenthal, "Introduction," in *American Sacred Space* (Bloomington: Indiana University Press, 1995), 15.

2. Roger Friedland and Richard D. Hecht, "The Politics of Sacred Place: Jerusalem's Temple Mount/al-haram al-sharif," in *Sacred Places and Profane Spaces: Essays in the Geographics of Judaism, Christianity, and Islam*, ed. Jamie S. Scott and Paul Simpson-Housley (Westport: Greenwood Press, 1991), 23.

3. The phrase was used by Colonel Frank Hall, a self-proclaimed "authority" on American Indians during a speech at the battlefield on the fortieth anniversary.

4. Robert M. Utley, text of centennial speech, Little Bighorn Battlefield National Monument, Crow Agency, Montana (hereafter LBNM).

5. Hayden White, quoted in James E. Young, *Writing and Rewriting the Holocaust: Narrative and the Consequences of Interpretation* (Bloomington: Indiana University Press, 1988), 15.

6. Edward S. Godfrey and James Marquisee, quoted in A. B. Ostrander, *The Custer Semi-Centennial Ceremonies* (Casper, Wyo.: Casper Printing and Stationery, 1926), 42, 47; Enos Poor Bear, quoted in "newspaper articles re: 110 Anniversary Ceremonies," LBNM.

7. Memorandum from Utley, June 3, 1975, and Edwin Bearss, September 18, 1987, in Historical Correspondence folder, National Park Service History Division files—Little Bighorn Battlefield National Monument, Washington, D.C. (hereafter Historical Correspondence, NPS).

8. I wish to thank Heather Huyck for allowing me to read written statements from the Billings hearings.

9. For Malcolm Wallop's report, see "Little Bighorn Battlefield National Monument," 102d Cong., 1st sess., Senate Report 102–73, October 3, 1991, pp. 8-9.

10. Robert M. Utley, "Whose Shrine Is It? The Ideological Struggle for Custer Battlefield," *Montana The Magazine of Western History*, 42 (Winter 1992), 70-74.

11. Douglas C. McChristian, "In Search of Custer Battlefield," *Montana The Magazine of Western History*, 42 (Winter 1992), 75–76.

12. "Testimony of Barney Old Coyote before the Sub-Committee on Public Lands and Parks, Interior Committee, United States House of Representatives, June 10, 1991," transcript, copy in author's possession.

13. Letters from William L. Guy to J. Leonard Volz, Midwest Regional Director of the Park Service, January 20, 1971, and February 12, 1971, Historical Correspondence, NPS; letter from Mrs. Thomas Beaverheart to the superintendent, July 27, 1925, in Don Rickey, Jr., *History of Custer Battlefield* (Billings, Mont.: Custer Battlefield and Museum Association, 1967), and in "Superintendent's Notes," *Battlefield Dispatch*, 9 (Fall 1990), 2.

14. Dennis L. Ditmanson, "Superintendent's Notes," *Battlefield Dispatch*, 7 (Summer 1988), 2-3.

15. Dennis L. Ditmanson, "Superintendent's Notes." This discussion appears in letters responding to an article about Russell Means's activities and the National Park Service's plan for an Indian memorial in *National Parks*, 63 (January/February 1989), 12. Responses appear in ibid., 63 (March/April 1989), 7; and ibid., 63 (July/August 1989), 7.

16. Dennis L. Ditmanson, "Superintendent's Notes," *Battlefield Dispatch*, 7 (Fall 1988), 4.

17. Bill Wells, "Little Big Horn Diary," *Little Big Horn Associates Newsletter*, 25 (May 1991), 4; Custer quoted in "Letters" in ibid., 25 (September 1991), 8.

18. I wish to thank Barbara Booher for sharing this correspondence with me. Letter from a Missourian to Booher, October 15, 1990, and from a Bostonian to Booher, October 16, 1990, LBNM.

19. Ben Nighthorse Campbell quoted in "Solemn Celebration Where Custer Fell," New York *Times*, November 12, 1992, and Denver *Post* November 15, 1992.

20. Letter from Brian Pohanka to Booher, November 3, 1990, LBNM.

1994 Little Bighorn Legacy Symposium

Steering Committee

Douglas C. McChristian, Steering Committee Chairman
Jon G. James, Secretary-Treasurer

Alan Clark	Joseph M. Marshall III
Paul Fees	John D. McDermott
Paul L. Hedren	Charles E. Rankin

Presenters

Robert M. Baker	Neil C. Mangum
Edwin C. Bearss	Joseph M. Marshall III
Colin G. Calloway	Douglas C. McChristian
Brian W. Dippie	John D. McDermott
Jeanne M. Eder	Joe Medicine Crow
Dan Flores	Joseph C. Porter
Richard A. Fox, Jr.	John Pretty On Top
Jerome A. Greene	Don G. Rickey
John P. Hart	Douglas D. Scott
Paul L. Hedren	Richard S. Slotkin
Paul Andrew Hutton	Charles Sooktis
Alvin M. Josephy, Jr.	Ruby Sooktis
John P. Langellier	Paul J. Stekler
Margot Liberty	Richard B. Williams
Edward T. Linenthal	

About the Contributors

COLIN G. CALLOWAY is Professor of History and Native American Studies in Dartmouth College in Hanover, New Hampshire. He is the author of *The American Revolution in Indian Country* (1995), *Crown and Calumet: British-Indian Relations, 1783–1815* (1987), and *The Western Abenakis of Vermont, 1600–1800* (1990). He has also edited *Our Hearts Fell to the Ground: Plains Indian Views of How the West Was Lost* (1996).

BRIAN W. DIPPIE, a specialist in the cultural history of the American West, teaches in the University of Victoria, British Columbia. His *Custer's Last Stand: The Anatomy of an American Myth* was recently reprinted as a Bison Book by the University of Nebraska Press.

DAN FLORES holds the A. B. Hammond Chair in Western History at the University of Montana, Missoula. His seventh book, an environmental history of Plains Indians and bison, is forthcoming from Yale University Press. Earlier books include *Jefferson and Southwestern Exploration* (1984), which won the Westerner's International award for best book on the West, and *Caprock Canyonlands: Journeys into the Heart of the Southern Plains* (1990).

RICHARD A. FOX, JR., a Montana native (Hardin), is an Associate Professor of Anthropology in the University of South Dakota. A historical archaeologist, he has conducted digs at Fort Abraham Lincoln, along the Custer trail, and at Little Bighorn battlefield. He is the author of *Archaeology, History, and Custer's Last Battle: The Little Big Horn Reexamined* (1993), which in 1994 won the Little Big Horn Associates literary award and was selected as a Choice Outstanding Academic Book.

JEROME A. GREENE is Supervisory Historian with the National Park Service in Denver. His books include *Evidence and the Custer Enigma* (1973), *Slim Buttes, 1876: An Episode of the Great Sioux War* (1982), and *Yellowstone Command: Colonel Nelson A. Miles and the Great Sioux War, 1876–1877* (1991). Greene is also editor/compiler of *Battles and Skirmishes of the Great Sioux War, 1876–1877: The Military View* (1993) and *Lakota and Cheyenne: Indian Views of the Great Sioux War* (1994).

JOHN P. HART is Associate Professor of Communication and Director of Forensics at Truman State University in Kirksville, Missouri. He has published widely in the field of communication and public policy. In 1991, he was invited to address the U.S. Senate on the symbolic aspects of renaming the Custer Battlefield. He is currently writing a book based on his dissertation, "Custer and the Tragedy of Myth."

PAUL L. HEDREN is the National Park Service Superintendent of the Fort Union Trading Post National Historic Site, Williston, North Dakota, and an oft-published historian of the northern plains Indian wars. His most recent book, *A Traveler's Guide to the Great Sioux War*, was published by the Montana Historical Society Press in 1996, as was *The Great Sioux War: The Best from Montana The Magazine of Western History* (1991), which he edited.

PAUL ANDREW HUTTON is Professor of History in the University of New Mexico, Albuquerque, where he also serves as Executive Director of the Western History Association. He is the author of numerous works on western history and popular culture, including *Phil Sheridan and His Army* (1985), which won the Ray Allen Billington Prize from the Organization of American Historians, and editor of *The Custer Reader* (1992), winner of the John M. Carroll Literary Award from the Little Big Horn Associates.

ALVIN M. JOSEPHY, JR., is the author of many award-winning books on Indians and the American West, including *The Indian Heritage of America* (1968), *The Civil War in the American West* (1991), and *The Nez Perce Indians and the Opening of the Northwest* (1965).

MARGOT LIBERTY has spent many years working with Northern Cheyenne history and tradition, after serving as a teacher on the reservation in the 1950s. She holds a Ph.D. in anthropology and is the author, with John Stands in Timber, of *Cheyenne Memories* (1967). She has written or edited two other books, *American Indian Intellectuals* (1978) and *Anthropology on the Great Plains* (1979), and more than forty articles and reviews. Her most recent book is *Working Cowboy: Recollections of Ray Holmes* (1995).

EDWARD T. LINENTHAL is Professor of Religion and American Culture at the University of Wisconsin, Oshkosh. He is the author of *Sacred Ground: Americans and Their Battlefields* (1993). His most recent book, *Preserving Memory: The Struggle to Create America's Holocaust Museum*, was published in 1995.

JOSEPH M. MARSHALL III was born and raised on the Rosebud Reservation in South Dakota. He has written widely on Plains Indian culture and history and has served as a consultant for several television documentaries on the West. His books include *On Behalf of the Wolf and the First Peoples* (1995) and *Winter of the Holy Iron* (1994).

DOUGLAS C. McCHRISTIAN served as Chief Historian at Little Bighorn Battlefield from 1988 to 1995. He is currently a historian for the Rocky Mountain System Support Office and is stationed at Fort Laramie National Historic Site. He is the author of *The U.S. Army in the West: Uniforms, Weapons, and Equipment, 1870–1880* (1995) and *An Army of Marksmen: The Development of United States Army Marksmanship in the Nineteenth Century* (1981).

JOHN D. McDERMOTT is a historian, interpretive planner, and heritage tourism consultant in Sheridan, Wyoming. From 1960 to 1986, McDermott was a federal historian and administrator, first with the National Park Service and then with the President's Advisory Council on Historic Preservation. His publications include *Dangerous Duty* (1993), a study of outposts that protected the Pacific Telegraph in the South Pass area of Wyoming and *Forlorn Hope* (1978), a book on the Nez Percé Indian war.

JOSEPH C. PORTER is currently a visiting member of the History Department at the University of Texas at Arlington. Nominated for the Pulitzer Prize in Biography, his book *Paper Medicine Man: John Gregory Bourke and His American West* (1986) won three awards including the Western Writers of American Spur Award for Best Western Nonfiction Book of 1986 and the Westerners' International Co-Founders Award for Best Book of 1986.

CHARLES E. RANKIN has been Director of Publications for the Montana Historical Society and editor of *Montana The Magazine of Western History* for the past seven years. He has published articles and essays on a number of topics involving western history, journalism history, and the Civil War and is editor or coeditor of two other volumes of essays, *Wallace Stegner: Man and Writer* (1996) and *Trails Toward a New Western History* (1991).

DOUGLAS D. SCOTT is Chief of the Division of Great Plains and Rocky Mountain Research of the National Park Service Midwest Archeological Center. He is author of *A Sharp Little Affair: The Archeology of the Big Hole Battlefield* (1994) and coauthor of *Archeological Insights into the Custer Battle: A Preliminary Assessment* (1987) and *Archaeological Perspectives on the Battle of the Little Bighorn* (1989).

RICHARD S. SLOTKIN is Olin Professor and Director of American Studies in Wesleyan University. His most recent book, *Gunfighter Nation: The Myth of the Frontier in Twentieth Century America* (1992), completes a trilogy on the American myth of the frontier and was a finalist for the 1993 National Book Award in Nonfiction. The first volume, *Regeneration through Violence: The Mythology of the American Frontier, 1600–1860* (1973) received the Albert J. Beveridge Award of the American Historical Association in 1973; the second, *The Fatal Environment: The Myth of the Frontier in the Age of Industrialization, 1800–1890* (1985) received the Literary Award of the Little Big Horn Association.

Index